CENTRAL AND LOCAL

GOVERNMENT

"Advance, Britannia!
Long live the Cause of Freedom!
God save the King!"

Rt. Hon. Winston Churchill, P.C., M.P.,
Prime Minister and First Lord of the Treasury,
Minister of Defence, Lord Warden of the Cinque Ports,
in a broadcast speech to the nation upon the
occasion of Victory in Europe,
8th May, 1945.

CENTRAL AND LOCAL GOVERNMENT

Second edition

R. E. C. JEWELL, LL.M. (Lond.)

of Gray's Inn, Barrister-at-Law
Examiner in Local Government Law and Practice
Fellowship Examination, Institute of Legal Executives

CHARLES KNIGHT & CO. LTD.
LONDON
1970

CHARLES KNIGHT & CO. LTD.
11/12 Bury Street, St. Mary Axe, London E.C.3.

Copyright © 1969 Charles Knight & Co. Ltd.

First edition 1966
Second edition 1970

Printed in Great Britain by
65 Offset Ltd.
London E.C.2.

SBN   85314 041 3 (soft cover)
         85314 045 6 (hard cover)

PREFACE TO THE SECOND EDITION

The last three years have witnessed a remarkable proliferation of changes in the law, in the machinery of government and in the organisation of public corporations. There have been reforms in the procedure of Parliament and the Royal Commission on Local Government in England has at last issued its Report, with a strong and equally voluminous Memorandum of Dissent. A short new chapter has been added to describe the Report.

Developments have been rapid and far-reaching in relation to some of the topics described in Part III. New methods of control of public expenditure are being considered and discussed, whilst great strides have been made in the training revolution in the field of personnel policy and management. The Radcliffe-Maud Report also impinges on the subjects of economic planning and regional government.

I am most grateful to my good friend Jack Wolkind, LL.M. (Lond.), Town Clerk and Solicitor, London Borough of Tower Hamlets, who has again made valuable suggestions and material freely available to me. The reorganisation of London Government remains the only viable attempt so far made in the area of regional government. I therefore hope and believe that my section on the new authorities in action in Chapter XV will be of interest to local government practitioners both in and outside the great Metropolis.

The book aims to develop the syllabus in Central and Local Government for the Intermediate Examinations of the D.M.A. and the D.G.A. It should also prove useful to students preparing for the new O.N.C. paper in Public Administration. At degree level one may express the hope that the modern approach could assist those reading Government for the B.Sc. (Econ.) Degree and also law students preparing for Constitutional and Administrative Law, both academically and professionally. Legal Executives may also benefit, having regard to the Fellowship Examination in Local Government Law and Practice of their Institute.

Finally, I have the pleasant task once more of thanking my publishers and printers for their patience, skill and perseverance. The book seeks to state the position obtaining at the end of October, 1969.

R.E.C.J.

GRAY'S INN,
LONDON,
October, 1969.

v

PREFACE TO THE FIRST EDITION

THIS book is based on the Central and Local Government syllabus for the Intermediate Examinations of the Diploma in Government Administration and the Diploma in Municipal Administration. In 1957 the D.G.A. was devised jointly by the Local Government Examinations Board and the Royal Institute of Public Administration; it was designed especially for the needs of Civil Servants, just as the D.M.A. had for many years provided an Administrative Examination for local government officers. My book falls into three parts, the first dealing with the central government; the second describing local government; and the third examining some modern problems of public administration.

I am deeply indebted to my good friend Jack Wolkind, LL.M. (Lond.), Town Clerk of the London Borough of Tower Hamlets, for perusing the first draft of the chapters on local government at a time when he was extremely busy in his official capacity. Mr. Wolkind made several valuable suggestions which have been incorporated in the text. I should however, emphasise that the responsibility for any errors or omissions is mine alone. I have not hesitated to indicate my views on controversial topics in accordance with the best traditions of a free society.

Finally, I should like to pay tribute to the patience, perseverance and skill of the publishers and printers, in both of whom I have indeed been fortunate. It is a matter of particular pleasure to me that the book is being published by Messrs. Charles Knight and Co., the Publishers of the Local Government Chronicle, the oldest journal devoted entirely to the fascinating subject of local government.

By means of Appendices and last-minute insertions at proof stage the book seeks to state the position obtaining at the beginning of July, 1966.

R.E.C.J.

GRAY'S INN,
LONDON.
July, 1966.

CONTENTS

PART I   THE CENTRAL GOVERNMENT

PART II LOCAL GOVERNMENT

CONTENTS

PART III   SOME PROBLEMS OF PUBLIC ADMINISTRATION

APPENDICES

TABLE OF CASES

TABLE OF STATUTES

PART I
THE CENTRAL
GOVERNMENT

CHAPTER I

THE MAIN CHARACTERISTICS OF THE
BRITISH CONSTITUTION

I.   THE SEPARATION OF POWERS

The American Constitution. The French writer Montesquieu, in his book *"L'Esprit des Lois"*, published in 1748, advocated a complete separation of the three branches of the Constitution—the Executive, the Legislative and the Judiciary. The author had visited this country and his doctrine of the separation of powers was to some extent based on a misinterpretation of the English scene. The doctrine had a profound effect upon the Founding Fathers when they were drafting the American Constitution in 1787; and it had some effect upon the author's native land of France. The Constitution of the United States of America is a written document, not easily susceptible of amendment; the aim is to provide a system of checks and balances.

The American Constitution has been described as rigid and inflexible; moreover, as America is a federation of States (the United States), it is necessary to have an allocation of powers as between the Federal Government on the one hand and the States' governments on the other. The President of the United States, who is the Chief Executive and Commander-in-Chief, can veto legislation but he cannot initiate it. He is elected at fixed four-yearly intervals and, since the successive tenures of President Roosevelt (1933-45), he cannot serve for more than two terms. His Administration must be drawn from outside the ranks of Congress, which is the Legislative organ and comprises the Senate and the House of Representatives. The members of these bodies are directly elected by the people but the Senate enjoys the distinction of being the only Upper House in the world which is more powerful than the Lower House. If the President wishes certain legislation to be introduced, he must prevail upon the Congressional leaders to meet his wishes: he is powerless in the legislative field without their co-operation. It has happened that the President was a member of the Republican Party and either or both Houses of Congress have had a Democrat Party majority. In these circumstances it has proved difficult for the President to obtain the legislation that he wishes; all he can do is to veto the legislation that he does not want.

In this way the Executive and the Legislative branches are separated under the American Constitution; on occasion the too rigid separation has hampered necessary executive action. Turning to the Judiciary, the Supreme Court of the United States has the power to declare legislation unconstitutional. This is logical, because there is a written Constitution; disputes may arise particularly in the case of demarcation of rights as between the States and the Federal Government. On the other hand, the President appoints the members of the Supreme Court. Such are the leading examples of the application of checks and balances under the doctrine of the separation of powers.

The British Constitution. The British Constitution is unwritten; like Topsy "it just growed". No single document enshrines the Constitution of these islands, although certain Acts of Parliament enjoy a peculiar sanctity and are hardly likely to be repealed Examples of such statutes are Magna Carta, 1215; the Bill of Rights, 1689; and the great Reform Act, 1832. The United Kingdom of Great Britain and Northern Ireland is not a federation, so that the Constitution is unitary, not federal. It has not been necessary to spell out solutions for possible disputes between the component parts. The British Constitution is therefore said to be unwritten and flexible. How far does it adhere to the doctrine of the separation of powers?

In the first place, the Executive in Britain is parliamentary: all members of the government are normally drawn from the two Houses of Parliament, with a preponderance in the House of Commons. This is in marked contrast to the American system and it is of course in clear breach of the doctrine because British Ministers belong both to the Executive and the Legislature. Montesquieu postulated his doctrine in the belief that fusion of any two of the branches militated against liberty. The effect of this fusion in our country has hardly had this effect. The most serious criticism that can be levelled is that it has perhaps led to Cabinet domination of Parliament, thus derogating from a desirable parliamentary control of the Executive. This state of affairs seems inevitable because stable government is required in a modern state; there would appear to be no serious threat to liberty if there are free elections, the sanction of the parliamentary question (diminishing in value though this is), and the preservation of the fundamental freedoms of speech, conscience, association and person.

Another exception, more apparent than real, concerns the House of Lords. This is the Upper House of the Legislature and, when sitting as a final court of appeal, represents the apex of the judiciary. Although by convention lay peers do not take part in the judicial work of the House of Lords, nevertheless the highest Court in the land is still notionally "the House of Lords", although it comprises only the Lords-of-Appeal-in-Ordinary. As these "law lords" are completely independent in the discharge of their judicial duties and take no great part in the legislative work of the Upper House, this is hardly an important exception to the doctrine.

The Privy Council may be said to exercise all three functions—legislative, executive and judicial. The Queen-in-Council has power to make Orders-in-Council under the royal prerogative (exceptionally, an Order-in-Council is delegated legislation made under the authority of a statute). An Order-in-Council may deal with legislative or executive matters; for example, it may promulgate a colonial constitution or it may ratify a treaty. However, a treaty which interferes with or alters the substantive rights of British subjects requires ratification by Act of Parliament. The Judicial Committee of the Privy Council, which hears appeals from certain parts of the Commonwealth and colonies, is a judicial body although technically it tenders advice to the Crown.

The Judiciary. The Lord Chancellor provides the largest single exception to the doctrine in this country. As Speaker of the House of Lords he is a leading member of the Legislature; as a prominent member of the Cabinet he is part of the Executive; and as Head of the Judiciary he has important judicial functions, notably in relation to the appointment of judges. He is in the same position as other Ministers in respect of the fusion of legislative and executive functions. It may on occasion be difficult for a Lord Chancellor to maintain a judicial and impartial approach if he is called upon to defend the action of a fellow member of the Cabinet: nevertheless the Judiciary of which the Lord Chancellor is head is manifestly independent in this country. This is ensured by the provisions of the Act of Settlement of 1700, whereby judges are appointed by the Crown during good behaviour and can be removed only upon an Address to the Crown by both Houses of Parliament. It may be argued that the Lord Chancellor, who is usually a politician, advises the Crown on appointments; but cases are not wanting, in the twentieth as in other centuries, in which our judges have rebuffed and withstood the pretensions of the Executive. In 1964 the technical doctrine of Crown Privlege in relation to discovery of documents, i.e., the claim of the Crown to withhold documents required in evidence, was considerably whittled down by Her Majesty's Judges. The independence of the judiciary is vital to a free society, and the cause of liberty is endangered in those countries where the machinery of government includes the administration of justice.

II. THE RULE OF LAW

The first meaning: absence of arbitrary power. All decisions and actions taken by the three branches of the Constitution should be informed with the spirit of the law, which is derived from the Common Law as developed in the courts and from Statute-law emanating from Parliament. The late Professor A. V. Dicey, Vinerian Professor of Law in the University of Oxford, in his book *"The Law and the Constitution"* (1885), postulated three aspects or meanings of the Rule of Law. In the first place, he said, the Rule of Law connotes an absence of arbitrary power or even of wide discretionary power on the part of the executive government. It should be remembered that the professor was writing in the late Victorian heyday when government interference with private lives was much less than it is today. Dicey lived to foreshadow the advance of administrative law and wrote a paper on the subject in 1915. This first meaning is still broadly true in so far as the fundamental liberties of the subject are concerned: freedom of the person, freedom of conscience, freedom of association and freedom of speech. In the economic and property spheres, however, the age-old conflict between public interest and private right has been largely resolved in favour of the public.

This is not to say that private right has been completely suborned: for example, compensation at current value in the open market is payable on the compulsory aquisition of land for public purposes such as education, housing or highways. Appeal lies to the Lands Tribunal, which is probably the best of our administrative tribunals and is composed of lawyers, surveyors and valuers. Appeal on a point of law lies from the Tribunal's decision to the Court of Appeal and thence, with leave, to the House of Lords. Thus, although the dispossessed property owner is probably loath to lose his land, he is at least reasonably certain of obtaining a fair price for it. Confiscation without compensation has never been part of the policy of any major political party in this country. Compensation has therefore been paid to the former owners or shareholders of nationalised undertakings, although political arguments may rage that it has been too much or too little.

It is not always realised that the compulsory acquisition of land is a far from recent development. A statute relevant to this subject was passed as long ago as 1845—the Lands Clauses (*Consolidation*) Act. The scale of activities has of course developed enormously. Powers were given by Parliament in the nineteenth century, following the Industrial Revolution, to railway companies and to gas and water undertakers. In the twentieth century, the advent of town and country planning and the development of local government services, particularly housing and education, has led to much greater powers of control over land.

The Town and Country Planning Act, 1968 authorises acquisition of land in the public interest, to secure overall development of an area, to provide for the relocation of population or industry or to achieve proper planning. This is the widest power of compulsory acquisition in any statute. Government departments and local authorities also have wide discretionary powers in relation to businesses; for example street traders, betting shop proprietors and the occupiers of caravan sites must obtain licences; in the last two cases, they must also seek planning permission.

We have seen that interference with property is mitigated by the statutory provisions that compensation on a fair and just basis is payable. The Rule of Law has also been invoked by the modern tendency to make greater provision for appeals in the ordinary courts of law against administrative action. The establishment of administrative tribunals to deal with such matters as rents, national insurance and aspects of the national health service has led to some anxiety. As a result, the Franks Committee on Administrative Tribunals and Inquiries reported in 1957, recommending appeals on points of law to the High Court from a large number of tribunals. The Report stressed the need for "openness, fairness and impartiality" and many of the recommendations have been implemented. Appeals lie to the High Court on a point of law from decisions of rent tribunals, national health service executive councils and industrial tribunals. Appeals lie similarly from planning decisions and orders made by the Minister of Housing and Local Government. Detailed procedural rules for planning inquiries were made in 1962 by the Lord Chancellor in an attempt to apply the criteria of the Report in this field. Further regulations have been made following the extended powers of planning inspectors under the 1968 Act.

The second meaning: equality before the law. Dicey's second meaning of the Rule of Law was that there should be equality before the law; there should be no special rules or privileges for officials of the government. Dicey was obsessed with a fear of the system of *droit administratif* in France, where there is a separate hierarchy of administrative courts. Just as Montesquieu in the previous century had misconstrued our system, so Dicey misinterpreted the French. The opinion of experts on French law is that their administrative courts have formed a bulwark of liberty for the individual, there being no bias in favour of the Administration or its officials, as Dicey feared.

There is no distinction between public and private law in England. This means that all matters are dealt with by the same system of courts, although there are divisions of the High Court based on subject-matter, for convenience. On the other hand, the growth of special or administrative tribunals has been said to derogate from the principle of equality before the law. The reforms already described have ameliorated the position; and, when acting judicially in the sense of deciding a dispute between parties, the tribunals must observe the rules of natural justice. This means that they must be impartial, must give all interested parties a fair hearing and must not arrive at their decisions from unworthy or improper motives or use a statutory power as a cloak for another purpose.

If they do any of these things, their decisions or orders can be set aside by the Courts.

Other exceptions to the doctrine of equality are the special positions of the Crown and of trades unions. Although the effect of the Crown Proceedings Act, 1947, was broadly to assimilate the position of the Crown to that of the subject in litigation, the Crown still possesses certain advantages (for example, Crown Privilege can still be claimed although its scope has been narrowed). Trades unions cannot be sued in tort; previous uncertainties in respect of the tort of intimidation have now been clarified by the Trades Disputes Act, 1965. The White Paper "In Place of Strife" (A Policy for Industrial Relations Cmnd. 3888, January 1969) stated that the Government intends, after further consultations (which became protracted) to introduce an Industrial Relations Bill. Amongst the bill's provisions would be one to enable a trades union to be sued in tort, except in the circumstances of a trade dispute.

The third meaning: law enforcement or public opinion? Dicey's third contention was that the law of the Constitution was the result of the ordinary law of the land. This is not nowadays considered to be very important and indeed his emphasis on law enforcement in relation to the Constitution has been largely discredited. The modern doctrine is that political considerations such as the effect of public opinion are more important. The most eminent protagonist of this now widely accepted view, until his death in 1965, was Sir Ivor Jennings.

III. THE SOVEREIGNTY OF PARLIAMENT

Internal and external sovereignty. Parliament is the supreme law-making body in the Kingdom and it is said to have both external and internal sovereignty. Great Britain is a sovereign state, in the sense that she owes allegiance to no other State; therefore we have external sovereignty. Difficult questions affecting both legal and political sovereignty might arise if Britain were to join the European Economic Community because this would, presumably, connote adherence to the Treaty of Rome. However, the implications of that Treaty seem to have been largely disregarded by de Gaulle during his long tenure of the Presidency of France (1958–1969).[1] Britain thus possessed the external sovereignty of an independent State.

The achievement of internal sovereignty has not been accomplished without a struggle, particularly with the Crown in the seventeenth century and to some extent with the courts. The common law judges in the early part of that century were of the opinion that they could declare an Act of Parliament void if it were "contrary to the reason of the common law". This is analogous to the position in the United States, where, as we have seen, the Supreme Court can declare legislation to be invalid if they consider it to be contrary to the Constitution.

However, since the enactment of the Bill of Rights by the Convention Parliament in the winter of 1688-9, the internal sovereignty of Parliament has been acknowledged by the courts. The judges confine their activities in this field to statutory interpretation and construction, upon which strict rules have been evolved. If the meaning of a statute is clear, the judges will give effect to it even if it means overruling a principle hitherto enshrined in the common law. It is only where the statutory provision is ambiguous or uncertain that the judges will endeavour to supply a meaning and even then they must try to evoke the intention of Parliament. They will apply the technical rules of statutory interpretation to prevent a palpable absurdity which Parliament cannot have intended; and they will invoke the common law presumption in favour of individual rights. For example, if a person's land is to be compulsorily acquired, the statutory authority must be loud, clear and unambiguous.

It sometimes happens that the courts arrive at decisions which are unpalatable to the Legislature. The position can be remedied, from Parliament's viewpoint, by enacting a statute. An interesting example is afforded by the decision of the House of Lords in the Burmah Oil Company Case in 1964. In 1942 valuable oil installations belonging to the company were destroyed in order to prevent them falling into the hands of the advancing Japanese. The action was taken on the authority of the prerogative power of the Crown in an emergency. In 1920 the House of Lords had decided that compensation was payable in respect of property requisitioned under such emergency powers because a statute specifically authorised it. That decision illustrated the sovereignty of Parliament because counsel for the Crown had argued that compensation, if it was payable at all, was only payable as an act of grace by the Crown. The case clearly established that where statute and prerogative powers cover the same ground, the statutory powers prevail and the prerogative is cut down to that extent. In the Burmah Oil case, the House of Lords decided that compensation was payable in respect of the destruction of valuable property as a result of the exercise of prerogative powers in an emergency.

As many millions of pounds were involved, the Conservative Government drafted a Bill to reverse the effect of the decision. The incoming Labour Government took up the draft and as a consequence the War Damage Act, 1965, was passed with retrospective effect and provided that the compensation was not payable after all. This furnishes an excellent example of the operation of the doctrine of the sovereignty of Paarliament, showing how the judgment of the highest legal tribunal in the land can be set aside. This procedure has been criticised as a breach of the rule of law because it deprived the oil company of the fruits of its litigation. The sovereignty of Parliament is coupled with a wide franchise and free elections so that the remedy, if required, is in the hands of the electorate.

Parliament and the Crown. The military victory of Parliament in the Civil

War did not long outlive the death of Cromwell but the Restoration did not provide an absolute monarchy, as Charles II was wise enough to realise. His brother was not so sensible and after his short reign and flight to France the political victory of Parliament was entrenched in the Bill of Rights. The most important provision was that there should be no taxation without the consent of Parliament. In practice, this has meant control of finance by the House of Commons, which had been in a dominant position in this field even before the Revolutionary Settlement of 1689. This had been one of the bitterest bones of contention with Charles I and such incidents as his levying of Ship Money and John Hampden's physical and legal resistance had helped to precipitate the Civil War. There has never been any doubt about parliamentary control of taxation since 1689.

The Bill of Rights also forbade the raising or keeping of a standing army within the Kingdom in time of peace without parliamentary consent. This notable provision has always ensured that the armed forces of the Crown are subject to the control of Parliament and also, nowadays, of Her Majesty's Government. The evolution of the constitutional monarchy has successfully prevented any further irruption of civil war.

Other important provisions of the Bill of Rights were that the election of members of Parliament ought to be free, that the freedom of speech and debates or proceedings in Parliament must not be questioned outside Parliament and that Parliaments ought to be held frequently. All this is axiomatic today but these provisions were very necessary in the context of the seventeenth centry struggle against the former autocratic powers of the Crown.

An echo of the Bill of Rights in this respect is still audible today when, at the Opening of Parliament, the Speaker claims certain formal privileges for the loyal House of Commons. Through the Speaker, the Commons claim collective access to the Sovereign in order to tender advice and that the most favourable construction should be put on their proceedings by the Crown. These formal privileges are now only of historic interest but the Speaker also claims the more substantial privileges of freedom from arrest and freedom of speech. The latter is naturally extremely important and is necessary to protect a member in carrying out his duties: speeches in Parliament are not subject to the law of defamation.

Successive Parliaments. It follows from the doctrine of the sovereignty of Parliament that a particular Parliament cannot bind succeeding Parliaments. It may attempt to do so but a future Parliament can always amend or repeal a statute: if it were otherwise, parliamentary supremacy would not exist any more. Some have argued that the existence of permanent statutes which are hardly likely to be repealed derogates from the purity of the doctrine. It is true that it is unthinkable that the existing or any future Parliament would seek to repeal Magna Carta, the Bill of

Rights or the Act of Settlement. Nevertheless, Parliament has the legal power to do so and in legal theory Parliament could do anything. Apart from the innate common sense of members of Parliament, there are political restraints. The repeal of the fundamental or constitutional statutes is unlikely, owing to the force of public opinion and to the political realism of parliamentarians. There is also a deeper reason, which is that members of all the three main parties, in Parliament and outside it, believe passionately in the cause of freedom and the preservation of the hard-won liberties of the British people.

Finally, despite statutory provision limiting the duration of Parliament, Parliament can prolong its own life beyond the limit. This has been done only in time of grave emergency during both the World Wars. Despite the fact that the Parliament Act, 1911, limited the duration of Parliament to five years, the second Parliament elected in 1910 prolonged its existence until 1918. Similarly, the Parliament convened in 1935 continued to function until the general election of 1945. Such necessary prolongations of life again aptly illustrate the operation of the doctrine.

IV. CONVENTIONS OF THE CONSTITUTION

Definition of Conventions. Conventions are not rules of law; they are practices which have developed during the slow evolution of the British Constitution. They help to ensure the smooth working of the administrative machine and contribute materially to stability of government. They have no legal sanction, which means that a court of law would not enforce a convention or punish anyone for not observing it; although a court might acknowledge the existence of a convention which was relevant in deciding a case. Their real sanction is political, for breach of a convention would probably affront public opinion. Conventions are respected and observed by the Queen, Ministers of the Crown and other members of Parliament. The flouting of any of the more important conventions would be likely to lead to political unrest. Most conventions are of long standing, but it can be said to be a twentieth-century convention that the Prime Minister of the day should sit in the House of Commons.

Conventions affecting the Crown. It is a convention that the monarch should not withhold the Royal Assent from a Bill which has passed through all its stages in both Houses. The royal veto has in fact fallen into disuse; it has not been exercised since the reign of Queen Anne. It is in any event inconceivable that Ministers would advise the Crown to withhold Assent from such Bills, since they would not have reached this stage without the sponsorship or support of the government.

By convention, the Queen acts politically only on the advice of her Ministers; this applies not only in Great Britain, but also in Canada, Australia and New Zealand. Thus the Monarch exercises the prerogative power of dissolution of Parliament only on the advice of the Prime Minister of the day. Thus, subject to the operation of certain conventions affecting the government, the Prime Minister can choose the date of a general election within the limit of five years set by the Parliament Act, 1911. The prerogative power of choosing a Prime Minister is also regulated by the convention that the sovereign, in doing so, must seek appropriate political advice.[1]

Conventions affecting the Government. The most important convention of the Constitution is that, if the government of the day is defeated on a vote of confidence in the House of Commons, it should resign or advise the Crown to dissolve Parliament. There is a technical distinction here between resignation and dissolution. If a government resigns, it is possible for a new one to be formed from a regrouping of forces in Parliament without recourse to dissolution and general election. With the growth of the two-party system and the greater use of disciplinary measures, this possibility is fairly remote today. It is much more likely that the Prime Minister would advise dissolution of Parliament, in which case the government would remain in office until the result of the general election was known. The reason for this is that Her Majesty's Government must be carried on at all times. No action would be necessary if the government were to be defeated in the Commons on a "snap vote" or on a procedural issue. The vote would have to be on a vote of confidence in the general policy of the government. In July, 1905, a motion in the name of the Conservative Prime Minister was defeated in the House of Commons; Mr. Arthur Balfour, as he then was, did not resign from office until the following December. A Liberal Government was formed and, almost immediately, Sir Henry Campbell-Bannerman advised the King to dissolve Parliament.

The second important convention affecting the government is the doctrine of collective ministerial responsibility. Ministers must stand or fall together in Parliament and in the country; they must defend each other's policies and the general policy the government is pursuing. The alternative is resignation, and by convention, a Minister who has resigned explains his reasons to Parliament.

Conventions affecting the Civil Service. There is also a doctrine of individual ministerial responsibility. A Minister is responsible, legally and politically, for his executive actions and for decisions taken in his name by the Civil Servants in the government department of which the Minister is in charge. With one or two exceptions, each Minister is the political head of a department staffed by Civil Servants. If anything goes wrong, the Minister must assume responsibility: he must defend his department in Parliament and give what explanations he can. He must not attack his Civil Servants, for they are precluded from active participation in politics and they would not, therefore, be able to defend themselves. In the last resort, a Minister of the Crown should resign if, under this doctrine, he finds himself responsible for some gross error of judgment or maladministration. In 1954 the Minister of Agriculture resigned following criticism of the action of Civil Servants in his department in relation to the disposal of certain land in Dorset. This was known as the "Crichel Down affair" and the resignation occurred despite the fact that the Minister had no detailed personal knowledge of the facts disclosed in the inquiry which had censured the Civil Servants concerned. The corollary is that a Civil Servant is directly responsible to his Minister and can be dismissed at any time (in theory the power to dismiss is vested in the Crown), although in practice Civil Servants enjoy a remarkable security of tenure.

Conventions relating to Parliament. By convention, Parliament is convened annually although the Meeting of Parliament Act, 1694, which is still in force, merely requires Parliament to meet every three years. Obviously, the pressure of business is such nowadays as to require an annual meeting and in fact there have been annual sessions of Parliament ever since the enactment of the Bill of Rights. The convention is therefore mainly of historical interest: Charles I had governed the country for eleven years without summoning a Parliament.

Before the enactment of the Parliament Act, 1911, there was a convention that the House of Commons should prevail in any dispute with the House of Lords. Proposals relating to the expenditure of public money may be introduced only by a Minister in the Commons. By convention, the Ministers of the Crown dealing with public finances must sit in the House of Commons. They include the Chancellor of the Exchequer, the Chief Secretary to the Treasury and the Junior Treasury Ministers. It is arguable that the Prime Minister could also be included, as he is the First Lord of the Treasury.

By convention lay peers may not attend the House of Lords when it is sitting in its judicial capacity as a court of appeal.

Finally, Parliament and its members represent public opinion in enforcing the observance of conventions by the Crown and the Executive. If a government were to refuse to resign or advise a dissolution following defeat in the House of Commons on a vote of confidence, this would be a matter for ventilation by members of Parliament. Public opinion would make itself felt in this and other ways so that the democratic processes available in this country could be invoked. During the spring of 1969, when it appeared possible that Labour M.P.s might revolt in such numbers against the government's industrial relations policy as to bring the government down, it was argued in certain quarters that the Queen could constitutionally refuse a dissolution if one was sought by the Prime Minister. The "Times" newspaper and others postulated the doctrine that the Monarch could refuse since it would not only embroil the Crown in politics but also in political in–fighting within one of the parliamentary parties. Moreover, as the government had been in office for more than three years a request for a dissolution and general election would hardly have been unreasonable.

1. This will be discussed more fully in Chapter II.

THE CONSTITUTIONAL MONARCHY

History of the Prerogative. The prerogative powers of the Crown have always been considerable. Under the feudal system of land tenure, all land was held from the King as feudal lord; this contributed to the absolute power enjoyed by strong Norman and Plantagenet Kings. It is true that the barons made King John submit to the provisions of Magna Carta in 1215, but this hardly affected the royal prerogative. Chapters 39 and 40, however, may be said to have influenced the spirit in which it was exercised:

> "39. No free man shall be taken or imprisoned or disseised or outlawed or exiled or in any way ruined, nor will we go or send against him, except by the lawful judgment of his peers or by the law of the land."

> "40. To no-one will we sell, to no-one will we delay right or justice."

The King was not only feudal lord but also head of the State, so that the prerogative power of the Crown was used to declare war and to make peace; to create hereditary peers of the realm of England; to tax; and to imprison. Full use was made of the royal prerogative by strong Kings such as Edward I and Edward III. The disturbed period of the Wars of the Roses was followed by the autocratic government of the Tudor monarchs. By the time of Queen Elizabeth I, however, Parliament was beginning to assert itself and to claim certain privileges, notably in relation to the supply of monies to the Crown. The Queen had no serious difficulties with her Parliaments as she knew when to compromise.

A new situation arose following the union of the crowns of England and Scotland. The first two Stuart Kings, in particular, believed in the theory of the Divine Right of Kings and this led to sharp differences of opinion with Parliament, eventually culminating in the Civil War.

The first trial of strength encountered by James I was with the judges over the prerogative power to issue a royal proclamation. In the famous Case of Proclamations in 1611 the Chief Justice of the Common Pleas informed the King that he could not sit in the courts himself and administer justice. Nor could the King alter the law by issuing a Proclamation, although he could by this means draw the attention of his subjects to the existence of certain offences and to the penalties prescribed. Thirdly, it was established that only Common Law courts could be created by the Crown. This was aimed at the so-called Prerogative Courts, such as the Star Chamber, which had been established by the Crown and were subject to royal influence. Their practice and procedure substantially differed from that of the Common Law courts. Finally, it was stated that the King could legislate only through Parliament.

Charles I, who believed in the Divine Right of Kings as a fundamental article of religious faith, gave the Royal Assent to the Petition of Right in 1628. It had been decided in the Five Knights' Case in the previous year that it was a sufficient answer to a Writ of *habeas corpus* to state that a prisoner was detained without cause by the special order of the King. This case is doubly interesting, for it concerned the levying of a tax imposed without parliamentary consent. It illustrated the discretion available to the Crown under an absolute prerogative power. The Petition of Right protested against both arbitrary imprisonment and taxation without the consent of Parliament. It also inveighed against such matters as the use of commissions of martial law and billeting of soldiers in peace-time. The King did not consider that his prerogative powers had been restricted in any way by the Petition of Right and proceeded to rule for eleven years without summoning a Parliament. Further protection was afforded against arbitrary committal by a statute in 1640, whereby the writ of *habeas corpus* was made available against the King and his council. In the following year the notorious prerogative court of the Star Chamber was abolished, an ominous prelude to the civil war.

At this time the judges were not independent of the Crown and were subject to royal whims and favour. A judge could be dismissed by the King after an unfavourable judgment. Not surprisingly, therefore, there were leading decisions in favour of the Crown on the question of taxation.

In 1606 it was held that the King could impose a duty on imported currants in order to regulate trade even though a statute forbade indirect taxation without Parliamentary consent. In 1637 it was decided that the King could levy a ship money tax on inland towns under his prerogative power to raise money to meet a national emergency. John Hampden, a Knight of the Shire and Member of Parliament for Buckinghamshire, was the man who had refused, on principle, to pay ship money. He was killed when fighting in the Parliamentary army in the early days of the ensuing Civil War.

The Civil War and the Bill of Rights. In brief, the issue between King and Parliament during the Civil War was whether the King was "above the law". The royalist lawyers argued that the King was above the law in the sense that his royal prerogative gave him an absolute discretion to act in the national interest, even if there was no emergency or national danger. The Parliamentary leaders were concerned to ensure the control of Parliament over certain matters, notably taxation, and to regulate other matters such as imprisonment.

The Civil War culminated in the victory of Parliament and the execution of the King in 1649. There was no King in office during the Commonwealth (1649-60) but the rule of Oliver Cromwell as Lord Protector was no less autocratic. The Restoration of the monarchy followed in 1660 and the reign of Charles II constituted a twilight period between the Commonwealth and the bloodless Revolution of 1688-9. Under this wise and tolerant King the doctrine of ministerial responsibility took root. Unlike his brother, James II was an ardent advocate of the Divine Right of Kings and a Roman Catholic to boot. His contribution was to use the prerogative to suspend and even dispense with laws in favour of his co-religionists. The excesses of this short reign ended in the flight of the King to France and the offer of the Crown from all the leading statesmen in the country to William of Orange, who ascended the throne as William III, his wife becoming Queen as Mary II.

The Bill of Rights was enacted by the Convention Parliament, which was so called because no monarch had summoned it, James having already fled the country and William not yet having landed at Brixham. The most important provision of the Bill relates to taxation and reads as follows:

"That the levying money for or to the use of the crown by pretence of prerogative without grant of Parliament for longer time or in other manner than the same is or shall be granted is illegal."

Since 1689 Parliament has controlled the supply and taxation of money without question; the dominant Chamber in this respect has always been the House of Commons.

Next, the Bill abolished the suspending and dispensing powers of the Crown. During the reign of James II it had been held in the courts that the King had a prerogative power to dispense with penal laws in particular cases, the monarch being the sole judge of the propriety of the act. This encouraged the King to suspend the Test Acts, the sequel being the acquittal of the Seven Bishops on a charge of seditious libel for refusing to read his Declaration of Indulgence. The Bill abolished the alleged suspending power and enacted:

"That the pretended power of dispensing with laws, or the execution of laws by regal authority, *as it hath been assumed and exercised of late,* is illegal."

The Bill also provided that the Crown should not maintain a standing army within the realm in peace-time without the sanction of Parliament. This was an obvious echo of the Parliamentary struggle in the Civil War and ensured the domination of the military by the civil power. We have already seen that the Bill protected the important principle of freedom of speech and debate in Parliament.

Finally, the Bill of Rights provided for the Protestant succession, these provisions being re-enacted a decade later in the Act of Settlement. The latter statute, as we have seen, ensured the independence of the judiciary from Crown patronage and influence. The Bill of Rights is a very important milestone in the evolution of the constitutional monarchy and entrenched the doctrine of the sovereignty of Parliament. It is a constitutional landmark of the greatest significance.

The Prerogative in Modern Times. The development of Cabinet government in the eighteenth century, and successive extensions of the franchise in the nineteenth century ensured that most of the prerogative powers of the Crown came to be exercised on political advice or even directly by Ministers. Thus the prerogative powers relating to foreign affairs are exercised on behalf of the Queen by the Foreign Secretary. Similarly, the Home Secretary acts on behalf of the Crown in the case of the prerogative of mercy. The opening, prorogation and dissolution of Parliament are all manifestations of prerogative powers of the Crown but their use is regulated by the advice of the Prime Minister of the day. The appointment and dismissal of Ministers are also prerogative powers and, in the case of Ministers of the Crown other than the Prime Minister, the Queen appoints and dismisses only upon his recommendation.

The Prime Minister is the political leader in the House of Commons who is most capable of forming a government. His capacity in this respect is based upon the support he can command in that House. Under the two-party system as it has evolved in the mid-twentieth century, the Prime Minister will therefore normally be the leader of the party with the largest representation in the House of Commons. Exceptionally, the Prime Minister may have to be selected as the leader commanding support in more than one party, as happened in 1924 and in 1929 when a minority Labour Government was sustained in office with the support of the Parliamentary Liberal Party. A grave national emergency may necessitate a realignment of forces resulting in a change of Prime Minister. This happened in 1916 when Asquith was replaced by Lloyd George as Prime Minister in the war coalition government drawn from the Liberal and Conservative Parties. In the situation which had arisen by Asquith's resignation, the King sent for Lloyd George because he was the choice of the majority in both parties.

In 1923 Bonar Law, the Conservative Prime Minister, resigned through ill-health and King George V was faced with the difficult task of choosing between Lord Curzon and Stanley Baldwin. At that time the Conservative Party was not in the habit of electing a deputy leader; another factor was that the last Prime Minister to have been in the House of Lords was the Marquis of Salisbury (1895-1902). The King was assisted in his choice under the prerogative power by advice from elder statesmen of the Conservatives. In the event the choice fell on Baldwin, probably because he was a commoner.

In 1940 Chamberlain, Prime Minister of a government which was technically a coalition but in reality predominantly Conservative, resigned after narrowly winning a vote of confidence in the Commons in which large numbers of his own side abstained. The country was at war and in a desperate situation, in the period between Narvik and Dunkirk. The name of Lord Halifax was canvassed as a possible successor but, fortunately for the country and the world, the indomitable Churchill was selected. Churchill had been hastily included in the government as First Lord of the Admiralty on the outbreak of war in 1939 after ten years in the wilderness, kept out of office by misguided and lesser men. He then formed a broad-based war coalition government, probably the best this country has ever known, its members drawn from the three political parties—Conservative, Liberal and Labour. It is believed that the reluctance of the Labour and Liberal leaders to serve under any other Conservative materially influenced King George VI in his decision.

In 1957 Eden, the Conservative Prime Minister, resigned through ill-health and on this occasion the Queen's choice lay between two commoners, Macmillan and Butler. The procedure adopted on a similar occasion in 1923 was followed and the Queen sent for Macmillan, having received advice from elder statesmen such as Churchill and Lord Salisbury that he was the more acceptable of the two to the party in power. It may be noted that both Baldwin and Macmillan had held the key post of Chancellor of the Exchequer at the crucial moment; and this was the last pre-war peace-time office held by Winston Churchill.

A more complicated situation arose in 1963 when Macmillan resigned the Premiership. On this occasion there were four contenders, of whom two were in the House of Lords. However, the Peerage Act, 1963, enabled peers to disclaim hereditary peerages and to seek election to the House of Commons. After much consultation and sounding of party opinion at all levels the outgoing Prime Minister advised the Queen that Lord Home was the popular choice of the party. Lord Home then disclaimed his peerages, fought a bye-election and entered the House of Commons as Sir Alec Douglas-Home. He was a peer for the first two weeks of his Premiership, but Parliament was not sitting. The unsuccessful candidates were the unfortunate Butler, Hogg (who had disclaimed the peerage of Hailsham) and Maudling. There was a sequel in 1965, when a method of election of the Conservative leader was formulated, and later Sir Alec resigned. Heath then replaced Douglas-Home and Maudling, who was the runner-up, became deputy leader. As the Labour Party elects a leader and deputy leader the personal choice of the sovereign should in future be easier in the event of the sudden death or resignation of a Prime Minister. A curious situation has, however, arisen following the resignation from the Labour Government, on somewhat obscure grounds, of Brown in March, 1968. He had held in succession the offices of Secretary of State for Economic Affairs and Foreign Secretary, having been initially designated First

Secretary of State. Following his resignation from the Government, Brown did not relinquish his post as Deputy Leader of the Labour Party, to which he had been elected in 1963. In the event of the death or incapacity of Wilson during the tenure of the Labour Government, Brown would hardly be regarded as a serious contender for the Premiership from his position outside the Government. The position will probably be regularised following the general election, after which new elections for the party posts can be held.

The Constitutional Monarchy. The transformation from absolute to constitutional monarchy has been achieved largely by the convention that the sovereign acts upon advice when exercising prerogative powers. In some cases, as we have seen, the prerogative is invoked on behalf of the monarch by Ministers of the Crown. Nevertheless, the prerogative powers are legally vested in the Crown, although their use is regulated by convention. It is inconceivable that the Queen would misuse the prerogative. She would not, for example, withhold her assent to a Bill which has passed both Houses. Such an action would inevitably involve the Crown in political controversy and, whilst a constitutional monarchy is no longer "above the law" it is certainly "above politics" in the partisan sense. The monarchs of the twentieth century have been eminently successful in this respect.

The Queen is Head of State[1] and also Head of the Commonwealth, which means that the republican and federal members acknowledge her as such, although they have their own Heads of State. As Head of State she had the right, as Walter Bagehot said, "to be consulted, to encourage and to warn" ministers in respect of their recommendations. It is possible for a constitutional monarch to have considerable political influence. Edward VII agreed to create a large number of Liberal peers in 1910 at the request of the Liberal Government in order to coerce the House of Lords; upon his death, George V also undertook to use his prerogative powers in this way but in the event the Upper House did not block the Bill which became the Parliament Act, 1911, and the action contemplated was not necessary. Again, Attlee seems to have taken the advice of George VI when nominating his Foreign Secretary in 1945.

We have seen that under the doctrine of the sovereignty of Parliament a statute will prevail in the event of a conflict with the prerogative. This can be reconciled with the legal position of the Crown by the fact that the Queen is an integral part of Parliament; technically she plays her part by giving the Royal Assent, albeit vicariously nowadays. Parliament is therefore accurately described as "The Queen-in-Parliament", just as the Privy Council is in theory "The Queen-in-Council". The prerogative power is manifested in the Privy Council by the making of Orders-in-Council, which concern action taken by the executive government of the country.

The Queen is said to be the fountain of justice because the Courts are the Queen's Courts and the administration of justice is carried on in her name. Judges, magistrates, and, more recently, the police have always been concerned with the maintenance of the Queen's Peace. Judges hold the Queen's commission, although the Queen cannot sit in court in person. The Queen is also described at the fountain of honour, as she has the prerogative power to create titles of nobility and to award honours. She is also Commander-in-Chief and Lord High Admiral; and officers in the armed forces of the Crown hold the Queen's Commission.

One of the more interesting of the prerogative powers is the right of the Crown to grant a Charter of Incorporation. This is the method used for the incorporation of a borough and nowadays the local authority concerned in the first instance petitions the Queen-in-Council. A committee of the Privy Council then considers the matter and advises the Crown whether or not the urban or rural district should be granted a Royal Charter of Incorporation.[2] Important differences flow from the distinction between chartered and statutory local authorities and this topic will be discussed in Part II. Charters have also been granted to some companies and professional bodies, and some boroughs have possessed their Charters for centuries. The designation "Incorporated by Royal Charter" is both honourable and dignified.

The royal prerogative has been described at the residual power of the Crown at common law. This means that it is not derived from any Act of Parliament but is something inherently connected with the sovereign and the mystique of monarchy. The evolution of the constitutional monarchy in the context of a democratic society based on free elections has meant, inevitably, that the residual power is much less than it was formerly, when the monarchy was absolute. The royal prerogative, its use now regulated by constitutional convention and its scope restricted by the sovereignty of Parliament, nevertheless plays an important part in ensuring the smooth working of the executive government of the country and the efficient functioning of Parliament. It is administratively convenient for Ministers of the Crown, particularly the Foreign Secretary, to take urgent executive action under prerogative powers. It is historically and symbolically appropriate for Parliament to be opened, prorogued and dissolved by the Queen. It is also good for the tourist trade and our invisible exports. Despite the cries of solitary republicans, this does not conflict with the modernisation of Britain.

1. In Great Britain, Canada, Australia and New Zealand.
2. Presumably this procedure will lapse following acceptance by the government of the main recommendations of the Royal Commission on Local Government in England.

CHAPTER III

POLITICAL PARTIES AND THE ELECTORAL SYSTEM

History of the Franchise. It has always been a prerogative power of the Crown to summon Parliament, the first having been convened by Henry III in 1265 at the instigation of Simon de Montfort. Initially the House of Lords was the more influential of the two Houses of Parliament, whilst for centuries the membership of the House of Commons was hardly representative of the people. Hereditary peers of the realm and the Lords Spiritual formed the composition of the House of Lords; and the feudal system was reflected in the membership of the House of Commons. The latter was dominated by the Knights of the Shires from the ancient hundreds and counties of England. With the development of trade in the Middle Ages the local merchants joined the squires and Knights in the representation of the Lower House. By the time of Queen Elizabeth I of England, each borough and county elected two members. As the franchise was still very restricted, and based on the holding of land, these members were always powerful landowners. It was, however, during the reign of this great Queen that the independent spirit of Parliament, and more particularly of the House of Commons, began to be manifested. This was not surprising, as the House of Commons included such men as Sir Walter Raleigh, although the Secretaries of State were usually in the Upper House, Lord Burghley (Cecil) being the outstanding example. The partnership between Crown and Parliament, with the Queen as the dominant partner, was an achievement to be frittered away by the upstart Stuart kings. The union of the crowns of England and Scotland brought with it monarchs who sowed the seed of their own destruction by their belief in the Divine Right of Kings.

As we have seen, Charles I did not summon a Parliament between 1629 and 1640 and this long period of arbitrary rule was the prelude to the Civil War. Despite the prevalence of democratic ideas in the Parliamentary Army, especially amongst the Levellers and the Diggers,[1] no material alteration occurred in the representation of the Commons during the Commonwealth (1649-60). Indeed, Cromwell ejected numerous members by force so that for a time the Lower House was even less representative than it had been before. The Restoration of the Monarchy in the person of Charles II was ushered in by the Cavalier Parliament, in which the royalists had largely ousted the puritan and independent republicans. It would be an oversimplification to say that the royalists became known as Tories and the republicans developed into Whigs, but this is a rough guide at any rate for the reign of Charles II. The Act of Uniformity, 1662, was unpalatable to a sizeable minority of Church of England clergy, who thus swelled the nonconformist ranks. In the Civil War the King and the established Church had stood against Parliament and the Puritans, who later split into other groups such as Independents (led by Cromwell himself) and Quakers. This broad political and religious division continued under Charles II, who sought to influence local government in the boroughs by the confiscation and reissue of royal charters. This King sought to appoint Tory magistrates: his brother and successor, James II, took the matter a stage further by attempting to increase the number of Catholic officers in the Kingdom. Because of this, he encountered difficulty with the Test Acts and embarked on the dangerous suspending of laws (and even dispensing with laws) which culminated in the Trial of the Seven Bishops, his flight, and, eventually, the prohibition against such powers in the Bill of Rights. It is noteworthy that the invitation to William of Orange came from practically all powerful political and religious groups in the land: Whigs and Tories, Anglicans and Puritans.

The revolutionary settlement of 1689 caused a fundamental change. Henceforth the Whigs were just as loyal to the Crown as the Tories and in fact the Whig Party dominated the governments formed during the reigns of William III and Anne. The Act of Union with Scotland was passed in the latter reign. The two Jacobite risings which occurred under the early Hanoverian Kings attracted mainly Catholic and Tory support, particularly in Scotland. The party system continued to develop in the eighteenth century: William Pitt the Elder (Lord Chatham) was a Whig, but his son, William Pitt the Younger, was a Tory. In general, the Tories represented the aristocracy and the old landowning families attached to the Established Church or the Roman Catholic Church: hence the normal rural alliance of squire and parson. The Whigs were the representatives of the merchants and rising middle classes although of course a Whig aristocracy also developed, a leading member having been the first Duke of Marlborough, the great soldier ancestor of Winston Churchill.

Many landowners controlled Parliament through the "rotten boroughs". In these pocket boroughs there were usually only a few electors and they would vote in accordance with the wishes of local landowners. On the other hand, new large towns such as Manchester had no representation at all. The long period of war against France and her Emperor, Napoleon I (1793-1815)[2] drained the country of money and manpower, leading to an aftermath of riot, insurrection and unemployment. Such was the situation in 1830, when radical thinkers such as Jeremy Bentham and Samuel Romilly were advocating reform in the parliamentary franchise and in the criminal law, which was harsh in the extreme, as was the civil government of the country. The stage was set for the enactment of the Great Reform Act of 1832, to which we now turn.

The Reform Acts. The Whig government, led by Russell, introduced the great Reform Bill but the House of Lords was reluctant to pass it after receiving the Bill from the Commons. Russell asked the King to create enough new Whig peers to ensure passage of the Bill through the House of Lords, but the King would agree to the creation of only six new peers. As a result of this, the government fell and the Tories took office under the Duke of Wellington. However, by this time the populace were aware that they were being deprived of new rights and there was riot and disaffection in many large centres of population. The Tory government soon fell and a new Whig government under Lord Grey was able to encourage Parliament to enact the Bill.

The Reform Act, 1832, laid the foundation of the modern system of representation and its main achievement was the redistribution of parliamentary seats. In the counties, the ancient forty shillings freehold franchise was coupled with the requirement of residence in order to become effective. Copyholders, leaseholders having leases for specified periods and tenants-at-will paying a rent of not less than fifty pounds a year were enfranchised. In the boroughs the existing qualifications were also retained, again subject to a condition of residence. The Act also provided that in the boroughs there should be a new qualification, based on the occupation of land having an annual value of ten pounds. The Act also, for the first time, laid down a statutory procedure for the registration of votes. These provisions had the effect of enfranchising the middle classes and of increasing the electorate by fifty per cent. On the other hand, the influence of the landowning classes was enhanced by the enfranchisement of tenants-at-will, who could easily be evicted from their land (voting was not yet secret). Having attacked the problem of the rotten boroughs by these reforms, the Act also restricted the system of patronage and nomination, thus depriving the Crown of its power to decide the composition of ministries and securing for them parliamentary, rather than royal, support. This tended to enhance the growing independence of the Cabinet and supremacy of the Prime Minister of the day.

The new electoral system ensured that the decision of the larger constituencies determined which party obtained an effective majority in the Commons; and that the monarch accepted that party's leaders as his Ministers. It led directly to a detailed organisation of political parties in Parliament and in the constituencies. The Act ensured that the final political arbiter was the electorate, thus vindicating the supremacy of the

House of Commons over the House of Lords. It also upset the former delicate constitutional balance between Crown, Lords and Commons. The Act was complemented by the great Municipal Reform Act, 1835, in relation to borough government. In 1852 provision was made for the appointment, on an address from both Houses, of Commissioners for the investigation of electoral abuses, with power to examine on oath. The Corrupt Practices Act, 1853, required an audit of election expenses. In 1858 the property qualification for members of Parliament was abolished.

Disraeli's Reform Act of 1867 reduced the qualifying leasehold or copyhold in the county franchise from ten to five pounds annual value and introduced an occupation franchise in respect of premises of twelve pounds annual value. The Act also introduced in the boroughs a household franchise conditional upon the payment of rates and a lodger franchise in respect of lodgings of ten pounds annual value. As the Act allowed registration of householders who paid rates through their landlords as an addition to rent, the electorate was doubled. This had the effect of placing the working-classes (or "the artisan masses" as described by some writers) in a clear majority of the electorate. In 1868 it was enacted that election petitions should be heard in the Court of Queen's Bench.

Gladstone's Ballot Act of 1872 introduced the vital principle of the secret ballot, thus clearing away the last vestiges of Dickensian "Eatanswill" and preventing intimidation. The Corrupt Practices Act, 1883, laid down that election expenses should be proportioned to the size of a constituency, that the objects on which money might be spent should be specified and that election agents should submit accounts to returning officers. Gladstone's Franchise Act of 1884 extended the householder franchise to the counties; this had the effect of trebling the electorate in the rural areas. The householder franchise now predominated in both boroughs and counties. In 1885 all boroughs with a population of less than 15,000 were merged in their counties for electoral purposes; the larger boroughs retained separate representation. All these valuable reforms in the nineteenth century based the right to vote upon occupation of property. It remained for the twentieth century to base the franchise upon residence.

Lloyd George's Representation of the People Act of 1918 enfranchised all adult males resident or occupying premises in borough and county constituencies. This Act also gave the vote to all women over 30, who or whose husbands, occupied premises or lands to the annual value of five pounds under the local government election law. Baldwin's Representation of the People Act of 1928 gave the vote to all adults resident in a constituency or who occupied premises there to the annual value of ten pounds or more or were married to persons thus qualified. The electorate now comprised virtually the entire adult population with women in a majority.

Attlee's Representation of the People Act of 1948 abolished the separate universities' and business premises vote (but the latter lingered on for 20 more years as an alternative qualification in local government elections). This Act also abolished the surviving two-member constituencies. The principle of "one man, one vote" was thus entrenched. Electoral law is now consolidated in the Representation of the People Act, 1949,[3] and its main provisions are described in the next section. Under the House of Commons (Redistribution of Seats) Acts, 1949–58, four commissions, each under the Chairmanship of the Speaker, keep the size of constituencies under review in England, Wales, Scotland and Northern Ireland. There are at present (1969) 630 Members of the House of Commons.

The machinery of elections. The electoral law is at present to be found in the consolidating Representation of the People Act, 1949.[3] The right to vote is now based on residence in a particular constituency on the "qualifying date", which is 10th October. The voters are adult British citizens who are not subject to any legal disability, such as being mentally disordered. Citizens of the Irish Republic are also entitled to vote if resident in this country. Special provision is made for absent voters, of whom the largest category comprises members of the armed forces who must make a service declaration enabling them to be registered in a particular constituency. They may vote by post or by proxy; in the latter case another person is nominated to vote for the absent voter. The 1969 Act reduces the voting age to 18 for both parliamentary and local elections and finally abolishes the non-residential and property qualifications in local government elections. A candidate in a local election must be qualified on the day of nomination and must remain so qualified on the day of election.

The Returning Officer is the Sheriff in a county, the Mayor or an alderman in a borough; on this officer is served the writ ordering him to cause an election to be held of a member to serve in Parliament. The electoral registration officer is the clerk of the county council, the town clerk in a borough or the clerk of the urban district council. This officer is responsible for compiling the register and this work is achieved partly by house to house canvassing (in the non-political sense!) and partly by the completion of forms by householders. Compilation of the register has to be ready by the end of November, based on residence on the preceding 10th October. Anyone so included in the register can vote in all parliamentary and local government elections taking place in the year commencing the following 16th February. The registration officer becomes "acting returning officer" early in the election campaign. It is his duty to declare the result of the poll and to make a casting vote in the event of a tie. In the latter eventuality some arbitrary but fair method must be used such as spinning a coin or cutting a pack of cards in which case it is advisable for the presiding officer to state in advance whether the ace is to count high or low!

A parliamentary candidate must give the returning officer a nomination paper signed by himself, his proposer and seconder and by eight other electors in the constituency. He must also deposit the sum of £150, which is returnable to him after the election if he polls one-eighth of the total votes cast, otherwise it is forfeited to the Crown. Nowadays this amount is usually provided by the candidate's political party and the major parties rarely lose a deposit. The reason for this curious deposit rule is supposed to be to discourage the lunatic fringe but as this is to be found in all parties anyway, perhaps it has now lost any justification it might ever have had.

An election petition is heard by Commissioners who are High Court Judges seconded to sit in an Election Court. This procedure is available where it is alleged that a member of Parliament was elected by means of corrupt or illegal practices. Bribery, treating, personation and undue influence comprise the former offences, which are serious and disqualify from electoral and candidacy rights. Illegal offences are less heinous and the court will grant relief from the statutory penalties if satisfied that they were not wilfully committed. Examples are omitting the printer's name from election literature or expenditure over the statutory limit,[4] both of which can occur in the heat of battle. The petitioner, who may be an ordinary elector or an unsuccessful candidate, must give £1,000 security for costs but again this is usually met by his political party. The Election Court certifies its findings to the Speaker of the House of Commons, which normally gives directions in conformity with the Court's decision. These may involve the issue of a writ for a new election or confirmation of the election of the successful candidate.

Another allegation which may be the subject of an election petition is that the election has been vitiated by some informality. In 1960 Lord Stansgate died, his heir being Mr. Anthony Wedgwood-Benn, M.P. Mr. Benn immediately resigned his seat and successfully fought a bye-election in his constituency of South-East Bristol. The unsuccessful Conservative candidate brought an election petition and the Court held that Mr. Benn was disqualified from membership of the House of Commons. This was because an hereditary peerage could not be surrendered even though no writ of summons had been applied for to attend the House of Lords. The interesting sequel to Mr. Benn's subsequent campaign was the Peerage Act, 1963, enabling hereditary peers to disclaim. Mr. Wedgwood-Benn was the first person to take advantage of the Act and he is now Minister of Technology in the Labour Government. The Benn case was the most classic recent instance of an election having been vitiated by an informality.

The candidate who polls the largest number of votes is elected and an elector can vote for only one candidate. This system tends to favour the large parties and does not always produce a very accurate reflection of national political opinion. One system postulated is that of the alternative vote, whereby the elector would list candidates in order of preference. If none obtained a clear majority the votes of the lowest would be shared according to the second preferences. Whilst this system would be more accurate than that obtaining at present, it would not secure adequate representation of minorities. However, it is believed that its introduction would at least double the number of Liberal seats. Under the system of proportional representation, there would be large multi-member constituencies and the elector would vote for the candidates in order of preference. A candidate obtaining a definite proportion of first preferences would be elected and his surplus votes allotted to second preferences. This would provide for proper representation of minorities and for this reason it is advocated by the Liberal Party. It would, however, probably lead to instability of government owing to the existence of a multiplicity of parties. This situation arose in France before the Fifth Republic and obtains to-day in Holland. A system of proportional representation is in operation in the Republic of Ireland. There are many permutations and combinations of the system whose advocates deny that a multiplicity of parties would necessarily result.

The Political Parties. We have seen that the Whig and Tory parties were beginning to emerge by the time of the reign of William III (1689–1702) and Mary II (1689–94). Originally the Whigs represented the rising middle classes and the Tories the landed aristocracy but as Whigs also began to enjoy royal favour a new Whig aristocracy developed. In the early eighteenth century the Whigs were for long periods the party of the establishment and the Tories were in opposition and therefore dissident. With their return to power under the Hanoverians the Tory links with the established order, particularly the Church of England, were soon reforged. Chatham was a Whig but his son, William Pitt the Younger, was a Tory, the latter's great political rival being Charles James Fox, renowned for his Libel Act and his encouragement of Wilberforce's campaign against slavery. Another great Whig leader at the end of the century was the Irishman Edmund Burke, who never achieved the office of Prime Minister. Burke enunciated the great constitutional principle that members of Parliament are representatives, not delegates. The later Whig leaders brought forward the great Reform Bill; Russell was the political leader, aided by such writers and jurists as Bentham and Romilly. The last of the great Whig leaders was Lord Palmerston; and the last Tory leader to be solely so described was Lord Derby.

The Tory party developed into the Conservative Party under Benjamin Disraeli, first Earl of Beaconsfield and the first Jewish Prime Minister (1874–80). He had previously served under Lord Derby and had brought forward the Reform Act of 1867. Conservatism under Disraeli was a strange mixture of limited social reform at home and Imperialism abroad. During his Premiership the Queen became Empress of India and Her Majesty's Government bought shares in the Suez Canal. An aggressive foreign policy and tension with Russia was reflected in the music-hall ditty of the time:

"We don't want to fight, but by jingo, if we do
We've got the ships, we've got the men, we've got the money, too!"

The founder of modern Liberalism, derived from the old Whig Party, was William Ewart Gladstone (1809–98), Disraeli's great rival. Gladstone had served as Chancellor of the Exchequer under Palmerston and later as Leader of the Opposition. He first became Prime Minister in 1868 and his government introduced the Ballot Act ensuring secret voting at elections. During his Midlothian Campaign in 1879, following the atrocities in Bulgaria, Gladstone called for "the expulsion of the unspeakable Turk bag and baggage from Europe". However, his name is more usually associated with ideas of peace, retrenchment and reform. His last period contained his valiant attempt to introduce Irish Home Rule but he was ahead of his time by some thirty years. Gladstone's later governments were also responsible for considerable extensions in the franchise, as we have already noted.

After ten years of quiescent Conservative rule under the Marquis of Salisbury (1895–1902) and Balfour (1902–5) a decade of Liberal Government ensued during which political controversy was acute and the parties sharply divided. The governments of Campbell-Bannerman and Asquith laid the foundations of the modern welfare state by introducing old age pensions and national insurance for the first time. The bitterest controversies arose over Lloyd George's Budget proposals to tax landed estates; the ensuing dispute over the powers of the House of Lords which resulted in the enactment of the Parliament Act, 1911; and, again, over the government's proposals for Irish Home Rule. Civil war on the latter question, at any rate in Northern Ireland, appears only to have been averted by the outbreak of the Great War. Winston Churchill, who had started his political life as a Tory democrat, was a leading member of the pre-war Liberal governments, as President of the Board of Trade, Home Secretary and First Lord of the Admiralty, the post he held in 1914 (and again in 1939). In 1916 Lloyd George succeeded Asquith as war Premier and, following the "khaki election" of 1918, formed his "government of hard-faced business men" which was largely Conservative and wanted to squeeze Germany "until the pips squeaked". The Liberal Party has never formed a government since the days of Asquith.

Meanwhile the Labour Party had been formed in 1900 in alliance with the trades union and co-operative movements to represent the working classes. One of its leaders, John Burns, became President of the Local Government Board in the pre-war Liberal Government. After the war the split in the Liberal Party ensured that the Labour Party replaced it as the radical opposition party. In 1924 the true Liberals, under Asquith, enabled a minority Labour Government to hold office for the first time under MacDonald. This situation occurred again in 1929 but the government fell in 1931 owing to a financial crisis, MacDonald deserting his party to form a so-called "National" government, which was in reality Conservative. The Labour Party is socialist and therefore differs sharply in economic matters from the other two parties. It is pledged to the common ownership of the means of production and the modern prototype of public corporation is largely the work of the Attlee Labour Governments (1945–51). The Wilson Labour Government, returned in 1964 after thirteen years of Conservative rule, spent most of its first year in office grappling with a serious inherited economic crisis. This, coupled with the dangers of a miniscule majority, effectively prevented this government from introducing many measures which can be described as socialist.[5] Socialists and Liberals can agree on many social questions, notably on aspects of the welfare state such as education, child care and welfare of the aged. The great divide is represented by nationalisation and economic policy.

Churchill. No account of our political parties would be complete without reference to the astonishing career of Winston Churchill. After his adventures as a war correspondent in the Boer War, Churchill crossed the floor of the House of Commons in 1905 to join the Liberals following many months of disagreement with his former leaders. Dropped from the government in 1915 as the scapegoat for the failure of the Dardanelles campaign, he returned to it after military service in the front line in France. He served as Secretary of State for War and Air and as Colonial Secretary under Lloyd George but lost his seat in the General Election of 1922, as a result of which Lloyd George fell from power, never to return. He had had a good innings, lasting continuously for seventeen years in office, the last six as Prime Minister. Churchill emerged as Conservative Chancellor of the Exchequer under Baldwin (1924–9) and played a rather flamboyant role in the General Strike of 1926. However, this brilliant man remained out of office for the decade before the war despite the fact that for most of this time Conservative-dominated governments were in power. There were three main reasons for this: his warnings about Nazi Germany, coupled with a demand for British rearmament from 1933 onwards; his intransigence on limited constitutional advance in India in 1935; and his support of the King (Edward VIII) during the Abdication Crisis of 1936. These attitudes made him unpopular, if not in the country, at any rate in his party, and, to some extent, even in Parliament. Churchill thoroughly denounced the shameful Munich Agreement of 1938 and, with the complete failure of Chamberlain's appeasement policy in 1939, was included in the government, together with Eden and Macmillan, on the outbreak of war.

The aftermath of the disastrous Norwegian campaign led to a motion for a vote of confidence in the government being tabled in the House of Commons. Many of the government's supporters arrived in uniform to complain of the incompetent conduct of the war. Amery, a former

Conservative Colonial Secretary and Secretary of State for India, said to Chamberlain "In the words of Cromwell, in the name of God, go!" The government won its vote of confidence but it was a Pyrrhic victory, many of its supporters abstaining. Chamberlain resigned and the King (George VI) eventually sent for Churchill to form a government, when it became clear that a coalition was in the national interest and that the Labour and Liberal leaders would serve under no other Conservative leader. From that day forth the country never looked back, not even in the darkest days of Dunkirk and the fall of France. Winston Churchill, the Tory aristocrat with the common touch, inspired the entire nation with his qualities of leadership. In him oratory based on both national and European patriotism was coupled with strategic military genius, a rare combination in a statesman. Churchill always remembered that he was the servant of Crown and Parliament, so that the use of wide emergency powers by the executive during total war did not tarnish the cause of freedom for which the nation fought. Incredible as it may seem, if his warnings of the thirties had been heeded, the war with all its slaughter and misery might not have occurred. For the whole of the period 1940–45 Churchill held the offices of Prime Minister, First Lord of the Treasury and Minister of Defence.

Churchill had been a Liberal and a Conservative; he was never a socialist. His time of greatness came late (he was seventy when the war ended) as leader of a coalition of the three parliamentary parties. Above all, he was a parliamentarian and a democrat. In 1945 the spirit of the times was in favour of radical change and social reform and against the temper of the Conservative Party, which he now led, but which had held office for so long between the wars. The people, notably the servicemen, gave a large majority to the Labour Party and Churchill became Leader of the Opposition. During this period he was able to give rein to his literary, as well as to his oratorical gifts, the latter being in evidence in his well-known Fulton and Zurich speeches. Finally, he became Prime Minister for the last time in 1951, retiring at the age of eighty nearly four years later. It was appropriate that this period should witness a certain easing of international tension and the accession and coronation of the present Queen. The old statesman was rewarded by the Crown with his knighthood of the Garter and it was therefore as Sir Winston that he was latterly remembered. He was also, until his death in 1965, the proud holder of the title of Lord Warden of the Cinque Ports. His successor in this ancient office is Sir Robert Menzies, the former Prime Minister of Australia.

Reform. A Speaker's Conference on Electoral Law was constituted in 1965, with the following terms of reference:-

To examine and if possible to submit agreed resolutions on the following matters relating to Parliamentary elections:

(a) Reform of the franchise, with particular reference to the minimum age for voting and registration procedure generally;

(b) Methods of election, with particular reference to preferential voting;

(c) Conduct of elections, with particular reference to:
   (i)   the problem of absent voting generally;
   (ii) use of the official mark on ballot papers, and of electoral numbers on counterfoils;
   (iii) polling hours;
   (iv) appointment of polling day as a public holiday;
   (v)   provisions relating to undue influence, and
   (vi) returning officers for county constituencies;

(d) Election expenses generally;

(e) Use of broadcasting; and

(f) Cost of election petitions and applications for relief.

There is a clear case for reform of registration procedure. At present there is a considerable time-lag between compilation of the forms sent to householders, compilation and printing of the register and the date of a general election.

It seems that we might profit by the adoption of the system used by our Canadian cousins. In Canada, dissolution of Parliament by the Governor-General acting on behalf of the Queen sets in motion the complicated election machinery. The Chief Electoral Officer will have been preparing for the election ever since completion of the last election. Immediately after the Dissolution Proclamation, local Returning Officers in each constituency complete plans for the recording of votes, set up polling divisions and polling stations, set enumerators at work compiling lists of eligible voters and appoint deputy returning officers. Lists of voters are printed and posted in public places enabling citizens to check them and to appeal where names have been wrongly omitted or included. The advantage of this system is that it encourages the electors to make sure of their voting rights at a time when political activity and interest is intense. It has also been suggested that use of computers would make the electoral register more effective and up-to-date.

At present, certain categories of absent voters are enabled to vote by post or, in some cases, by proxy. These include the service voters, that is, servicemen serving in this country or overseas, Crown servants serving abroad and the wives of both classes residing with them. Physically handicapped persons and those whose work takes them outside their constituency of registration can vote by post. The absent voters list does not, however, include persons living abroad other than the service voters, or persons on holiday. Each ballot paper is stamped with the official mark before being handed to the voter; the aim is to ensure secrecy of the ballot and to prevent the tendering of forged papers. It may be that, with modern developments, this precaution is no longer necessary. The allocation of broadcasting time and questions of legal liability under the Representation of the People Act, 1949, have caused difficulty in the recent past. A clear lead from the Conference on this stormy subject would be welcome in view of the powerful modern influence of television.

Representation of the People Act, 1969 amends the electoral law. It lowers the voting age to eighteen and, if otherwise qualified, a person who is of voting age on the date of the poll at a parliamentary or local government election shall be entitled to vote as an elector, whether or not he is of voting age at the qualifying date. Consequential amendments to the law are made in relation to inclusion of names on the registers of electors. The category of persons enabled to make a service declaration is extended to include merchant seamen. Convicted persons detained in penal institutions are legally incapable of voting.

The Act increases the limits on candidates' election expenses in both parliamentary and local government elections. Pending[6] a parliamentary or local government election the Act forbids broadcasting of any item about the constituency or electoral area if any candidate takes part in the item and the broadcast is made without his consent. The Act now permits a parliamentary candidate's political affiliations to be briefly included on his nomination paper and on ballot papers.

The Act abolishes the non-resident qualification for voting at local government elections and the property qualification for election to or membership of a local authority. The main provisions of the Act come into force so as to have effect with respect to the registers of electors to be published in 1970 and the elections for which those registers are used.

1. These were indigenous, Australia was not then discovered.
2. The period of the war, with one brief interlude; the duration of the Empire was shorter.
3. As amended by the Representation of the People Act, 1969.
4. This has been increased by the 1969 Act.
5. The Labour Party was returned to power in 1966 with a substantially increased majority but continued to grapple with the endemic economic crisis.
6. The operative periods are defined and are different in the various cases of parliamentary general elections, parliamentary bye-elections, ordinary local government elections and casual local vacancies.

CHAPTER IV

THE DEVELOPMENT OF CENTRAL GOVERNMENT

IN BRITAIN SINCE 1830

Introductory. The word "Ministry" in this connection means a department of State whose powers are vested either by law or convention in a single person who is responsible to Parliament for every act performed by that person, i.e., Minister of the Crown. Ministries have often been designated Boards, particularly in the nineteenth century. Examples still with us are the Treasury Board and the Board of Trade, the latter case still exemplifying the one-time practice of according the style of President to the relevant Minister. The Boards of Ordnance and of Health retained those titles until their abolition. Similarly, the Boards of Education and of Agriculture retained those titles until their reclassification as Ministries in this century. The word "Board" indicates an authority of more than one person which is convened and makes decisions but is not itself directly responsible to Parliament, although a Minister of the Crown is usually answerable for all or part of its activities.

Developments in the field of finance were of primary importance in the early period. In 1834 the old Exchequer office was abolished and revenue was thereafter paid into the Bank of England, where an account was opened for the Comptroller General, whose salary was charged on the Consolidated Fund. From 1832 an effective system of Appropriation Audit existed in the Navy, enabling Parliament to see how supply voted was actually spent. In 1842 this system was extended to the Army and Ordnance votes. In 1849 Civil Estimates were laid before the House of Commons for the first time. In 1866 the office of Comptroller General was combined with that of an Auditor General, whose business was (and still is) to ensure that expenditure had been approved by Parliament and that it had been duly spent on the objects to which it has been appropriated.

Poor Relief. As long ago as 1601 a Statute of Elizabeth I authorised the levying of rates for the relief of the poor, the ancestor of our modern rating system. In 1833 a Royal Commission was appointed to inquire into the state and administration of the poor law. One of the most active members of this Commission was Edwin Chadwick, an enthusiastic disciple of Jeremy Bentham, the great legal and social reformer. Bentham's *"Principles of Utility"*[1] aimed at the "greatest happiness of the greatest number"; the practical aspects of the doctrine were concentrated in a belief in centralised control and direction of local government. Following the Report of the Royal Commission the Poor Law Amendment Act, 1834, was enacted, setting up a body of Poor Law Commissioners with power to group parishes into unions for the purpose of poor relief and with detailed executive control over the local poor law administration. The main features of the Act, apart from establishing the Board of Commissioners, were the constitution of elected boards of guardians for the purposes of local administration and the withdrawal of out-door relief to the able-bodied.

Chadwick was appointed as the first Secretary to the Poor Law Commissioners, whose wide powers relating to the union of parishes made available for common use all workhouses in the union, although each parish remained separately chargeable for its own poor. The detailed responsibilities of the Commissioners included the following matters:

(i) the government of workhouses and education of children therein;

(ii) the management of parish poor children under an Act of 1767.

(iii) superintending, inspecting and regulating the houses wherein such poor children were kept and maintained;

(iv) apprenticing the children of poor persons;

(v) guidance and control of all guardians, vestries and parish officers.

By the time of the accession of Queen Victoria in 1837, the annual expenditure for the relief of the poor had been reduced by three million pounds. The Commissioners had wide powers of making orders, inspection and audit, and could dismiss officers. The duration of the Commission was extended until an Act of 1847 set up a new Commission, subsequently known as the Poor Law Board. The latter comprised persons appointed by the Crown and always included the Chancellor of the Exchequer, the Home Secretary, the Lord President of the Council and the Lord Privy Seal. The President of the Poor Law Board was a Minister of the Crown with a seat in Parliament. His functions were transferred to the President of the Local Government Board in 1871.

Medical attention was available under the Poor Law and some enterprising guardians of the poor had developed general hospitals, which were subsequently transferred to local authorities and, later, to hospital boards. The Local Government Act, 1929, abolished the boards of guardians and transferred their functions to local government. The National Assistance Act, 1948, finally abolished the Poor Law and transferred many of the formerly local functions to the National Assistance Board. The Board's duty was to assist, in cash or in kind, persons who are without resources or whose resources, including national insurance benefits, need supplementation. The Ministry of Social Security (since merged into the Department of Health and Social Security–see Chapter VI) was established in 1966, responsible for the administration of social security cash benefits. The N.A.B. was abolished and a Supplementary Benefits Commission set up in its place. The guiding principle, following the war-time Beveridge Report, an invaluable modern social document, is that no person in this country should be allowed to fall below a certain level of subsistence. County and county borough councils are still welfare authorities for certain functions under the 1948 Act, under the general supervision of the Secretary of State for the Social Services. They must provide residential accommodation for needy persons and are enabled to provide facilities for the disabled.

Thus has the wheel turned full circle, for the Poor Law which was amended by the Whigs in the reforming zeal of 1834 was later eradicated by the modern Labour Party, which partially replaced it with the Welfare State, building on foundations laid by the Liberals.

Public Health and Local Government. The Reports of the Poor Law Commissioners had drawn attention to grave defects of sanitary conditions, for in some cases in the towns, streets and rivers were little better than open sewers. Epidemics of cholera caused grave anxiety, particularly in 1847. The Commissioners urged that public health and poverty were related and, under Chadwick's influence, Parliament enacted the Births and Deaths Registration Act, 1836, enabling accurate and relevant records to be kept. This statistical information, coupled with the dire sanitary conditions prevailing, led to the passing of the Public Health Act, 1848.

This Act set up a general Board of Health as the central authority and provided that local boards could be constituted at the request of the local inhabitants or at the behest of the General Board, in the latter case if the death rate was high enough to warrant such action. A borough council could adopt the Act, thereby becoming the sanitary authority for the area of the borough. The 1848 Act enabled necessary action to be taken at local level on such matters as sewerage, paving, street lighting, water supply, burial grounds, public nuisances and control of offensive trades. Provision was also made for confirmation of bye-laws by a Secretary of State, appointment of officers and the levying of rates for these purposes. The Local Government Act, 1858, abolished the General Board and increased the power of the local boards; central control, such as it was, was shared between the Privy Council and the Local Government Department of the Home Office.

Many general and local Acts of Parliament were passed in the mid-nineteenth century dealing with vaccination, sanitation, removal of nuisances and prevention of disease. Nevertheless, a century ago the position of local government in this country was chaotic; indeed, it has been described as a chaos of areas, a chaos of authorities, a chaos of franchises and a chaos of rates. This was due to the development of the *ad hoc* boards of guardians to deal only with poor relief, boards of health administering only public health matters, burial boards, improvement commissions, highways districts and so on. Each authority administered only one service, over widely differing and conflicting areas and subject to the whims of similarly composed electorates; they also each levied rates for their various purposes. Central direction, which was not very well co-ordinated, came from the Privy Council, the Home Office, the Board of Trade, the Poor Law Board and the Medical Office.

A Royal Sanitary Commission reported in favour of the reconstruction of local government in 1871 and in the same year the Local Government Board was created under a President responsible to Parliament. This replaced the Poor Law Board and received powers from other departments. The Public Health Act, 1875 (some parts of which are still in force) provided a uniform code, for local government at this time was still almost exclusively concerned with matters of public health and sanitation. Under this Act, the borough councils and boards of guardians became public health authorities. The Local Government Act, 1888, transferred the administrative functions of the county magistrates to elected county councils and enabled larger boroughs to qualify for the status of county boroughs. The Local Government Act, 1894, created urban and rural districts in the counties and transferred public health and sanitary powers to their elected councils. These Acts still provide the basis of the structure of local government, which in the twentieth century replaced the former system of *ad hoc* boards and comprehended a large number of important services such as housing and highways. The impact of later local government statutes (e.g., those of 1933 and 1958) and the development of general local authorities will be described in Part II.

History of Education. The state did not begin to interest itself in education until the nineteenth century, such schools as there were having been provided by private benefactors. In 1811 the Church of England formed the National Society and three years later an undenominational British and Foreign School Society was formed. In 1833 Parliament voted small sums to both societies and from 1839 onwards the Education Committee of the Privy Council inspected the schools and allocated the grants. This Committee comprised the Lord President of the Council, the Lord Privy Seal, the Home Secretary and the Chancellor of the Exchequer. It was charged with the duty of superintending the appropriation of sums voted by Parliament for the purpose of promoting public education. In 1856 an Education Department was created within which was included the Establishment for the Encouragement of Art and Science developed by the Board of Trade. The Department was represented in Parliament and in the government by a Vice-President. At this stage the Department had a large measure of control but did not own any schools; local control of such a vital service was non-existent.

The great educational watershed of the nineteenth century was undoubtedly Forster's Elementary Education Act of 1870, enacted during Gladstone's first Administration. This Act provided the basis for educational advance for three-quarters of a century and gave the Education Department powers to secure the provision of efficient elementary schools by local School Boards, which were elected bodies empowered to levy an education rate. The board schools were set up alongside the pre-existing voluntary or "non-provided" schools which had been established privately, mainly by Church foundations. The school boards also provided higher grade and evening schools until restrained by the famous Cockerton judgment in 1901, which upheld the disallowance on audit of such expenditure. Meanwhile the Technical Instruction Act, 1889, had given the new county councils powers to provide secondary education.

In 1899 a Board of Education was established with a President responsible to Parliament; the new Board embraced the former functions of the Education Committee of the Privy Council and the Science and Art Department. With the creation of this new government department, the time was ripe to introduce the recently created local authorities to their most important function. The new Board of Education also acquired powers from the Board of Agriculture and the Charity Commission.

The Balfour Education Act of 1902 abolished the school boards [2] and transferred their powers to 378 local education authorities. The Board of Education was empowered to enforce the duty of providing efficient elementary education and the school-leaving age was raised from twelve to thirteen. The Board could also decide disputes between local education authorities and between the latter and managers of schools. The education rate was now levied for both the provided and non-provided schools, the former, the public elementary schools, being wholly maintained by the local authorities (assisted by government grant, replacing the former "assigned revenues" for education). The support of the voluntary or non-provided schools from the rates led to religious dissension, since nonconformists strenuously objected to the payment of rates in aid of denominational schools. The preservation of the denominational character of the voluntary schools was achieved by securing that a majority of the managers were to be appointed by the religious foundations.

The Fisher Education Act of 1918 raised the compulsory school attendance age to fourteen and required practical or advanced instruction to be made available in secondary schools, the local education authorities having to submit schemes in order to qualify for grants. It is curious that it generally takes a war to prod Parliament into raising the school-leaving age; it was raised at the end of the Boer War and towards the end of both World Wars.

The modern system of education. The Butler Education Act of 1944 was the next great milestone, replacing the Board with a Ministry. This Act raised the school-leaving age to fifteen and enables the Minister to increase it to sixteen by Order-in-Council. The Act's main achievement, however, was to end the system of elementary education and to divide public education into three stages—primary, secondary and further education. Primary schools provide education for children under twelve, secondary schools for children over twelve and colleges of further education for pupils over compulsory school age. Education must be provided in secondary schools for children up to the age of fifteen and there must be accommodation for those over that age who wish to remain at school.[3] It is the duty of the Minister to promote the education of the people and to secure the effective execution by local authorities, under his control and direction, of the national educational policy. Provision was made for the constitution of managers of primary schools and governors of secondary schools, and for an agreed syllabus on religious education in schools. No fees are to be charged in county (the former provided) or voluntary (non-provided) schools and the managers and governors of the latter now receive a government grant of 80 per cent. of expenditure. County and County borough councils are the local education authorities but delegation schemes can be made enabling the day-to-day administration of primary and secondary education to be delegated to county district councils (non-county borough, urban and rural district councils). Under the London Government Act, 1963, the Inner London Education Authority has replaced the London County Council Education Service; and the twenty Outer London Borough Councils are local education authorities. The twelve Inner London Boroughs are represented on the Inner London Education Authority.

For many years since the war the Minister of Education has hovered on the brink of the Cabinet but with the publication of the Robbins Report on Higher Education in 1963 a radical reorganisation of central administration was set in hand. In April, 1964, the Minister was replaced by a leading member of the Cabinet designated Secretary of State for Education and Science. He is assisted by two Ministers of State, one having responsibility for higher education (including the allocation of money to the University Grants Committee, a function formerly discharged by the Treasury) and the other being responsible for primary and secondary education. The last Minister of Education was Sir Edward Boyle,[4] the first Secretary of State Mr. Quintin Hogg; the first Labour Secretary of State was Mr. Michael Stewart (now Foreign Secretary), who was succeeded by Mr. Anthony Crosland (now Secretary of State for Local Government and Regional Planning). Subsequent Secretaries of

State have been Mr. Patrick Gordon-Walker and Mr. Edward Short. It can thus be seen that both major parties attach considerable weight to this key post in the government.

The transfer of children from primary to secondary schools at the age of eleven based on a competitive examination has led to public disquiet in recent years, owing to the tender age at which this examination is or was taken. With the development of comprehensive schools in the field of secondary education many authorities have felt able to abolish the so-called "eleven plus examination". In effect, the selection then takes place in the secondary schools, and a good comprehensive school is staffed and organised in such a way as to ensure that each child receives education in accordance with his age, ability and aptitude. The main criticism of these schools is their great size but this is also a social factor in encouraging classlessness (all the children of whatever origin wear the school uniform) and therefore the system is an attractive one to socialists. There is no doubt that many of these comprehensive schools are now achieving fine results. The London Borough of Enfield encountered some difficulties in attempting to introduce a system of comprehensive education in the borough.

In *Bradbury v. Enfield London Borough Council* (1968) L.G.R. 115, the main heads of decision were:

> (i) A change in the age range and sex of pupils is a fundamental change in the character of a school equivalent to "ceasing to maintain" it.
>
> (ii) Statutory requirements as to public notices must be complied with by the local education authority.
>
> (iii) Complaint could be made to the Minister about establishing new schools in advance of submitting plans conforming with prescribed standards and obtaining the Minister's approval (or his direction of exemption).

In *Lee v. Enfield London Borough Council* (1968) L.G.R. 195, an injunction was granted to restrain a local education authority from implementing a revised scheme for admission to a grammar school in contravention of its articles of government (which provided for taking account of parental wishes, suitability of education and school records).

In *Lee v. Department of Education and Science* (1968) L.G.R. 211, a voluntary controlled grammar school over 400 years old had been subjected to a scheme to allow an unusual type of comprehensive intake. The time for making statutory representations had been limited to less than five days. It was held that this was unreasonable and a denial of rights; the minimum period should have been four weeks, especially having regard to the fact that the procedure had been invoked during the summer holidays.

The Education Act, 1968—amends the law as to the effect of and procedure for making changes in the character, size or situation of county or voluntary schools to enable special age limits to be adopted for existing as well as for new schools.

The Civil Service. At the beginning of our period a patronage system of entry into the Civil Service obtained in this country and this led to grave scandals and abuse. The clerks entered the service at about the age of eighteen, obtaining their places purely on recommendation and without examination. The Treasury attempted to reform the patronage system by examining candidates for entry and placing them on a year's probation if accepted. Other departments used either examination or probation as a method of selection but both were inclined to be perfunctory. In 1853 the Northcote–Trevelyan Report condemned patronage and urged the merits of Open Competition. In 1855 a Civil Service Commission was established to enquire into the qualifications of candidates and to issue certificates to those considered suitable for employment. By Order-in-Council in 1870 the principle of Open Competition by written examination was made universal throughout the whole Civil Service, except for a few appointments made by the Crown or by the head of a department where special reasons exist for dispensing with an examination. This system of recruitment remains to this day, the Commissioners exercising an independent control of selection of candidates without any external or political pressure. In practice Civil Servants enjoy security of tenure, although technically they are subject to dismissal at the pleasure of the Crown under prerogative powers.

The Civil Service Selection Board makes regulations, subject to Treasury approval, for entrance examinations. Professional and technical officers are recruited by special examination or by selection after interview. There are three main classes or divisions in the Service:—Administrative, Executive and Clerical.

The Sixth Report of the Estimates Committee of the House of Commons,[5] which deals with recruitment to the Civil Service recommended a full-scale inquiry into the structure, recruitment and management of the Civil Service as a matter of urgency, possibly by means of a Royal Commission. There is a tradition in the Civil Service that a good administrator must be an amateur and this is reflected in the method of recruitment, particularly to the Administrative Class. This Class has been recruited mainly from among the younger arts graduates of the older universities. Fewer and fewer of such candidates have been entering the competitive examinations, partly because the modern graduates, particularly those from the provincial or "red-brick" universities, are no longer attracted. The Treasury was apparently alarmed at the prospect of a grave shortage of administrators but it was not prepared to make any changes in its methods of selection, which positively encouraged the present shortage of specialists. It is rare, if not unheard of, for a specialist such as an engineer, a lawyer or a scientist to head a government department as Permanent Secretary.

The following extracts from the Report are instructive and need no comment:

"There does not appear to have been any fundamental questioning of the basic structure, despite the wide range of experience available for this purpose both in private industry and commerce, and in the public service elsewhere.[6] In particular your committee find it hard to accept that the task of government justifies the unique significance attaching to the Administrative Class and that only a select few are fitted to undertake this work. . .

"It appears. . . that the Civil Service Commissions's procedures concentrate on keeping people out rather than attracting them."

There has been no difficulty in recruiting the Executive Class since 1963 and the Treasury believe that, as the number of potential recruits among school-leavers falls, recruitment of graduates will correspondingly increase. On the other hand, two out of every three senior scientific posts remain unfilled and there is also a serious shortage in certain professional classes.

The Report concludes that detailed examination might lead to changes in the follow three areas:

    (1) the extent of mobility within the Civil Service and between the Service and other occupations;

    (ii) the need for professional training;[7]

    (iii) the supply of qualified manpower.

The need for greater mobility between the Service and the outside world is stressed. The Report also postulates an administrative "cadet" grade and a smaller executive class of a higher standard. The former idea was, of course, pioneered many years ago by the London County Council.

The Prime Minister announced in the House of Commons in March, 1966, the appointment of a committee to examine the structure, recruitment and management, including training, of the Home Civil Service and to recommend any changes which they think necessary to ensure that the service is properly equipped for its role in the modern state. The chairman was Lord Fulton and the committee included Sir Edward Boyle and representatives of industry, the universities and the public service.

The Fulton Report was published in June, 1968 and recommended abolition of 1400 separate grades in the Civil Service, which should be replaced by a single, unified grading structure. No posts should be reserved for particular groups unless uniquely qualified (e.g. doctors for medical posts). Merit should be preferred to seniority in relation to promotion. Professional and technical specialists should have the same chance as administrators of achieving managerial responsibility. Inter-change with other forms of employment should be encouraged by late entry into the Service from business, the professions, public corporations, local government and the universities, in some cases on a temporary basis. A Civil Service College should be established to foster improved training facilities.

The Report has been implemented to the extent that, from 1st November, 1968, a new Civil Service Department was created, the Prime Minister being the Minister for Civil Service, assisted by the Lord Privy Seal; questions in the House of Commons on the Civil Service were answered by the Paymaster General.[8] Treasury functions relating to management of the Civil Service were transferred to the new Department. These functions include recruitment, pay, pensions, conditions of service, pay and pensions of the Armed Forces and certain public sector functions. The independence and political impartiality of the Civil Service Selection Board in the selection of individuals for appointment is said to have been safeguarded. Certainly the C.S.S.B. operates a very fair and comprehensive selection procedure with considerable professional expertise. In the case of some specialist appointments the final decision lies with the relevant Ministry, whose board members and assessment procedures based on a single interview, may not be so up to date. It might be advisable, therefore, for the C.S.S.B. to take over the recruitment function completely, assisted if necessary (as at present) by Ministry assessors. The size of Final Selection Boards has recently been reduced from 7 to 5 members.

The first government department to implement the Fulton Report was the Ministry of Public Building and Works which has replaced its separate and parallel hierarchies of professional and administrative staff by a unified system. Directors and managers responsible for a "block" of functions are drawn from both professionals and administrators in equal proportions. A controller-general is now responsible for directorates of finance and establishments, evaluation of completed projects, relations with the construction industry, the universities and professional institutions. The Civil Service Commission aim to introduce a new Qualifying Examination in 1971.

1. Utilitarianism.
2. The School Board for London was not replaced until 1904.
3. To an upper age limit of 19.
4. The first was Mr. R.A.Butler, as he then was.
5. House of Commons 308, H.M.S.O. 26s. (September 1965).
6. Notably local government.
7. Here the Treasury might have taken a leaf out of the book of the London Boroughs Training Committee.
8. Until October, 1969, when this function was transferred to a Minister without Portfolio.

CHAPTER V

THE COMPOSITION AND PROCEDURE OF PARLIAMENT

The Crown and Parliament. Parliament is made up of three component parts—the monarch, the House of Lords and the House of Commons—and is therefore sometimes described as the Queen in Parliament. The title to the Crown can be affected by statute: the Act of Settlement, 1700, provided for the Protestant succession and the Abdication Act, 1936, excluded the Duke of Windsor. With the evolution of the constitutional monarchy, the considerable prerogative powers of the Crown are exercised on political advice, that is, the advice of the Prime Minister or other senior Minister of the Crown such as the Home Secretary or the Foreign Secretary.

A Parliamentary session is opened annually by the sovereign, either in person or by commission. Nowadays the Queen usually performs the ceremony of the Opening of Parliament in person. This normally takes place in November, at the beginning of the Parliamentary year. General elections tend to take place in October but the timing is of course within the discretion of the Prime Minister. In 1966, for example, the election was held in March and the Opening of Parliament occurred in April. The Queen's Speech, which has been prepared by Her Majesty's Ministers, contains an outline of governmental achievements and aspirations and of proposed legislation in the new session. The Speech is delivered in the House of Lords,[1] the members of the House of Commons being also present. A debate on the Speech follows in the Commons but first, in accordance with tradition, members assert their historic right to deal with the "redress of grievances before supply". In other words, the members of the representative House of Parliament attend to the rights and liberties of the subject, before turning their attention to voting monies (supply) to the Crown in its capacity as the executive government of the country. The ensuing debate has been described as "the grand inquest of the nation".

The Crown is intimately involved with all the pauses in the parliamentary time-table except one, adjournment, which it is convenient to describe here. Each House has complete control of its adjournment and is not affected by the adjournment of the other. An adjournment of business may be from day to day, over a week-end or for longer periods at Christmas, Easter, Whitsun and in the summer. The two Houses of Parliament technically stand adjourned during the long summer recess (in 1965 it lasted from 5th August to 26th October).

A session is ended under the prerogative power of prorogation. The Crown also has power, again on the advice of the Prime Minister, to accelerate or postpone the Opening of Parliament. It was postponed for two weeks in 1963 to enable the then Prime Minister, Lord Home, to disclaim his peerage and to emerge, following a bye-election, as Sir Alec Douglas-Home, M.P. Parliament normally returns for a few days before being prorogued; this enables completion of all the stages of bills which have not yet received the Royal Assent. This is necessary because otherwise they would have to be introduced afresh and pass through all their stages again in the new session. In 1965 the Rent Act and the Murder (Abolition of Death Penalty) Act were dealt with in this way and receive; the Royal Assent on the day Parliament was prorogued.

Finally, Parliament is dissolved by the Crown on the advice of the Premier. Under the Parliament Act, 1911, Parliament must be automatically dissolved within five years of its first summons. In 1964 the outgoing Conservative Government remained until only two weeks of this period were left. Recent practice has been to dispense with prorogation at this stage, because a Dissolution Proclamation terminates the existence of a Parliament, whereas prorogation merely ends a session. The Proclamation orders returning officers in the various constituencies "to cause an election to be made of a member to serve in Parliament". The election campaign then gets under way and a new Parliament is summoned.

A fresh Government is formed, whichever party wins the election, because members of the pre-existing government, which remain in office during the election period, surrender their seals of office to the Crown when the result is known. Even if the party formerly in power wins the election the Adminstration formed by its leader is technically a new and different government; there will in any case probably be a redistribution of some portfolios.

The Queen also plays her part in giving the royal assent to bills which have passed all their stages in both Houses. Nowadays this is a formality and is given by a royal commission which always include the Lord Chancellor. Bill are accumulated for royal assent at certain times of the year, notably in April and in July or August. The assent has not been withheld since the reign of Queen Anne (1702-14) and it is inconceivable that this would happen to-day, since this would immediately embroil the Crown in party politics. The political neutrality and impartiality of the Crown is essential in a constitutional monarchy.

The House of Lords. The Upper House of Parliament is still largely hereditary and the customary division of its members is into the Lords Spiritual and the Lords Temporal. The former comprise the Archbishops and twenty-four senior bishops of the Established Church of England. The Lords Temporal can be classified into three distinct groups:

    (i) Hereditary peers of the realm;
    (ii) Lords of Appeal in Ordinary;
    (iii) Male and female life peers.

An hereditary peerage may have been created, under the royal prerogative, in respect of the realms of England,[2] Scotland,[2] Great Britain[3] or the United Kingdom (of Great Britain and Northern Ireland). The Lords of Appeal in Ordinary are life peers created under the Appellate Jurisdiction Act, 1876; they are the "law lords" who constitute the House of Lords when sitting judicially as the highest Court of Appeal in the land. The Life Peerages Act, 1958, enables the Crown, on the advice of the Premier, to create male and female life peers. It is possible that, in due course of time, the intelligent use of this power may transform the composition of the House of Lords. Lady Spencer-Churchill was created a life peer under this Act.

The composition of the House of Lords has also been affected by the enactment of the Peerage Act, 1963. This Act was passed largely as the result of the persistence of one man, Mr. Anthony Wedgwood-Benn, M.P.[4] In 1960 Lord Stansgate, an hereditary peer, died and his eldest surviving son, Mr. Benn, resigned his seat in the Commons and fought and won a bye-election. An election court found that he was disqualified from membership of the House of Commons because he automatically inherited the peerage of Stansgate upon the death of his father. He was therefore a member of the Upper House and could not enter the Commons, notwithstanding the fact that he had failed to apply for a writ of summons to the Lords. A Joint Select Committee of the two Houses of Parliament reported on the need for reform in 1962 and as a result the Peerage Act tied up several loose ends. In the first place, it enables the male heir to an hereditary peerage to disclaim the peerage; this does not have the effect of extinguishing the peerage because the *next* heir, upon the death of his father, can elect either to assume the peerage or to disclaim. Mr. Benn was the first to take advantage of these provisions and soon re-entered the House of Commons; others to follow suit included Sir Alec Douglas-Home and Mr. Quintin Hogg (formerly Lord Hailsham).

The Act also dealt with the position of Scottish and Irish peers and peeresses in their own right. Hitherto, Scottish peers had met at the beginning of each Parliament to elect sixteen representatives to sit in the House of Lords. In view of the changes in the composition of that Chamber since the Act of Union in 1706 it was felt that it was inequitable to exclude any[5] and so all Scottish peers can now sit in the Lords. On the other hand, there had been no election of Irish representative peers since 1919 and the last died in 1961. The Act therefore excludes Irish peers as such from the Lords but they are eligible to vote and stand in parliamentary elections if qualified by residence. Finally, the curious position of hereditary peeresses in their own right was cleared up. In 1922 the House of Lords, in its judicial capacity, held that such a person, who is the only surviving child of an hereditary peer who had died, was not eligible to sit in that House. The Act provides that an hereditary peeress in her own right can now sit in the House of Lords.

In recent years an attempt has been made to deal with the problem of the "backwoodsmen" in the House of Lords. These are the comparatively large numbers of hereditary peers who are not interested in parliamentary and public affairs. In 1958 a Standing Order of the House enabled a peer to apply for leave of absence. Peers and their wives can thus enjoy the ceremonial occasions such as the Opening of Parliament, whilst the "backwoodsmen" peers can avoid the necessity of attending sittings. The experiment appears to have worked well, under a "gentlemen's agreement". Expenses are paid on a daily basis for attendance whilst Parliament is sitting. Pressure on the House of Commons is alleviated by the introduction of some bills in the Upper House.

A White Paper on House of Lords Reform was published in November 1968 and included the following proposals. The reformed House should be a two-tier structure comprising voting peers with a right to speak and vote and non-voting peers with a right to speak. Voting members would be exclusively created peers but might also include some peers by succession if created life peers. The reformed House should include a suitable number of peers able to speak with authority on Scotland, Wales, Northern Ireland and the regions of England. The reformed House should be able to impose a delay of six months on the passage of an ordinary public bill received from the Commons on which there is a disagreement; the bill should then be submitted for the Royal Assent provided that a resolution to that effect had been passed in the Commons. The period of delay could run into a new session of Parliament. The House of Lords should be able to require the Commons to reconsider an affirmative order or to consider an negative order to which the House of Lords disagreed but its power of final rejection should be removed. Law lords and bishops should continue to sit in the Lords and all peers should be qualified to vote in Parliamentary elections. The proposals have been attacked on the ground that they would place too much patronage in the hands of the Prime Minister of the day. On the other hand, the second chamber as at present constituted is unrepresentative and remote from the people. The present voluntary abstention of backwoodsmen would be continued under the new arrangements. The voting House would consist of about 230 peers distributed between the parties so that the government had a small majority over opposition parties but not over the House as a whole. The balance would be held by the "cross-benchers", i.e. those without a specific party allegiance. This is alleged to be unworkable in some quarters, but the second chamber has never been subject to the same rigid party discipline as the House of Commons and it would be much fairer than the present system. In 1969 a bill was introduced on the composition and powers of the House of Lords but it was dropped by the government, partly because of the determined opposition of right wing Conservatives and left wing socialists, and partly to make room for an industrial relations bill which, in turn, was dropped.

The House of Commons. There are at present 630 members of the House of Commons, elected on the basis of universal adult suffrage, as we saw in Chapter III. There are four Parliamentary Boundary Commissions,[6] charged with the task of reviewing the areas and size of parliamentary constituencies within narrow limits. Their last review was effective at the general election of 1955; the current review is in process of completion and the Government proposes to reduce the number of parliamentary constituencies from 630 to 626. The recommendations of the Boundary Commission are to be implemented in full for constituencies in Greater London, where local government has been reorganised. The figure recommended by the Boundary Commission for the United Kingdom was 635 but the intention is to wait until after revision of local government areas following implementation of the Royal Commission Reports before making any other alterations. In due course, the Commission would be asked to recommend divisions for certain abnormally large constituencies outside Greater London.

This has led to a first-class constitutional crisis because the Conservative Opposition in Parliament alleges that the real reason behind the Labour Government's proposals is that reorganisation based on the Commissioner's Report would be injurious electorally to the Labour Party. The pre-existing legislation required the Home Secretary to lay Orders before Parliament "as soon as may be" and Conservative lawyers were of the opinion that he could be compelled to do so through the Courts by means of the prerogative order of *mandamus*. However, the strategy adopted in the House of Lords at committee stage of the House of Commons (Redistribution of Seats) Bill (No. 2) in July, 1969, was to amend the Bill in that sense. The net result of the Lords amendments would have been to compel the Home Secretary to lay draft Orders-in-Council before Parliament in respect of each report of the Boundary Commission on or before 31 March, 1970.

The Labour Government's answer was to table amendments to the Bill and to substitute an undertaking that the process of redrawing parliamentary boundaries would begin by 31 March, 1972. Such alterations would be on the basis either of new local government boundaries following implementation of the Redcliffe Maud Report or of the current recommendations of the Parliamentary Commissioners. The Home Secretary's amendments were laid in the Commons on 24 July, 1969, a day before Parliament adjourned for the long summer recess. They remained on the table throughout the recess after which the Bill was due to return to the Lords.

If the House of Lords again reject the Commons amendments, the bill would fall as Parliament is due to be prorogued in the autumn. In that event, the governments's intention is to reintroduce the bill as they want it in the new session of Parliament. Using the procedure available under the Parliament Acts the bill could become law by August, 1970. Meanwhile, a general election might be called in which case the bill would again fall if the election took place before August, 1970. A general election must in any event be held at the latest by the spring of 1971—See Appendix II.

A member of the House of Commons must be an adult British or Irish subject who is not legally disqualified (e.g., by reason of being an alien, a bankrupt, a convicted person, a mentally disordered patient or a peer). He must also be resident in this country and this applies to Irish subjects, who are technically aliens, so that special provision was made for them in this respect under the Ireland Act, 1949. Apart from three special cases, which can be summed up in the phrase "not subject to any legal disability", the old basis of disqualification used to be the holding of an office of profit under the Crown. The crucial test is the payment of salaries wholly out of monies provided by Parliament but, with the growth of public corporations and independent commissions, it began to be realised that the test was not wide enough in scope. Accordingly, the House of Commons (Disqualification) Act, 1957, lists in its Schedule a large number of public bodies, members of which are debarred from membership of the Commons.[7] The Act also names certain individual offices, such as town clerks, clerks of the peace and directors of the Bank of England, whose holders are similarly disqualified. Orders can be made under the Act disqualifying holders of offices created since 1957. The Schedule to the Act lists the following offices whose holders are absolutely barred from seeking election to the House of Commons (or from sitting there if by any chance they managed to secure election):

    (i)   Clergymen of the Church of England, Church of Ireland, Presbyterian (Established) Church of Scotland and Roman Catholic Church;

   (ii)   All major judicial offices;[8]

  (iii)   Civil Servants, whether permanent or temporary;

  (iv)   Members of the regular armed forces of the Crown;

   (v)   Members of police forces;

  (vi)   Members of legislatures of countries outside the Commonwealth;

(vii)   Members of numerous boards and commissions, e.g., the National Coal Board, the Central Electricity Generating Board, the Electricity Council, the Gas Council, the Area Gas Boards, the Area Electricity Boards, the Independent Television Authority, the Universities Grants Committee, the Monopolies Commission.

The aim here is to restrict the power of "the over-mighty subject" and the possibility of undesirable pressures from vested interests. The restriction is limited to membership of the governing bodies of these organisations; it does not apply to their employees.

The Act specifically retains the resignation Stewardships of the Chiltern Hundreds and the Manor of Northstead, thus preserving a link with the old law. These are sinecure offices of nominal value under the Crown and thus technically "offices of profit". A member of the House of Commons who wishes to resign his seat before a general election is held therefore applies for one of these Stewardships. The Act also provided that the maximum numbers of office-holders in the House of Commons should be seventy but this was raised to ninety-one by the Ministers of the Crown Act, 1964. Any dispute relating to an alleged disqualification can be referred to the Judicial Committee of the Privy Council for advice.

The machinery of parliamentary elections and the procedure for challenging an election by petition have already been described in Chapter III see pp 24-26. above. It remains for us to give a brief account of the privileges of the House of Commons and of the rights and duties of its members. At the Opening of each Parliament the Speaker of the House of Commons lays claim, on behalf of the Commons, to freedom of speech and debate; freedom from arrest; and the right of collective access to the Crown in order to tender advice. The most substantial of these is the first and it is guaranteed by the Bill of Rights, which enacts that the freedom of speech and debates or proceedings in Parliament ought not to be impeached or questioned in any Court or place outside Parliament. No action lies in the courts in respect of defamatory statements *made in the House*. The Parliamentary Papers Act, 1840, protects the publication of defamatory matter by authority of either House in *Hansard*, the official publication of Parliamentary proceedings. The Act also protects publication of fair and accurate extracts from papers published by Parliamentary authority. The Committee of Privileges of the House of Commons examines matters referred to it from time to time.[9]

Another privilege of the House of Commons is the right to regulate its own composition and procedure, although this is not claimed at the Opening of Parliament. The House has the right to suspend or expel members and the Speaker issues a warrant for the issue of a writ for an election to fill a casual vacancy. The courts will define the limits of parliamentary privilege in a proper case but they will not interfere with internal procedure. Thus Bradlaugh, the atheist M.P., was refused a declaration and injunction in connection with his exclusion from the House of Commons, which would not allow him to take the oath. Under the Oaths Act, 1888, an affirmation may now be made in lieu of an oath.

In December, 1968, the government tabled a motion to rescind a resolution of the House of Commons passed in 1762 under which it was technically a breach of parliamentary privilege to report proceedings of the House of Commons. This resolution has been literally more honoured in the breach than the observance but it is significant that the government has taken this action, which has been warmly welcomed by the fourth estate in general. Perhaps some of those who allege that freedom is under attack in this country should ponder this development.

The privileges of the House of Lords are substantially the same as those of the Commons; and aliens, bankrupts and convicted persons are also disqualified from the Upper House.

Members of the House of Commons dispose of considerable collective power in relation to their privileges and the legislative process. The individual power of a back-bencher is, however, limited owing to the arrangements for party discipline based on the Whip system. A member can ask a Minister questions at "Question-Time", which is usually the first business of the day. Questions are not tabled more than twenty-one days ahead. A member can also raise issues of urgent public importance on a motion for the adjournment and can participate in general debates. It is within the Speaker's discretion whether a question can be put down and within that of the relevant Minister whether it is in fact answered. Oral supplementary questions may also be asked. This method is supplemented by a Parliamentary Commissioner for Administration, whose duties are described in Chapter VI.

Parliamentary Procedure. The Speaker of the House of Commons is responsible for the maintenance of order and can suspend an unruly member from a sitting of the House; This is an example of his considerable disciplinary powers. Although originally a party politician, on election to the Speaker's chair he becomes an impartial arbiter, charged especially with the protection of minority rights. The Speaker is therefore chosen because he is trusted by members of all parties to assert their privileges and rights, to check occasional unseemly behaviour and generally to uphold the great dignity and prestige of the representative House of Parliament. Subject to the rulings of the Speaker, which are final, the internal procedure of the House of Commons is regulated by Standing and Sessional Orders. The former are permanent and are sometimes amended.

The Speaker leaves the Chair when the House is dealing with finance in a committee of the whole House; the Chair is then taken by his Deputy, the Chairman of Ways and Means. This also is an ancient and historic office and the committee is literally dealing with ways and means of raising the revenue required for government expenditure. The Chancellor of the Exchequer normally makes his annual Budget speech in April to this committee. Five or six Standing Committees are nominated by the Committee of Selection and their composition reflects the strengths of the political parties in the House. These are the Committees which usually deal with the Committee stage of a public bill. There are also Select Committees, which are smaller and deal with specialised matters such as Privileges, Procedure, Public Accounts and Statutory Instruments.

The Lord Chancellor is Speaker of the House of Lords, but, unlike his counterpart in the Commons, he is a member of the Government. He does not enjoy, or need, such disciplinary powers as are available to the Speaker of the House of Commons. The two Speakers, if necessary with their Counsel, consult together in case of disagreement between the two Houses. Each House has a Leader, who is a member of the government and responsible for the arrangement of business after consultation with the Whips ("the usual channels"). The Leadership of the House of Commons is often combined with some other office such as Lord President of the Council.[10]

A public general bill is one which is public in the sense that it will affect the nation as a whole and general in the sense that it will alter the general law (in some cases providing new law). Recent examples are the Town and Country Planning Act, 1968; and the Representation of the People Act, 1969. A public bill is usually introduced by a Minister of the Crown, having been first considered by the Legislative Committee of the Cabinet. It will represent government policy and its subject-matter will probably have been briefly mentioned in the Queen's Speech. After the formal first reading, the bill is printed; and it should be noted that a bill can originate in either House. The procedure described below therefore applies to both Houses.

The next stage of a public bill is the second reading when there is a debate on general principles, but no amendments are allowed. Following a recommendation of the Select Committee on Procedure, second readings of non-controversial bills are now taken by a Second Reading Committee. The bill is next "committed" to a Standing Committee, or if it is a measure affecting finance or constitutional rights, to a Committee of the Whole House. Here the real work on the bill is achieved, detailed amendments are made, each clause and line is scrupulously examined and the bill is knocked into shape. At report stage the full House decides whether to accept the changes wrought in Committee; usually it does so. On third reading only amendments to make the meaning clear are permitted. The bill then goes to the other House where all these stages, including the important Committee stage, are repeated. It is then returned with any amendments; disagreements between the Houses are usually resolved by the two Speakers but, in case of deadlock, the provisions of the Parliament Acts are available to ensure that the will of the Commons prevails. The bill is finally presented for the Royal Assent. There is a separate procedure for money bills, which are a type of public bill, and this will be described below in the section on the Parliament Acts.

The Parliament Acts. Under the Parliament Acts, 1911–49, a public general bill, if passed in the same form in the Commons in two successive sessions may be presented for the Royal Assent if it is rejected by the House of Lords on both occasions. This is subject to the proviso that not less than one year has elapsed between the second reading in the first session and the final reading in the third session in which it passed the

Commons. The delaying period was originally two years under the 1911 Act and was reduced to one year by the later amending Act, which did not affect any of the other provisions of the main 1911 Act.

The 1911 Act also provides that a money bill shall receive the Royal Assent if it is not passed by the Lords within a month of its receipt from the Coons. The House of Lords thus has virtually no power at all over money bills and one might say that such bills are merely sent to the Upper House as a courtesy and for information only. The certificate of the Speaker of the House of Commons that a bill is a money bill is final and conclusive and cannot be challenged.

The 1911 Act also limited the maximum duration of Parliament to five years and required the consent of the House of Lords to a bill extending this period and to the enactment of local bills. The effect of the Parliament Acts is to ensure the domination of the House of Commons in any dispute. In the case of money bills, the control of the Lower House of Parliament is now absolute and expresses in statutory form the aspirations of the Commons in this respect ever since the Civil War. In view of the basis of selection of the Speaker, it is extremely unlikely that his wide powers in relation to money bills would ever be exercised in an arbitrary or perverse manner.

It is arguable that the House of Lords could use its delaying power to embarrass a government in the fifth year of a Parliament because this would force the issue during the ensuing general election. The Commons will consider any Lords' amendments to a non-money bill and representatives of the two Speakers can usually settle differences. The House of Commons accepted some of the amendments made by the Upper House to the Government's important Rent Bill, which became law as the Rent Act, 1965.

Methods of curtailing discussion. The first method is the closure and this is used to end a debate. The closure motion is "that the question be now put" and the member moving it must be supported by at least one hundred members in the House of Commons. If the Speaker or Chairman of Ways and Means accepts the motion and it is carried on a vote being taken, no further debate is permitted and there must be another vote of the substantive motion before the House, that is, whatever was being discussed before the closure was moved.

The "guillotine" procedure entails the allocation of a fixed time to discussion of the contents of a bill, or of different parts of it. The guillotine falls on the expiry of the time and there must be no further debate on the clauses which have not been discussed. Under the "Kangaroo" procedure the Speaker at report stage or the Chairman at committee stage can select amendments for debate; a vote is eventually taken on all amendments, including those which have been omitted.

All governments have found it expedient to use these devices in order to get urgently needed legislation on the statute-book by a particular date.

If it has been decided that the guillotine is to be used, this will be announced on behalf of the government by the Leader of the House of Commons. The official Opposition usually protests vigorously upon the invocation of these procedures, particularly the "guillotine". They are undoubtedly an interference with the freedom of expression of individual members of Parliament and therefore a government will bring them into play with some reluctance. On the other hand, if the Opposition indulges in time-wasting tactics, the government of the day may be forced to use these methods in order to achieve the passing of legislation for which it considers that it has a mandate from the electorate. Moreover, as we have already seen, it is necessary for government-sponsored bills to receive Royal Assent before the prorogation of Parliament.

Local Bills and Private Members' Bills. A local or private bill is one introduced by a local authority or public corporation to alter the law in respect of the responsibilities of the public body concerned; the aim is usually to enlarge the powers of the authority. A local or private Act of Parliament therefore has only limited, application and should be distinguished from a public general Act which affects the whole country. The promoters must give public notice in the *London Gazette* and in the local press and must present a petition for leave to introduce the bill. Copies must be deposited[11] with the Clerk of the Parliaments and in the Committee and Private Bill Office. The first and second readings are usually formal, but there may be a debate on second reading if there are objections. The Committee stage is said to be judicial, because promoters and opponents are represented by Parliamentary Counsel. The latter have only a right of audience; the right to vote in Committee remains with the members of Parliament. Reports of government departments are considered at this stage and objectors often demand the inclusion of clauses to protect their interests. Report stage and third reading follow in the usual way and all the stages are duplicated in the other House, after which the bill is presented for the Royal Assent.

Certain days are allotted to private members' bills but such bills cannot authorise expenditure. Under the "Ten-Minute Rule" procedure, motion for leave to introduce a bill may be heard on any day. Such motions used to be heard after "Question-Time" but in the 1965–66 session of Parliament they were taken towards the end of the evening as an experiment. The bill falls after introduction under the "Ten-Minute Rule", the aim of the mover being to attract publicity to the subject-matter. If a member is lucky in the ballot he will need still more luck for his project to reach the statute-book, because the government of the day can easily scotch a private member's bill through its control of parliamentary business. A recent successful example is the private member's bill which became law as the Civic Amenities Act, 1967.

Delegated Legislation. An Act of Parliament may delegate authority to the Privy Council or to a Minister to make rules, regulations or orders; since the Statutory Instruments Act, 1946, these have been known collectively as statutory instruments. Orders-in-Council may be made by the Privy Council under the prerogative powers of the Crown, for example to ratify a treaty or to promulgate a colonial constitution. Such prerogative Orders-in-Council are original, not delegated, legislation, since they emanate from the inherent prerogative power of the Crown. But some statutes authorise the Privy Council to make an Order-in-Council, for example to bring an Act into force; this type of Order-in-Council is an example of delegated or subordinate legislation, and is a Statutory Instrument. The vast majority of Statutory Instruments, however, are made by Ministers of the Crown under the authority of an Act of Parliament. Recent examples are the Secretary of State for Employment and Productivity *Order,* 1968 made under the Ministers of the Crown (Transfer of Functions) Act, 1946; the County and Voluntary Schools (Notices) *Regulations,* 1968 made under the Education Act, 1944; and the Iron and Steel Arbitration Tribunal *Rules,* 1968, made under the Iron and Steel Acts 1949–67. They may be described as Orders, Rules or Regulations but they are all technically Statutory Instruments. Owing to the great complexity of modern legislation, it is necessary for provision to be made enabling Ministers to fill in administrative details in this way. There are certain parliamentary safeguards to prevent abuses following the recommendations of a Committee on Ministers' Powers in 1932.

In general, a Statutory Instrument must lie on the Table of each House of Parliament for forty days and is subject to either the affirmative or the negative procedure. Under the former, which is used in the more important cases including financial instruments, it is incumbent upon a Minister of the Crown to move a resolution approving the order. It is usual for the resolution to be carried in view of the government's majority and the disciplinary powers available to it.

Under the negative procedure, the instrument remains on the Table and comes into effect at the end of the laying period unless a "prayer" is successfully moved against it. In this case the prayer would be moved by a back-bencher but he is unlikely to succeed unless he can point to some radical defect in the instrument.

A Select Committee of the House of Commons was set up in 1944 and it draws the attention of the House to any Statutory Instrument which:

    (i) imposes a charge on the public revenues;

    (ii) excludes challenge in the courts;

    (iii) appears to make unusual or unexpected use of the statutory power;

    (iv) purports to have retrospective effect, there being no authority for this in the parent Act;

    (v) has been unjustifiably delayed in publication or laying;

    (vi) has not been promptly notified to the Speaker where the instrument has come into operation before laying on account of its urgency;

(vii) is not clear in meaning.

The first head illustrates the jealous control over finance rightly exercised by the House of Commons in the spirit of the Bill of Rights.

The second term of reference has been retained as a precautionary measure, although the general trend since the publication of the Franks Report in 1957 has been to encourage and provide for such challenge. Publication is by Her Majesty's Stationery Office; and the sixth head refers to the safeguard of reference to the two[12] Speakers in such cases as guardians of the interests and rights of Parliament. A statutory instrument can be declared null and void in the courts on the ground that it is *ultra vires* the enabling statute. Therefore the instrument must be within the scope of the Act and must fulfil the statutory purpose.

The bye-laws of local authorities have certain peculiarities and will be described in Part II;[13] they are a form of delegated legislation.

Reform in Parliamentary Procedure.[14] Politicians of all parties, academics and students of politics have for some years been pressing for reform. The recent increase in members' pay has perhaps established, at any rate for the time being, a corps of adequately paid members of Parliament. A member of the House of Commons now receives an annual salary of £3,250 "chargeable to the Vote of the House of Commons. This amount is currently under review". Regular attenders at the House of Lords can claim expenses of 4½ guineas a day during sittings of Parliament.

The Houses of Parliament are situate within the royal Palace of Westminster for which the Lord Great Chamberlain, an officer of the Queen's Household, has always been responsible. However, in March, 1965, Mr. Harold Wilson, the Prime Minister, announced in the House of Commons that "the control, use and occupation of the Palace of Westminster and its precincts would be permanently enjoyed by the House of Commons". Accordingly, the Speaker of the House of Commons is responsible for that part of the Palace occupied by the House; and the Lord Chancellor, as Speaker of the House of Lords, is responsible for that part occupied by the peers. The control of Westminster Hall, the oldest part of the Palace (which accommodated the Lying-in-State of Sir Winston Churchill towards the end of January, 1965), and of the crypt chapel is vested jointly in the Lord Great Chamberlain, representing the Queen, and the two Speakers. The Chamberlain retains his existing functions on royal occasions such as coronations and the Opening of Parliament. The Minister of Public Building and Works is responsible to the Queen-in-Parliament for the day-to-day management of Westminster Hall and of the crypt chapel and for the fabric of the Palace. These re-arrangements represent a useful advance in the control of parliamentary accommodation and the Select Committee Report on the Palace of Westminster has recently recommended the establishment of two service committees from the government front benches and two from the Opposition. A Services Committee was constituted in 1966 and, amongst other matters, it considered the possibility of the televising of Parliamentary proceedings. The opening of Parliament in April, 1966, was televised.

Other reforms which have been advocated include an extension of "Question-Time"; more time for private members' bills; and more free votes. We have already noted (pp.50 and 52, *ante*) the minor procedural reforms introduced in relation to second reading committees and the "Ten-Minute Rule". However, the government has rejected the recommendation of the Select Committee on Procedure that the administrative parts of a finance bill should be taken in committee. Finance bills will therefore still be taken in a committee of the whole House. A previous recommendation to transfer the Committee stage "upstairs" (i.e., to a Standing Committee) had foundered on the rock of the inalienable right of back-bench members to intervene, subject to the Speaker's discretion, at all stages of a money bill.

There were several reasons for the implementation of the recommendation that questions should not be tabled more than twenty-one days ahead. First, members had often to wait at least a month before getting a reply to an oral question. Next, not enough questions had been answered daily and this led to an undesirable growth in the number of supplementary questions. Finally, there was what the Leader of the House described[15] as the pre-emption of the order paper through members putting down questions weeks ahead, thus taking priority over other members.

These reforms can be summarised as useful but limited. One has only to compare the facilities afforded to the legislators of other countries such as Canada and the United States to realise that our professional politicians still labour under considerable disadvantages. For example they have to meet all secretarial expenses out of the annual salaries payable. It is true that they also enjoy free first-class rail travel between Westminster and their constituencies, but the ardours and financial cost of top-level political work in this country are hardly recompensed in a generous fashion. The old prejudice against professional politicians and all that the concept implies lingers on even into the third quarter of the twentieth century.

The allocation of more time to private members is desirable from two points of view. Not all legislation should emanate from the government; it should be leavened by the ideas of the independent back-bencher, if such an animal still exists. The second point is linked with the campaign for more free votes in Parliament. The back-bench member of Parliament should have more influence, if not more power. The twentieth century development of political party organisation, inside and outside Parliament, has led to the domination of Parliament by the Executive, i.e., the government. This trend should be reversed, and one way of assisting such a development would be to allow more free votes when the "Whips are off" and members are enabled to vote according to conscience. A system of proxy voting for sick M.P.s was suggested during the 1965–66 session[16] and this would undoubtedly enhance the dignity of Parliament. It would be a pity, however, if the ultimate introduction of voting machines were to coincide with such a loss of independence that the men could not be distinguished from the machines. Members of the stature of the late Sir Winston Chruchill and the late Aneurin Bevan are still needed at Westminster.

The **Constitutional Commission.** In the spring of 1969 the Prime Minister announced that a Constitutional Commission would investigate the relationship between the constituent parts of the United Kingdom—England, Scotland, Wales, Northern Ireland, the Channel Islands and the Isle of Man. The terms of reference of the Commission are "to examine the present function of the central legislature and government in relation to the several countries, nations and regions of the U.K." The Northern Ireland Parliament at Stormont, Belfast, is elected on the basis of universal suffrage. The Ulster Government has responsibility for internal matters such as education, housing, health, welfare, police, law and order. The United Kingdom Government and Parliament is responsible for the defence and foreign affairs policy of Northern Ireland and, indeed, for all matters appertaining to the Crown; substantial subsidies are payable. The U.K. has the residual power of control, including the right to intervene on such matters as the administration of justice and public order and internal security. The Company vote in local elections is to be abolished at an early date and further review of the franchise will take place on the restructuring of local government. Where powers under the Special Powers Act are in conflict with Britain's international obligations, they will be withdrawn when this can be done without undue hazard. A Parliamentary Commissioner is to be appointed in Northern Ireland for central government matters. Finally, local authorities are to be told to allocate houses on the basis of a comprehensible and published scheme.

It is convenient here to mention the proposal, aired in certain quarters, that there should be a written Bill of Rights. The basis for this is said to be the increasing powers of the State and, in particular, the bureaucracy. Dozens of officials now have rights of entry to private houses and there is no protection of the right to privacy which is increasingly invaded by representatives of the Press. The gravamen of the discussion is whether a comprehensive Bill of Rights could rectify all these matters or whether they should be put right in separate legislation, having regard to subject matter and enforceability. The author inclines to the latter view.

1 By the Lord Chancellor if the opening is by royal commission.
2 Before the Union of the two countries in 1707.
3 After the Union.
4 Now Minister of Technology (as expanded).
5 There are only 32.
6 For England, Scotland, Wales and Northern Ireland.
7 They can sit in the Lords.
8 Borough Recorders, Chairmen and Deputy Chairmen of Quarter Sessions are disqualified only in respect of the constituencies in which they serve in these judicial offices.
9 E.g. in 1958 the correspondence between an M.P. and the London Electricity Board was treated as *prima facie* privileged, but the House, on a free vote, decided not to pursue the matter.
10 The holder need not be a peer.
11 By 27th November, i.e. early in the new session.
12 There is a Special Orders Committee in the House of Lords with similar terms of reference.
13 See Chapter XIII.
14 This matter will be considered further in Chapter XX.
15 Debate in House of Commons, 27th October, 1965.
16 H.C. Paper No. 361 (12th November, 1965).

CHAPTER VI

THE ADMINISTRATION

Upon being commissioned to form a government by the Queen, the Prime Minister and First Lord of the Treasury nominates some of his leading parliamentary supporters for membership of the Cabinet, which nowadays includes some twenty Ministers. In recent years the practice has developed of designating a senior Minister as First Secretary of State. The Inner Cabinet is grouped round the Premier and First Secretary and includes the Chancellor of the Exchequer, the Lord Chancellor, the Home Secretary, the Foreign Secretary and the Leader of the House of Commons. Other important members of the Cabinet include the Defence Secretary, the Education Secretary, the Employment and Productivity Secretary, the Social Services Secretary, the Local Government and Regional Planning Secretary and the Minister of Technology. The word "Secretary" in this connection is being used as a form of shorthand for "Secretary of State". The full title of the Foreign Secretary, for example, is "Her Majesty's Principal Secretary of State for Foreign and Commonwealth Affairs".

Originally there was only one Secretary of State, the Keeper of the King's secrets. Under the Tudors there were two Secretaries and in the course of time others were added. The distinction between a Secretary of State and a Minister of the Crown used to be that the former was a creation of the royal prerogative and the latter a creation of an Act of Parliament. In the latter case this is still true but some recent Secretaryships have been created by statute and, in any event, a Secretary of State is also a Minister of the Crown. The historical evolution is interesting, even fascinating, but there is not the time to describe it in an elementary textbook of this nature. Suffice it to say that, in general, a Secretary of State heads a more important department and has more power and influence than a Minister.

We shall be describing below some of the main government departments, from which it will be seen that the Lord Chancellor and the Chancellor of the Exchequer are extremely powerful Ministers on a level with the chief Secretaries of State. There are also the sinecure office holders, of whom the Lord President of the Council is nowadays a leading member of the Cabinet. Usually at least three members of the Cabinet are in the House of Lords but Mr. Wilson's government includes only two peers in the Cabinet; there are, however, a dozen peers amongst the junior Ministers. All the other members must be drawn from the House of Commons, where the Prime Minister and the Treasury Ministers must sit. It is a twentieth century convention that the Premier should be in the Commons: apart from Lord Home's brief spell of two weeks as Prime Minister whilst Parliament was in recess, there has been no Premier in the House of Lords since 1902.[1] Apart from the difficulty of conducting the nation's affairs from the Upper House in view of the dominance of the Lower, it could be argued that the Premier is technically a Treasury Minister in view of his designation as First Lord of the Treasury.

The present size of the Administration can be envisaged when it is realised that the Ministers of the Crown Act, 1964, increased the total numbers of Ministers who may sit and vote in the House of Commons to 91[2]. They include not only Cabinet Ministers but Ministers of Cabinet rank not in the Cabinet (this means that they are in charge of a government department, e.g., Minister of Transport), Ministers of State, Law Officers and Parliamentary Secretaries. The Ministerial Salaries Consolidation Act, 1965, is the current authority for the salaries of Ministers, Opposition Leaders and Whips and for the payment of pensions to former Prime Ministers. We now turn our attention to the examination and description of some of the more important offices and departments.

The Treasury. The political control of the Treasury is divided between the Prime Minister, in his capacity as First Lord, and the Chancellor of the Exchequer. There was until 1956 a single Permanent Secretary to the Treasury, the top post in the Home Civil Service. Owing to pressure of work two Joint Permanent Secretaries were appointed; and in 1963 the post of Secretary to the Cabinet held by one of them became a separate office. The Prime Minister's Office thus includes the Secretary to the Cabinet and the Cabinet Secretariat.[3] Since 1968 the Permanent Secretary to the Civil Service Department has been Head of the Home Civil Service, responsible to the Prime Minister for management and establishment policy. The word "management" today is one of the most overworked in our vocabulary and means what the speaker or writer thinks it ought to mean. In this connection it means the detailed control of the actual work of government departments as distinct from staffing and recruitment, which is the "establishment" function.

The Chancellor of the Exchequer is assisted by the Chief Secretary to the Treasury, a political post first created in 1961. The Chief Secretary is particularly concerned with the collation and preparation of the estimates annually presented to Parliament. The spending departments submit their estimates to the Treasury which, in the time-honoured tradition, usually reduces them before they reach the House of Commons. As soon as the estimates have been collated in this way in the autumn they are examined by that House's Select Committee on Estimates, which has the power of examining the Civil Servants responsible. The Permanent Secretary to the Treasury is responsible for finance, the Civil Public Sector and the Economic Section.

The Comptroller and Auditor-General is a public official whose salary and security of tenure are on the same sound basis as those of the judges.[4]

The Chancellor of the Exchequer presents his annual budget speech in April or May to the Committee of Ways and Means, a committee of the whole House of Commons. The budget deals with methods of raising revenue, particularly taxation, during the coming year. By convention, the Queen and the remainder of the Cabinet are informed of the proposals shortly beforehand; and they are subsequently embodied in the annual Finance Act. The Budget Speech, made to a packed House of Commons, usually contains a review of the past financial year, which begins on 6th April. The Chancellor of the Exchequer has power to make orders on financial matters at any time: for example, he can vary the rates of purchase tax. He was formerly assisted in one aspect of his work by the establishment in 1962 of the National Incomes Commission, now superseded by the National Prices and Incomes Board. A White Paper containing an analysis of national income is published at the same time as the Budget.

Permanent statutes authorise the collection of much of the revenue, such as Customs and excise duties; any alteration in their rates must be included in the Budget. Income tax and surtax must be authorised annually and the Speech will deal with any proposed variations, usually in an upward direction, of the standard rate of income tax. Under the Provisional Collection of Taxes Act, 1968, the financial resolutions relating to variation of existing taxes are passed in Parliament immediately after the Budget speech and come into operation straightaway, so that taxes can be collected on the new basis. This is subject to certain safeguards, the main one being that the Finance Bill should be presented for the Royal Assent within four months, i.e., before Parliament adjourns for the long summer recess. The Finance Act, 1965, was a very long and complicated measure and introduced a new Capital Gains tax and a new Corporation tax on companies; it received the Royal Assent on 5th August, 1965. The 1968 Act applies to repeal, renewal and variation of taxes and replaces the 1913 Act.

The annual Budget procedure has been criticised as archaic and unsound in the modern age. It might be necessary to adjust taxation in the autumn rather than the spring although such devices as the purchase tax regulations are open to the Chancellor of the Exchequer. It might be preferable to have quinquennial Budgets with minor adjustments in the interim, coupled with forward planning of the nation's economy.

The First Report from the Select Committee on Procedure, 1968/69 (published by H.M.S.O., September, 1969) recommends that the Select Committee on Estimates should be replaced by a Select Committee on Expenditure. The new Committee would discuss strategy and policies in projections of public expenditure for several years ahead; and it would examine new managerial methods to implement strategy and execute policies, as reflected in the annual estimates. The Committee would also assess results and value for money on the basis of annual departmental accounts. The Committee's Report is linked with government proposals in a Green Paper On Public Expenditure and is considered in more detail in Chapter XIX.

The Home Office. Until the very recent advent of the First Secretary of State the Home Secretary was the senior Secretary of State: to give him his full title, he is Her Majesty's Principal Secretary of State for the Home Department. His antecedents can be traced right back to the original Secretary of State of the absolute monarchy. A modern Home Secretary can be described as a residuary legatee amongst Ministers because his department has assimilated so many functions. The historic origins of the office ensure that he has a special link with the Crown: for example, he exercises the prerogative of mercy on the Queen's behalf in criminal cases and petitions to the Crown are presented to the Home Secretary where no other procedure is available. He is also the Cabinet's liaison officer with the government of Northern Ireland, which has legislative autonomy in domestic matters such as education, health and welfare.

The Home Secretary's most important functions relate to the maintenance of law and order, for which he is responsible throughout England and Wales.[5] He therefore controls, directly or indirectly, the various police forces; and he is the co-ordinating Minister responsible for the fire protection and Civil Defence services, which are administered at local level by the elected local authorities. In the area of the Metropolitan Police District, which is approximately the same as Greater London, the Home Secretary is the police authority, acting through a Commissioner and Assistant Commissioners. In the area of a county borough the local police force is responsible to a Watch Committee of the corporation; in the area of a county it is responsible to a police committee of the County Council. Under the Police Act, 1964, a Watch or police committee must have two-thirds of its members drawn from the local council and one-third from the local magistracy. The Home Secretary has wide powers to order amalgamation of two or more police forces in the public interest to promote greater efficiency;[6] an amalgamation creates a "combined police force" on which serve an equal proportion of members of the constituent councils and of the local justices. The small enclave of the City of London has its own separate police force for the square mile of the City, responsible to the Common Council of the Corporation. The Home Secretary has an Inspectorate of Constabulary to report to him on the efficiency or otherwise of local police forces. A Home Office grant of 50 per cent. of the cost of the police service is made to the local police authorities, including the Receiver of the Metropolitan Police who controls administration, buildings and finance in the District. The Home Secretary has the power to withhold or reduce the police grant if he is dissatisfied with the standards achieved but the power is rarely invoked as withdrawal of funds tends to increase, rather than decrease, inefficiency. A more efficacious power is that to order an amalgamation. He also has the right to veto the appointment of a chief constable and even to order the removal of a name from a "short-list" for the post: this is sometimes done to further the departmental policy of discouraging "in-breeding" so that, for example, a deputy chief constable of a county police force is encouraged to seek promotion outside that particular force. The opportunity was taken in the Police Act, 1964[7] to tie up a number of loose ends. The constitutional position of the police is obscure, since they are neither Crown servants nor local government officers. However, the Act enables a citizen aggrieved by, for example, an alleged false imprisonment, to sue the Chief Constable in tort and, if he is successful, any award of damages or costs will be recoverable from the police fund. The Act also extended a constable's jurisdiction (or "bailiwick") to the whole of England and Wales, thus answering to some extent the advocates of a national police force, with its attendant dangers of centralised bureaucracy and undesirably tight political control. Co-operation between local police forces has increased, particularly in criminal and road traffic matters, and criminals can now be followed over local government boundaries.

The Home Secretary exercises the prerogative of mercy on behalf of the Queen. The glamour surrounding this power will doubtless disappear as a result of the abolition of capital punishment in this country. However, the prerogative is available in respect of less serious crimes and can be used not only to grant remission of sentence but also to order a reprieve or even a free pardon in a clear case. The former Prison Commission has been replaced by the Prison Department of the Home Office, the Secretary of State being responsible for the administration of prisons and borstals. There is also a Probation and After-Care Department at the Home Office dealing with the probation service available in the Courts and the welfare of released prisoners, including recidivists ("old lags"). It is appropriate, therefore, that the Criminal Law Revision Committee should present its Reports to the Home Secretary.

The Home Secretary is assisted by a Minister of State and two Under-Secretaries of State. The Immigration and Nationality Department of the Home Office deals with control of immigration under legislative powers; and with the naturalisation and deportation of aliens. In the latter respect, the Home Secretary is said to have an absolute discretion since his actions cannot be challenged in the courts. The possible controls are either political, by means of parliamentary question or protest meeting; or diplomatic, whereby the ambassador or consul of the alien's country of origin may make representations on his behalf. The prerogative power lingers in this field, although statute has also intervened. The overall effect is illiberal and alien to this country's best traditions. The deportation power has been used as a cloak for extradition at the instance of a foreign power, but the undertaking given in the last Parliament but one to amend the Fugitive Offenders Act, 1881 (in relation to fugitives from Commonwealth Member States) has now been redeemed.[8] There is now statutory provision for appeal against immigration decisions.[9]

The Secretary of State is the senior Minister responsible for the smooth running of the machinery of parliamentary and local government elections and deals, for example, with applications for alterations in the boundaries of electoral wards; in case of dispute, the Home Secretary will decide who the returning officer should be in a particular constituency.

The Home Secretary deals with a mass of miscellaneous matters affecting the welfare of the community. Thus he is the Minister responsible for the child care service, administered locally by the elected authorities under the Children Acts and centrally in the Children's Department.[10] His approval is required for the appointment of a children's officer in a county or county borough. He is responsible for the administration of "summer time"; firearms; burials and cremation; and liquor licensing. Recent legislation dealing with such diverse matters as street offences (this relates to the activities of prostitutes, not road traffic), licensing, betting and gaming has emanated from the Home Office.

The Lord Chancellor. We noticed in Chapter I that the Lord Chancellor is the biggest single exception to the doctrine of the separation of powers. He is a leading member of the Cabinet and is the principal constitutional expert in the government. The office of Lord High Chancellor is of great antiquity and antedates that of the original Secretary of State. He receives an additional salary as Speaker of the House of Lords, where he not only presides but also acts as chief government spokesman. He is also Head of the Judiciary and *ex officio* entitled to preside over the House of Lords in its judicial role and the Judicial Committee of the Privy Council. He is also Head of the Chancery Division of the High Court and President of the Supreme Court of Judicature. He advises the Crown on the appointment of High Court Judges, county court judges, metropolitan and stipendiary magistrates and borough recorders. He appoints and may dismiss lay justices of the peace[11] and is *ex officio* a member of the Rules Committee of the Supreme Court; from time to time he promulgates Rules of the Supreme Court. The Council on Tribunals reports to the Lord Chancellor, who may make procedural rules on their recommendation. His responsibility for ecclesiastical partronage is greater than that of the two Archbishops. There is a small Lord Chancellor's Department to which standing committees on law reform report. A recent development was the establishment of a law commission under the Law Commission Act, 1965.

The four Commissioners, under the Chairmanship of Mr. Justice Searman, are charged with the duty of reviewing the law and making recommendations as to its reform, codification and consolidation in the light of modern needs and conditions. A start has been made on the law of contract; the law relating to personal injuries; landlord and tenant; and family law. A fruitful field in the public law sector might well be planning law and compulsory purchase procedure, where anomalies and injustices remain, despite numerous recent statutes and statutory instruments (e.g., the consolidating Inquiries Procedure Rules, 1965). Such bodies as the Land Registry, the Public Trustee and the Public Records Office also come within the purview of the Department.

The functions that would be performed by a Continental Minister of the Interior or Minister of Justice are shared between the Lord Chancellor and the Home Secretary. There is a considerable overlap in relation to the administration of justice in the inferior courts; whilst the Lord Chancellor appoints the lay magistrates, the Home Secretary controls such matters as the financing of court buildings, magistrates' courts' committees and the probation service. The burden of work upon an active Lord Chancellor is immense and he rarely has time to exercise his privilege of sitting in one of the higher Courts.

The Law Officers of the Crown. The Attorney-General and his deputy the Solicitor General are selected from practising barristers in the House of Commons who support the party or coalition in power. The Lord Advocate and the Solicitor-General for Scotland are not required to sit in Parliament. The law officers represent the Crown in litigation and act as general legal advisers to the government. Whilst the Lord Chancellor advises mainly on constitutional questions the Attorney-General may also assist in this field, as in the Rhodesian crisis of 1965–66. But the main function of the law officers is to appear for the Crown in civil proceedings and public prosecutions. At one time they received separate fees as members of the Bar for this work but nowadays they rely on their parliamentary salary and expenses.

The Attorney-General is said to be the "protector of public rights" and therefore an applicant for a declaratory judgment of the High Court on the law may seek to join the Attorney-General in the action. If the Attorney-General agrees to this it strengthens the applicant's case: he is said to have a *prima facie* case, that is he has a case worth investigating, one that is not merely frivolous or imaginary. The Court will not adjudicate upon a hypothetical case: there must be a set of facts for it to examine. An action for a declaration may be instituted by an ordinary citizen in his capacity as an elector or ratepayer, or by a local or public authority. The procedure has been invoked to prevent a local authority from acting without statutory authorisation; and by a local authority to restrain an individual from flouting the law. As disobedience of a declaratory judgment is not contempt of court an application is often coupled with an action for an injunction, which is enforceable. It sometimes happens that a fine is an inadequate remedy if good profits are being made and this procedure is the only method of securing compliance with the law.

Foreign and Commonwealth Affairs. The Foreign and Commonwealth Relations Secretary acts on behalf of the Crown in foreign affairs and makes extensive use of prerogative powers, for example to declare war, make peace and assent to a treaty. However, there are certain constitutional and parliamentary safeguards.

A declaration of war made under the prerogative would have little practical effect if Parliament refused to vote the necessary supplies to carry on a war. The point is somewhat academic, since a Foreign Secretary is hardly likely to take such drastic action without the knowledge of parliamentary support. Similarly, if a treaty adversely affects the substantive rights of British subjects, for example by creating new crimes or restricting liberty, an Act of Parliament is necessary for its application in this country. The Foreign Secretary is the principal representative of the United Kingdom in international matters such as negotiations with other countries and at the United Nations. He is assisted by three Ministers of State, one of whom (Lord Caradon, formerly Sir Hugh Foot) is permanently attached to U.N. Headquarters in New York, whilst another (Lord Chalfont) is "Minister for Disarmament" at Geneva; and by two Under-Secretaries of State. (a junior Minister).

The Foreign and Commonwealth Relations Secretary also deals with external affairs relating to the independent Member States of the Commonwealth. These comprise those where the Queen is Head of State as in the United Kingdom, Canada, Australia, New Zealand and Malta; and those which have their own Head of State, usually a President,—the African and Asian Members. All Member States acknowledge the Queen as Head of the Commonwealth, thus preserving the link with the United Kingdom. Just as the Foreign Office, on behalf of the Crown, deals with the Ambassadors of foreign powers (who are accredited to "the Court of St. James") it also maintains diplomatic relations with the High Commissioners of Commonwealth countries and is the channel for communicating general developments in foreign affairs to Commonwealth Members. There was established in January, 1965, the new Diplomatic Service, an amalgamation of the Foreign Service, the Commonwealth Service and the Trade Commissioner Service of the Board of Trade. Its overseas members provide the staffs of British Embassies, High Commissions, Consulates and permanent delegations to international bodies.

Some other functions of the three former departments, i.e., the Foreign, Commonwealth and Colonial offices, were assimilated in 1961 in the Department of Technical Co-operation, which in 1964 was absorbed in the new Ministry of Overseas Development, assisted by a Parlimentary

Secretary. This Department provides technical assistance and advice to under-developed countries. The United Kingdom is still responsible for certain protectorates and colonies and the new Department is one method of executing commitments under the United Nations Charter.

Defence. Except in war-time, there used to be no separate Ministry of Defence; during the second world war Churchill held the portfolio in addition to the Premiership. Until 1947 the First Lord of the Admiralty and the Secretaries of State for War and Air were members of the Cabinet. In that year a separate Ministry of Defence was created to co-ordinate defence, the individual service ministers losing their seats in the Cabinet but remaining "Ministers of Cabinet rank". A considerable reorganisation of Defence was effected in 1964, the aim being to have a much more unified Defence Department more or less on the Pentagon or MacNamara model. The Minister, already in the Cabinet, was redesignated Secretary of State, thus becoming a leading member of the Cabinet. On the other hand the service ministers lost their ancient and resounding titles and became Ministers of Defence for the Army, the Royal Navy and the Royal Air Force, assisted by an Under-Secretary of State. The Secretary of State and the Ministers are assisted by the Chief of the Defence Staff, Chief of the Naval Staff and First Sea Lord, Chief of the General Staff (Army) and Chief of the Air Staff. These latter are senior service appointments. In addition to the usual Civil Service staff under a Permanent Under-Secretary, there are specialist appointments such as a Chief Scientific Adviser. A further reorganisation in 1968 replaced the three Ministers of State with two Ministers of Defence for the whole range—one for Administration and one for Equipment.

The Secretary of State for Defence is in a powerful position and must be one of the key figures in any government. One of the effects of the disappearance of the Board of Admiralty is that the Queen is now Lord High Admiral.

Comprehensive reviews of defence commitments were completed in 1966 and 1968.

Department of Health and Social Security. The former separate Ministries of Health and Social Security have been amalgamated to form a new Department of Health and Social Security headed by the Secretary of State for Social Services (a new appointment) with effect from November 1, 1968. He is assisted by two ministers of State and two Under-Secretaries of State. The new Department has a tremendous amount of planning and legislation in prospect. The Secretary of State has inherited from the old Ministry of Health the Report of the Royal Commission on Medical Education and that Ministry's Green Paper on the administration of the Health Service; and from the old Ministry of Social Security the Seebohm Report on the Social Services. Moreover, the following passage occurred in the Queen's Speech: "Our social security

schemes will be kept under close review. My Government will publish for
discussion proposals for a new scheme of national insurance founded on
earnings-related benefits and contributions". A White Paper on this
subject was published in 1969 and legislation is expected in the next
session of Parliament. The Secretary of State is also the Cabinet Minister
responsible for co-ordinating the whole range of social services.

The Medical Education Report postulates extensive vocational
training in general practice to make it a coherent speciality and the
medical schools have managed to escape the restrictions on university
spending. The Green Paper on the NHS provides tentative proposals on
the administrative structure of the Medical and Related Services in
England and Wales as a basis for discussion. Its main suggestion is the
creation of new Area Health Boards (or Authorities) to replace existing
Executive Councils, Regional Hospital Boards, Boards of Governors and
Hospital Management Committees. It is also envisaged that certain
community and local health services should be performed by the new
boards and thus leave local government, a proposal in conflict with the
Seebohm Report and one which has naturally been hotly contested by
some of the local authority associations. Even aspects of public health and
port health are included in the Paper in this connection. Aspects of
organisation of the proposed boards are considered in some detail in
Chapter 3. The main proposal of the Seebohm Report is for unified
control of one Ministry. At present child care and Children's legislation is
the responsiblity of the Home Office at central level and this should, of
course, be transferred to the new Department. Paragraph 137 of the
Report states:

"A high level of citizen participation is vital to the successful
development of services which are sensitive to local needs and we do
not see how at present this can be achieved outside the local
government system".

The Report also emphasises the contribution of voluntary bodies in this
field and co-ordination of this work at local level is surely essential; it also
calls for creation of a new governmental inspectorate of local social
services. Local government, reformed or unreformed, is the obvious
vehicle for administration of the social services comprising personal
health; child care; welfare of the aged, mentally disordered and physically
handicapped; and perhaps some aspects of housing and public health
(transfer of these functions at central level would involve the Ministry of
Housing and Local Government).

The Department of Employment and Productivity. The Secretary of
State for Employment and Productivity Order 1968 (S.I. 1968 No. 729)
transferred to the new Secretary of State all functions of the old Ministry
of Labour, which was dissolved. The Order came into operation on May
15, 1968. The Minister, who is also designated First Secretary of State, is
assisted by a Minister of State and an Under-Secretary. Responsibility for

the administration of the prices and incomes policy was transferred to the new Department from the D.E.A. Thus the National Board for Prices and Incomes reports direct to the Secretary of State who is also responsible for the prices and incomes legislation and administrative action arising under it.

The Department inherited the Employment Exchange Service which derived from the Labour Exchanges set up by Winston Churchill in 1908 when he was President of the Board of Trade. They were subsequently transferred to the Ministry of Labour on its inception in 1919. The modern service includes the Occupational Guidance Units set up in 1966 and this has greatly helped many affected by redundancy or wishing to change their employment; there are now 24 such units in Britain and nearly 100 guidance officers. Employment Exchanges now provide a housing information service for employers and workers and a resettlement transfer scheme for unemployed. Placing officers at the exchanges have been trained at Government Training Centres, at technical colleges and in industry. A Dictionary of Occupations is available to the 900 employment exchanges in Britain. Special services include the Professional and Executive Register, the Commercial Register, an advisory nursing service, Disablement Resettlement and a Hotel and Catering Service. The Department's Training Within Industry (T.W.I.) service offers courses to develop the skills of supervisors employed in industry and is very popular; it is used also by some of the industrial training boards. There are also special Courses for supervisors employed in offices, hospitals and in retail distribution. The Training Development Service of T.W.I. provides for the training of skilled operators as instructors. Special facilities are available in Development Areas, including weekly training grants and the loan of government instructors and Instructor Training College lecturers.

Industrial Relations Officers and Technical Officers advise employers on such matters as manpower use and planning, recruitment, labour turnover, training, communications, redundancy, productivity and demarcation agreements. Employment exchanges throughout Britain pay unemployment benefit as agents for the Department of Health and Social Security. In 55 local offices an experiment has been undertaken in payment by post and eventually computers will be used.

The Secretary of State makes the "Board" and "Levy" Orders under the Industrial Training Act, 1964 regulating and defining the activities of the industrial training boards, of which there are now 26 (e.g. engineering, shipbuilding, construction, iron and steel, furniture and timber, hotel and catering, civil air transport, road transport, chemical and allied products, distributive industry, printing and publishing, paper and paper products). Broadly, the "Board" Order defines the appropriate industry and the "levy" order authorises the imposition of a levy on the annual emoluments paid by employers in that industry. Provision is made for appeal to an industrial tribunal but the only valid grounds are either that the employer is not within the industry as defined or that there has been an arithmetical or clerical error in calculation of the levy. An industrial tribunal has a legally qualified chairman and two lay members, one drawn from a panel of employers' associations and one from a panel of trades unions. Appeal lies on a point of law to the High Court. The tribunals also hear appeals under the Redundancy Payments Act, 1965 (this now constitutes about 80% of their work), under the Selective Employment Payments Act, 1966 and certain other miscellaneous appeals (Contracts of Employment Act, 1963; London Government Act, 1963). In general, an employee dismissed owing to redundancy can claim redundancy pay if he has at least 104 weeks' continuous full-time employment with his employer. The 1965 Act is very technical and specialist industrial advice is necessary in redundancy appeals. Reference may be made to the Departments' pamphlets "Dealing with Redundancies" and "The Redundancy Payments Scheme," a Revised Guide to the Act (2nd Revision, July 1967).

One of the main functions of the Department is to encourage training and we have already seen that the employment exchanges and I.T.B.s play their part here. The boards' powers extend to all forms of training and to all occupations in industry, they raise levies and pay grants to employers who train to approved standards. A Central Training Council advises the First Secretary on training matters. The Youth Employment Service is shared between the Department and local education authorities. C.T.C.s provide vocational training in skilled trades. The Department runs free courses at 21 Industrial Rehabilitation Units in industrial areas.

The Department administers the safety, health and welfare provisions of the Factories Act, 1961 and the Offices, Shops and Railway Premises Act, 1963. The Industrial Health and Safety Centre is part of H.M. Inspectorate and is a permanent exhibition. There is also a Wages Inspectorate acting under the Wages Council Act 1959. The settlement of industrial disputes is an important function of the Department and if the arbitration machinery fails then the Secretary of State is the final arbiter between the contending parties in the sense that the department's experienced and well-tried conciliation machinery is then used.

The Board of Trade. The Board of Trade deals mainly with commercial matters and during the last century it was given powers in respect of railways and shipping. It subsequently relinquished control of railways to the Ministry of Transport. Nowadays it administers such matters as bankruptcy, winding-up of companies and the regulation of weights and measures.[1 2]

The President of the Board of Trade is assisted by two Ministers of State, one with special responsibility for exports, and by a Parliamentary Secretary. There are departments dealing with Commercial Relations and Exports, Standard Weights and Measures, Insurance, Companies and Bankruptcy, Patent Office and Industrial Property, and Enemy Property.

In October, 1969, the Board's functions relating to distribution of industry and investment grants were transferred to the enlarged Ministry of Technology. Consequently, the Board is mainly concerned with overseas trade, exports and invisible earnings. It continues to publish the monthly trade figures and to be responsible for the distributive and service trades.

The Sinecure Offices. There are some offices in which the duties are said to be nominal, but the holder still receives a Ministerial salary. The Prime Minister in recent times has usually allotted special tasks to the holders of the sinecure offices. Thus the Lord President of the Council may also be Leader of the House of Commons, and the Lord Privy Seal may be leader of the House of Lords, in which case they are respectively responsible for the arrangement of business in the two Houses of Parliament.

The Lord President of the Council is a leading member of the Cabinet and had duties in relation to the Privy Council, over whose meetings he is entitled to preside. The Privy Council Office has a small staff under the Clerk to the Council, who summons its members to meetings. It was created under the royal prerogative and the Privy Council (technically, the Queen-in-Council) still exercises the prerogative by making Orders-in-Council. Most Orders-in-Council today, however, are statutory because they are made under the authority of an Act of Parliament. This type of Order-in-Council is a form of delegated legislation.

The Lord Privy Seal has no departmental duties because his authority is no longer required for payment of money. The Paymaster-General now exercises this function; this is another sinecure office, whose last holder was concerned with decentralisation and devolution, participation of the individual in the decision-making processes of democracy; youth; home information policy; and answering questions in Parliament on the new Civil Service Department. These functions have now been transferred to a Minister without Portfolio in the Cabinet. Since October, 1969, the Paymaster-General has been in effect second-in-command at the enlarged Ministry of Technology, with special responsibility for industrial policy. The Chancellor of the Duchy of Lancaster has recently been assigned special responsibility for detailed negotiations with the European Economic Community, under the general guidance and control of the Foreign Secretary. The Chancellor of the Duchy of Lancaster administers the Crown estates in the County Palatine of Lancaster, which has a separate Chancery Court.[13] This Minister appoints County Court judges and justices of the peace within the Duchy. In addition there are often Ministers without Portfolio, in other words without special departmental duties.

Other Ministers. We have now described some of the leading Ministries and departments of State. Others affecting local government will be encountered in Part II, notably the Minister of Housing and Local

Government, the Minister of Public Building and Works, and the Secretary for Social Services. There is a separate Secretary of State for Scotland with a seat in the Cabinet, responsible for the co-ordination of police and local government services in Scotland. Scots law is based on Roman Law, the Civil Law of the Continent of Europe, and is therefore a separate and distinct system. Scotland also has a different system of local government and education. The Scottish Department is located partly in Edinburgh and partly in London; it has separate branches for Agriculture, Education and Health. Since 1964 there has also been a Secretary of State for Wales in the Cabinet, although the English systems of law and local government are applicable to Wales. It was the former practice to attach responsibility for Welsh affairs to a senior Cabinet Minister such as the Home Secretary or the Minister of Housing and Local Government. Certain planning functions have been transferred to the new Secretary of State, whose appointment was generally regarded as an acknowledgement of nationalist sentiment. This brings the number of Her Majesty's principal Secretaries of State up to nine, which is a convenient figure, for by long tradition one Secretary of State can act in lieu of another in case of emergency. In 1964 a Ministry of Technology was created to co-ordinate scientific research, formerly the responsibility of the Lord President of the Council; and in 1969 this Ministry was greatly expanded to incorporate the Ministry of Power and most of D.E.A.

Conclusion. We have seen that a Cabinet Secretariat was set up in 1916 and that the Secretary to the Cabinet became a separate office in 1963.

During the first world war a distinguished former Liberal Lord Chancellor, Lord Haldane, presided over a Departmental Committee on the Machinery of Government, which reported in 1918. The Haldane Report summarised the functions of the Cabinet as follows:

  (i) final determination of policy to be submitted to Parliament;
  (ii) supreme control of the national executive in accordance with policy prescribed by Parliament;
  (iii) continuous co-ordination and delimitation of the several departments of State.

Since then, the trend has been towards Cabinet domination of Parliament owing to the power of the two-party system and the disciplinary measures available to the Prime Minister of the day. The Cabinet puts into effect the policy publicised at the general election.

In 1932 the Donoughmore Report of the Committee on Ministers' Powers was issued, reporting on the powers of Ministers in relation to delegated legislation and the exercise of judicial powers. The influence of the Report could be discerned in the establishment in 1944 of the Select Committee on Statutory Instruments, which still functions. The Report of the Franks Committee on Administrative Tribunals and Inquiries appeared in 1957 and led to certain legislative and administrative action which will be discussed in Chapter VIII.

In August, 1965, the Select Committee on Procedure recommended the establishment of specialist committees of M.P.s to examine the administration of government departments, particularly those concerned with defence, foreign affairs and the social services.

Select Committees of the House of Commons have been set up to consider agriculture; education; race relations and immigration; and science and technology; and the PCA. in 1967/68.

The Select Committee on Nationalised Industries was established in 1956. The Select Committee on race relations has done much useful work in examining the practical effects of legislation and has produced an informative report on the problems of coloured school leavers. Finally, a Parliamentary Commissioner for Administration has been appointed to investigate grievances against central government departments.[14] This is based on the idea of the "Ombudsman", a Scandinavian concept introduced in New Zealand in 1962. The British Parliamentary Commissioner is an independent officer appointed by the Crown and dismissible only upon parliamentary motion. He reports annually to Parliament and acts only at the instance of a Member of the House of Commons who considers that a complaint of personal injustice should be investigated. Subject to certain exclusions in the public interest the Commissioner investigates complaints against government departments; in due course this excellent innovation, especially advocated by the Lord Chancellor, will doubtless be extended to complaints against local authorities and public corporations.

In July, 1969, the Prime Minister, in an answer to a question in the House of Commons, said that the Government accepted in principle that an ombudsman system should be established for investigating complaints of maladministration in local government. A start could be made in London, Birmingham, Manchester and other large cities. The local system would be separate from that of the Parliamentary Commissioner, although similar in scope. The appointment of a Health Service Commissioner was also being considered in the light of the future administrative structure of the National Health Service. A new hospital advisory service is being established to help the public with information but this would not be concerned with the investigation of complaints.

M.H.L.G. deal with 20,000 planning complaints annually and it is thought that the figure for local authorities approaches half a million. Extension of the "ombudsman" system to local government is therefore desirable. Some local authorities already have their own internal "ombudsman" (e.g. London Borough of Haringey,) but this is not quite the same thing. The activities of the Parliamentary Commissioner for Administration are beginning to bite in the central government field. The Foreign and Commonwealth office has set up a Parliamentary Commissioner Unit and, as a "Guardian" leader recently (18th September, 1969) puts it "Sir Edmund (Compton) has made careful civil servants still more careful when it comes to the rights of people".

1. Lord Salisbury (1895-1902).
2. Previously it was 70; it has now been increased to over 100 by the Ministerial Salaries Consolidation Act, 1965. There are at present 82 members of the Commons in the Government and 15 peers.
3. Formed in 1916.
4. His salary is charged on the Consolidated Fund; he is dismissible only upon an Address to the Crown from both Houses of Parliament.
5. The Secretary of State for Scotland is responsible for Scotland.
6. It is proposed to reduce the number of police forces in England and Wales from 117 to 49.
7. Following the Report of the Royal Commission on the Police, 1962.
8. Fugitive Offenders Act, 1967.
9. Commonwealth Immigrants Act, 1969.
10. This may be transferred to the Secretary for Social Services if the Seebohm Report is implemented.
11. Except in the County Palatine of Lancaster, where this is the function of the Chancellor of the Duchy.
12. Under the Weights and Measures Act, 1963.
13. As has the County Palatine of Durham.
14. Parliamentary Commissioner Act, 1967.

CHAPTER VII

THE PUBLIC CORPORATIONS

The Nationalised Industries. The nationalisation of the means of production, distribution and exchange remains a basic tenet or article of faith in the Constitution of the Labour Party. So far, however, only the basic industries of coal, electricity, gas and transport have been nationalised and another air corporation has been established. All this action was taken during the first post-war Parliament of 1945–50, when the Labour Government under Mr. Clement Attlee[1] had a commanding majority in the House of Commons.[2]

Coal. The coal industry was the first to be nationalised, under the Coal Industry Nationalisation Act, 1946, which established the National Coal Board. The Board's organisation is centralised and functional: each Board member has executive responsibility for an assigned departmental task.[3] The Fleck Report published in 1955 found very little to criticise in the organisation of this nationalised industry but recommended a certain amount of devolution which has been carried out.

Organisation of the Board's management structure underwent a fundamental change in March 1967, when the industry's five-tier organisation which was established in 1947 was replaced by a three-tier structure consisting of the National Board, Coalfield Areas and Collieries.

Since 1947 the number of mines has been more than halved through mergers and closures, resulting in fewer but larger units. This was the major reason for the reorganisation.

There are 17 Areas each headed by an Area Director who is assisted by a Deputy Director (Mining) and a Deputy Director (Administration). The Area Director is directly accountable to the Board for managing the Area. The Departments at Area are directly responsible to the Area Director and functionally responsible to the equivalent department at Headquarters, the Area Head answering functionally to the appropriate Director-General or Head of Department.

The collieries, of which there are now about 310, are managed by colliery managers, agent-managers or colliery general managers (depending on their size and complexity) who are accountable to the Area Director for the safe and efficient management of their collieries. The Director is assisted in this task by the Deputy Director (Mining) and the Production Manager whose assignment comprises that colliery.

A typical N.C.B. Area produces nearly 70 million tons of coal a year, employs up to 20,000 men and has a turnover of about £55 million. The reorganisation is expected to save up to £15 million a year.

Great Britain is divided into eight Sales Regions,[4] and the Sales Regions are sub-divided into Sales Districts, 79 in all. This organisation comes under the Marketing Department of the Board.

Electricity. Electricity was nationalised next under the Electricity Act, 1947, which constituted twelve Area Boards in England and Wales. The way had been paved for this development by the establishment of a national grid in 1926. Recommendations in a Herbert Report in 1956 led to the enactment of the Electricity Act, 1957, setting up a Central Electricity Generating Board and an advisory Electricity Council.[5] The Area Boards were given more power following the dissolution of the Central Electricity Authority created by the 1947 Act. The function of the Generating Board is to maintain an efficient and economical supply of electricity in bulk in England and Wales, whereas the Area Boards plan the distribution of supplies. In 1954 the North of Scotland Hydro-Electric Board and the South of Scotland Electricity Board were set up. The Minister of Power announced in Parliament in July, 1969, that the present Electricity Council would be renamed Electricity Authority and its members reduced from 21 to 12. The new Authority would have greater powers over C.E.G.B. and A.E.B.s thus strengthening the central direction of the industry. It would control the C.E.G.B. capital expenditure programme and the A.E.B.'s pricing policies. It would also keep under review the performance of individual boards. Within the context of centralised control of strategic policy the area boards would still be responsible for day to day management. Thus the much greater flexibility of 1957 which replaced the rigidly centralised structure of 1947 is to yield to a compromise between the two in the seventies. The aim is to obtain central direction of major policy together with managerial responsibility and local initiative at area level.

Gas. The Gas Act, 1948, provided for an advisory Gas Council and twelve Area Gas Boards. The Gas Council includes the Chairmen of the area boards and co-ordinates manufacture of plant, education and research. The Area Boards manufacture and supply gas and are really powerful units; the Electricity Act, 1957, virtually places the Area Electricity Boards on the same footing. The Gas Act, 1965, gave the Gas Council power to manufacture, acquire, store and distribute gas; it is planning a national pipeline network for natural gas found under the North Sea.

Transport. Transport has been something of a political shuttlecock; the Transport Act, 1947, nationalised railways, canals, docks and inland waterways. The London Passenger Transport Board had been created in 1933 to administer all public transport in the London traffic area, so that in effect this Board continued under another name. An Act of 1953 denationalised road haulage but the present position is governed by the Transport Acts, 1962—68. There are now, as there were originally, separate Boards for British Rail, London Transport, British Transport Docks and British Waterways. The powerful British Transport Commission was abolished: it furnished an example of the "over-mighty subject", if ever there was one. Dr. Beeching as Chairman of the British Railways Board presided over a drastic reorganisation of the railway system resulting in numerous closures up and down the country, against which the protests of Transport Users Consultative Committees[6] were generally of little avail. In 1965 a National Ports Authority was constituted.

Transport Act, 1968
Part I: "Integration of Freight Transport Services"
  A National Freight Corporation is charged with the duty, in conjunction with the Railways Board, of securing the provision of properly integrated services for the carriage of goods within Great Britain by road and rail; and that goods are carried by rail whenever this is efficient and economic. In addition, the Corporation is empowered to provide sea and hovercraft transport, to consign and store goods and to operate harbours. A Freight Integration Council has the duty to consider any matter relating to the provision of an integrated transport service by the N.F.C., the Railways Board, the Docks Board, the Waterways Board, the Scottish Group, B.O.A.C., B.E.A.C., the British Airports Authority and the Minister of Posts and Telecommunications. Such matters will normally be referred to the F.I.C. by the Minister of Transport or by the Scottish Secretary. The new body replaces the Nationalised Transport Advisory Council, which is abolished.

Part II: Passenger Transport Areas
  The Minister by Order can designate Passenger Transport Areas and Executives outside Greater London, which is being dealt with separately under the Transport (London) Act, 1969. The members of P.T.A.s will be appointed mainly by the local authorities, not more than one-sixth by the Minister. P.T.E.s each comprise a Director-General and two to eight members appointed by the P.T.A. after consultation with him. Before making an order the Minister must consult local authorities affected and give an opportunity to make representations to anyone providing road passenger transport services by stage carriages within or to and from that area. The reorganisation of passenger transport in P.T.A.s can be effected

by means of transfer to P.T.E.s of local authority transport undertakings, planning of passenger transport services in designated areas on a long term basis and transfer of control of bus services to P.T.A.s.

Part III: Bus and Ferry Services

A National Bus Company has been constituted with power to carry passengers by road, whether in or outside England and Wales, to carry passengers by vessel or hovercraft in certain circumstances, to carry luggage, to store goods, to let passenger vehicles for hire, to carry on business as travel agents and to enter into necessary agreements. A Scottish Group is given similar powers and can carry passengers by road, sub-way or water or by hovercraft, whether in or outside Scotland.

Local traffic commissioners may grant a permit for certain bus services in lieu of a road service licence. This includes a permit for use on a route being used to provide school transport under the Education Acts subject to the vehicle not belonging to the local education authority, to their consent and to certain other safeguards. The commissioners have power to revoke or suspend operation of a permit, the normal duration of which will be three years.

When considering whether or not to refuse, suspend or revoke a public service vehicle licence on the ground of alleged unfitness the traffic commissioners shall consider any representations made by trade unions or associations, chief officers of police and local authorities. Matters to be considered include previous conduct, drivers' hours, maintenance of vehicles, their proposed or previous use and financial resources.

Any local authority running public service vehicles under statutory powers may run them as contract carriages, subject to the approval of the Minister. Such a local authority may also acquire or dispose of public service vehicle undertakings.

PART IV: Further Provision as to Boards, New Authorities and Transport services

The composition of the Railways Board has been revised and the requirement for Regional Railway Boards is abolished.

The N.F.C. and the Railways Board must review their organisation: and the Boards and new authorities must promote research and development. The Railways Board can now provide and manage hotels in any part of Great Britain and, with the Minister's consent, elsewhere, and limited powers to make such provision are given to the Waterways Board, the Bus Company and the Scottish Group. None of the new authorities are to be regarded as the servant or agent of the Crown or as enjoying any status, immunity or privilege of the Crown and their property is not to be regarded as property of, or property held on behalf of, the Crown.

New provision is made for railway closures and reasonable opportunity to make representations to the Minister must be afforded in such cases. The scope of Transport Consultative Committees is extended to cover the N.F.C. and any of its subsidiaries and any of the Boards except the Waterways Board.

Air. In 1939 the British Overseas Airways Corporation was established, followed by the British European Airways Corporation in 1946. The Civil Aviation Act, 1949, enables the Minister of Transport to control civil airfields and local authorities to maintain aerodromes.[7] Since 1960 an Air Transport Licensing Board has supervised the issuing of air service licences. This put the two air corporations in the same position as private companies in that they have to apply to the Board for a licence; appeal against refusal lies to the Minister. The government has a controlling interest in the British Aircraft Corporation and Hawker Siddeley (Aviation), the two major aircraft manufacturing companies.

Iron and Steel. The Iron and Steel Act, 1967 brings into public ownership the 14 principal companies concerned with the production of steel in Great Britain and provides for the continued control of the development by other companies of substantial production facilities in the basic fields of iron and steel-making. The British Steel Corporation comprises a chairman and from 7 to 20 other members appointed by the Minister of Technology; The Corporation holds the securities of the nationalised companies, has power to carry on iron and steel activities and the sale of iron and steel products. Its general duties are to promote the efficient and economical supply of iron and steel products; to avoid undue preference or unfair discrimination between consumers; to promote exports of iron and steel products; and to promote research and development. The Minister may give the corporation specific directions on organisation and general directions on matters affecting the national interest. The Corporation must submit an annual report to the Minister who must lay it before both Houses of Parliament. The Minister may authorise the Corporation to purchase land compulsorily. The Iron and Steel Consumers' Council has been reconstituted. Provision is made for the compensation of holders of certain securities now to vest in the Corporation and disputes are settled by the Iron and Steel Arbitration Tribunal.

The Corporation must secure that the combined revenues of the Corporation and all the publicly-owned Companies are sufficient to meet their combined charges properly chargeable to revenue and to establish and maintain a general reserve; the Minister may give it specific directions of disposal of surplus revenue and the general reserve. Borrowing powers are subject to the consent of the Minister and the approval of the Treasury. The Corporation must annually submit the Report and audited accounts and those of the publicly-owned companies to the Minister, who must lay them before Parliament.

Ministerial Control. The Minister of Technology can give general mandatory directions to the coal, electricity and gas boards and councils. Similar powers are available to the Minister of Transport in relation to the air corporations and transport boards respectively. These powers are not often used but in the last resort they can ensure conformity with national policy. The relevant Ministers also have power to appoint and dismiss members of these public corporations; and they control the allocation of funds provided by Parliament for capital development.

Post Office Board. Direct responsibility for the General Post Office was transferred from the Postmaster-General to the Post Office Board by the Post Office Act, 1969. The Board is a public corporation and is no longer directly answerable to Parliament. The new Board controls the national and local postal, telephone and telegraph services. Local post offices collect duties and taxes as agents for the government and issue motor taxation, radio and television licences. Current expansion will continue in telephone installation, data transmission, telex operations and other branches of telecommunications. The Minister answerable to Parliament is now the Minister of Posts and Telecommunications.

The British Broadcasting Corporation was created in 1927 and incorporated by a Royal Charter which is periodically renewable by the Crown after a debate in Parliament. The Corporation operates under a licence granted by the Minister, who has power to revoke it and to require the broadcasting of official announcements. The right to take entire control of broadcasting has never been exercised by the government, not even during the last war, so that the cause of freedom was not tarnished or impaired. The Corporation staff work under a Director-General responsible to the governors of the B.B.C.; they are not Civil Servants. The governors, like the members of other public corporations, are specifically disqualified from membership of the House of Commons. They are appointed by the Minister, technically on behalf of the Crown owing to the existence of the Charter, after consultation with the Premier. There are Regional Advisory Councils for England and a Council for Northern Ireland and National Broadcasting Councils for Scotland and Wales.

The Independent Television Authority was established in 1954 to encourage competition between independent programme companies. It hires transmitting stations to commercial companies, such as Associated Television and Granada, which supply programmes and receive revenue from advertisements. The Authority can intervene to ensure that programmes are impartial and accurate, and that they conform to accepted standards of good taste. The Minister is also responsible for Cable and Wireless, nationalised in 1946.

The Minister is not responsible for the day to day administration of the public corporations under his control. This is the province of the governors of the B.B.C., the members of I.T.A. and of the Post Office Board. The Minister is said to be responsible for overall policy control and to this end he has powers of appointment and dismissal of members and power to issue directions. The line is difficult to draw on occasion and the distinction between policy control and daily administration will be discussed towards the end of this chapter (p.81) under the rubric "Accountability to Parliament"

Social Service Corporations. Hospitals are administered by fifteen Hospital Boards and, at a more local level, by Hospital Management Committees. The teaching hospitals remain autonomous under their governors. General medical, dental and certain ancillary services are the responsibility of National Health Service Executive Councils and the local general practitioners. Local authorities administer certain personal health services. All these matters are regulated at central government level by the Secretary for Social Services under the terms of the National Health Service Act, 1946. The Minister has the usual power to give mandatory directions to the Boards and to appoint or dismiss their members. Hospital Boards are not Crown servants but their relationship with the Minister is closer than that of the other public corporations with their respective Ministers and they are thus subjected to a more detailed control.

The National Assistance Board (now replaced by the Supplementary Benefits Commission) was set up in 1948 to help persons with limited or non-existent means of support[8] It is staffed by Civil Servants and acts through local advisory committees and local offices. The Secretary of State[9] presents the Commission's report to Parliament and is generally responsible for policy matters, such as laying down new scales of assistance by regulations. Nevertheless it is not a government department and the Minister cannot therefore interfere with its daily administration.

The law on development corporations in new towns is now to be found in the consolidating New Town's Act, 1965. The first step is for the Minister of Housing and Local Government to make a draft order designating the site of a new town. After considering any objections at a public local inquiry the Minister is empowered to confirm his draft order. Next, the Minister must by order establish a development corporation to acquire and manage land, carry out building and provide water and other services. When the new town has been developed the Minister dissolves the corporation and its assets vest in the Commission for the New Towns,[10] which is not a servant or agent of the Crown. The Commission must maintain and enhance the value of the land transferred to it and act generally in the interests of the inhabitants. The Commission may use the services of local authorities as agents. Its members are appointed by the Minister, who can give it a general mandatory direction.[11] The legislation thus affords an interesting example of the replacement of one type of public corporation (the development corporation) by another (the New Towns Commission).

Accountability to Parliament. We have seen that there is considerable ministerial control over the public corporations but parliamentary control is decidedly more tenuous. There may be a parliamentary debate upon a public corporation whose affairs are before the House owing to the presentation of the Annual Report and Accounts by the Minister. A motion for the adjournment may relate to the public sector but, in accordance with time-honoured practice, such a motion will be accepted only if it is urgent and of definite public importance. Again, the nationalised industries may be mentioned in the Queen's Speech, in which case questions about them can be raised in the ensuing debate.

A question may be tabled in Parliament about a public corporation, or matters relating to it, for example the Minister of Technology might be questioned on a policy of exporting coal. We have seen that sometimes there may be difficulty in distinguishing between questions of policy and questions of daily administration. Export of coal would fall into the former category; the installation of a computer at the Board's headquarters would be in the latter.

As a result of difficulties encountered during the teething troubles of public corporations in the 1945—50 Parliament, certain rules have been evolved. The Speaker of the House of Commons must decide whether or not to allow a particular question; he would normally allow a question on mandatory directions given by a Minister to a Board "in the national interest" unless matters of state security were involved. Exceptionally, the Speaker may allow a question even if a Minister has previously refused to answer it. As the protector of minority rights, the Speaker may consider that the question is material enough to warrant an answer. However, the last word lies with the Minister, who can refuse to answer, but persistent refusal to answer reasonable questions would at least lead to political criticism and might lead to the dropping of the Minister from the government.

The last and perhaps most efficacious form of parliamentary control is by Select Committees. Originally, examination of the accounts of the public corporations was discharged by the Select Committee on Estimates and the Public Accounts Committee. Since 1957 a Select Committee on Nationalised Industries has assumed this responsibility, which extends to reports as well as accounts. It has reported each session and has examined the operations and policies of all the major nationalised industries, including the Post Office. In 1968[12] it reported on ministerial control and recommended separate treatment for securing of the public interest and supervision of efficiency. To this latter end a new Ministry of Nationalised Industries should be established. The public interest would continue to be defended and accountability to Parliament to be represented by the Ministries of Power[13] and Transport and the Board of Trade.

Parliamentary control is limited for several reasons. Debates on public corporations are comparatively infrequent, owing to the pressure of competing demands on parliamentary time. Oral questions are often not reached in Parliament: again, the allocation of time is restricted. Finally, the Select Committee on Nationalised Industries appears to work very slowly, presumably on account of the many other preoccupations and duties of its members.

Constitutional Position of the Public Corporations. We have seen that Ministerial control of the public corporations is extensive, although it is probably fair to say that it is exercised unobtrusively. There is a strong case for greater accountability to Parliament and more facilities should be afforded for Parliamentary debates and questions on these important matters. In general, neither the Board members nor their employees are Crown servants: this has been established judicially in the Courts in the cases of the B.B.C. and the Transport boards.[14] The public corporation is not therefore in the same position as a government department; the relevant Minister will answer only for overall policy control. In view of the fact that the corporations now exercise a monopoly over the basic industries, consumer protection should be strengthened. The Transport Users Consultative Committee appeared to be able to do little but protest in face of the recent Beeching steamroller, resulting in many railway closures. Similarly, very little is heard of the Domestic and Industrial Coal Consumer Councils and of the Electricity or Gas Consultative Committees. The Parliamentary Commissioner for Administration has rightly been limited in his scope to the central government departments in the first instance. Some criticism has been levelled at the fact that he will not initially be concerned with local government, but local authorities are at least elected by the people. If the majority of the electors do not choose to exercise their franchise, that is their loss. There seems to be a more cogent case for extending the field of the Parliamentary Commissioner to the public corporations, with their mighty resources, powerful members appointed by Ministers and, often, apparent contempt for the consumer.

In fairness it may be said that some limited attempts are made in the field of public relations. The London Electricity Board, for example, occasionally sends out leaflets explaining increases in charges. This aspect of the work of the Boards should be encouraged, in place of the futile advertising which the Minister of Power had to check recently in relation to gas and electricity. The provision and supply of cookers, refrigerators and washing-machines should be co-ordinated in the public interest, which should prevail over commercial interests.

In conclusion, it may be instructive to examine a recent Report by the Select Committee on Nationalised Industries on London Transport[15] which found that the Board was failing to carry out either of its two statutory duties; to provide adequate services and to make a profit. The Minister of Transport is in the process of a thorough examination of the conditions under which the Board operates. It is believed that the Ministry view is that if the Board cannot provide adequate services *and* make a profit, the financial obligation would have to yield. Presumably this would require amending legislation, a particular feature of nationalised transport, but the conclusion is justified and accords with the principle postulated above. The government appears to be moving gently in the direction of a direct government subsidy. The London Transport Board has replied[16] to certain detailed criticisms in the report, particularly those dealing with alleged delay in the construction of the Victoria Line extension and, in this connection, Ministry restrictions on capital expenditure are cited. The Board also rejected criticism of its labour relations and its efforts to achieve increased productivity. The Board has been in existence, in one form or another, since 1934. In the writer's opinion it has provided, on the whole, an excellent system of public transport in the Metropolis during the last thirty years, although signs of deterioration have appeared recently. Comparison has only to be made with rural areas or with the Continent to realise that there are many services inferior to those provided by London Transport.[17]

Independent Boards and Commissions. Certain boards have been established whose main purpose is the internal regulation of production, the object being to encourage declining industries. Examples are the Milk, Egg, Potato and Tomato Marketing Boards which have flourished during and since the war, some having fallen by the wayside in recent years. There are also licensing and registration bodies such as the Area Traffic Commissioners whose function is to license the operators of public service vehicles and approve routes.

Following the enactment of the Race Relations Act, 1965, a Race Relations Board has been established to investigate complaints of racial discrimination. The Act of 1968 set up a Community Relations Commission.

The special character of the Metropolis has led to the establishment of *ad hoc* institutions to carry out particular functions. Thus the Metropolitan Water Board is responsible for water supply in a large area of Greater London. This Board was created in 1902 and comprises nominees from all the local authorities in its area. The Port of London Authority controls the docks and wharves of the river Thames up to Teddington Lock. Its members include representatives of local authorities and of Trinity House, itself an *ad hoc* institution of some antiquity (1514) and mainly concerned with pilotage.

The Forestry Commission has a Chairman and five unpaid Commissioners, the Minister of Housing and Local Government being answerable for it in Parliament. It is responsible for afforestation on a large scale and in general deals with tree preservation in the grand manner, whereas local planning authorities make tree preservation orders on a more local and limited basis.

The University Grants Committee is responsible to the Secretary of State for Education and Science for higher education, and funds are allocated on the basis of its recommendations to the universities, including the new technological universities. Its membership comprises a Chairman, two Vice-Chairmen and some twenty other members well versed in academic life.[18]

Industrial Training Boards. Nearly thirty ITBs have now been constituted under the Industrial Training Act, 1964, to spread the cost of training more evenly throughout the country by means of statutory levies and grants. This represents an interesting constitutional innovation since the DEP has the power to define whole industries very widely for the purpose. Demarcation disputes in this respect are dealt with by industrial tribunals. The engineering industry imposed the heaviest levy and therefore many employees sought transfer to another industry but often without avail, for decisions rested purely on legal interpretation of the relevant orders.

1   Lord Attlee.
2   The steel industry which was denationalised by the Conservative Government has been renationalised (Iron and Steel Act, 1967).
3   E.g. production, welfare, labour relations.
4   Including one each for Scotland and Northern Ireland.
5   In 1958.
6   There is also a Central Transport Consultative Committee.
7   E.g. Manchester, Southend-on-Sea.
8   E.g. retirement pensioners and unemployed persons.
9   See p.34, *ante.*
10 E.g. Crawley, Hemel Hempstead, Hatfield and Welwyn.
11 As he can to development corporations, which require his assent to development or acquisistion of land.
12 H.M.S.O. 371 –I, £1 net.
13 Now Mintech.
14 The only exception appear to be the S.B.C. which is staffed by Civil Servants but its *member* are not Crown servants.
15 Published 31st August, 1965.
16 On 3rd December, 1965.
17 See Ch.XV for the latest reorganisation.
18 The Select Committee on Education and Science has recommended establishment of a Higher Education Commission.

CHAPTER VIII

THE ADMINISTRATION OF JUSTICE

Independence of the Judiciary. It is vital, in a free society, for the judges to be wholly independent of the Executive. This happy state of affairs was not achieved in Britain until 1714, when the relevant provisions of the Act of Settlement took effect. Until then, judges had been subject to royal favour in that the King could appoint or dismiss a judge at will in the exercise of the royal prerogative. Such a state of affairs was bound to limit the independence of the judiciary but nevertheless on occasion a courageous judge would fearlessly advise the monarch on the law. Thus in the *Case of Proclamations*, as we have seen, Sir Edward Coke told the King that there were limitations on the prerogative powers to change the law. The royalist lawyers in the Civil War period held the King to be "above the law"; the effect of the Revolutionary Settlement in 1689 was to place the Crown "under the law". Thus the evolution of the constitutional monarchy, which did not blossom into full flower until the twentieth century, was intimately linked with the achievement by the judiciary of independence from the Crown.

The Act of Settlement, 1701, ensured the Protestant succession and vested the title to the Crown in the Electress of Hanover and her descendants. It also enacted that, from the accession of the House of Hanover, judges were to hold their commissions "during good behaviour" and that the only method available to dismiss a judge would be the presentation of an Address by both Houses of Parliament to the Crown. The initiative must come from the House of Commons and the judge has a right to be heard. The procedure has been invoked only once, in 1830, in the case of an Irish judge.

The relevant provisions of the Act of Settlement are now to be found in the Supreme Court of Judicature (Consolidation) Act, 1925 The Lord Chancellor has power to remove county court judges and magistrates.

In modern times the independence of the judiciary from the influence of the Crown is important in the sense that the Crown in its public aspect is the executive government of the country—Her Majesty's Government.

The principle is no longer important in relation to the person of the monarch since we now have a constitutional monarchy and the Queen acts on the advice of her Ministers. As a result of the provisions of the Act of Settlement, the judges have protected the rights of the individual against the Executive whenever this has been necessary in litigation. For example, in 1765 it was decided that a Secretary of State has no power to issue a general search warrant, or to order an arrest except for treason. At that time, only a justice of the peace had such powers and this is still basically the position.[1] It is well recognised, two centuries later, that a Secretary of State or a Minister of the Crown has no such power, which would be oppressive in the hands of a Minister. Other cases to illustrate the principle of judicial independence are not lacking in this century. Thus, in 1923, the Court of Appeal ordered the issue of writ of *habeas corpus* directed to the Home Secretary "commanding him to have the body of Art O' Brien immediately before this court". The ancient writ of *habeas corpus* ("you have the body") is in the last resort the main protection of the individual against unlawful detention or imprisonment. Again, in 1921, the House of Lords refused to countenance as an "Act of State" (an act of sovereign power against which there is no redress) the confiscation of money from an American subject arrested in Ireland for illegal drilling. This was because he was technically a friendly alien, despite his hostile act for which he was later imprisoned, and an Act of State cannot be perpetrated against a friendly alien or against a British subject. The reason is that a British subject owes allegiance to the Crown, which in return offers its protection; a friendly alien is said to owe local allegiance and comes within the ambit of the protection of the Crown. This was the law, despite a purported ratification of the unlawful confiscation by the Chief Secretary for Ireland.[2]

The Organisation of the Courts. The organisation of the civil courts is based on the Judicature Acts, 1873–75, as subsequently amended.[3] These Acts created a Supreme Court of Judicature comprising the Court of Appeal and the High Court of Justice. The High Court has three divisions, which were formed from amalgamations or reclassifications of the old Courts of Common Law and Chancery, which for centuries had dispensed justice at Westminster Hall. The Queen's Bench Division hears actions in contract and tort, for example where a plaintiff is suing for damages for breach of contract or for personal injuries sustained in a road accident caused by negligence. The Lord Chief Justice's Court is in this division. The Lord Chancellor is the titular head of the Chancery Division and the Master of the Rolls, his deputy, is President of the Court of Appeal. The Chancery Division hears cases on administration of estates, trusts, mortgages, dissolution of partnerships and wardship of infants. These are known as "equity matters" and are inherited from the old Court of Chancery and the days when the Lord High Chancellor, as Keeper of the King's Conscience or "King's eye", sought to ameliorate the hardships

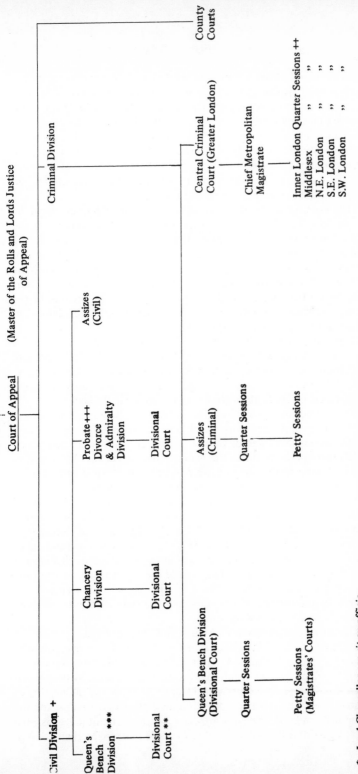

House of Lords *

(Lords of Appeal in Ordinary)

Court of Appeal

(Master of the Rolls and Lords Justice of Appeal)

Civil Division +

Criminal Division

Queen's Bench Division ***

Divisional Court **

Chancery Division

Divisional Court

Probate +++ Divorce & Admiralty Division

Divisional Court

Assizes (Civil)

County Courts

Queen's Bench Division (Divisional Court)

Assizes (Criminal)

Central Criminal Court (Greater London)

Quarter Sessions

Quarter Sessions

Chief Metropolitan Magistrate

Petty Sessions (Magistrates' Courts)

Petty Sessions

Inner London Quarter Sessions ++
Middlesex   ,,
N.E. London   ,,
S.E. London   ,,
S.W. London   ,,

*   Lord Chancellor can sit ex-officio
\+   Criminal Appeal Act, 1066 abolished the Court of Criminal Appeal from 1.10.66
**   Including the Lord Chief Justice's Court
\++   Administration of Justice Act, 1964
***   This may include a new Admiralty and Commercial Court
\+++   This may be reconstituted as the Family Division

of the Common Law with equitable principles. Unfortunately equity has now developed into an arid and soulless body of doctrine with little or no relationship to its noble origins. The work of the Probate, Divorce and Admiralty Division is fairly obvious from its title: thus it can give a valid title to a will by a grant of probate or it can grant letters of administration if there is no will; it can grant decrees of dissolution of marriage, the Queen's Proctor having power to intervene where collusion is alleged; and cases of collisions at sea, where apportionment of blame is material, can be heard with the assistance of nautical assessors.

The Lord Chancellor, after consultations with the Bar Council and the Law Society, has formulated provisional proposals to reorganise the P.D.A. Division. A new Family Division is contemplated, having jurisdiction over matrimonial causes, wardship,[4] adoption and guardianship of infants. Thus it would inherit jurisdiction from both the P.D.A. and Chancery Divisions. A new Admiralty and Commerical Court would be formed as part of the Q.B.D. from an amalgamation of the existing Admiralty Court and Commercial Court. Legislation to implement these proposals is expected in due course.

Appeal lies from all three Divisions of the High Court to the Court of Appeal and thence with leave to the House of Lords. The Appellate Jurisdiction Act, 1876, authorised the Crown to create nine[5] Lords-of-Appeal-in-Ordinary as life peers and the "law lords" sit as the judicial House of Lords, the highest court of appeal in the land.

We must not overlook the civil side of Assize. There are seven Circuits with a number of Assize towns in each and the Assize Judges visit as many of these as possible three or four times a year. They hear cases which would otherwise be heard in the various Divisions of the High Court in London. Owing to the unfortunate prevalence of divorce cases, special Divorce Commissioners have been appointed for this work.

Turning to the administration of the Criminal Law, the Central Criminal Court[6] is the Assize Court for Greater London and sits monthly except in August. It includes High Court Judges and the Recorder of London. The criminal work of Assize is of very ancient origin and can be traced back to the circuits of the royal justices of the early Plantagenet Kings. To this day, the Assize Judges hold the Commissions of Oyer and Terminer (Norman-French for "hear and determine") and General Gaol Delivery. In other words, they try prisoners charged with crimes and those detained in gaol or released on bail.

The Royal Commission on Assizes and Quarter Sessions under the Chairmanship of Lord Beeching recommends a drastic reorganisation of the system of courts (Cmnd. 4153, H.M.S.O., published 29th September, 1969). The Report recommends that Crown Courts staffed by two tiers of judges should replace Assizes and Quarter Sessions for the hearing of criminal cases. The top tier would comprise High Court judges and the second tier would be formed from a new bench of circuit judges assisted by a few part-time Recorders. Civil cases would be heard by High Court or circuit judges and would be separated entirely from the criminal list. Circuit judges would be existing county court judges and full time judges exercising criminal jurisdiction. The reasons for the proposed changes include great delays under the existing procedure, archaic conditions and location of some courts and unnecessary travel by judges and supporting staff. The recommendations should make for greater convenience and speedier trial of cases. Courts should be continually available at a few larger towns and regularly at smaller ones. High Court judges would try the more serious offences, circuit judges and recorders the less grave.

The Lord Chancellor would be responsible to Parliament for the Higher Court system and the cost of administration of the courts would be transferred from local to central government. Six areas would be devised, each with administrative headquarters and staff under a circuit administrator. Advisory committees comprising members of the public and of the legal profession should be established at court centres to help in the investigation of complaints.

The Court of Criminal Appeal was established in 1907 and included the Lord Chief Justice and other High Court judges. It had power to vary sentence or quash convictions and appeal lies with leave to the House of Lords.[7] Divisional Courts of the Queen's Bench Division exercise both civil and criminal jurisdiction, for they have power to issue prerogative orders, and writs of *habeas corpus;* they can determine appeals from Quarter Sessions and hear appeals from other inferior courts.

The inferior Courts. So far we have been dealing with what are quaintly described as Superior Courts of Record. County courts were established in 1846 and have limited civil jurisdiction, which latterly has included housing, landlord and tenant litigation and rent restriction. County court judges must be barristers or solicitors of at least seven years' standing and appeal from their decisions lies to the Court of Appeal. Coroners' Courts hold inquests into violent or unnatural deaths; the verdict of a coroner's jury may lead to a warrant for arrest for murder. Coroners, who must be legally or medically qualified, also hold inquests into treasure trove.

The justices of the peace, or lay magistrates, can trace their origin to the Justices of the Peace Act, 1361. They have met in the counties four times a year in Quarter Sessions since then. Except for a chairman of the bench, justices do not have to be legally qualified[8] and they are unpaid. The Lord Chancellor appoints them, after consulting local Advisory Committees. Since 1950 Magistrates' Courts Committees have been responsible for the appointment of clerks to the justices, for the division of counties into petty sessional divisions and for the provision of courses of instruction for magistrates. At least two magistrates must conduct summary trials, which deal with minor crimes. More serious crimes, known as indictable offences, can be tried by the justices if the accused agrees. They can also act as "examining magistrates" in order to conduct a preliminary examination of a person charged with an indictable offence.

In such a case the accused person can be committed for trial at the next Assizes or Quarter Sessions.[9]

Justices on a county commission of the peace serve in petty sessions, which deal with summary offences and preliminary examinations. There are also specially constituted Juvenile Courts to hear charges against persons under seventeen; and Domestic Courts to deal with separation, maintenance and guardianship orders.[10] In most cases, appeal from the justices in petty sessions lies to the County Quarter Sessions.

The smaller boroughs form part of the county for the purposes of the administration of justice. The larger boroughs have their own commissions of the peace, separate from the county commission. Some boroughs also have their own Quarter Sessions, which may have been granted to them under their Charters. A Recorder presides over Borough Quarter Sessions; he is appointed by the Lord Chancellor from the practising Bar. The justices in Quarter Sessions hear appeals from Petty Sessions and deal, at first instance, with all but the most serious of indictable offences. Appeal in criminal cases lies by way of case stated from Quarter Sessions to a Divisional Court of the Queen's Bench Division.

The system of stipendiary magistrates was inaugurated in London as long ago as 1792 and was extended to other urban areas in 1863. A stipendiary receives a salary and must be legally qualified. Any borough with a separate commission can petition for the appointment of a stipendiary, who is appointed by the Crown from the legal profession and normally[11] sits alone. The Chief Metropolitan Magistrate at Bow Street has wider powers than other magistrates. There are certain peculiarities in the administration of justice in Greater London. An Alderman of the City of London, who is not necessarily legally qualified, is *ex officio* a justice of the peace and can sit alone (no other lay magistrate has this power). Under the Administration of Justice Act, 1964, there are five separate Commission areas for Greater London: Inner London, Middlesex, N.E. London, S.E. London and S.W. London. The last three were formerly parts of the administrative counties of Essex, Kent and Surrey. The London Commission areas are treated as counties for the purposes of commissions of the peace, Quarter Sessions and Magistrates' Courts. Whole-time Chairmen of Quarter Sessions are appointed by the Lord Chancellor from the legal profession. The Act also provides for the integration of the summary jurisdiction of the Metropolitan stipendiary and lay magistrates in Inner London (the old County of London), and for committees of magistrates to exercise the functions performed by Magistrates' Courts Committees elsewhere. The Act was passed following the reorganisation of local government in Greater London.

Administrative Tribunals. The twentieth century has witnessed the development of special administrative tribunals, whose function is to act as agents for the central government in dealing with policy matters, in some cases at local level. They are to be distinguished from the public corporations on the one hand and from the local authorities on the other. Public and local authorities are administrative units which may, on occasion, exercise judicial functions. Administrative tribunals, despite their title, perform functions which would otherwise be carried out by the ordinary courts; and they often act judicially or quasi-judicially, in the sense of adjudicating in disputes between parties. One of the parties may be, and usually is, a government department or local authority; the other (or others) an aggrieved citizen or citizens. When exercising judicial functions, the so-called "rules of natural justice" must be observed by a tribunal. These are, first, that the tribunal must be impartial and, secondly, that all parties concerned must be given an opportunity to be heard. Another rule, which is really an extension of the first, is that there must be no malice or improper motive for arriving at the decision. The reasons usually advanced to justify the establishment of special tribunals are that their procedure is quick, cheap and informal, and that questions arising out of a social service or government function are better decided by persons with relevant specialised knowledge. There is also the advantage of decentralisation, and the fact that otherwise the ordinary courts would be overburdened. It is therefore appropriate to give a brief outline of the subject of administrative tribunals under the main heading of "Administration of Justice".

The best of our administrative tribunals is undoubtedly the Lands Tribunal, which was established in 1950 to adjudicate upon disputes between individuals and public authorities on such matters as compensation payable in the case of compulsory acquisition of land and rating valuation appeals. It also deals with the highly technical matter of applications for discharge or modification of restrictive covenants. Its members are appointed by the Lord Chancellor and the President is a distinguished lawyer:[12] the other members must be experienced lawyers or valuers. An appeal on a point of law lies direct to the Court of Appeal.

The Lands Tribunal exercises purely judicial functions and is more or less on the same footing as a Division of the High Court. It is concerned to ensure that compensation payable for compulsory acquisition is based on the current market value[13] of the land, that is the price the land would fetch in a sale on the open market, assuming that there is a willing purchaser and a willing vendor. The development levy to be charged by the Land Commission would have to be deducted after sale if development of the land in the planning sense is envisaged.[14] The other main aspect of the Tribunal's work is to hear rating valuation appeals from local valuation courts appointed from panels of local authority members; these courts hear appeals in the first instance from valuation officers of the Inland Revenue who calculate the rateable value of property on the basis of which rates are levied.

A fairly detailed description of the Lands Tribunal has been given but there are thousands of administrative tribunals and several categories.

Examples of other tribunals exercising judicial functions are the Special Commissioners of Income Tax and the Solicitors (Discipline) Committee.

There are other tribunals whose functions are mainly administrative covering matters of policy laid down by Parliament in the public interest (in the sense of the sum of collective individual interests). A leading example is the Transport Tribunal established in 1948, which heard applications for increases in fares in the London Transport area until 1969 and hears road haulage appeals. It has a legally qualified President and its other members are qualified in transport business, commerce and finance. Appeal lies on a point of law to the Court of Appeal and it reports annually to the Minister of Transport, who lays the report before Parliament. Whilst the matters with which the Transport Tribunal deals may hit the individual citizen directly in his pocket, there are also many other citizens likewise affected; by contrast the Lands Tribunal is dealing with individual landowners and ratepayers. Again, there are numerous other tribunals of the administrative type such as Rent Tribunals, Rent Assessment Committees and National Health Service Executive Councils. Some are fact-finding tribunals whose procedure has been laid down in detail by ministerial regulations, e.g., Pensions Appeal Tribunals and National Insurance and Supplementary Benefits Appeal Tribunals. As noted previously, industrial tribunals have been established to hear industrial training levy appeals: applications for redundancy payments; S.E.T. appeals; contracts of employment appeals; and other miscellaneous industrial matters. The Chairmen are legally qualified and appeal lies on a point of law to the High Court. Some cases, on S.E.T. and industrial training, have reached the House of Lords.

The arbitrary development of some of these tribunals led to the appointment of the Franks Committee on Administrative Tribunals and Inquiries, which reported in 1957. As a result, wherever possible, legally qualified chairmen are now appointed, written notice of decisions and the reasons for them are given to all parties and appeal now lies on a point of law to the High Court from a number of administrative tribunals. The Tribunals and Inquiries Act, 1958, set up a Council on Tribunals to review the administration and working of a large number of tribunals, including those mentioned above. The Council reports annually to the Lord Chancellor and the Secretary of State for Scotland.

Statutory Inquiries. Many statutes authorise a Minister to hold a public local inquiry where objections are raised to the proposed action of a local authority or public corporation. The most common case is the making of a draft compulsory purchase order to acquire land; in order to become effective, the order must be confirmed by a Minister. Inevitably, landowners affected will object and a local public inquiry is usually held.[15] Compulsory purchase of land is authorised for such purposes as the provision of hospitals, houses, schools and roads, so that here we can see most clearly the age-old conflict between public interest and private right. When an inquiry is ordered, it is conducted on behalf of the relevant Minister by an inspector from his department (the Franks Report recommended that the inspectors should be drawn from the Lord Chancellor's Department, but this has not been implemented).

The Minister, acting through his inspector, is said to be acting quasi-judicially at this stage. This means that the inspector must observe the rules of natural justice: he must be unbiassed and allow all the objectors to present their case against the acquisition or planning restriction. But the inspector has no power of decision, he can only make a recommendation to his Minister, who alone can decide. After the inquiry is ended, the Minister makes an order and he need not follow his inspector's advice, although he usually does. The Minister in arriving at his decision is said to be acting in a matter of policy laid down by Parliament; he is no longer adjudicating in a dispute as he was, through his inspector, at the inquiry. The rules of natural justice cannot be invoked at this stage; the courts can intervene only if there has been an error of law. The Town and Country Planning Act, 1968 enables inspectors to make certain decisions after holding an inquiry.

Again, there had been disquiet on some aspects of local inquiries and this, too, was considered by the Franks Report. There is a very limited right to challenge a compulsory purchase order once it has been confirmed and notice of this confirmation has appeared in the local press. Within six weeks of publication, it can be challenged in the High Court on the grounds that it is *ultra vires* the enabling Act of Parliament or that the applicant's interest has been substantially prejudiced by non-compliance with a statutory procedural requirement. Once the six weeks have elapsed, no challenge is possible, not even if fraud or bad faith are alleged. In 1959 these limited rights of appeal to the High Court were extended to various planning decisions, orders and appeals.[16] The new Law Commission might well examine this question with a view to strengthening the rights of individuals affected by town and country planning and compulsory purchase; the grounds of appeal and the time-limit could well be enlarged.

As a result of the famous "chalk-pit case" in 1960 new procedural rules were made by the Lord Chancellor in 1962 to cover local inquiries on compulsory purchase and planning[17] matters. The allegation in this case was that the Minister of Housing and Local Government had received "new factual evidence" after the close of the inquiry (but before he made his decision) from technical officers of the Ministry of Agriculture. The implication was that this evidence or advice had materially influenced him in making the decision and that therefore the inquiry should be re-opened. The new Rules provide that, in such circumstances, a new inquiry should be held, but there is doubtless scope for pedantic lawyers and others to debate *ad infinitum* whether or not new material constitutes new factual evidence.

The Council on Tribunals has a duty to report to the Lord Chancellor on the need for procedural rules for statutory inquiries, and it so happened that the chalk-pit affair exploded upon the body politic whilst this matter was being considered. The promulgation of the new Rules in 1962 was therefore a welcome development, although the original "chalk-pit case" could not, unfortunately, be re-opened. The Rules provide for forty-two days' notice to be given to objectors, who must, twenty-eight days before the inquiry, be given a written statement of reasons for the draft order. There is also provision for legal representation at the inquiry and for the views of government departments affected to be conveyed to the objectors so that the latter can prepare their case adequately. The inspector's report must be published when the Minister's decision-letter is sent to all parties, and must include his findings of fact as well as his recommendations.

The Franks Report was concerned to establish the principles of 'fairness, openness and impartiality', and it considered that the judicial, rather than the administrative, function of tribunals should be emphasised. Governmental action has followed, by means of administrative and legislative procedures. The former include Ministry circulars urging local authorities to give reasons for decisions and explaining legislation and Statutory Instruments. The latter comprise the Tribunals and Inquiries Acts, 1958–66, and what is now the Town and Country Planning Act, 1962, the Town and Country Planning (Inquiries Procedure) Rules, 1965, and the Compulsory Purchase (Inquiries Procedure) Rules, 1965. Although matters are not yet perfect, the Rule of Law is now more in evidence in this field than it was a decade ago.

In June, 1969, the Law Commission published its Paper on Administrative Law,[18] which seeks appointment of a Royal Commission to consider the subject. A citizen can sue the Crown and a poor man can get legal aid and advice. The Council on Tribunals and the Parliamentary Commissioner for Administration also play their part in supervision of administrative tribunals and redress of grievances in a limited field respectively. At present, however, there is no redress in the shape of damages following an unlawful act by or on behalf of the State or one of its agencies. The Law Commission suggests that lawyers are the proper champions of the rights of the individual and their powers should be strengthened to this end. It also wants an examination and simplification of the procedure for reviewing tribunal and other decisions by means of the prerogative orders.

This is undoubtedly a case for this archaic procedure (application for the prerogative orders of *certiorari* to bring up and quash a decision, prohibition to prevent excess of jurisdiction and *mandamus* to compel performance by a public authority) to be replaced by the declaratory judgment. Although an action for a declaration does not necessarily result in a sanction by court order it is often coupled with an injunction which must be obeyed. In any event. this could easily be remedied by legislation.

1. By statute a High Court judge (in the case of official secrets) and a police superintendent (in case of sedition in the armed forces) can issue a general search warrant.
2. A Cabinet post no longer in existence.
3. The law is now mainly to be found in the Supreme Court of Judicature (Consolidation) Act, 1925.
4. There would be power to transfer wardship questions to the Chancery Division if property matters were in dispute.
5. Increased to eleven by the Administration of Justice Act 1968, which also provided for a maximum of thirteen judges of the Court of Appeal, 70 puisne judges of the High Court and 97 County Court judges.
6. Housed in the Old Bailey building in the City of London.
7. The Court of Criminal Appeal was abolished and its jurisdiction transferred to the Court of Appeal (Civil Division) by the Criminal Appeal Act, 1966.
8. Compulsory legal training for justices is envisaged in a White Paper (Cmnd. 2856, December, 1965).
9. Or, of course, he may be discharged.
10. Appeal lies to the High Court.
11. Except in Greater London since 1965.
12. At present Sir Michael Rowe, Q.C, who succeeded the first President, Sir William FitzGerald, Q.C., on 1st January, 1966.
13. Subject to certain exceptions, mainly in the field of housing (slum clearance).
14. This topic will be dealt with in more detail in Part III.
15. A public inquiry must be held in case of slum clearance; in other cases the Minister may afford a private hearing instead.
16. Town and Country Planning Act, 1962 (a consolidating Act).
17. Now consolidated in Rules made in 1965.
18. Paper No. 20, Cmnd. 4059, H.M.S.O. 2s.

PART II
LOCAL GOVERNMENT

CHAPTER IX

THE DEVELOPMENT AND STRUCTURE OF

LOCAL GOVERNMENT SINCE 1830

THE BOROUGHS AND THE COUNTIES

The great Reform Act of 1832 which enlarged the parliamentary franchise was swiftly followed by the Poor Law Amendment Act, 1834, and the Municipal Corporations Act, 1835. At the beginning of this period reform was in the air, partly owing to the teaching and writing of Jeremy Bentham (1748–1832), the great legal and social philosopher, who propounded the theory of Utilitarianism. According to this the aim should be the achievement of the greatest happiness of the greatest number of people. Curiously enough, Bentham's doctrines have been useful both to the proponents of "laissez-faire"[1] and to the advocates of collectivism. In the latter respect, Bentham was one of the forerunners of the sociological school of jurisprudence which believes that law must have a social purpose. Law is not an arid body of doctrine but a living discipline allied to the concept of liberty and, in a free society, reflecting both the legitimate aspirations of the common people and changing social conditions. In the field of local government, Bentham advocated that the areas in which local authorities were to act should be governed solely by ease of administration. The other main impetus to reform could be discerned in the liberalism of the old Whig Party which resulted initially in the enactment of the Reform Act. By this "Great Charter of 1832" the rotten boroughs were swept away and many new and rising centres of population received parliamentary representation for the first time.

During the course of centuries, many ancient towns and cities had received Charters of incorporation from the Crown, in the exercise of the royal prerogative. During the reign of Charles II many Charters were called in and re-issued in order to ensure Tory and royalist control. A Charter had the effect of incorporating the Mayor, Aldermen and

Burgesses[2] of a borough. Some boroughs were also cities as being seats of an Archbishop (Canterbury and York) or of a diocesan bishop (e.g. London, Durham and Winchester). There were certain peculiarities about the City of London, as we shall see later: suffice it to say, for the present, that the ancient City Corporation possesses several Charters issued to it by various monarchs. As long ago as the sixteenth century some boroughs provided street lighting, water supply and fire brigades. However, royal intervention and "laissez-faire" doctrines led to inertia and incompetence under municipal obligarchies which were unrepresentative and often corrupt. The Municipal Corporations Act, 1835, vested borough government in the mayor, aldermen and councillors. The corporations were made responsible for the local police force (under the control of borough Watch Committees) and were empowered to make bye-laws for good government and prevention of nuisances.

The municipal franchise was based on rateable occupation of property. The act extinguished ancient trading rights within boroughs and provided for publicity for proceedings of the new councils and for the publication and auditing of accounts. The Act also abolished the old system of electing borough justices by municipal corporations. The law was consolidated in the Municipal Corporations Act, 1882.

In the counties, the Crown was represented, as it is today, by a Lord Lieutenant and a Sheriff. However, by 1830 local administration had passed out of their hands to the local justices of the peace. During the previous century the justices in Quarter Sessions had administered the "county business" after dealing with their judicial work. They were assisted not only by the clerk of the peace but also by such officals as the county surveyor, since the repair and maintenance of certain highways and bridges came within their purview. In addition, the justices had statutory powers over poor law administration, maintenance of public order and licensing of ale houses (the last two matters being not unconnected on occasion!). By the beginning of our period, Parliament had for some time habitually sent bills affecting local administration to the justices for their expert opinion. In this way, as Professor Plucknett points out,[3] "the opinion of the Knights of the Shires often decided the fate of bills which dealt with local government." The reform of municipal government in 1835 did not lead to a corresponding alteration in county affairs. The justices of the peace continued more or less undisturbed until 1888, largely owing to their excellent record stretching back to 1361 and even earlier. Their powers even extended to the levying of rates but this was generally accepted despite the nomination of justices of the peace by the Crown.

The growth of *ad hoc* **authorities.** We have already described the effect of the Poor Law Amendment Act, 1834, in Chapter IV *(pp. 33 et seq.).* Here Benthamite principles were observed and implemented by Chadwick, a disciple of Bentham. In particular, strong central control was achieved we are concerned to note here that, under the Act, local administration was vested in elected boards of guardians, following the union of parishes and workhouses. A purely local administration of the poor law was thus supplanted by one in which the local element was subjected to strong central guidance and direction in the guise of the Poor Law Board.[4] Following a report by Chadwick, the Commissioners had investigated sanitary conditions by 1842.

During the early part of the nineteenth century a large number of elected *ad hoc* authorities had been created. An *ad hoc* authority is one formed for a sole specific purpose, in contradistinction to the modern local authority, which is a *general* authority administering several services. Thus at the beginning of our period there were such bodies as highway boards, local boards of health, burial boards, improvement commissioners, boards of guardians, poor law parishes and unions. These were joined later in the century by school boards and school attendance committees (see Chapter IV, pp. 35–6, *ante*).

In 1845 a Royal Commission recommended that water supply, drainage, paving, repairing and cleansing of streets should be carried out in each area by a single authority subject to certain central controls.

The local boards of health were perhaps the genesis of the modern system of local government, because the Public Health Act, 1848, which constituted the boards, also enabled a borough council to adopt the Act and become the sanitary authority for its area. Local boards of health were created either at the request of the inhabitants or by order of the Central Board of Health if the death rate was high. It will be recalled that the Act was passed owing to the severe outbreak of cholera in 1847 (see p. 34, *ante*). The boards administered such matters as sewerage, paving, lighting, water supply and burial grounds. Thus although they were "ad hoc" in the generic sense of public health, there was a glimmering of overlapping functions, for example in relation to burial boards. As late as 1883, however, there were 18 different kinds of rates, elections were held on varying franchises and they were by no means uniform in other respects. The position at this period has been described as "a chaos of areas, a chaos of franchises, a chaos of authorities and a chaos of rates."[5]

Although the General Board of Health was dissolved in 1854 Parliament came to realise that central control was too diffuse. Following the Report of a Royal Sanitary Commission the Local Government Board was established in 1871, replacing the Poor Law Board and exercising general supervisory control over local services. The Royal Commission had also indicated that general local authorities were preferable to a proliferation of *ad hoc* authorities. This led to the next great land-mark, the Public Health Act, 1875, which is still in force to some extent. This Act definitely designated borough councils as the local authorities for public health matters; in other areas, urban and rural, public health powers were transferred in general to the boards of guardians. The Act codified the law of public health and established urban and rural sanitary districts. Not all urban areas were (or are even today) governed by borough councils, so that outside the boroughs it was necessary to make use of improvement commissioners and local boards of guardians for this purpose. The rural districts comprised the remainder of the poor law unions. The Act of 1875 imposed on urban and rural sanitary authorities definite powers and duties relating to public health and the general provisions of the Act are strictly limited to the discharge of those powers and duties. Thus, in every later Act conferring or imposing on urban district or rural district councils[6] fresh powers or duties (such as housing), new general provisions have had to be enacted. On the other hand, general powers conferred on a borough council by the Municipal Corporation Acts, 1835–1882, cover the activities of the corporation acting through its council; but they do not extend to the corporation when it is discharging other specific statutory functions such as public health and housing. In the latter case, authority for action taken must derive from the Public Health Acts or from the Housing Acts.

Nineteenth Century Reform. Reform in the counties was ushered in by the Local Government Act, 1888, under which most of the administrative functions of the justices of the peace were transferred to new elected county councils. The most important functions of the new councils initially related to highways. We have here to make a distinction between a geographical county and an administrative county. A large geographical county like Yorkshire was divided into three administrative counties:— North Riding, West Riding and East Riding, each with its own county council. Similarly the geographical county of "famous Lincolnshire" was divided administratively into three Parts: Holland-with-Boston, Kesteven and Lindsey, each having a county council. Other examples are furnished by the separate county councils of East and West Suffolk and East and West Sussex. In general, administrative counties were based on the old geographical counties of England and Wales, and a link between the old and the new was maintained in that, in most instances, the clerk of the peace became also clerk of the county council. As we shall see in Chapter XVI, the pattern is slowly changing with the trend towards larger administrative units, so that some of the smaller administrative counties are being absorbed into their larger neighbours. Rutland, however, which is the smallest county, successfully resisted a shot-gun marriage with Leicestershire in 1964.

The 1888 Act also created county boroughs out of the larger municipalities: in general, a minimum population of 50,000 or more was a pre-requisite for this status at that time. Until 1888 all municipal boroughs were the same, both in relation to internal composition and functions. After the Act came into force, they remained the same as regards internal composition; that is, with rare exceptions,[7] they were all incorporated by Royal Charter, each having a Mayor, Aldermen and Councillors. But a big distinction must be made in respect of their functions, for the county borough council is the most powerful unit of local government, exercising all conceivable local government functions. Initially, these were few, but as twentieth century legislation piled function upon function on local authorities, all were absorbed by the county borough councils administering the larger towns and cities. On the other hand, the non-county borough councils administering the smaller towns exercise only limited functions, because some of the more important functions are the responsibility of the county councils. By contrast, the county borough councils, although of course remaining physically within the area of the administrative counties in which they were situated, were no longer subordinate to the counties and became completely autonomous units of local government. In some cases old historic cities like Canterbury were able to claim county borough status although their population fell considerably below 50,000. The reason was that they already possessed certain privileges by being "counties of cities"[8] which meant that they had separate courts of quarter sessions and commissions of the peace and therefore appointed their own sheriffs and coroners. In these circumstances, it was considered appropriate that they should acquire the more powerful status of a county borough. As we shall see in Chapter XVI, the minimum population figure has been increased to 100,000[9] and it is doubtful whether Canterbury will retain its county borough status indefinitely.

The Local Government Act, 1894, established smaller authorities operating within the system of county administration. It reclassified urban sanitary authorities other than borough councils as urban district councils and rural sanitary authorities as rural district councils. The smaller, or non-county, borough councils, together with the two types of district council, became responsible for the important allied functions of housing and public health. The "two-tier" or divided system of local administration was born, contrasting with the unitary county borough system. In both systems, the genesis of the *general* local authority can be discerned, as opposed to the *ad hoc* authority.[10] The 1894 Act also created parish councils in the rural parishes, thus adding a third tier in the rural districts of the counties. If there is no parish council, responsibility devolves upon the parish meeting, which comprises all the local government electors of the parish.

The Twentieth Century. The great Public Health Act, 1875, remained the basis of public health law until the enactment of the consolidating Public Health Act, 1936. The close connection of public health and housing is illustrated by the fact that slum clearance powers are given to deal with houses "unfit for human habitation" and surveys and reports are made by public health inspectors. There had been some housing legislation in the nineteenth century culminating in the Housing of the Working Classes Act, 1890, which provided for slum clearance and the erection of new houses. Borough councils became housing authorities for these purposes and were joined in 1894 by the new urban and rural district councils. Housing legislation during the twentieth century has been prolific, partly owing to housing shortages caused by wars and partly owing to special problems in relation to rural areas and housing finance. Housing will be examined in more detail in Chapter XI: suffice it to note that references to the "working-classes" were expunged as far as possible by the Housing Act, 1949 (the expression was so embedded in the legislation that it was impossible to dislodge it entirely). Parliament has enacted six housing statutes during the last decade.

We have already noticed that many important Acts of Parliament were enacted relating to education, casting important duties upon education authorities, notably in 1902 and 1944. A Housing and Town Planning Act was passed in 1909; town and country planning was subsequently divorced from housing, although it is difficult to separate them completely. A lukewarm attempt was made to deal with planning control in an Act of 1932 but it was not until 1947 that the legislature really came to grips with this subject. As in the case of education, planning was transferred to the larger authorities—the county councils and county borough councils—when the importance of the function came to be realised. Occasionally Parliament has taken away functions from local authorities, for example administration of hospitals, national assistance, gas and electricity distribution[11] and rating valuation assessment. The main trend during the century, however, has been to give local authorities new or extended functions requiring local administration of a high order.

Following the Report of the Chelmsford Committee, the Local Government Act, 1933, provided local authorities with a constitutional code in the shape of a framework of general powers. Thus the Act deals with such matters as the appointment of officers, the provision of office accommodation, the acquisition of land for general purposes, the enactment of bye-laws, the promotion of private bill legislation and finance. The more important of these matters will be described in more detail in succeeding chapters. For the moment, it is sufficient to note this important landmark in the development of local government. The 1933 Act also made a useful classification of the second-tier authorities in the county system: non-county borough, urban district and rural district councils can be described collectively as "county district councils". The reforming Local Government Act, 1958, dealt mainly with Finance and Areas and its effect will therefore be described in Chapters XII and XVI. Both these matters are now in the melting pot following the appointment of Royal Commissions on Local Government in England and in Scotland (see Chapter XVII).

Chartered and statutory authorities: the doctrine of *ultra vires*. We have seen that boroughs outside London have achieved their status by means of incorporation by Royal Charter, in the vast majority of cases. All other local authorities are creatures of statute: county councils, urban district councils, rural district councils, parish councils, parish meetings, rural borough councils.[12] The common law origin of a county borough council remains, despite the acquisition of new functions under Act of Parliament when that status is attained. Originally, there were no county boroughs and they have come into existence only since 1888. Despite their more numerous functions, the internal composition and structure of a county borough is exactly the same as that of a non-county borough. In the first instance, the Charter constituted the legal authority for any action taken by a borough council; but with the growth of legislation affecting all types of local authority, a borough council could also be governed and regulated by statutory provision. In the case of a conflict between an Act of Parliament and the common law, the statute prevails.[13] Since a Charter is granted under the exercise of the royal prerogative, which is the residual power of the Crown at common law, a statutory requirement would prevail over a provision in the Charter. In the case of the purely statutory local authorities, they must be able to point to an Act of Parliament authorising action taken.

This brings us to the well-known doctrine of *ultra vires* (beyond the powers). As applied to local government, this means that a local authority can do only those things which it is authorised to do by Act of Parliament. This has been held to cover matters considered to be reasonably incidental to the main purpose and, if necessary, borderline cases can be tested in the Courts. The doctrine applies to all local authorities including borough councils, but in theory the latter can perform acts under the authority of their Charters provided that they are not contrary to a statute. The qualification is necessary owing to the principles stated above, which are based on the doctrine of the sovereignty of Parliament. Nowadays the theoretical distinction between Chartered and statutory corporations in relation to the doctrine of *ultra vires* is rather artificial and academic. There are so many statutes affecting local government that there can be few, if any, activities of a borough council today which are not regulated by legislation. Certain accounts of borough councils are subject to the scrutiny of the district auditor, who will automatically check that tthere is statutory authority for the relevant expenditure.

The application of the *ultra vires* rules may be illustrated by a case[14] where the Attorney-General, on the relation of a ratepayer, obtained a declaration that Fulham borough council[15] had acted *ultra vires* by installing a municipal laundry with the latest contrivances operated by officers employed by the council. It was held that this went beyond the powers given in the Baths and Wash-houses Acts, 1846–47. Since then, some local authorities have obtained the necessary powers by local Act of Parliament.

Another example of the application of the doctrine is afforded by an Australian case[16] which went on appeal to the Judicial Committee of the Privy Council. The Municipal Council of Sydney had power under a statute to acquire land compulsorily in order to carry out improvements in the city. A compulsory purchase order was made under these powers but the real reason was that an appreciation in value of the area resulting from a street extension scheme should accrue to the local authority which had met the cost of making the new road. The Judicial Committee indicated that a local authority authorised to take land for specific purposes would not be allowed to exercise its powers for different purposes. In other words, the action taken was *ultra vires* the enabling statute.

A more recent illustration of the *ultra vires* rule was furnished by the case[17] of the pensioners who were allowed by Birmingham Corporation to travel free on their municipal transport system. A ratepayer tested the legality of this in an action for a declaration and the free travel was held to be *ultra vires* the powers of the Corporation, as no statutory authority existed and the Charter did not provide for such a contingency. An Act of Parliament was enacted in the same year[18] that the declaratory judgment was issued. This statute gave certain local authorities in the Midlands permissive power to provide free transport for certain classes of persons, including pensioners. These permissive powers were extended to all local authorities in England and Wales by the Travel Concessions Act, 1964, which enables concessions to be made to school children as well as to pensioners. The Transport Act, 1968, enables local authorities to arrange with P.T.Es for travel concessions for pensioners, blind and disabled persons.

An Act passed in 1963 gives a local authority power to incur expenditure *in the interests of its area or inhabitants,* where the expenditure is not otherwise authorised.[19] Such expenditure is limited to the product of a penny rate. Subject to this limitation, this novel statutory provision has provided local authorities with considerable discretion and has enhanced their financial freedom of action since the relevant payments cannot be challenged by the district auditor. It is important that the expenditure should not have been authorised under any enactment. It is now open to local authorities to incur expenditure on such items as mayoral regalia (which in the past was often provided by public subscription or a generous benefactor) or on "twinning" arrangements with Continental towns under which civic representatives exchange useful and informative visits.

TABLE 1

LOCAL GOVERNMENT LANDMARKS

1832 Reform Act. Reorganisation of "rotten boroughs" for purpose of the parliamentary franchise.

1834 Poor Law Amendment Act—control of poor law authorities.

1835 Municipal Corporations Act. New powers given to borough councils (municipal corporations) and regulation of their internal composition and government.

1848   Public Health Act. Creation of General Board of Health: control of local boards.

1870   Elementary Education Act—local school boards created.

1871   Local Government Board created.

1875   Public Health Act: borough councils, urban and rural sanitary districts constituted public health authorities.

1882   Municipal Corporations Act.*

1888   Local Government Act—county councils and county borough councils constituted.

1890   Housing of the Working Classes Act.

1894   Local Government Act—urban district councils, rural district councils and parish councils created.

1902   Education Act—education functions given to local authorities.

1909   Housing and Town Planning Act.

1918   Education Act: more powers to local authorities.

1919   Acquisition of Land (Assessment of Compensation) Act.

1925   Rating and Valuation Act.

1929   Local Government Act—boards of guardians abolished, de-rating introduced (see Chapter XII).

1932   Town and Country Planning Act.

1933   Local Government Act: Code of general powers.

1936   Public Health Act.* Housing Act.*

1944   Education Act.

1947   Town and Country Planning Act.

1948   Local Government Act—valuation assessment functions transferred to Inland Revenue (see Chapter XII).

1949   Housing Act.

1957   Housing Act.*

1958   Local Government Act—Finance, Areas, Delegation.

1959   Highways Act.* Town and Country Planning Act. Mental Health Act.

1961   Housing Act. Rating and Valuation Act.

1962   Town and Country Planning Act.*

1964   Housing Act.

1965   Control of Office and Industrial Development Act.

1966   Local Government Act. Rating Act.

1967   General Rate Act.* Civic Amenities Act. Housing Subsidies Act.

1968   Rent Act. Town and Country Planning Act.

1969   Housing Act. Representation of the People Act.

*Consolidating statutes.

1.   The economic theory, now largely discredited, of leaving things as they are.
2.   I.e. inhabitants or citizens (in a city).

3. Taswell-Langmead's English Constitutional History (11th Edn., p.196).
4. Originally the Poor Law Commissioners.
5. Rathbone and Peel, Local Administration.
6. The successors-in-title of the sanitary districts.
7. E.g. Barnstaple, created a borough by Act of Parliament.
8. Or "counties of towns".
9. Although other factors are also material.
10. The boards of guardians lingered on until 1930.
11. Nationalisation removed these functions from some local authorities and private undertakings.
12. See Chapter XVI.
13. *Attorney-General v. De Keyser's Royal Hotel Ltd.* [1920] A.C. 508.
14. *Attorney General v. Fulham Corporation* [1921] 1 Ch. 440.
15. A metropolitan borough created by statute, now incorporated in the London Borough of Hammersmith.
16. *Municipal Council of Sydney v. Campbell* [1925] A.C. 338.
17. *Prescott v. Birmingham Corporation* [1955] Ch. 210.
18. Public Service Vehicles (Travel Concessions) Act, 1955.
19. Local Government (Financial Provisions) Act, 1963, s. 6.

CHAPTER X

THE INTERNAL ORGANISATION OF LOCAL

AUTHORITIES

POLITICAL PARTIES AND THE MACHINERY

OF ELECTIONS AND MEETINGS

The national political parties nowadays run candidates in local government elections, the general trend being for the Labour Party to dominate the urban areas and for the Conservatives to hold sway in the rural counties and districts. For a long time local elections were non-political in the sense that candidates were independent of party influence. Nevertheless, many so-called independent bodies, such as the Independent Ratepayers' Associations, were in reality rarely distinguishable from the Conservative interest; and, until comparatively recently, the Conservatives in London stood as Municipal Reform candidates. Until about ten years ago local government provided a useful training ground for membership of Parliament, but the tendency now is for bright young men to seek parliamentary election without bothering first to serve on a local authority. The alleged decline of local government, coupled perhaps with youthful impatience, is postulated as a reason for this development. Each of the national parties has a local government section or division at their headquarters, with paid officers dealing with such matters as party organisation for local elections and research. The Conservatives allocate the last session of their annual party conference to discussion of local government affairs, and hold a separate local government conference in the spring. The Liberals appear to be more successful in local elections that they are in Parliament but they are still very much the third party in both cases. Some of the longer-serving members of Parliament are also councillors or aldermen; one or two even manage to serve as Mayor or Lord Mayor of a town or city as well. In general, the same local party agent can service both local and parliamentary elections, although the constituency areas are not necessarily identical.

The same electoral register is used for both parliamentary and local elections. Residence on the qualifying date in accordingly the main basis of the franchise. However, the property qualification lingered on in local government as an alternative basis of qualification.[1] An adult British or Irish subject[2] can be registered if he is resident in the area. Special provision is again made for service and other absent voters and persons unable to go to the polling station may vote by post.

Candidates in local elections must be adult British or Irish subjects registered as local government electors *or* resident within the area during the whole of the preceding twelve months[3]. The main disqualification for election is the holding of any paid office or other place of profit in the gift or disposal of the local authority or of any of its committees. Recorders and coroners are disqualified under these provisions which do not, however, apply to sheriffs, returning officers, mayors and chairmen.

A councillor who resigns cannot be appointed to a paid office under the council until twelve months later even though he receives no remuneration. Other disqualifications include bankruptcy or making a composition with creditors; surcharge in a sum of over £500 and conviction and sentence of imprisonment for not less than 3 months.[4]

County council elections are held between the 3rd and 15th of April, all other local government elections between the 3rd and 15th of May. The Home Secretary fixed the polling day for borough council elections; the county council decides in the case of all other local elections. Public notice must be given and nominations must be in writing, signed by a proposer, a seconder and 8 other local government electors,[5] and must contain the candidate's written consent and a statement of his qualifications for election.

The returning officer has power to reject a nomination paper only on the grounds that the particulars of the candidate or persons subscribing the paper are not as required by law. He cannot decide any question raised with respect to the disqualification of the candiate. The returning officer's decision can be challenged subsequently by means of election petition. Election offences and election petition procedure are the same as for parliamentary elections. No deposit is required of candidates in local elections.

The county council usually appoints its clerk to be returning officer in county elections but the mayor acts for him if an electoral division is wholly within a borough. The clerk of the district council is returning officer in urban and rural district elections; the clerk of the rural district council acts in parishes. The returning officer in a borough is the mayor but if it is divided into wards, an alderman is assigned to each ward. If the nominations exceed the vacancies, a poll is held by secret ballot. This is the usual procedure, but there are two other possibilities. If the nominations correspond to the vacancies, the returning officer declares the candidates elected. If the nominations are less than the vacancies he declares those candidates elected, the remainder being filled by the retiring councillors who gained the highest number of votes at the previous election.[6] Casual vacancies normally necessitate bye-elections but if one occurs within 6 months of the end of the term of office, the seat remains vacant until the next election; and a parish council or rural borough council fills a casual vacancy by co-option. The most common reason for a casual vacancy is the election of aldermen but continuous failure to attend council or committee meetings for 6 months is another reason. The 1969 Act makes special provision for casual vacancies occurring in boroughs or districts subject to annual elections.

Councillors and Aldermen. We have described the procedure for the election of councillors; let us now examine what happens to them once they are elected. First, it is fundamental that all councillors, once elected, are entitled to serve for three years, unless they die or become disqualified. A general election of councillors is held every three years in the counties, rural boroughs and parishes, and in some county districts.

In the boroughs one-third of the councillors are elected annually; this is aptly described by Sir William Hart[7] as "the system of partial renewal", which is also the normal method in the urban and rural districts. However, exceptionally the County Council orders triennial elections to be held in the area of an urban or rural district. The electoral area of a local authority may be a division or a ward or the local government unit itself, owing to the enormous variation in size within all types of unit. There are even some very large parishes: it should be noted that, where there is no parish council, the parish meeting comprising all the local government electors can exercise limited functions. Elections in rural districts, rural boroughs and parishes are now held simultaneously. The table opposite sets out electoral areas, representation and incidence of elections in relation to the different types of local authority.

A councillor or an alderman may be elected by his fellow-councillors and aldermen to be Mayor of a borough or Chairman of a county council. Aldermen are to be found only in counties and boroughs.[8] A councillor may be elected as chairman of the council of an urban district, rural district, rural borough or parish. Candidates for the office of Mayor or Chairman must be qualified for membership of the council and the election of Mayor is the first business at the annual meeting immediately following the general election of a proportion of the councillors in a borough in May. In the counties the annual meeting is held in April: in the other statutory local authorities it is held in May. The expression "annual meeting" does not mean that it is the only meeting, merely that it is the first meeting in the council year. The person presiding, that is the chairman of the meeting until a Mayor or Chairman has been elected, has a casting vote in the event of a tie. A deputy or vice-Chairman is appointed

TABLE 2   LOCAL ELECTIONS

Local Government Area	Electoral Area	Representation	Incidence of elections
Greater London	Parliamentary Division	1 Councillor for each division	Triennial (all Councillors retire en bloc)
Administrative County	Electoral Division (usually comprising one or more non-county boroughs or districts and divided into polling districts)	1 Councillor for each division	Triennial (all Councillors retire en bloc)
Borough (including County Borough and London Borough)	Ward (unless the borough is the electoral area), usually divided into polling districts	3 Councillors for each ward, as a general rule	Annual ($\frac{1}{3}$ retire annually); triennial in Greater London
Urban District	Ward (unless the urban district is the electoral area)	3 Councillors for each ward, usually	Annual (unless triennial under County Council order)
Rural District	Rural borough, parish, ward of parish or combination of parishes	Number of Councillors for each area is fixed by County Council	Annual (unless triennial under County Council order)
Rural Borough	Rural borough, unless divided into wards in the order providing for its inclusion in the rural district or subsequently so divided by the County Council	Fixed by County Council	Triennial
Parish	Ward of a parish or parish	Fixed by County Council	Triennial

from council members.

Aldermen in counties and boroughs are elected by councillors from among councillors and persons qualified to be councillors. They constitute one-third the number of councillors[9] and one-half of their number retire triennially, when the election of aldermen takes place at the annual meeting. The aldermanic principle was first introduced in the Municipal Corporations Act, 1835, and was applied to the new county councils by the Local Government Act, 1888. The system of indirect election has been attacked as undemocratic and unrepresentative, to some extent, of the wishes of the electorate and it has the curious effect of causing bye-elections to be held to fill the consequential vacancies. It is rare for an alderman not to have been a councillor first, although one may be selected from those "qualified to be councillors". The most recent opportunity to get rid of the aldermanic system was not taken; it was preserved in Greater London under the London Government Act, 1963. Aldermen tend, of course, to be the most senior and experienced council members and one is often elected Mayor or Chairman. It is important to remember that, apart from their method of election and longer tenure of office, an alderman is inherently no different from a councillor. They are both *members* of the council and an alderman has no more powers than a councillor except those which may accrue to him as Mayor or Chairman or as a powerful committee chairman. It is possible for an alderman or a councillor to hold such positions. The defence usually advanced for preservation of the system is that it ensures stability and continuity, particularly where political control changes. It is open to the party in power to claim all the aldermanic vacancies and this often happens nowadays. The Royal Commission on Local Government in England 1966—69 recommends the abolition of the office of alderman.

Mention should here be made of the vexed question of payment of council members. Reasonable allowances are payable to a mayor or chairman and limited allowances are payable to members in respect of financial loss, travelling and subsistence on "approved duty". The scales are revised periodically by the Minister of Housing and Local Government but there is general recognition that the system is out of touch with reality. The Maud Committee on Management submitted an interim report on remuneration of councillors to the Minister in June, 1966. It is recommended that councillors should receive an annual flat rate allowance.[10] The Wheatley Report on Scotland recommends payment of councillors.

Finally, it should be noted that a member of a local authority is under a duty to disclose his interest in any contract or other matter before the council or any of its committees, and he must abstain from discussion and voting. This has been another difficult matter, despite the fact that the Minister has power to remove disabilities if the numbers affected are so great as to impede the transaction of business. The original provisions are in the 1933 Act, as amended: the Local Government (Pecuniary Interests) Act, 1964, provides that the duty to disclose and abstain does not apply when the interest is remote or insignificant. Difficulties have arisen in the past in the case of councillors, who were also council house tenants, participating in housing debates and decisions on rent rebate and differential rent schemes. The courts have held that a councillor may be "interested" in this special sense even if he takes part and votes against his interest; he can still be convicted and fined. In one case[10] a councillor was managing director of a building firm which had not tendered for work to the council for some years; he was nevertheless convicted because he had taken part in a housing committee debate on direct labour building. The courts have interpreted the law very strictly in the past and there is much scope for argument on what exactly is "remote or insignificant". Corruption may take place much less openly, as is possible in the field of planning decisions, and it may well be that quite different provisions are necessary to deal with it. If so, the disclosure of interest provisions could be swept away together with the *ultra vires* rule, since they are both remnants of a nineteenth century approach.

Council Meetings and Committees. A council must hold an annual meeting and at least three other meetings during the year; in addition, the Mayor or Chairman may call a meeting at any time and may be required to call one on the requisition of members. Nowadays most councils hold more than four meetings a year and in the urban areas monthly meetings are common. Notice of the time and place of a council meeting must be published at the council offices or town hall three clear days beforehand; and a summons to attend specifying the business and signed by the clerk or town clerk must be sent to each member. Minutes of meetings must be kept by the clerk and his assistants and must be signed by the chairman at the next meeting; on payment of a shilling, a local government elector can inspect the minutes at the council offices and make copies of extracts. A quorum of members must be present in order to transact business: in general, a quorum is one-third of the members, except in the case of a county council, where a quarter suffices.

The committee system is fundamental to local government and chairmen of committees are powerful members of local authorities. Membership of committees is fixed by the council and may include persons who are not members of the authority;[11] but the number of co-opted members may not exceed a maximum of one-third of the total membership. A council can remove a member from a committee before his term of office expires. A council can *refer* a specific matter to a committee, which then prepares a report for consideration by the full council. In such a case the recommendation of the committee is not effective until ratified by the council. On the other hand, a council may *delegate* specific matters to a committee: in this case the committee has full executive power so that its decisions are immediately effective. The general rule is that such a committee cannot delegate its executive powers to a sub-committee. A local authority may delegate any of its functions to a committee, except the powers to levy a rate or issue a precept or borrow money.[12] A county council must have a finance committee; there is no mandatory requirement in the case of other local authorities but in practice they all have finance committees as it would be impracticable for them to operate otherwise. The finance committee chairman is a kind of local Chancellor of the Exchequer, since his committee co-ordinates the estimates of the spending committees and he presents the estimates to the council. Similarly, the Leader of the Council has been described as a local Prime Minister.

In a number of cases a local authority must appoint specific committees by statute and in general the council may not initiate action except on a recommendation or report of such a committee. Thus a majority of the education committee of a county council or county borough councils[13] must be elected members and it must contain members with local knowledge of education. This means that just under half of the members of an education committee may be co-opted, but very few authorities make full use of this provision. A local education authority may delegate powers to an education committee. A county council or county borough council, in its capacity as local health authority, must appoint a health committee and can in general only act on its report, save in urgent cases. A majority of the health committee must be council members and the committee minutes must be open to inspection. Business may be referred to this committee or health functions may be delegated to it. Similarly, a local welfare authority must have a committee to which it may delegate welfare functions. The committee must include women and persons with special knowledge of welfare and the majority must be council members. Save in urgent cases, an authority must not exercise welfare functions without considering a committee report. Except for the requirement as to women, there are similar provisions in relation to the children's committees which county councils and county borough councils must appoint and to which these councils may delegate functions relating to deprived children and child life protection.

The majority of members of a planning committee of a county council, county borough council or joint board must be members of the appointing authority, which may delegate all its planning functions to the committee. It has been held that the minutes of a planning committee exercising delegated powers are not open to inspection, because they are not technically the minutes of a local authority. On the other hand, the minutes of a committee exercising referred powers, if submitted to the council for approval, are part of the minutes of the council and are therefore open to inspection. A planning committee may delegate functions to a sub-committee, the majority of which must be members of the appointing committee or of the local district councils.[14]

A power may be conferred directly by statute on a committee: thus in a county the police authority is a committee of the county council known as the police committee, and in a county borough it is a committee of the borough council known as the Watch Committee. In both cases, two-thirds of the members of the committee are council members appointed by the council and one-third are magistrates appointed by Quarter Sessions.

Local authorities have a general power to make standing orders on such matters as the quorum, proceedings and place of meeting of committees. In 1963 the Ministry of Housing and Local Government issued its second edition of Model Standing Orders (Proceedings and Business of Local Authorities) for the guidance of councils. Fair and accurate reports of meetings of local authorities and their committees are privileged, unless the publication is proved to be made with malice[15] but this "qualified privilege" does not extend to meetings to which the public and the press are denied admission. Meetings of local authorities and education committees must be open to the public and this applies where a body resolves itself into committee or where a committee comprises all the members of the local authority. Unfortunately some councils have evaded the spirit of the Public Bodies (Admission to Meetings) Act, 1960, by the simple device of removing one member from such a committee. The public and press can be excluded whenever publicity would be prejudicial to the public interest, for example when the council is receiving advice from its officers. A town clerk may wish to advise his borough council that proposed action is *ultra vires* and it would not be in the public interest for this to be reported. The press can demand copies of agenda and supporting documents.

Many authorities have a general purposes committee, sometimes a general purposes and law committee, since it is convenient to have a residual committee to deal with matters outside the scope of other committees. In some cases, all the other committee chairmen serve on the general purposes committee, which is then one of the most powerful committees of the council.

A further refinement has recently taken place in the urban district of Basildon, Essex. There, an executive committee of nine members submits new policy proposals to the council for approval and it is, in fact, the only committee reporting to the council. All other committees, except education, comprise two members of the controlling party; but a "shadow" chairman from the minority party attends all formal meetings but cannot vote. These committees report to the executive committee and a record of committee decisions is available to councillors. Advisory groups of members assist the committees periodically. Other reforms at Basildon include the institution of "question-time" before council meetings and the appointment of a town manager, which will be discussed below. The prelude to this, under the late town clerk and first town manager, was the abolition of all sub-committees, except for education, and maximum delegation to committees, chairmen and vice-chairmen, with the corollary of greater delegation to officers and the establishment of panels and study groups. The Basildon experiment repays study and certainly deserves success as an exercise in streamlined local democracy.

Another radical reorganisation of committees has been undertaken in the city and county borough of Newcastle-upon-Tyne. There the "principal city officer with town clerk" persuaded the city council to accept his report recommending a reduction in the number of its committees from 37 to 8. The case for this was partly based on the fact that, formerly, in some months about a hundred committee meetings were held; and this must have meant a considerable strain upon the 60 councillors and 20 aldermen. Two of the main principles underlying the report were that members should not do the work for which officers are paid, and decision-taking and day-to-day administration should not be delayed. Since April, 1966, the eight Newcastle committees have controlled municipal relations; resources planning; public safety; health and social services; education and leisure; housing; public works and transport; and civic enterprises. The municipal relations committee deals with such matters as staffing, establishments and remuneration; the flow of communications; relationships between the council, staff, public and Parliament; and the administration of justice. The resources planning committee combines the functions of the former finance and planning committees, allocates resources between the various services and generally co-ordinates the work of the corporation. These are the two key committees of the council and party meetings are held to decide policy beforehand; officers attend such meetings of the majority party, which are treated as if they were ordinary committee meetings.

The council's representatives on the Watch Committee are drawn from the public safety committee, which controls the fire service and civil defence. The civic enterprises committee deals with markets and street trading and maintains corporation property, including the airport and the quay. No committee has more than 18 members and many decisions are delegated to officers. This radical recasting of the committee system in Newcastle is to be applauded and it seems likely to result in greater efficiency and a lessening of the burden on the elected member.

Major Departments and the Local Government Service. A local authority has a general power to appoint such officers as it thinks fit, but there are certain mandatory requirements. Thus, a county council must have a clerk, a medical officer of health, a treasurer, a surveyor, a chief education officer, a children's officer and a chief welfare officer. A county borough council must have all these officers; county district councils must have a clerk, a treasurer, a medical officer of health, public health inspectors and a surveyor.[16] A parish council may appoint a clerk or treasurer. Under the 1933 Act, the clerk, treasurer and surveyor must be "fit" persons;

presumably this means something more than mere physical fitness, but the term is nowhere defined. A medical officer of health must be a qualified medical practitioner; and the Minister of Health has made regulations governing the qualifications and duties of medical officers of health and public health inspectors, neither of whom can be dismissed without that Minister's consent. In general, local government officers hold their appointments "at the pleasure of the council" but ministerial consent is necessary for the dismissal of a clerk of the council. In some cases a minimum standard of professional and technical qualification is ensured, as in the case of chief fire officers under regulations made by the Home Secretary. A local education authority cannot appoint a chief education officer without consulting the Secretary of State for Education and Science, who may veto an appointment. Similarly, the Home Secretary must approve the appointment of a children's officer or a chief constable.

The senior and co-ordinating chief officer is the clerk or town clerk and local authorities usually require this officer to have legal qualifications. Solicitors have a virtual monopoly in this field, particularly in the boroughs, where well over ninety per cent of town clerks are solicitors. There has however, been a recent interesting development in that some enterprising authorities have made appointments apparently based on the American "city manager" concept. In 1965 the City and County Borough Council of Newcastle-upon-Tyne appointed a "Principal City Officer with Town Clerk". The successful applicant was formerly a production planning executive at Ford's and received a salary of over £8,000 per annum. He has now returned to industry. In Newcastle the need to co-ordinate redevelopment of the City, particularly in relation to the housing and planning committees, led to the formation of what has been described as a city cabinet. This experiment will be examined in more detail in Part III. We turn now to the examination of the more orthodox Clerk's Department. We have seen that the Clerk of the County Council is usually also Clerk of the Peace and that a town clerk generally holds this position if the borough has a separate commission. As the clerk is normally also the council's chief legal adviser, it would seem logical that he should be a lawyer. It is true that some of the larger counties and county boroughs have a separate Legal Department headed by a Solicitor as chief officer; in such cases the clerk or town clerk can devote himself wholly to administration. In any event, the clerk will be expected to advise on procedure in Council and in Committee and he and his staff including the deputy clerk and assistant clerks, will service the council's committees. In other words, the clerk's department is responsible for the preparation of agenda and minuting of all council and committee meetings.

The clerk is the administrative arbiter in any dispute between other chief officers, the final court of appeal of course being the council itself. A good clerk of the council (and most fall into this category) is able, by virtue of his expertise, experience and personality, in most instances to persuade his colleagues that the correct course of action is the one he recommends. More local authorities, especially in London, are making Maud-type appointments of chief executives drawn from the professions.

We turn now to the Treasurer's Department; the treasurer or comptroller is usually a qualified accountant, since the practice is for local authorities to require such qualification in their advertisements, although again there is no mandatory requirement. The treasurer reports to the finance committee, controls the internal audit and advises the Council and fellow officers on financial matters generally. Just as the Leader of the Council, the policy-making leader of the majority party, works closely with the town clerk, so does the chairman of the finance committee rely upon the services of the treasurer and his deputy and assistants. It may be interpolated here that the Mayor and town clerk[17] are associated on ceremonial occasions rather than on political or policy matters. Some former treasurers have been appointed chief executive offices.

The treasurer must disobey orders of his council if they are manifestly illegal: thus he must not sanction expenditure which would be *ultra vires*.

With the advent of "organisation and methods" and the corresponding search for greater administrative efficiency, the "O and M" teams settled initially in the town clerk's department. The fashionable modern term is "management", which covers a multitude of sins, and with the arrival of the computer these matters have tended to come increasingly within the province of the treasurer, who presumably talks the same language as the computer. The larger computers can talk to one another, such is progress.

An engineer and surveyor usually heads a department of that name and reports to the highways and bridges committee or communications or roads committee. The larger and more forward looking authorities appoint Architects and Planning Officers with separate departments. The town clerk is closely concerned with these chief officers because he must carry out the Council's policy and instructions in relation to building new houses, slum clearance, town and county planning, and highway maintenance and improvements.

The Medical Officer of Health is in charge of the Public Health Department, assisted by a chief public health inspector and other inspectors with multifarious duties relating to public health and housing.[18] The Medical Officer may have to act under the direct orders of the Minister of Health if there is an outbreak of infectious disease in his area: in these circumstances the Minister, not the local authority, can be sued for any tort committed by the Medical Officer during the emergency.

The chief education officer, sometimes styled director of education, reports to the education committee of the council and is one of the most powerful chief officers. Normally the town clerk or clerk services the education committee but in one or two authorities this is done by the education officer, who in any event provides clerks from his department to attend meetings of governors and managers of schools. There may or may not be a separate children's committee; in some authorities there is a single committee for child-care, personal health and welfare, including mental welfare, to which the three chief officers report. This trend will be accentuated if the Seebohm Report is implemented.

If an officer has an interest in any contract he must disclose this fact in writing unless it is remote or insignificant; and he must not accept any fee or reward other than his remuneration. An officer must account for money or property committed to his charge. An authority can ratify a decision made by an officer if it is *intra vires*. A local authority is now bound by a contract entered into on its behalf by a duly authorised officer.[19]

Full-time local government officers must contribute to a superannuation scheme and may transfer from one authority to another without detriment to their rights. Local authorities have a general discretion to pay reasonable remuneration but this is now determined by the National Joint Council for Local Authorities' Administrative, Professional, Technical and Clerical Services.[20] This applies to general staff but not to the chief officers and their deputies described above. The Employers' side of the N.J.C. comprises the Local Authority Associations—the Association of Municipal Corporations,[21] the County Councils Association, the Urban District Councils Association and the Rural District Councils Association.[22] The dominant body on the Staff Side of the N.J.C. is the National and Local Government Officers Association (N.A.L.G.O.), whose members include officers of the nationalised electricity, gas and hospital services. Other bodies on the staff side include the National Union of Public Employees. N.A.L.G.O.'s National Executive Council elected by its members has a Service Conditions Committee and a Local Government Committee; every branch is represented on a District Council which reports to the former committee. Every branch is also represented at the Annual Conference, the policy-making body. The employers meet the staff at branch level, where individual local authorities are directly represented; at provincial level, where several authorities are represented; and at national level, where members of the provincial council assist the local authority association representatives. If agreement is not reached, a claim on the application of recognised terms and conditions is settled by the Department of Employment and Productivity.

1   It was abolished by the Representation of the People Act, 1969.
2   Who is not under any legal disability.
3   The 12 months preceding the date of nomination for election.
4   This disqualifies if the surcharge or imprisonment was within 5 years before or since election.
5   Except in rural districts, where the signatures of proposer and seconder suffice.

6   In case of a tie, the choice is determined by drawing lots.
7   The distinguished former Clerk of the Greater London Council and author of "Local Government Law and Administration".
8   Except rural boroughs.
9   One-sixth in Greater London.
10 Rands v. Oldroyd [1959] 1 Q.B. 204.
11 Except in the case of a finance committee.
12 See Chapter XII, pp. 140-141, *post*.
13 Or joint education board.
14 Certain county planning functions can be delegated to these councils (see Chapter XI. p. 124, *post*).
15 In which case an action for libel would lie.
16 Except in a rural district, where the council *may* appoint a surveyor under the general provisions.
17 Or the chairman of the council and the clerk.
18 These will be described in detail in Chapter XI.
19 Corporate Bodies (Contracts) Act, 1960.
20 Representing the Clerical Division; the Administrative and Professional Division; and the Technicians and Technical Staffs Division.
21 To which all councils of county boroughs, non-county boroughs, London Boroughs and rural boroughs can belong.
22 The National Association of Parish Councils is not represented, as parish councils are administered mainly on a voluntary basis.

CHAPTER XI

THE FUNCTIONS OF LOCAL AUTHORITIES

The functions of local authorities are many and varied and it is not possible to give a detailed account in a work of this nature. An outline of four of the most important groups of functions follows, but it should be borne in mind that special provisions apply to Greater London (see Chapter XV). This account therefore relates to local authorities in England and Wales, outside Greater London.

A. Education, Health and Welfare
Education[1]

The modern system of public education in this country derives from the war-time Education Act, 1944. The local education authorities are county councils, county borough councils and joint education boards; there is provision for the establishment of joint education committees. A Joint Education Board is a corporate body which can be formed to administer education over a wider area and it can hold land, borrow money and precept upon its constituent authorities. A Joint Committee, on the other hand, has no corporate status, no independent financial powers and cannot hold property; its constitution is contained in an agreement between the appointing authorities.

Arrangements for the delegation of education functions furnish an excellent example of the working of the county or "divided" system of local government (as distinct from the unitary county borough system which is self-contained) and, secondarily, of the usefulness of the "county district" classification. Schemes for divisional administration constitute within each division of a county a "divisional executive", comprising representatives of the group of county districts within the executive area. The expression "county district" is a term of art and embraces a non-county borough, an urban district and a rural district. A county district council can therefore be the council of any of these types of local authority; a district council is merely an urban or a rural district council. Some county district councils are "excepted districts"; such a council has been excepted from the county scheme of divisional administration by Ministerial order enabling it to administer certain aspects of primary and secondary education in its area. The excepted district thus exercises the functions that would otherwise be performed by the local divisional executive or, to put it another way, the excepted district is the divisional executive. This was done for historical reasons because under the 1944 Act the smaller authorities ceased to be fully responsible for elementary education. The county council retains financial and policy control but the day-to-day administration of the schools is in the hands of the excepted district. The minimum population figure for such delegation schemes is 60,000; the Secretary of State has a discretion to vary this limit if special reasons exist and rural district councils have been included since 1958.

Local education authorities must provide primary, secondary and further education. Authority exists in the 1944 Act to raise the upper limit of the compulsory school age to 16. In general, pupils are to be educated in accordance with the wishes of their parents and their different ages, abilities and aptitudes; and no fees must be charged. It is the duty of parents to send their children to school or to make other satisfactory provision; this can be enforced by means of school attendance orders and by prosecution in the magistrates' courts.

County schools are those established by a present or former authority; voluntary schools are maintained by a local education authority but were originally established by a religious or charitable foundation. Managers or Governors[2] of a county school are appointed by the local education authority from members of political parties in the area; in the case of voluntary schools, a proportion are "foundation" managers or governors. In the case of voluntary aided schools, governors or managers are responsible for outstanding liabilities, necessary alterations to buildings, and external repairs; the authority is responsible for internal, playground and playing field repairs, maintenance expenses and repairs necessitated by ancillary use of the premises.[3] Managers or governors receive a direct grant from the Minister of 80 percent of the cost of alterations and repairs. In the case of special agreement schools, grants have been made by the authority and the position of managers and governors is similar to those of aided schools.

The managers or governors of voluntary controlled schools merely provide the premises; the authority is fully responsible for maintenance, alteration and repair. In county controlled and special agreement schools, the authority can appoint or dismiss teachers except that in the voluntary schools managers or governors can control appointment or dismissal of "reserved teachers" responsible for religious instruction. Teachers in voluntary aided schools are appointed by managers or governors within limits set by the authority, which can veto appointment or require dismissal, other than dismissal of "reserved teachers" on religious grounds.

In general, teachers employed by local education authorities must be recognised as 'qualified" by the Secretary of State. The majority of teachers who have completed their training in and since 1963 have undertaken a three year course. Considerable progress has been made in recent years in the provision of training for mature students. Teachers' training colleges had been established, maintained and governed by local education authorities or voluntary bodies; and university Institutes of Education had been associated with the maintenance of academic standards. The Robbins Report on Higher Education (1963) recommended fundamental changes to bring the colleges under the control of university Schools of Education. In December, 1964, the government decided to leave the colleges under local or voluntary control, but closer academic links with the universities were to be encouraged. They were renamed Colleges of Education, as suggested by the Robbins Report.

Control of the colleges is divided between local education authorities and governors, as in the case of secondary schools. A significant difference, however, is that the governors of a college of education include a substantial proportion of the teaching staff. A study group[4] has recently recommended that the governing body should not draw more than 55 per cent of its membership from councillors; the remaining governors would be academic staff, practising teachers and outside specialists in education. They also propose that the governors should be consulted on the estimates and should take as many decisions as possible, including determination of the number and grading of lecturers within the financial allocation and with the assistance of the local education officers and inspectors.

The Education (No. 2) Act, 1968, provides that the governing bodies have greater autonomy and they are no longer sub-committees of the local education authority.

The staff of polytechnics are now eligible for membership of the local authority by whom they are employed.

The White Paper on "A Plan for Polytechnics and Other Colleges" (Cmnd. 3006) has now been implemented and the Secretary of State has designated some 30 Polytechnics in England and Wales as the main higher education centres within the further education system. In inner London, for example, a new polytechnic is to be formed from the merger of Holborn College of Law, Languages and Commerce with Regent Street Polytechnic; and the City of London Polytechnic will incorporate the City of London College, Sir John Cass College and a new unit to be built.

The Open University, based on the concept of the "University of the Air" has now been given its Charter. It is designed to help part-time and mature students who are unable, for one reason or another, to undertake full-time study.

The remuneration of teachers until 1945 was dealt with by a Burnham Committee, which was named after its first chairman. Following the enactment of the 1944 Act, the Minister appointed a new Burnham

Committee with an independent chairman, 26 representatives of the authorities and 26 representatives of the teachers. The Committee's duty was to submit agreed salary scales to the Minister for his approval. The Minister could not compel negotiations nor could he modify the scales; his only course was to reject them if he disapproved. This state of affairs was unsatisfactory and in 1963 new scales had to be introduced by statute. Finally, the Remuneration of Teachers Act, 1965, set up committees under an independent chairman and including representatives of the Secretary of State. The Act provides for arbitration in default of agreement and for orders made under it to have retrospective effect. All teachers in maintained schools are paid by the local education authority and their conditions of service are negotiated between the local authority associations and the teachers' organisations, of which the National Union of Teachers is the most prominent.

Special provision must be made for handicapped children and for further education of persons over compulsory school age. Maintained special schools now have governing bodies which are not sub committees of the local education committee. Authorities must arrange free transport or pay reasonable expenses to a pupil if his school is not within "walking distance"[5] of his home.

Under the Public Libraries and Museums Act, 1964, library facilities must be provided by the councils of counties and county boroughs, and by most non-country borough and urban district councils. Joint Boards may be constituted and charges may be made for failure to return books within due time. The Act enables local authorities to provide and maintain museums and art galleries.

Health and Welfare

Although the National Health Service Act, 1946, transferred hospitals to Hospital Boards, the local authorities remained responsible for the personal health services. The authorities had to submit proposals under the Act to the Minister of Health for health centres, maternity and child welfare, midwifery, health visiting and home nursing, vaccination and immunisation, ambulances, prevention of illness and after-care and domestic help. Owing to financial stringency few health centres have been established; the aim is to co-ordinate medical, dental and pharmaceutical services under one roof in order to provide a better service to the public. Local health authorities can now give advice on contraception[6]

The National Assistance Act, 1948, created the National Assistance Board but certain welfare functions are discharged by the local authorities.

Local welfare authorities submitted schemes of administration to the Minister of Health for modification or approval. Welfare authorities must provide residential accommodation for the aged and infirm and for persons in urgent need of temporary accommodation. There is power to inspect homes for the aged, disabled or mentally disordered. Authorities must promote the welfare of blind, deaf, physically handicapped and mentally disordered persons and can use voluntary agencies for these purposes. Personal health and welfare powers have been supplemented by the Mental Health Act, 1959, in relation to mentally disordered persons.

County councils and county borough councils administer the Children Acts, 1948–58, under the general guidance of the Home Secretary. They must take into care any child under 17 who is an orphan or who has been abandoned or lost or whose parents or guardians cannot provide for him. An authority may by resolution assume parental rights and a court may commit a child to the care of a local authority. Such children may be boarded out in foster homes or placed in homes run by the authority. There is provision for the parents to contribute towards maintenance of their children.

The Children and Young Persons Act. 1963, provided, for the first time, that local children's authorities have a duty to *prevent* or diminish the need to receive children into care. This power enables such a local authority to make grants to individual families. It is well-known that prevention is better than cure and many organisations concerned with child care, such as the Association of Children's Officers, had long been pressing for such a provision.

The Local Government Act, 1958, enabled certain personal health and welfare functions to be delegated to county district councils. Again, the minimum population figure of 60,000 was taken, the Minister of Health having a discretion in the matter. Where schemes for the divisional administration of education apply to school health services, divisional executives may be constituted to administer child welfare and child life protection.

A White Paper on "The Child, the Family and the Young Offender" published in August, 1965, emphasised the need to improve the structure of the services connected with the family and prevention of delinquency. The government believe that these services should be organised as a family service and accordingly, in December, 1965, set up an independent committee under Mr. Frederick Seebohm to review the personal social services. The committee was sponsored jointly by the Home Secretary, the Secretary of State for Education, the Minister of Housing and Local Government and the Minister of Health.

A report presented to the Prime Minister in December, 1965, disclosed an alarming proportion of children living in dire poverty in the midst of the affluent society and one hopes that urgent reforms will take cognisance of this problem.

The main conclusion of the Seebohm Report was that all major authorities should have a unified social service department under a chief officer who would have no other duties and would report to a separate social service committee. This would embrace services relating to children, the aged, the disabled, the handicapped and some social services now discharged in health (e.g. home help, meals on wheels), education (e.g. school care committees) and housing (e.g. housing estate management and rent collection) departments. The Report also called for more manpower, more extensive training, improved buildings and research. The chief officer should not be subordinate to any other departmental head and should work as a member of a team under the leadership of the clerk. He should be a trained social worker and a gifted administrator. The Secretary of State for Social Services should be involved in his selection.[7] There should be close liasion between the departments and the Supplementary Benefits Commission.[8] The contribution made by voluntary bodies was also recognised by the Seebohm Committee. The unification should provide an effective family service. Housing should be discharged by the same tier as local health, education and welfare. The aim should be to provide "one door on which to knock". The Local Government Grants (Social Need) Act 1969[9] enables a new specific grant to be paid to local authorities on account of expenditure which, in the opinion of the Secretary of State, is incurred in respect of "special social need" in urban areas. The Government has launched an experimental community development project in areas of serious social need to unite all existing services in Coventry, Liverpool and Southwark. D.H.S.S., Home Office, D.E.S. and M.H.L.G are co-operating in this neighbourhood–based experiment which is attracting 75 per cent grant under the government urban programme.

The Green Paper on the National Health Service recommended that some seven hundred local health authorities should be replaced by forty area health boards, which would inherit the functions of executive councils, R.H.B.s, H.M.C.s and boards of hospital governors. These proposals are very unpopular in local government circles. A consensus in favour of a two tier solution appeared to be emerging, with Regional authorities as the first tier and district executives based on districts served by one or more hospitals as the second tier. Election should be the basis of representation on these bodies. Both the A.M.C. and the R.D.C.A. have urged that hospitals should be returned to local government; the R.D.C.A. would go further and advocates the transfer of all health services to local government. The government is believed to be working on a plan for a unified health service and the Secretary of State is to announce his plans in the autumn of 1969.

The Health Services and Public Health Act 1968 extends powers in N.H.S.A. 1946 re provision of midwives and home helps and enables charges to be made and local health authorities to provide and to charge for residential accommodation. The authorities must keep a register of premises where children are looked after under the Nursery and Child Minders Regulation Act 1948. Accommodation can now be provided under the National Assistance Acts in premises managed by a voluntary body and local authorities have wide powers to promote the welfare of old people. Statutory provisions on notifiable diseases are extended (e.g. a family doctor must notify the local medical officer of health if he suspects that his patient is suffering from cholera or smallpox).

B.   Town and Country Planning

Parliament first turned its attention to this subject in the Housing and Town Planning Act, 1909, which enabled borough and urban district councils to make town planning schemes. A similar Act of 1919 required local authorities to prepare schemes and in 1925 they were given extended powers. The Local Government Act, 1929, brought the County Councils into the picture for the first time and empowered them to act jointly with other authorities for this purpose. The Town and Country Planning Act, 1932, required county borough and county district councils to make planning schemes and authorised the appointment of joint committees. The local planning authorities passed resolutions to prepare schemes, which became effective when approved by the Minister of Health,[10] who could also make interim development orders. Much of the war-time legislation was incorporated in the Town and Country Planning Act, 1947, which provided the basis of all subsequent planning law, which was consolidated in the Town and Country Planning Act, 1962.

Local planning authorities are county councils, county borough councils and Joint Boards. Control of development[11] may be delegated to county district councils with a minimum population of 60,000; the Minister of Housing and Local Government has discretionary power to authorise delegation to a council with a lesser population. The 1947 Act required the preparation of development plans, subject to review at five-yearly intervals. The plans define sites and allocate areas of land for specific uses (residential, commercial, industrial, etc.) There is also a very wide power to *designate* as subject to compulsory acquisition land allocated by the plan for *any* of the functions of *any* Minister, local authority or statutory undertaker. This is the widest power of compulsory purchase contained in any statute; and it applies also to land in a comprehensive development area, that is, an area which is to be replanned on a large scale owing to war damage, bad lay-out, obsolete development, re-location of population or industry or replacement of open spaces. The Minister made Regulations in 1965 to simplify the form and content of development plans and in the same year a Working Party reported on the Future of Development Plans. There is provision for objections to be made to the Minister on quinquennial review and for a local inquiry or private hearing to be held. If a compulsory purchase order is made in respect of designated land, the Minister may disregard any objection which amounts in substance to an objection to the provisions of the plan defining the proposed use of the land. The reason for this is that objectors had their opportunity on the occasion of the last review of the plan. An owner-occupier of land allocated for a particular use can serve a purchase notice on the local authority if its rateable value does not exceed £750 and provided that he can prove that the designation has caused ' blight" to settle on the land. This means that he has been unable to sell property except at a price substantially lower than current market value. The local authority may serve a counter-notice denying this and the matter is then settled by the Lands Tribunal. A local authority may carry out development or grant building leases to private developers. It must, however, secure alternative accommodation in advance of displacing residents. The 1968 Act provides that local planning authorities shall make substantive plans for strategic planning and allows them also to make local plans.

We now turn to "control of development" which can be delegated in the counties and which really means dealing with applications for planning permission. The Act defines development as:-

(a) the carrying out of building, engineering, mining or other operations in, on, over or under land; or

(b) the making of any material change in the use of buildings or land.

Some years ago the Ministry, presumably trying to be helpful, indicated that a material change of use is a change of use which is substantial. However, the Act does give examples, such as the use as two or more dwellings of a building previously used as a single dwelling; and the formation or layout of means of access to a highway. Again, certain operations and uses are declared not to be development, such as internal works of maintenance and improvement, the use of existing buildings or land within the ground[12] used for the comfortable enjoyment of a dwelling-house; or the use of land or buildings for the purposes of agriculture or forestry. Application may be made to the local planning authority to determine whether a proposed operation or change of use constitutes development.

An applicant for planning permission need not be the landowner but, if he is not, he must notify all owners or publish a notice in the local press; and notice must be given to any agricultural tenants. The law was changed in this respect in 1959 because prospective purchasers were seeking planning permission without the knowledge of landowners; and agricultural tenants need special protection owing to their general insecurity of tenure. An authority must not deal with "bad neighbour development" (e.g. construction of public conveniences) until 21 days after advertisement in the local press. "Outline planning permission" can settle an application in principle, leaving points of detail to be filled in later: the developer can then go ahead with siting and design before submission of final plans.

A local planning authority may grant or refuse planning permission and may attach conditions or limitations on its duration. Permission may be granted for development which is contrary to the development plan so long as it is not a substantial departure and does not injuriously affect the amenity of adjoining land. Appeal lies to the Minister within 28 days and his decision can be challenged within 6 weeks only on the grounds that it is *ultra vires* or that the applicant's interest has been substantially prejudiced by non-compliance with a statutory requirement (the "challenge procedure"). The Minister may "call in" applications for his initial decision.

An authority may not grant permission to erect or enlarge an industrial building over a certain limit unless the Minister of Technology issues an industrial development certificate. The Control of Office and Industrial Development Act, 1965, enabled the Minister to reduce the limit, which he has done in certain areas, and also introduced control of office building. An office development permit must now similarly be obtained before planning permission can be granted. Under the Industrial Development Act, 1966 an industrial development certificate will in future attach to the *project,* not to the *land.*

There are now stringent provisions for the enforcement of planning control. A local planning authority may serve on the owner and occupier of land an enforcement notice specifying the alleged contravention and the action to be taken to put the matter right. It is important that the notice should be served within four years of the contravention[13] and that it should specify a period of not less than 28 days at the end of which it takes effect *and* a period of compliance. An enforcement notice which does not specify *both* periods is null and void and can be set aside in the courts. Appeal lies on several specified grounds to the Minister and from him to the High Court. When an enforcement notice has become effective, the authority may enter the land and do any necessary work, charging the owner with the cost. Fines may be imposed and an enforcement notice is not now discharged by compliance. Until 1960 it was so discharged and there were cases of individuals moving structures from field to field, causing the local authority to invoke the enforcement procedure all over again after each move. The only way to deal with such evasions and flouting of the law was by means of an injunction issuing from the High Court but the strengthened enforcement procedure has probably made this unnecessary.

Planning. Under the Town and Country Planning Act, 1968, certain appeals are to be decided by inspectors instead of by the Minister of Housing and Local Government (e.g. planning decisions, tree preservation orders, refusal of established use certificate, control of listed buildings).

A material change in use can be caught by an Enforcement Notice at any time provided the change occurred after the end of 1963. But if the material change is to use as a single dwelling house the development will be safe whenever it occurred. Building operations still enjoy the protection of the four year rule.

Penalties for breach of an enforcement notice are increased (in general from £100 to £400). A stop notice can now be served following an enforcement notice to prevent breach of planning control during the 28 day period between its service and coming into operation. This only applies to building operations (not to material change of use) and there is provision for compensation.

All permissions granted before January, 1968, are subject to an implied condition that the development must be begun within five years.[14] Time limits on future permissions will be in the discretion of the local authority. The Act also gives more extensive powers for conservation of buildings of special architectural or historic interest.

The classic *raison d'etre* of planning law is the preservation of local amenities in accordance with a central direction of policy laid down by Parliament. To this end, local planning authorities may make tree preservation orders and building preservation orders. In the former case, there is overlapping with the powers of the Forestry Commission. The latter orders relate to buildings of special architectural or historic interest; the Ministry has compiled lists of such buildings and *prima facie* a listed building should be protected. The challenge procedure applies to these powers.

The Civic Amenities Act, 1967, enabled local planning authorities to designate "conservation areas" of special architectural or historic interest and for the preservation and enhancement of their character and appearance. At least six months notice must now be given of works affecting listed buildings and the penalties for contravention of a building preservation order are increased. The Act also provides for more adequate provision in respect of the preservation, planting and replacement of trees. As noted above, the 1968 Act has built on these provisions which were introduced as a private members' bill by Mr. Duncan Sandys.

Advertisement Regulations control the display of advertisements in the interests of amenity and safety; there are more stringent checks in areas of special control but in general they must be clean, tidy and safe, road safety requirements nowadays being a important factor to be considered. Where local amenity is seriously injured by the condition of any garden, vacant site or other open land, an abatement notice may be served on the owner and occupier. Appeal lies to the local magistrates court, as it did in the case of ordinary enforcement notices until 1960.

The Countryside Act, 1967, redesignated the National Parks Commission as the Countryside Commission, responsible for the promotion of public enjoyment of the countryside. The Act provides for the creation of Country Parks on the coast and in the countryside, in order to relieve pressure on the National Parks. Exchequer grants to National Parks and areas of outstanding natural beauty will be continued and extended to include the Country Parks, amenity tree planting and increased public access to open country. Local authorities are given extended powers to provide amenities in Country Parks, camping and picnic sites.

The Commons Registration Act, 1965, provides for the registration of common land and of village greens. The registration authorities are the Greater London Council, county councils and county borough councils and rights of common will no longer be registered under the Land Registration Acts, 1925–36. The purpose of the new Act is to establish what land in England and Wales is common or a town or village green, what rights of common exist and to place on record who claims ownership of the land. Local authorities opened registers for this purpose in 1967. Commons Commissioners appointed by the Lord Chancellor from the legal profession resolve disputes and they may be assisted by technical assessors. Registers are open to public inspection and adequate publicity and information must be given by the local registration authorities. The Act does not affect rights of access to commons, nor does it extend to land that forms part of a highway. The New Forest, Epping Forest and the Forest of Dean are exempted from registration and the Minister may by order exempt other land if it is already regulated by statute, if no common rights have been exercised over it for at least 30 years and if the landowner is known.

Compensation for compulsory acquisition is payable under the Land Compensation Act, 1961, and is based on the current market value of the land, assuming a willing purchaser and a willing vendor. Valuers must take into account the existing use of the land and planning permissions already in force. The Lands Tribunal is available to decide disputes on the correct amount of compensation. Where permission has been refused or is conditional and the owner claims that his land is useless to him in its existing state,[15] he can serve a purchase notice on his county borough or county district council. The latter may not be the planning authority but it was selected as being more local than the county council. If the Minister confirms the notice it has the same effect as a compulsory purchase order.

Finally, it should be noted that the Town Development Act, 1952, authorises development in the shape of the expansion of existing towns in order to decentralise population and industry. The ' exporting'' local authority sends its "overspill" population to the "receiving" local authority and pays to the latter a contribution equal to the central subsidy.

The Minister of Housing and Local Government announced in Parliament in March, 1966, the establishment of a planning centre for environmental studies. The object is to give an impetus to research in the environmental field and to make a major contribution to understanding the nature of cities. Lord Llewelyn-Davies, professor of architecture at London University, is chairman of the governing body. The planning centre is an independent trust and has a budget of nearly £1 million spread over five years. Sixty per cent of this has been contributed by the Treasury and forty per cent by the Ford Foundation. The centre will commission universities to undertake the necessary research and it is estimated that about five projects should be completed in the next five years.

The Minister also stated, in May, 1966, that he had selected five old cities for pilot studies of preservation and change. These are Bath, Chester, Chichester, King's Lynn and York.

C. *Housing and Public Health*
Housing

Borough, urban and rural district councils are both local housing authorities and local public health authorities. The close historical connection between the two services can be discerned in the procedure for slum clearance. Public health inspectors, who are local government officers, must inspect houses in their areas and the medical officer of health must make an official representation to the local housing authority when he thinks that a house is unfit for human habitation. The Housing Act, 1957,[16] re-enacting the old law, postulates nine standards of fitness: repair; stability; freedom from damp; internal arrangement; natural lighting; ventilation; water supply; drainage and sanitary conveniences; and facilities for the preparation and cooking of food and for the disposal of waste water. If a local authority is satisfied that a house is capable of being made fit at reasonable cost, a repairs notice may be served.[17] If it is not complied with, the authority may do the work and recover the cost; appeal lies to the local county court.

If a local authority considers a house to be beyond repair at reasonable cost a repairs notice is served on the owner, the person in control of the house and mortgagees asking them to make representations. If the authority does not receive and accept an undertaking to do the repairs, it may make a demolition order, a closing order or a compulsory purchase order. A closing order is sometimes made where, although human habitation is undesirable, the property is protected as a listed building or is subject to a building preservation order. A closing order is also useful where demolition would adversely affect adjoining habitable property. A right of appeal in each case lies to the county court.

So far we have been dealing with the individual unfit house but it may be necessary to go in for slum clearance on the grand scale, especially in the big cities. Accordingly, where there are numerous unfit houses in an area a local housing authority may deal with them collectively by passing a resolution declaring the area to be a clearance area or a redevelopment area and must send a copy of its resolution to the Minister. The authority may make a clearance order requiring the owners to clear the site, purchase the land and demolish the buildings or allow redevelopment by property companies. The clearance procedure is used where the houses are unfit or by reason of their bad arrangement or the narrowness of the streets are dangerous or injurious to health and demolition is the most satisfactory solution. Redevelopment procedure can be invoked only if the area contains at least fifty houses, of which a third are overcrowded or unfit and the authority considers that the area should be redeveloped as a whole. In both cases there is detailed provision for publicity in the local press, the holding of local public inquiries in case of objection, challenge procedure in the courts and submission of the order for ministerial confirmation. Land subject to a clearance order may be purchased[18] by the local authority if it is not developed within 18 months. A redevelopment plan shows areas to be used for streets and open spaces as well as houses. Land purchased may include   sanitary islands" of fit houses in a sea of unfit dwellings, and adjoining land. Demolition can be postponed if the houses can be made temporarily fit and are now owned by the authority, which can ask the Minister to make an order taking houses out of a clearance order. When a redevelopment plan becomes operative, the local authority can acquire land to rehouse those displaced.

In general, compensation is based on current market value in relation to fit houses which have to be acquired in a clearance or redevelopment area. In the case of condemned property in such an area, however, the basic rule is that no compensation is payable and the owner is left with the site cleared of buildings and available for development in conformity with building regulations and planning control. In the case of compulsory purchase of an unfit house, the compensation payable by the local authority is based on site value but this must not exceed the market value of the site with the useless house on it, since a cleared site available for development may be more valuable than one containing slums. The Minister may order an extra payment to be made if the house has been well maintained and an owner of a house used for business purposes will receive full compensation.[19] Discretionary payments may be made in respect of removal expenses and losses caused by disturbance of trade or business.

Several Housing Acts have attempted to deal with the problems of overcrowding and houses in multiple occupation, notably those of 1957, 1961 and 1964. None appear to have been very successful, perhaps because they have not been rigidly applied and enforced. The Acts prescribe penalties for offences and drastic powers are available under the 1964 Act to make a control order in respect of a house in multiple occupation if this is necessary to protect the safety, welfare on health of the occupants. There is a right of appeal to the county court and the effect of an order is to give the local authority right of possession, management and insurance. In effect, the authority displaces the owner for five years and in fact the Act describes the owner as "the dispossessed proprietor '. He must be paid compensation in lieu of rent and allowed access. The 1969 Act defines a house in multiple occupation as one occupied by persons who do not form a single household.

We now turn to the more positive and stimulating aspects of housing administration, the provision of new houses. This can be done by means of acquisition, erection of houses, conversions and improvements; and shops, recreation grounds and amenities can also be provided to service housing estates.

A local housing authority is responsible for the general management and control of its houses and flats, which it can regulate by means of bye-laws and tenancy agreements. The amount of rents is within the discretion of the authority but they must be reasonable and subject to periodical review. Reasonableness may be a question for the courts, which expect local authorities to act as trustees for the general body of ratepayers and to balance this duty against that owed to a special class such as council tenants. Unduly low rents must not cast too heavy a load on the general rate fund; and the treasurer and auditors must be satisfied with the position of the housing revenue account. Provided that these criteria are met, a local housing authority can perfectly well operate a differential rents scheme or a rent rebate scheme based on tenants' incomes; or it may prefer to charge standard rents, leaving the poorer tenants to apply to the Department of Health and Social Security for rent relief and thus cast the burden on taxation rather than the rates. Local authorities must primarily allocate their housing to tenants who have been living in insanitary or overcrowded houses and to those with large families. Council tenants must not assign or sub-let without consent. In practice, much council housing has to be allocated to those dispossessed by planning and road widening schemes as well as by slum clearance.

The housing manager plays an important part in local housing administration and many local authorities issue tenants' handbooks. Implementation of the Seebohm Report may result in transfer of housing management to a new unified local Social Service department.

The 1964 Act set up a Housing Corporation to promote the development of housing societies. Cost-rent societies provide housing at rents reflecting cost, without profit or subsidy; co-ownership societies enable a group to own collectively, each householder having a long lease. Local authorities may also help housing associations to provide housing by acquiring land and selling or leasing it to such associations. Authorities may sell or lease houses and may impose covenants and conditions limiting the price of resale within five years and limiting the rent payable.

Subject to certain conditions, county councils and local housing authorities can lend money for house purchase to the full value of the property. These powers extend to building, conversions, repairs and improvement of houses. Local housing authorities can also make discretionary improvement grants for conversions and improvements, subject to several conditions, and towards the provision of certain standard amenities such as a hot and cold water supply, fixed bath and water closet. The authority must be convinced that the dwelling will be satisfactory for at least 15 years. An applicant who is refused a grant may ask the authority to state the reason. The 1964 Act enabled an authority to declare an area to be an improvement area in order to provide standard amenities.

The main purpose of the Housing Act, 1969, was to implement the proposals outlined in the White Paper "Old Houses into New Homes"[20] Part I incorporates the proposals for increasing the maximum amount of improvement and standard grants and for making conditions for them more flexible. The minimum estimated cost of works to qualify for an improvement grant is £100. An improvement grant must not exceed half of the approved expense of the works nor a certain limit (£1,200 if the dwelling is provided by conversion of a house comprising three or more storeys, £1,000 in other cases). The Act also enables local authorities to pay special grants for works executed in respect of houses already having some standard amenities. Provision is made for the Minister to contribute towards the cost of improvement, standard and special grants. Part II contains new area improvement powers, which replace the improvement area provisions contained in the 1964 Act. In order to declare a general improvement area the local authority must pass a resolution to that effect and publish an article in the local press and send a copy of the resolution, report, map and statement to the M.H.L.G. In London the G.L.C. exercises the improvement area powers, subject to L.B.C. agreement.

Part IV (Houses in Multiple Occupation) enables a control order under the 1964 Act to be followed by a C.P.O. Provisions as to registration of such houses are strengthened. In general this is a remarkably wide-ranging Act, as can be seen from its Long Title. No more 1964 Act areas are to be declared and in those already initiated a local authority can elect to use the 1964 Act powers or to use the powers under the new Act. The 1969 Act also contains fresh provisions as to payments for unfit houses, noted above. It also redefines a house in multiple occupation as one occupied by persons who do not form a single household.

The Rent Act, 1968, consolidates the Rent Acts, including most of the Rent Act, 1965, under which controlled or regulated tenancies can have their rents reviewed, at the instance of landlord or tenant, by rent officers. Counties, county boroughs and London boroughs are registration areas whose clerks and town clerks are responsible for appointment, dismissal (with M.H.L.G. consent) and allocation of work of rent officers, whose terms of employment are, however, otherwise regulated by schemes made by M.H.L.G. Appeal on determination of fair rent lies to rent assessment committees appointed by the Minister for each registration area; there is no appeal on a point of law to the High Court but decisions can be reviewed by means of the prerogative orders. The Rent Act provisions as to determination of fair rent are applied by the Housing Act, 1969, to controlled tenancies certified by the local authority as having all standard amenities for the exclusive use of occupants, and as being in general in good repair and fit for human habitation. Procedure is laid down as regards application for such qualification certificates, registration of rent after issue and appeal to the county court against refusal to issue. The effect of the issue of a qualification certificate is to specify a tenancy as a regulated tenancy under the Rent Act, 1968.

Housing finance is extremely intricate: the principle under the 1961 Act was that the general housing subsidy depended on the state of the local authority's finances. An authority charging economic or realistic rents received a higher rate of subsidy from the Ministry. Extra subsidies are given to certain large towns and cities with acute slum clearance problems *and* which have already incurred considerable expenditure on clearance projects. As already noted, special social need in urban areas now attracts grant and this can include housing.

The Housing Subsidies Act, 1967, introduced a new form of general subsidy aimed to relieve housing authorities from high rates of interest by payment of a subsidy assessed to amount to the excess over four per cent of the actual rate of interest paid. Extra subsidies continue to be paid for dwellings provided to meet special needs or which are unusually expensive.[21] This Act also introduced an Option Mortgage Scheme designed to help house purchasers whose income is too low to enable them to obtain full tax-relief at the standard rate on their mortgage interest. Borrowers can elect to have *either* an Option Mortgage under which the Government pays a subsidy to the lender *or* an ordinary mortgage with normal tax relief. A brief Guide to the Option Mortgage Scheme was published by H.M.S.O. in 1967. The Act also enables the Housing Ministers to enter into arrangements with insurance companies to provide guarantees to enable loans up to 100 per cent to be made where the valuation or purchase price is not more than £5,000. This scheme was evolved with the co-operation of the Building Societies Association and the British Insurance Association. Orders have been made designating as qualifying lenders under the option mortgage scheme building societies with trustee status, development corporations, the Commission for the New Towns and M.H.L.G. and the Secretaries of State for Scotland and Wales.

A Working Party reported on the Housing Revenue Account's present principles and practice in May, 1969 and described its function, scope and purpose.

The National House Builders Registration Council keeps a register of house-builders and requires all on the register to submit to various disciplines in the interests of purchasers. N.H.B.R.C. has power to remove builders from the register, taking into account standards of work including after-sales service.

Public Health

Public health functions may be discharged by joint boards and port health authorities as well as the councils of county boroughs and county districts. The Minister of Housing and Local Government may by order constitute a port health authority having jurisdiction over the port and its waters and comprising one local authority[22] or a joint board representing local authorities and the harbour authority. As already noted, the modern public health authorities in part replaced the old sanitary districts; they are therefore responsible for sanitation and buildings. The local authorities must accordingly maintain and repair the public sewers and are under a general duty to provide such public sewers as may be necessary for effectual drainage.[23] An authority can construct public sewers in streets and through private land but in both cases notice must be given and in the latter case compensation may be payable. If a private developer proposes to construct a drain or sewer he may be required to construct it so as to form part of a general system, the authority bearing the extra cost. An owner or occupier of premises has the right to drain into a public sewer. Where plans are submitted under building regulations the authority must reject them unless adequate provision is made for drainage. Subject to certain conditions, the local authority may require new buildings to be drained into a sewer. If an existing building has no satisfactory drainage system or if a drain is defective, the owner may be compelled to carry out remedial work. The medical officer of health and public health inspectors may require stopped-up drains to be remedied within 48 hours of service of a notice. If a drain is believed to be defective the authority may excavate for testing purposes, reinstating and making good if it is in order.

Until recently, local authorities made building bye-laws which were confirmed by the Minister of Housing and Local Government. This procedure has now been short-circuited, after a long delay. The 1961 Act authorised this Minister to make building regulations to replace the byelaws but in 1964 responsibility was transferred, logically enough, to the Minister of Public Building and Works. A general election and a change of government intervened but at last the Building Regulations, 1965, emerged.[24] They were made by statutory instrument and regulate numerous matters previously covered by the building bye-laws. The Regulations are made by the Minister and applied locally by the authorities. Plans submitted under building regulations must provide for satisfactory sanitary accommodation; and the local authority may require installation of water closets in place of other types provided that a sufficient water supply and sewer are available. The authority can require alteration or removal of new buildings which contravene the regulations or which have been erected without plans having been deposited; it also has powers to deal with dilapidated or dangerous buildings. It is important to distinguish between public health control under the building regulations and planning control of development, which in general are administered by different classes of local authority (except in county boroughs).

Next, a local public health authority can invoke the abatement notice procedure to deal with nuisances which are `prejudicial to health". If service of notice does not jolt the occupier to put the matter right, the local justices can make a "nuisance order" requiring abatement and execution of works. Appeal lies to quarter sessions and non-compliance subjects the defaulter to fines and enables the authority to do the work and recover the cost from the occupier. The courts have held that lack of internal decorative repair[25] and noisy animals[26] cannot be statutory nuisances; but in another case[27] a woman was held to have committed a nuisance in allowing 69 uncontrolled cats to roam at will, the results being offensive. A special type of nuisance order can be sought, under the Noise Abatement Act, 1960, by the local authority or the aggrieved occupiers of land or premises. Notices prohibiting recurrences of nuisances can now be served and justices can made a nuisance order if a prohibition notice is disregarded [28].

One of the most important duties of a public health authority is refuse collection: this is almost a personal service, amongst this welter of sewers, drains, sanitation and nuisances. The authority may undertake the removal of house refuse and if the council passes a resolution to do so, the duty can be enforced by an occupier of premises in the area. It can also remove trade refuse but in this case reasonable charges can be made and the duty can again be enforced. In the former case the authority may require the provision of regulation dustbins.

Public health inspectors are also involved in enforcement of the food and drugs legislation, in which they are assisted by the public analyst; and in smoke control enforcement under the Clean Air Act, 1956, but the latter powers are permissive only[29] Notice of occurrence of certain notifiable diseases must be sent to the medical officer of health, who must inform the local authority, which has power to add to the number of such diseases. Authorised officers of a local authority have a right of entry at all reasonable hours under the Public Health Acts, on giving at least 24 hours notice and if they are refused entry they may apply for a warrant from the justices. Finally, the occupier of land to be used as a caravan site must hold a site licence granted by the local authority, but only if planning permission has been given.[30] This is subject to certain exceptions and conditions may be imposed which reasonably relate to the use of the land for stationing caravans. The Caravan Sites Act 1968 restricts eviction, secures establishment of sites for use of gypsies and controls unauthorised occupation.

D. Highways and Bridges

The Minister of Transport is the highway authority for motorways and trunk roads but he can delegate his functions to local authorities, who can act as his agents to carry out repair and maintenance works. A county council is the highway authority for all roads in its rural districts and for county roads[31] in its non-county boroughs and urban districts. Non-county borough and urban district councils are the local highway authorities for all non-county roads[32] within their areas; but if such a borough or urban district has a population of 20,000 or more its council may claim to repair and maintain the local county roads. The council in effect then becomes the local highway authority for such "claimed" roads, but the county council must contribute to the cost of repair and maintenance. The county council may delegate repair and maintenance of both county and non-county roads to a rural district council. Despite delegation, the roads remain the property of the county council, whose approval must be obtained for necessary works. These arrangements for the local administration of highways are based on the consolidating Highways Act, 1959, and furnish two interesting exceptions to the general principles of county administration. In the first place, this is the only major service which is not common to the three types of county district council, the rural district council being the "odd man out". Secondly, the arrangements for delegation deviate from the usual minimum population figure of 60,000. It is true that a council whose area (if a borough or urban district) contains a minimum population of 20,000 and which claims maintenance of county roads becomes the highway authority for those claimed county roads. However a borough or urban district council with a lesser population may seek delegation of responsibility for county roads and a rural district council may ask for delegation. In addition, there are "special roads" designed for particular classes of heavy traffic and any highway authority can be responsible for them; usually it is the county council or county borough council.

The Minister can direct that a road shall be a trunk road and both he and the local highway authorities can construct special roads and acquire land for construction and improvement of highways. Local authorities can acquire by agreement with the owner land near a highway if this is desirable to prevent the erection of buildings detrimental to the view from the highway or to preserve amenities. A link with the principles of planning legislation can be discerned here.

Highways repairable by a highway authority are now known as "highways maintainable at the public expense". Under the Highways Act, 1835, which was the governing statute until 1960, they were "highways repairable by the inhabitants at large" and originally this had a literal meaning. As time went on the surveyors of highways came to authorise the necessary work on the authority of local highway boards, the predecessors in this respect of the local authorities, which now have a positive duty to maintain and repair such highways. Local highway authorities are now[33] liable both for mis-feasance (negligent or unskilful repair) and non-feasance (complete lack of repair).

Where a bridge across a river carries a maintainable highway the local authority is responsible for repair of the bridge; in the county system, if the county council is liable it can delegate the function to a county district council. The Minister is responsible for bridges carrying motorways or trunk roads. British Rail is responsible, as successor in title to the old railway companies, for any bridge which was built over or beneath a railway in substitution for a highway, which had been rendered unsuitable by the original works. The body responsible for repair of a bridge built before 1835 must repair the road on each side of it up to a distance of 300 feet. If the bridge was built after that date, the authority responsible for the highway before it was built remains liable for repair. Public highways and bridges must be maintained in a condition fit to accommodate ordinary traffic, in accordance with prevailing conditions. The fact that nowadays this connotes enormous lorries carrying huge loads which should travel by rail is just unfortunate; it may be that integration of road and rail transport under the Transport Act, 1968, will remedy the situation.

A highway authority has power to make up private streets under the "Code of 1892"[34] or the "Code of 1875".[35] The former applies in all rural districts and in boroughs and urban districts which have adopted it. The latter applies in all other urban areas. The 1892 Code is preferred for its flexibility and apportionment provisions and is in fact operated by about 80 per cent of local authorities. The county council acts under the 1892 Code in rural districts but if highway functions have been delegated the rural district council acts as agent for the county council. Under both Codes, the frontagers of houses in private streets can be compelled to "make up" the street, that is to pave, sewer and light it. Whereas under the 1875 Code apportionment is made on a pure frontage basis, under the 1892 Code the local authority may apportion the cost on the basis of degree of benefit to particular premises. The latter system is much more equitable; the necessary works will be more beneficial to a house at the corner of the street than to one in the middle. There are detailed rights of appeal, both to the local justices an to the Minister of Housing and Local Government. This Minister is concerned, rather than the Minister of Transport, because paving, sewering and lighting are all matters which touch upon public health. The Advance Payments Code was introduced in 1951[36] and requires payment of the estimated cost of street works or security to be given by developers to the local authority before new buildings are erected in private streets. The code applies to boroughs and urban districts and may be applied by order of the Minister to rural districts on the application of the county council after consultation with the rural district council. If more than half of the total frontage of the street is built up and the code has been applied to at least one building, a majority of the frontagers may compel the local authority to make up the street.

A highway authority may prescribe building lines and improvement lines for houses and make new street bye-laws. There is authority to break up streets in various statutes and procedure is laid down in the Public Utilities Street Works Act, 1950. The theory is that breaking-up of streets for the purposes of local authorities and public corporations should be co-ordinated, so that opening up by the public health authority to look at the sewers is not followed by breaking-up by the Area Gas Board to repair a gas main and then by the Area Electricity Board to examine a cable. However, this seems to remain a pious hope, perhaps because the various bodies are not sufficiently "down to earth".

There is a detailed and complicated procedure for stopping up and diversion of a highway, each of which can be ordered by a magistrates' court. A highway can be stopped up as unnecessary or diverted if the proposed new road is "nearer or more commodious to the public". These are Highways Act powers but a local authority may also extinguish a public right of way over land purchased for slum clearance; and the Minister of Transport may authorise stopping up or diversion to enable development to be carried out in accordance with planning permission. There are the usual provisions for publicity, public inquiry in case of objection and challenge in the courts.

A highway authority has a common law duty to prevent and remove obstructions; and, under the Highways Act, it can prosecute persons who cause an obstruction of the highway. It is desirable to make use of this modern statutory power rather than to rely on obscure provisions in old local Acts, some of which were enacted over a century ago.

A rural district council may provide lighting by order of the Minister and the Parish Councils Act, 1957, enables parish councils to provide street lighting. County councils can enter into street lighting agreements with their county district councils, which exercise permissive powers. The Minister of Transport may make agreements for the lighting of trunk roads. As the powers are permissive only, a street lighting authority is not liable for accidents arising from a failure of light; but if it puts an obstruction in a road, it must warn the public. Local authorities may prosecute persons who drop and leave litter in any public place.[37] Local authorities have powers to number houses and to name and alter the names of streets.

Capital grants are payable to local highway authorities towards the cost of construction or improvement of principal roads. Expenditure on road maintenance is now grant aided through the rate support grant[38] payable to county and county borough councils.

1. The Minister has been replaced by a Secretary of State.
2. Primary schools have managers: secondary schools have governors.
3. E.g. as an evening institute for further education.
4. Report of the Study Group on the Government of Colleges of Education Department of Education and Science (H.M.S.O., 3s.).
5. Over 3 miles for children over 8; over 2 miles for children under 8.
6. National Health Service (Family Planning) Act, 1967.
7. Compare the existing position relating to education officers and chief officers of police.
8. Which recently replaced the National Assistance Board.
9. Which has retrospective effect from 1st April, 1968.
10. The Minister then in charge of local government.
11. But not preparation and review of development plans.
12. Technically, the curtilage.
13. The 1968 Act confines the four-year rule to building operations (see below)
14. Subject to certain exceptions (e.g. planning permissions granted by development order or where express time limits have been inserted by the local planning authority).
15. "Incapable of reasonably beneficial use" in the planning jargon.
16. As amended.

17. On the person having control of the house.
18. By agreement or compulsorily.
19. The Housing Act, 1969, authorises additional payments to owner-occupiers of unfit houses and larger payments for fully well maintained unfit houses.
20. Cmnd. 3602.
21. E.g. where there is urgent need and a subsidy is a cushion against unreasonably high rates or rents; to promote industrial mobility; tall blocks of flats; expensive sites; extra expense to prevent subsidence or to preserve amenity.
22. E.g. the Common Council of the City of London Corporation.
23. Public Health Acts. 1936–1961.
24. They were operative from 1st February, 1966 and have already been amended.
25. *Springett v. Harold* [1954] 1 All E.R. 568.
26. *Galer v. Morrissey* [1955] 1 All E.R. 380.
27. *R. v. Walden-Jones, ex parte Cotton* [1963] Crim. L.R. 839.
28. Public Health (Recurring Nuisances) Act, 1969.
29. The Clean Air Act 1968 prohibits the emission of smoke from industrial or trade premises and empowers the Minister to compel local authorities to make smoke control orders.
30. Caravan Sites and Control of Development Act, 1960.
31. The old "classified" roads.
32. The old "unclassified" roads.
33. Since 3rd August, 1964.
34. Private Street Works Act, 1892, now in the Highways Act, 1959.
35. Public Health Act, 1875, now in the Highways Act, 1959.
36. New Streets Act, 1951, now in the Highway Act, 1959.
37. Litter Act. 1958.
38. See next Chapter.

CHAPTER XII

LOCAL GOVERNMENT FINANCE

RATES

The councils of boroughs, urban districts and rural districts are rating authorities; the Metropolitan Police Receiver, the G.L.C., County Councils, joint boards and parish councils are precepting authorities. A rating authority *collects* the rates from the ratepayers in its area; a precepting authority *requires* a rating authority to collect rates payable to the former. A precept is a demand from one authority to another to collect rates. In a rural area, the rural district council is the rating authority and receives precepts from the county council and from all parish councils in the rural district. The amounts in these precepts are added to the rural district's own requirements and the whole collected by the R.D.C. The reverse side of the rate demand shows all the services provided, the amount in the £ charged to each and the local authority responsible for each service.

The general rate, which after collection is payable into the general rate fund, is at a uniform amount in the £ on the rateable value of each hereditament[1] in the area of the local rating authority. This is known as the "rate poundage", in other words so many shillings in the pound. The number of shillings can exceed twenty but this does not mean that the ratepayer is drained of every penny he possesses. For example, Henry Hopkins lives at No. 1, Acacia Avenue, Bigtown, of which he is the owner-occupier. The rateable value of this desirable property has been assessed at £200. Bigtown Borough Council declare a rate poundage of fifteen shillings in the £. This means that Henry will have to pay the rating authority £150 during the course of the financial year. The local rating authority passes a resolution in February or March declaring the rate poundage for the ensuing financial year, which for local government purposes begins on April 1st. Notice of the rate must be given within seven days after it is made by notice in public places or in the local press, and forms of demand note have been prescribed by the Minister of Housing and Local Government. As we have seen, the demand note must contain certain specific information. The demand note issued by a county borough council will be much simpler than that of a county district council because there will be no precepting authorities to complicate the issue in the unitary system. A ratepayer has a right to be given a statement of rates payable in respect of any hereditament for which he is liable. If he wishes to challenge the legality of a rate demand note,[2] the ratepayer can appeal to Quarter Sessions. If a ratepayer does not pay within seven days of demand, the rating authority may seek a distress warrant in the local magistrates' court. If a warrant is issued, the defaulter's goods[3] can be seized from his home.

In practice, a rating authority will wait a good deal longer than a week before invoking this drastic procedure. A warrant of commitment to prison may not be issued unless wilful refusal or culpable neglect is established to the satisfaction of the Court. A person aggrieved by the levy of distress upon his goods may appeal to Quarter Sessions.

In 1964 Parliament provided for grants to be made to rating authorities by reference to the proportion of elderly persons in their areas and for mitigation of hardship to residential occupiers attributable to the increase in the level of rates.[4] For many years some progressive authorities have accepted payment by monthly, or even weekly, instalments. Demand notes are usually sent out half-yearly, in some areas quarterly, so that the system connotes prompt payment of fairly large sums. The Minister has encouraged local authorities to operate instalment payments and in 1966 local rating authorities were required by statute[5] to allow payments by this method on the request of rateppayers.

Until 1950 local rating authorities were responsible for assessment of rateable values as well as for the collection and spending of the rates but in that year valuation assessment functions were transferred to valuation officers of the Board of Inland Revenue. In theory, a new valuation list must be prepared quinquennially but in fact the last three were in 1939, 1956 and 1963. The incidence of wars and Rent Acts has served to defer preparation of a new list in each case; and under the Local Government Act, 1966 the revaluation due to take place in 1968 was postponed until 1973. The valuation officer has power to require owners and occupiers of hereditaments to furnish him with returns; to obtain information from his colleague the local Inspector of Taxes as to annual values, and to inspect premises. An aggrieved ratepayer may serve a proposal to amend the list on the valuation officer, who may also make a proposal. The rating authority may make a proposal to include a hereditament if the valuation officer refuses to do so. The valuation officer must notify his proposals to the rating authority and to occupiers, who may lodge objections. Appeal from the valuation officer's decision lies to the local valuation court, a local administrative tribunal drawn from a panel of members appointed under a scheme prepared by the county council or the county borough council and approved by the Minister. Local valuation courts sit in public and have now been brought within the purview of the Council of Tribunals so that their constitution and working can be reviewed by that body. The valuation list can be altered following agreement by the parties or by direction of the court. Appeal lies from the local valuation court to the Lands Tribunal, which is composed of lawyers and expert valuers.

Valuation Assessment Appeal Procedure

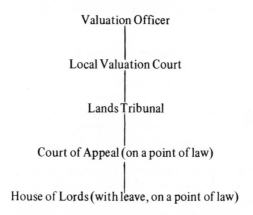

Valuation Officer

Local Valuation Court

Lands Tribunal

Court of Appeal (on a point of law)

House of Lords (with leave, on a point of law)

Rates are levied on the *occupiers* of property as a general rule; a rating authority has a permissive power to rate the owners of small properties if their rateable values do not exceed £56.[6] Modern rating law derives from a statute enacted as long ago as 1601[7] and the original basis was relief of the poor. Over the centuries the courts of law have evolved certain tests of rateable occupation:—

(i) *Actual Occupation.*

Thus empty houses are not rateable,[8] but it has been held that seaside bungalows which remain empty in the winter but are ready for letting in the summer are rateable. Similarly, empty warehouses ready for use are in rateable occupation.

(ii) *Exclusive Occupation.*

A mere lodger is not in rateable occupation but a flat is classified as a separate hereditament and the tenant is therefore rateable. Although rates may be payable by the landlord under a lease or agreement, the demand note would be properly served by the local rating authority upon the tenant as occupier.

(iii) *The possession must be of some value or benefit.*

Local authorities have been held rateable in respect of

premises occupied for library purposes because the occupation is beneficial in the sense that public duties are being discharged. But "land struck with sterility" is not rateable, for example, a public park, unless substantial income is derived from refreshment kiosks, amusement arcades, etc.

(iv) *The possession must not be temporary.*

As one judge said, the occupation must be as a settler, not as a wayfarer. It has been held that a caravan occupied as a dwelling-house is in rateable occupation. But if the use is only occasional, it would not be rateable for the occupation would then be too transient.

There is a detailed statutory formula for the calculation of the rateable value of a dwelling-house. In the first place, the *gross value* is the reasonable annual rent payable on the basis that the tenant pays usual rates and taxes and the landlord pays the cost of repairs, insurance and maintenance. In order to calculate the *rateable value,* certain deductions are made for repairs, insurance and maintenance. This is the figure entered in the valuation list by the valuation officer. What happens if the house is owner-occupied and there is no tenant paying rent? If there is no tenant, it is necessary to invent one and so the amorphous figure of the hypothetical tenant enters upon the scene. The valuation officer must seek another house as similar as possible to the owner-occupied house in every respect except one, which is that the second house *is* let. He works out his assessment on the second house and then, other things being equal, applies it to the first, which thus acquires a hypothetical tenant paying rent.

Until 1963, valuations were based on rental values obtaining in 1939 but the artificiality of this was accentuated by the operation of the Rent Act, 1957, which enabled many rents to soar to dizzy heights. The position now is that rateable values are calculated by reference to estimated current rental values. Alterations to the valuation list are to be based on the "tone of the list", owing to the postponement of revaluation until 1973. This means that a hereditament is to be given the rateable value that it would have had if it had been valued when the list was being prepared and the property and the locality had been the same then as at the time of valuation. With the concept of fair rents and extension of rent control under the Rent Act, 1965,[9] the calculation of rateable values on this basis should eventually reach a fair middle-of-the-road level. Offices, shops, mines, factories and workshops are assessed on a slightly different basis. The rateable value of commercial and industrial hereditaments is the reasonable annual rent payable on the basis of the tenant paying all usual rates and taxes and bearing the cost of repairs, insurance and maintenance. In this case the valuation officer makes all the calculations but in the case of a dwelling-house the statutory deductions for repairs insurance and maintenance are laid down in statutory instruments made from time to time by the Minister of Housing and Local Government.

Until 1963 industrial hereditaments were not fully rated and a temporary concession was made in respect of shops. In 1929 industrial and freight-transport hereditaments were relieved of three-quarters of their rates; in 1958 this was reduced to a half and the partial de-rating was finally abolished in 1963, when the 20 per cent temporary concession to shopkeepers also terminated. Agricultural land and buildings were fully de-rated in 1929 and do not therefore appear at all in the valuation list. This has not been altered, despite the apparent prosperity of British agriculture and the heavy subsidies payable following the annual price review in the spring.[10] The incidence of land drainage rates and charges is minimal and does not compensate for agricultural de-rating. Crown property is technically exempt from rateability owing to the doctrine of the royal prerogative: it would be inappropriate to compel the Crown to pay rates. Nevertheless, the Treasury makes a contribution in lieu of rates in respect of Crown property on the basis of valuation by the Treasury Valuer, who is of course a colleague of the valuation officer, since the Board of Inland Revenue is a department of the Treasury. For this purpose, Crown property includes police stations, owing to the law enforcement duties of the police and their historic connection with the maintenance of the Queen's Peace. In this case, the police authorities make contributions to the rating authorities in aid of the rates in much the same way as the Treasury Valuer does in respect of other Crown property. Places of public worship are also exempt and this includes church and chapel halls, unless they are let for payment which exceeds the expenses of letting. Thus those responsible for a church hall let for bingo sessions would have to submit a return to the valuation officer showing the balance of receipts over expenses.

The Rating and Valuation Act, 1961, clarified the law relating to remissions and exemptions of hereditaments occupied for charitable and ancillary purposes. There is provision for certain hereditaments to be charged no more than half the rate: these include those wholly or mainly used for charitable purposes, almshouses and houses occupied by clergymen. Moreover, the local authority has a discretion to remit or reduce further payment of rates in respect of such hereditaments and to remit or reduce rates of hereditaments occupied by certain non-profit making organisations. The latter comprise those whose main objects are charitable, religious, educational, recreational or devoted to social welfare, science, literature and the fine arts.[11]

There are certain other exemptions and special cases. The Secretary of State for Education and Science and the Minister of Housing and Local Government have jointly made regulations on the valuation of county and voluntary schools based on the estimated cost of providing school places. In accordance with the principles outlined above, if a voluntary school is a charitable organisation the local authority *must* give a 50 per cent remission, which it *may* increase. Other miscellaneous exemptions include public sewers, garages for certain classes of invalid carriages and land occupied for specified purposes by land drainage authorities.

Special provision has been made for the rating of hereditaments occupied by electricity, gas, transport and water undertakings. The Boards of British Rail and British Waterways make payments in lieu of rates to the Minister of Housing and Local Government for distribution to the local rating authorities. Premises occupied by any of the transport boards as a dwelling house, hotel or place of public refreshment are fully rated. There is a statutory formula for the payment of rates by the Central Electricity Generating Board and the Area Electricity Boards; but premises used as a dwelling-house or showrooms and premises occupied by the Electricity Council are rated in the ordinary way. Again, the Area Gas Boards are rateable under a statutory formula having regard to the number of therms consumed, now governed by the Gas Act, 1965. Premises occupied for operational purposes by the Gas Council are not liable to be rated but gas showrooms are rated in the ordinary way. Water undertakings have been assessed since 1963 under a complicated formula in the Rating and Valuation Act, 1961. Rating and valuation law is now contained in the consolidating General Rate Act, 1967.

Grants and Loans. Grants in aid of services administered locally were made by the central government in the mid-nineteenth century. At that time the government began to make "percentage grants" to specific authorities so that they could depend upon receiving a specific proportion of the cost from monies voted by Parliament, the remainder being raised by rate. One of the first of these percentage grants was the police grant, which was introduced in 1856. The Local Government Act, 1888, however, abolished most of the old percentage grants and replaced them with "assigned revenues". Under this system the proceeds of taxes of a local character were assigned to the use of local authorities. This had the curious effect that the cost of education was for a time subsidised by the duty on whisky and other spirits. Changes in the national taxation and fiscal policy rendered the system of assigned revenues somewhat cumbersome and unrealistic so that it was finally abolished by the Local Government Act, 1929.

Meanwhile percentage grants had become payable for a number of services including not only the police but also education, highways, housing and some health services. Under the scheme of the 1929 Act, new "block grants" were paid in lump sums to local authorities in respect of all the remaining services, but shortly after the end of the last war percentage grants were payable in respect of town and county planning and local health and welfare services. This, then, was the system in operation until the enactment of the Local Government Act, 1958. Under that Act, a "general grant" or block grant became payable for most of the main services, including education, health, welfare, planning and fire protection. Specific grants remained payable in respect of police, civil defence, housing, planning and roads.

The general grant was payable to all county councils and county borough councils and the total amount available for distribution was prescribed in a General Grant Order made by the Minister of Housing and Local Government every two years in December. The amount was calculated by reference to estimates submitted by the local authority and the Minister must take into account the current level of prices, costs, remuneration and expenditure; any probable fluctuation in demand for the services and the need for their development. The Order had to be approved by the Commons and the Minister had power to vary the amount during the two years. If the Minister was satisfied that a local authority has failed to achieve or maintain reasonable standards he could submit a report to Parliament and, if the report was approved by the Commons, he could reduce the amount of general grant payable. The yardstick here is the average standard achieved by other authorities in the area, taking into account also those postulated by the relevant government departments. Similarly, a specific grant was not payable unless the appropriate Minister was broadly satisfied with the service provided. Thus the power to withhold a substantial unit grant for housing tended to ensure that local rehousing schemes conform to standards prescribed by the Minister. There is no appeal against a Minister's decision to withhold a grant.

The 1929 Act provided for the payment of general exchequer grants to county councils and county borough councils, based on a complicated "weighting" formula taking into account such matters as rateable value, children under five, the unemployed and, in the counties, population per mile of road. This system was replaced in 1948 by "exchequer equalisation grants" payable to the poorer authorities, i.e. those falling below a defined minimum standard of financial resources. Again, a "weighted population" formula was used, similar to that of 1929. The 1948 Act also enabled county councils to pay capitation grants to their county district councils.

The financial aspects of the 1958 Act were an attempt to strengthen local government by slackening the financial control of the central government departments. It is doubtful whether this worthy aim has been achieved, since the total grant contribution of the government still considerably exceeds the income of local authorities from rates.[12] The exchequer equalisation grants were replaced by "rate deficiency grants" and the capitation grants were abolished Rate deficiency grants were payable to the councils of county boroughs, counties and county districts if their actual product of a rate of a penny in the £ was less than the national standard penny rate product. The formula was modified in the counties if the population was less than seventy per mile of road.

The Minister could reduce a rate deficiency grant if a reasonable standard was not being maintained by a local authority, subject to approval of his report by the House of Commons. These drastic default powers have never been invoked in relation to either the rate deficiency grant or the general grant. This is not only evidence of the general good behaviour of local authorities but also of the fact that withdrawal of necessary finance would be hardly likely to promote efficiency.

Local government finance was entirely recast by the Local Government Act, 1966, which provides for the payment of rate support grants to local authorities and abolished the general and rate deficiency grants. After consultation with the local authority associations, M.H.L.G. determines the total central government grant, excluding housing subsidies. He continues to take into account the factors postulated in the 1958 Act (level of prices, costs, etc.). Grants to local authorities for rate rebates under the Rating Act, 1966, and specific grants are deducted from this total and the balance remaining constitutes the rate support grant.

The total is made up of a resources element, a needs element and a domestic element. The resources element (payable to all local authorities except parish councils) replaces the rate deficiency grant and is payable to any local authority with rate resources lower than the national average. The needs element is in substitution for the general grant and is based on population and other objective factors corresponding to the "weighting" formulae used in older legislation. This is payable to county and county borough councils, G.L.C. and L.B.C. but not to district councils. The domestic element is payable only to rating authorities and enables a deduction to be made in rate poundages on residential property (which must be passed on to the domestic ratepayer in reduced rates). The intended reduction for 1969/70 is 1/3d. in the £.

The Act abolishes the specific grants for school milk and meals and provides for specific grants for development and redevelopment; public open space; reclamation of derelict land; port and airport health; and special expenditure due to the presence in an area of substantial numbers of immigrants from the Commonwealth whose language or customs differ from those of the community.

When the Minister has completed his calculations, he makes a rate support grant order, operative for not less than two years. The order must be laid before the House of Commons together with a report, for approval. There is provision for the making of supplementary grants (subject to the same procedure) owing to inflationary pressure. The Act enables any Minister concerned with a local service to reduce any of the elements paid to a local authority if it has fallen below an average standard, subject to allowing it to make representations and to the safeguard of laying a report before Parliament. It can thus be seen that the 1966 Act continues some well-entrenched notions: consultations; criteria to consider in formulating estimates; special aid to poorer authorities; grants for special need; and default powers. Rate support orders were made in 1966 and 1968 and the next is due in 1970.

It is often necessary for the cost of expensive works to be financed by loans charged on the revenues (including rates) or land of a local authority. In this way the capital cost is spread over a period of years, and loans will be sanctioned only if the works are of a permanent nature and will continue to benefit the local ratepayers.

A general borrowing power is contained in the Local Government Act, 1933. Provided that statutory authority exists for the purpose of the loan, a local authority may borrow money to acquire land or buildings, to erect buildings, to undertake permanent works or to meet any other expense[13] which the Minister of Housing and Local Government considers should be spread over a number of years. This Minister is the sanctioning authority,[14] even for such services as education. The relevant Minister will consider the legality of the project and the financial resources of the local authority.

The normal maximum period for the repayment of a loan is sixty years and, once sanctioned, it is charged upon all the revenues of the borrowing authority. Since 1958 local authorities have been able to operate consolidated loans funds, with the Minister's consent. This is a device for the pooling of all money borrowed.

Borrowing powers may be obtained by a local Act of Parliament for purposes for which no general power exists, but strict proof of estimates is required by Parliamentary Standing Orders and returns of expenditure must be made to the Minister. Local authorities may borrow from the open market or from the Public Works Loans Board. Until about fifteen years ago the Board offered a lower rate of interest but the government increased the rate to that prevailing in the open market. Local authorities can also borrow from their reserve or superannuation funds if the money is not currently required for those purposes. Local authorities have powers of investment through L.A.M.I.T. (Local Authorities Mutual Investment Trust). The scope of such powers made collectively through L.A.M.I.T. has been extended by the Local Authorities Mutual Investment Trust Act, 1968.

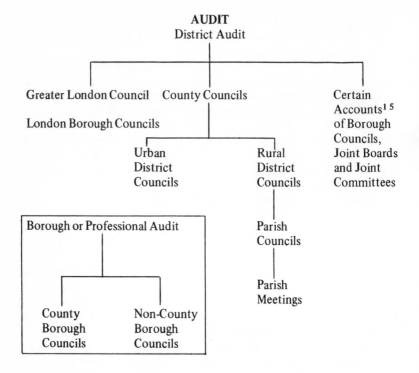

AUDIT
District Audit

Greater London Council   County Councils   Certain Accounts[15] of Borough Councils,

London Borough Councils

Urban District Councils   Rural District Councils   Joint Boards and Joint Committees

Borough or Professional Audit   Parish Councils

County Borough Councils   Non-County Borough Councils   Parish Meetings

Under the system of district audit, the local authority must prepare a financial statement, and for seven clear days before the audit a copy of every account and all relevant vouchers and receipts must be available for inspection at the Council Offices by "any person interested". Notice of these facilities must be given by advertisement in the local press. An "interested person" can make copies or extracts or depute an agent to do this; he is entitled to have a skilled person at his elbow, such as an accountant. "Persons interested" include electors, ratepayers, contractors, landowners, shopkeepers and officials of trades unions whose members are employees of the local authority.

A local government *elector* may be present or may be represented at the audit and may object to any of the accounts. The qualification for the right to object to the accounts is thus more restricted than that for the right to inspect. The district auditor is a Civil Servant, being an official of the Ministry of Housing and Local Government. His powers are very wide and he can require the production of documents and can interrogate the officers responsible for them. It is the duty of the district auditor to disallow every item of the account which is contrary to law and to surcharge the amount of any expenditure disallowed upon the person responsible, be he an elected member or an appointed officer. At the conclusion of the audit he certifies his allowance of the accounts, subject to any disallowance or surcharge. An item will be "contrary to law" if it is illegal in the sense that there is no statutory authority for the expenditure, which is accordingly *ultra vires*. Expenditure has been held to be contrary to law if it was unreasonable in extent, even though the objects were lawful. This is illustrated by the decision of the House of Lords in 1925 in the *Poplar Wage Case*,[16] a decision which inhibited reasonable freedom of action in local government for many years.

The council of the Metropolitan Borough of Poplar[17] was authorised to pay its employees reasonable wages and resolved to pay its manual workers wages in excess of those paid to similar workers by other local employers. The actual wage involved was £4 a week, but it should be borne in mind that this was over forty years ago. The district auditor disallowed most of the excess over the ordinary prevailing rates of pay as unreasonable and therefore contrary to law. He was upheld in the High Court, reversed in the Court of Appeal and finally vindicated in the House of Lords on the ground that the expenditure was excessive and therefore unlawful. The Council was held not to have acted as a proper trustee of the ratepayers' money. The surcharged councillors, whose leader was George Lansbury, later leader of the Labour Party, refused to pay but the surcharge was later remitted by the Minister of Health.

Twenty years later, a rather more liberal decision of the Court of Appeal[18] allowed the payment of children's allowances by a local authority to its employees; the total amount having been held to be reasonable. But in the *St. Pancras Rents Case*,[19] the shadow of Poplar returned, the court holding itself to be bound by the older decision of the House of Lords. In that case, the council of the Metropolitan Borough of St. Pancras[20] was responsible for requisitioned properties and had a statutory duty to review the rents of the tenants from time to time. Owing to its dislike of the policy of the Rent Act, 1957, the council decided not to increase the rents of these tenants but to pay the balance of the increased rent to the landlords. The councillors concerned were surcharged by the district auditor and at the hearing of the appeal the Lord Chief Justice said that the council had in effect made a gift of the increase to the landlords. The case had several interesting features, one being that the councillors concerned disregarded the advice of their town clerk, always an unwise thing to do. Perhaps this will not matter so much in the future, when town managers have replaced the legally qualified town clerks. In the *St. Pancras Case* the district auditor's surcharge was upheld but the case had an even more unfortunate sequel. Appeal lies to the High Court but if the surcharge is in respect of a sum not over £500, there is a choice between appealing to the Minister or to the High Court. Some councillors appealed to the Minister, who in the circumstances relieved them from the surcharge; others appealed to the High Court, which upheld the surcharge. The net result was that quite fortuitously, fewer people had to pay the same total sum of money. That procedure was invoked in respect of a sum of £200. On a second surcharge of £1,400 the appeals had to go to the High Court and on this occasion both groups of councillors sought a declaration to avoid disqualification from council membership and applied for relief from personal liability. The court awarded the declaration but refused relief from personal liability. In general, the Minister's decision on appeal is final; and a person may apply for a declaration by the High Court or by the Minister that he acted reasonably or believed that his action was authorised by law. The Court or the Minister can relieve a councillor from payment of surcharge in whole or in part if satisfied that he "ought fairly to be excused". If the surcharge is in a sum exceeding £500, relief can be sought from disqualification from membership of a local authority for a period of five years; and such relief was obtained by the surcharged councillors in the *St. Pancras Case,* as noted above.

No expense paid by a local authority may be disallowed by the district auditor if it has been sanctioned by the Minister. Nevertheless, if the relevant payment is *ultra vires,* a local government elector can seek an injunction or declaration in the High Court and, if he is successful, this should have the effect of preventing a recurrence of the illegal expenditure. There is provision for the Minister to direct the district auditor to hold an extraordinary audit of accounts on giving three days' written notice to the local authority. After completion of the audit the local authority must make an abstract of accounts and give notice in the local press that it can be inspected. Local authorities contribute to the cost of district audit by a stamp duty based on the volume of transactions within the audited accounts.

Owing to its method of incorporation by royal charter, a borough is not ordinarily subject to district audit. However, the district auditor is required by statute to examine certain important borough accounts. Subject to this, and to the possibility of voluntary adoption of District Audit, borough councils have either an elective or a professional audit. In neither case is there any power of disallowance or surcharge but steps are presumably taken by a borough council to deal with any adverse factors disclosed in an auditors' report. Under the system of elective audit, two auditors are elected by the local government electors (the "elective auditors") and one is chosen by the Mayor from council members ("the Mayor's auditor"). An elective auditor must be qualified to be a councillor but must not be a member or officer; no other qualifications are necessary. The borough treasurer must print an abstract of accounts after an elective or professional audit. A borough council may by resolution[21] adopt the system of district or professional audit; the City Council of Manchester adopted the latter system in 1956.[22] The professional auditors must be appointed in writing under seal, must belong to a professional body and can require production of documents. Professional audit is probably more efficient than elective audit but they both lack the effective sanctions and frequently the expertise of the district auditor.

Reform. The system of local government finance has long been criticised but it is so entrenched that many attempts at reform have foundered. Rates in particular have been attacked as regressive in contradistinction to taxation, which is said to be progressive because it takes into account social factors such as earning power and family responsibilities. Although the method of valuation for rating purposes of dwellinghouses may be fair, the occupiers and ratepayers of two identical properties may be in very different circumstances: one may be wealthy, the other may be a pensioner. The remedy postulated by the Liberal Party is the rating of site values: under this system, buildings on the land would be ignored for rating valuation purposes. On the other hand, the value of the site could be enhanced considerably by the grant of planning permission for a profitable purpose and site value rating would take account of this. Even under existing procedures, the actual cost of land has been taken as the best evidence of the value of a school site. However, neither the Conservative Party nor the Labour Party favour the rating of site values, so that it is unlikely to be introduced.

Another suggestion, made by a study group of the Royal Institute of Public Administration in 1956, is that there should be a form of local income tax to be collected and spent by local authorities. Ever since the war all employers, including local authorities, have collected tax from their employees on behalf of the Inland Revenue under the P.A.Y.E. system. It was thought that this system could be extended to the collection of a small local tax of 3d. to 6d. in the £. This would be collected by all employers in the area of a local authority and the total amount deducted from employees' salaries and wages would be passed to the local authority. The objection to this idea was that people would be taxed in respect of their work places rather than their homes, and that some local authorities, with numerous offices, factories and workshops in their areas, would benefit much more than others in the rural and more sparsely populated districts. The laudable object was to try and give local government a source of revenue independent of rates and grants but the idea foundered on the objections and was not implemented, although variants are possible. The Royal Commission Report refers vaguely to the need for a wider tax base but gives no definite lead.

Under the rating law, based as it is on the concept of actual and beneficial occupation of land and buildings, unoccupied or empty property was not rateable until recently. A local Act of Parliament enabled the City of London Corporation to collect a proportion of the rates on such properties but this was the only exception. We have already noticed that seaside bungalows and warehouses are borderline cases, the acid test being whether they are ready for occupation or storage, even though they were empty during part of the rating year. There is a strong case for the rating of empty property envisaged in the Local Government Act, 1966, especially in view of the numerous large office blocks which remain unoccupied for months or even years in some of our cities. If the rating system is retained, it may well be that there should be a shift of emphasis from occupation to ownership as the test of rateability. Moreover, the rating of empty or vacant hereditaments would encourage owners to utilise their properties to the fullest possible extent.

The abolition of the de-rating of agricultural land and buildings is long overdue in an era of farming prosperity, especially as the partial de-rating of industrial and freight-transport hereditaments was abolished in 1963.

The Rating Act, 1966, enables local rating authorities to allow rebates to domestic ratepayers with low incomes. It is estimated that rebates will average about £15 million annually. Ratepayers who qualify for a full rebate are entitled to a remission of two-thirds of the amount by which their rates exceed £7 10s. a year. A childless married couple earning £10 a week would qualify for full remission; an increased wage being permissible in the case of a married couple with dependent children. The new Act provides an example of a useful minor reform, especially as it is coupled with the right of domestic ratepayers to elect to pay their rates by instalments. Those who can apply for rate rebates include owner-occupiers and tenants of private and council property.

We have already seen that the history of grants-in-aid or government grants has been somewhat chequered. At the present time, the government meets approximately 60 per cent of local government expenditure by means of grant. Education is by far the most costly of the services provided by local authorities and many students of politics and public administration have advocated transferring its total cost to the Exchequer. This has been resisted by the spokesmen of local government on the grounds that such a development would weaken local control still further. The police services constitute another candidate for greater contributions from the central government, which currently makes a specific grant of 50 per cent of the net expenditure. Although subject to a measure of local control, the police are not really a local government service and the police grant could well be increased materially without detriment to the local authorities. Again, should the government shoulder a greater share of the burden of expenditure on the roads?

The Minister of Transport is already responsible for trunk roads and motorways and important aspects of national policy are often linked with road widening and other schemes in relation to the lesser roads. The compromise solution which is expected to be implemented in the case of education could well be extended also to highways, so that the Ministry grants to local authorities could be increased.

There is no doubt that the payment of rates is much more unpopular than payment of taxes, partly owing to the method of collection and partly due to a feeling of injustice in some cases. Palliatives such as payment by instalments do not appear to be enough. The solution may well be for the Exchequer to assume greater responsibility for expenditure on the more important and expensive services, such as education, highways, housing and the police; a significant proportion of the expenditure, however, should still be met locally.

1 A plot or parcel of land, usually with a building on it.
2 E.g. on the ground that the authority has not followed the correct procedure in making or giving notice of the rate or that it contains an arithmetical or clerical error.
3 With certain exceptions.
4 These grants ceased in 1967/68.
5 The Rating Act, 1966.
6 And the owners are entitled to a discount.
7 Poor Relief Act, 1601.
8 A rating authority can now by resolution charge half the normal rates on properties unoccupied for over three months (General Rate Act, 1967).
9 Now largely consolidated into the Rent Act, 1968.
10 The Royal Commission Report recommends the re-rating of agricultural land and buildings.
11 The last three items were formerly covered by legislation enacted in 1843.
12 The proportion is about 60:40.
13 E.g. promotion of a local Act of Parliament.
14 With one minor and diminishing exception.
15 E.g. education, child care, health, welfare, rate collection.
16 *Roberts v. Hopwood* [1925] A.C. 578.
17 Now incorporated in the London Borough of Tower Hamlets.
18 *Re. Walker's Decision* [1944] 1 All E.R. 614.
19 *Taylor v. Munrow* [1960] 1 All E.R. 455.
20 Now incorporated in the London Borough of Camden.
21 The resolution must be passed by not less than two-thirds of council members at a specially convened meeting and confirmed at an ordinary meeting not less than a month later.
22 The City Council of Gloucester adopted the district audit system in 1966.

CHAPTER XIII

POWERS OF LOCAL AUTHORITIES

Bye-laws. A bye-law is a special form of delegated legislation made under procedure laid down in the Local Government Act, 1933. County councils and county borough councils can make bye-laws for the good rule and government of their areas and for the suppression of nuisances. Those made by a county council are operative in urban and rural districts and may be enforced by the councils of such districts. There is a common procedure for making bye-laws under the 1933 Act.[1] After being made under the seal of the council, a bye-law must be submitted to the confirming authority, who is in general the Home Secretary. However, the Minister of Housing and Local Government is the confirming authority in the case of public health bye-laws and it may well be that a bye-law "for the suppression of nuisances" may appertain to the public health field. In such a case the Home Office and the Ministry consult together and if they resolve that it is the Ministry's concern the bye-law is confirmed by the Minister of Housing and Local Government. We have already noted that building bye-laws have been replaced by building regulations made by the Minister of Public Building and Works; but there are of course many other public health matters upon which bye-laws can be made.

The council must publish in the local press notice of its intention to make the bye-law, after which objectors have a month in which to object to the confirming authority. At the end of this period the bye-law is submitted for confirmation. In deciding whether or not to confirm a bye-law, the Home Secretary or the Minister will consider whether it is in fact necessary, having regard to local conditions and national policy. He must of course also be satisfied that the proposed bye-law is *intra vires* and that it is not likely to be set aside by the courts on other grounds. Confirming authorities have issued sets of model bye-laws based on experience: this helps the local authorities to avoid pitfalls and encourages uniformity in the country as a whole. A bye-law may be confirmed or rejected—a confirming order fixes its date of operation in the area of the local authority. After confirmation a copy of the bye-law must be available for public inspection and sale at a cost not exceeding a shilling. Numerous statutes authorise the making of bye-laws[2] and an enabling Act will fix the penalty for non-compliance: this does not usually exceed £5.

In the early years, the courts laid down four judicial tests of the validity of bye-laws. In the first place, a bye-law must be reasonable. Thus in 1898 the House of Lords held that a bye-law made by Kent County Council prohibiting any person from playing music or singing in any place within 50 yards of a dwelling-house after being requested to desist was reasonable. It was said in this case that there is a presumption of reasonableness in favour of bye-laws made by local authorities because they are bodies of a public representative character entrusted by Parliament with delegated authority. Their bye-laws should be supported if possible, since local authorities are elective, not nominated, bodies. The onus of proof in the courts is therefore on the person alleging that a bye-law is unreasonable. A bye-law will be declared void as unreasonable, however, if it discriminates unfairly between different classes of people, if it is manifestly unjust, if it discloses bad faith or if it is oppressive. The second judicial test is that a bye-law should be certain in its terms and clear in its meaning. On this principle, a bye-law providing that "no person shall wilfully annoy passengers in the streets" has been held too vague and uncertain and was therefore set aside as void.

A third and most important principle is that a bye-law must not conflict with the positive provisions of common law or statute. The function of a bye-law is to supplement the law, not to override it; it must therefore be consistent with the general law. This is in accordance with the doctrine of the sovereignty of Parliament, for bye-laws constitute a type of subordinate legislation. Only Parliament can change the general law. The fourth and last of the judicial tests is that a bye-law must be *intra vires* its enabling legislation. This is a fundamental principle, not unconnected with the third test. There have not been many actions in the courts on the validity of bye-laws in recent years, partly because the judicial tests are so well known and partly because the system of issuing model bye-laws by the central departments has helped local authorities to avoid errors. Finally, it should be noticed that other Ministers may confirm bye-laws. For example, the Secretary of State for Education and Science is the confirming authority for bye-laws made under the Public Libraries and Museums Act, 1964, and the Minister of Transport confirms bye-laws made under the Highways Act, 1959.

Acquisition of Powers. If a local authority wishes to acquire new powers which are not covered by existing legislation, it must seek to promote a local or private bill in Parliament. The parliamentary procedure has already been described (see p. 52, *ante*) but we must now consider the preliminary action to be taken by the local authority. Ten clear days' notice of a council meeting convened to promote a local bill must be given in the local press and the resolution to promote it must be carried by a majority vote. The resolution is then published in the local newspapers and submitted for approval to the Minister of Housing and Local Government. In urban areas, promotion of a local bill by a borough council or by an urban district council requires the approval of the local government electors. In these cases, public notice must be given of the deposit of the bill in Parliament and a town's meeting must be called. The decision of the town's meeting is final, unless a poll is demanded by one hundred electors or one-twentieth of the electorate, whichever is the less, or by the council itself. If the proposal is then rejected by the electorate, the bill must be withdrawn. Town's meetings have been described as "undemocratic hindrances to local legislation"[3] and there is a campaign to abolish this somewhat archaic procedure. Its abolition has been recommended thrice in the last forty years, the last time by the Joint Committee on Private Bill Procedure in 1955. When the local Bill has been finally deposited in Parliament, another confirmatory resolution must be passed. If a council wishes to oppose a local bill promoted by another authority, the same procedure must be followed in relation to resolutions and publicity. It should be realised that local bills can also be introduced in Parliament on behalf of public corporations and there may well be a conflict of interest between local government and a nationalised industry, as well as between differing types of local authority.

Local authorities often used to obtain new powers by means of the provisional order procedure. Numerous Acts of Parliament gave Ministers power to make provisional orders, in the old days "for the execution of useful works". The local authority had to apply to the Minister for an order, after having given interested parties an opportunity to object by means of a notice in the local press. If objections were raised, a local inquiry was normally held and the Minister then made a provisional order. The order had no force until included in a Provisional Orders Confirmation Bill, a special kind of local bill subject in other respects to the usual parliamentary procedure for a local bill. If a petition was presented before confirmation the petitioner could appear before the Select Committee in both Houses and oppose the order. An advantage of the procedure was that it enlisted a measure of government support in Parliament but it came to be regarded as rather cumbersome, having to pass through all stages of a local bill in both Houses. It is little used today, having been largely replaced by special parliamentary procedure.

The Statutory Orders (Special Procedure) Acts, 1945–1965, enable an order to be made by a Minister, who lays it before Parliament after compliance with preliminary proceedings in the enabling Act. If no procedure is specified, notice must be given in the *London Gazette* and in the local press. The notice must state the procedure for lodging objections and the Minister has a discretionary power to hold a local inquiry. Petitions may be lodged within twenty-one days of laying before Parliament. All petitions are referred to the Chairman of Ways and Means and the Lord Chairman of Committees who report to each House if objections have been made and if they can be received. Petitions for amendment pray for specific amendments and are referred to a joint committee of both Houses; petitions of general objection pray against the order generally but are referred to a joint committee only if either House of Parliament so resolves.

The Joint Committee consists of three members of both Houses and it can report the order with or without amendment; in the latter case, it comes into operation on the day the report is laid before Parliament. If the order is amended it will take effect on a day fixed by the Minister. If the Minister has second thoughts arising from the petitions and objections, he may withdraw the order or resubmit it to Parliament by means of a Provisional Order Confirmation Bill. Many statutes passed since 1945 provide for orders made under them to be subject to special parliamentary procedure and it has been extended to earlier legislation by Order-in-Council. The advantage of this post-war procedure to Parliament and to local government is that it is much quicker. Special parliamentary procedure was applied to the power to repeal, alter or amend local Acts for public health purposes[4] but in 1962 provisional order procedure was restored in order to ensure greater parliamentary scrutiny in these matters.

Acquisition of Land. There are a great number of statutes affecting the power of local authorities to acquire land; these include the Local Government Act, 1933: the Public Health Acts, 1875–1961; the Land Compensation Act, 1961; the Town and Country Planning Act, 1962; and the Compulsory Purchase Act, 1965. All local authorities have a general power to acquire land by agreement by means of purchase, lease or exchange of land. This covers the acquisition of land in advance of requirements and in this case Ministerial consent is necessary, as it is for loan sanction in connection with acquisition by agreement.

County councils can acquire land compulsorily for the purpose of any of their functions under a public general Act of Parliament. County borough councils and county district councils can acquire land compulsorily for public health purposes. We have already seen that development plans may allocate land for the purpose of *any* of the functions of a local authority; education, health, welfare, housing, highways, planning or whatever. If the land is expressly designated as subject to compulsory purchase, a local authority[5] may be authorised to acquire the land compulsorily.

The first step is for the local authority to make a compulsory purchase order (C.P.O.) describing the land and to publish a notice in the local press, indicating where the order and map may be inspected and how objections may be made. A similar notice must be served on owners, occupiers and lessees of the land. The draft order is then sent to the relevant Minister who must hold a local inquiry or private hearing if there are objections. If the Minister confirms the order the authority must give public notice of confirmation in the local press and this publication is the date upon which the order comes into effect. A C.P.O. can be challenged within six weeks of this date by a special appeal to the High Court to quash it on the grounds that it is *ultra vires* or that the interests of the appellant have been substantially prejudiced by failure to comply with a statutory requirement. An aggrieved person must invoke this challenge procedure quickly, for if proceedings are not started within six weeks, the order may not be questioned in any legal proceedings whatsoever, even if fraud or bad faith are alleged. This is the effect of a majority decision in the House of Lords fourteen years ago.[6] However an acquiring authority must exercise its powers within 3 years from date of operation of C.P.O.

Special parliamentary procedure must be followed if objection is made to a C.P.O. affecting land belonging to a local authority or held inalienably by the National Trust. This procedure also applies if the C.P.O. relates to the site of an ancient monument unless the Minister of Public Building and Works has certified that the acquiring authority has undertaken to safeguard the monument. Similarly, special parliamentary procedure applies if the C.P.O. relates to commons, allotments or open spaces, unless the relevant Minister certifies that the land is required for road widening or that it will be replaced by equally suitable land.

A county council can acquire land for a parish council after holding a local inquiry. The resultant C.P.O. is subject to Ministerial confirmation or modification in the ordinary way. The county council then acquires the land and conveys it to the parish council, which has the right to appeal to the Minister if the council refuses to make an order. In a recent case,[7] a parish meeting was convened to consider the transfer of certain land to a county council. *B* proposed that he should acquire part of the land but did not move any amendment to the resolution. With the support of more than five other electors he demanded a poll. The resolution to transfer all the land to the county council was carried on a show of hands and subsequently on a poll. Later the land was conveyed to the county council. *B* brought an action claiming declarations that a poll was validly demanded, that no poll had been taken and that the subsequent proceedings were invalid. The Court of Appeal held that no poll could be validly demanded on a question which had not been put to the meeting as a resolution or amendment and that, since the land had already been conveyed, relief could not be granted.

When a C.P.O. has become operative, the acquiring authority may serve on the owner a Notice to Treat and this has the same effect as if the owner had entered into a contract to sell to that authority. The Lands Tribunal is available to settle disputes on compensation payable if the parties cannot agree. The acquiring authority may at any time after service of Notice to Treat give Notice of Entry on the land, to take effect not less than fourteen days after service. If Notice to Treat is not served within three years of the coming into force of the C.P.O., the order lapses.

Some boroughs hold what is known as corporate land, which is "land belonging to, or held in trust for, or to be acquired by or held in trust for, a municipal corporation otherwise than for an express statutory purpose". Rents and profits derived from such land are transferred to the general rate fund in order to benefit the borough as a whole. A borough council can acquire land by agreement to be held as corporate land even if it has no power under its Charter to hold land.

Relations between authorities. We have seen that in the county or "divided" system, which contains two tiers of local government, considerable delegation in the exercise of functions is possible. A county council can delegate, subject to the appropriate Minister's consent, important aspects of the education, health and welfare services and also control of development under planning legislation to county district councils. The Minister must approve the delegation scheme and the minimum population figure for a county district in this connection is 60,000 although the Minister has a discretion to allow delegation if the population is less than this. The county council retains financial control and is the local authority for the service, the county district councils being responsible for daily administration. Provided that the participants do not contest the legal aspects of delegation "like mediaeval schoolmen",[8] delegation can be successful.

We now turn to a description of the local government associations, which have an honourable and important part to play in representing the various classes of local authority.

The local authority associations are recognised by government departments as representative national bodies and are consulted on legislation and subordinate legislation, circulars and policy matters. Government departments often seek the views of the associations informally on the practical application of proposals. Departmental committees often invite the associations to submit memoranda of evidence and government departments frequently assemble small working parties to examine special problems such as model standing orders or rate support grants. The associations may be asked to nominate representatives to serve on working parties. An example of their influence is afforded by the Housing Act, 1961, which enables the Minister of Housing and Local Government to abolish or reduce exchequer subsidies by order but provides that the Minister, before making an order, shall consult with local authority associations.

The Association of Municipal Corporations. This is the oldest of the local authority associations, having been founded in 1873 at a time when all municipal boroughs enjoyed the same status and, subject to certain local variations, exercised the same functions. With the creation of the new county boroughs under the Local Government Act, 1888, the membership embraced both types of municipal corporation: the county borough council and the non-county borough council. The metropolitan borough councils established under the London Government Act, 1899, became eligible for membership. They ceased to exist in 1965 and the new London Borough Councils are members of the Association, whose present constitution states that it shall consist of municipal corporations in England, Wales and Northern Ireland, and such assemblies or commissions of towns or places in the Channel Islands or the Isle of Man as the Council may from time to time approve. At present there are 392 corporations in membership, including the London Boroughs.

The object of the Association is to watch over and protect the interests, rights and privileges of municipal corporations as they may be affected by legislation; and to take action in respect of any other subjects in which municipal corporations generally may be interested. It takes no action in cases where a conflict of interest is disclosed between county boroughs and non-county boroughs. The Association is organised and governed in much the same way as a borough council. It has a council of about 150 member corporations. The City of London and the six largest cities are parmanent members of the Council, the remaining county boroughs and the London boroughs serving by rotation. The non-county borough and Northern Irish members of the Council are elected by ballot from among themselves. Each elected member corporation is entitled to send three respresentatives to Council meetings but voting in Council is on the basis of one town-one vote. The Council normally meets four times a year; it manages the Associations affairs, decides its policy and elects the standing committees. There is a full-time Secretary, who is a former town clerk of Blackpool. It has separate standing committees on Children; Education; Fire Service; General Purposes; Health; Highways and Transport; Housing; Law; Libraries, Museums and Art; Markets and Slaughterhouses; Police; Rating; Town Planning; and Welfare.

The wide range of the Association's activities is also illustrated by the Report of its 1968 Annual Conference. The speeches included one on "Productivity, Prices and Incomes" by Lord Peddie (a Deputy Chairman of the Prices and Incomes Board) and another by Lord Morris of Grasmere (Chairman, L.G.T.B.) on Training in Local Government.

The County Councils Association. Leading officers of the Society of Clerks of the Peace of Counties gave valuable advice to the President of the Local Government Board on the Local Government Bill, which subsequently became the Act of 1888. Members of the Society drew the attention of their respective councils to the desirability of forming a County Councils' Association. It should be recalled that, in most cases, the clerks of the new county councils were also clerks of the peace. The Association was accordingly formed in 1889 and in the following year county councils received statutory authority to pay subscriptions to it. The first annual meeting of the County Councils Association was held in 1891.

The Association consists of 58 county councils in England and Wales and its objects are to watch over and protect the interests, rights and privileges of county councils, as representatives of the county electorate, as they may be affected by legislation of general application to counties. The Association obtains and disseminates information on matters of importance to county councils generally, and in other respects takes action in relation to any subjects in which county councils may be interested. The present President of the Association is Viscount Amory,[9] the present Secretary was formerly Clerk of the Cheshire County Council. The Association has an Executive Council comprising representatives from each county council and separate committees on such matters as Education; Children; Health and Welfare; Planning; Highways; Police; Fire; Civil Defence; Agriculture; and Local Government Finance. Representatives of county councils serve on all these committees. The Parliamentary and General Purposes Committee has a Local Government Reorganisation Sub-Committee, which have been very busy in recent years. The Association is represented on some thirty negotiating bodies, and there is a separate Association of County Councils in Scotland. The London County Council was not a member of the Association, nor is the Greater London Council, which is not technically a county council.

The Urban District Councils' Association. This Association is the direct lineal successor of the Association of Local Boards of Health, which were the predecessors of the original urban district councils that came into existence in 1895.[10] In effect, the Association merely changed its name to the Urban District Councils' Association and has been continuously in existence under that name ever since. In 1895 less than a hundred urban district councils were in membership, there being over 700 such authorities at that time. However, the membership gradually increased until 100 per cent membership was achieved some thirty years ago. This has been maintained, so that all the 522 urban district councils in England and Wales are members of the Association today. Any member or former member of the Association whose district has been constituted a borough is eligible for membership. The object of the Association is by complete organisation more effectually to watch over and protect the interests, rights and privileges of urban district councils as they may be affected by legislation; in other respects to take action in relation to any other subjects in which such councils may generally be interested, and to promote such measures as may from time to time be deemed advisable. The rules provide for the appointment of a President and 18 Vice-Presidents who are members of either House of Parliament and interested in local government. All these officers serve on the Association's Executive Council, which also includes an honorary treasurer and a councillor and the clerk of each of 18 urban district councils elected on an area basis. The Association has a Secretary and a Deputy Secretary and the wide range of its activities can be gleaned from the subject of motions debated at the 1969 Annual Conference; these include such subjects as improvement and codification of the laws of compensation, housing advances, SET, tree preservation and agricultural land policy on green belt perimeters.

Rural District Councils Association. The Association was formed in 1895 following the creation of rural district councils as successors to the rural sanitary authorities established twenty years earlier. A council of management consisting of 21 councils was appointed; it is interesting that of these Croydon and Bromley are now the major portions of new London Boroughs and Havant is an urban district, whilst three of the others have ceased to have an independent existence. In 1895 there were 675 rural district councils, now there are 469, all in membership of the Association, full membership having been achieved in 1953. The objects of the Association are to protect the rights and interests of the rural district councils as they may be affected by legislation; to assist in maintaining a high standard of administration of the public services in rural districts; to take action in relation to any other matters with which such councils may be concerned and to promote such measures as may be deemed advisable from time to time.

As a result of revision of the constitution in 1945, there are now 48 seats on the council of the Association; at present there are 25 councillors and 23 clerks. The 42 county branches have their own constitutions and give their views to the Association. The present population in rural districts in England and Wales is nearly ten millions or one-fifth of the population. The Association is represented on a large number of national and negotiating bodies. It has a President and Vice-Presidents most of whom are members of one or other of the Houses of Parliament. The Council of the Association meets four times a year and is assisted by several committees on such matters as Housing and Planning; Finance; Public Health; and Local Government Reorganisation. The Association holds an Annual Meeting and Conference; its income is principally derived from subscriptions and since 1959 it has had a full-time Secretary and Deputy Secretary, assisted by supporting staff.

National Association of Parish Councils. This Association was formed in 1947, having grown out of a Parish Councils Advisory Committee of the National Council of Social Service. The new Association received a small grant from the National Council and, following the precedent of the Advisory Committee which had been founded with about a thousand affiliated parish councils, local associations had been formed in every county by 1951. At the end of 1968 there were over six thousand parish councils in membership of the National Association.

The Association went through many vicissitudes in its early days but it had an active and successful Secretary, Mr. Charles Arnold-Baker, who has been in office since 1953. The Association publishes a handbook on

Constitution and Powers of Parish Councils, which became a best-seller in the world of parishes. Parish councils had been abolished in Scotland in 1929 and it is thought that parish councils in England and Wales owe their survival to the patronage of the National Council of Social Service, which kept interest in them alive. In 1953 the conflict between the powerful A.M.C. and the C.C.A. led to the enlistment of the N.A.P.C. on the latter's side and its participation in the Four Associations' Report. The Association was thus drawn into the main current of local government reorganisation and participated in discussions and conferences. The enactment of the Parish Councils Act, 1957, gave parish councils a number of permissive powers, including street lighting. The Association also runs an insurance service and an advisory service for its members, the latter service now being under the direction of the deputy secretary. One of the main aims of the Association is to resist urban encroachments: parishes vary enormously in size, some having populations of less than 300 and others, notably in Lincolnshire, containing more than a thousand inhabitants.

The Association of Councillors. The Association of Councillors was formed in 1963 to serve the interests of all members of local authorities. It is not, like the various local authority associations, confined to one particular class of local authority. Its other objects are to provide information and educational facilities for such members, to institute and carry on research into matters connected with local government, to exchange information and to provide a forum for discussion and to make any necessary representations. An example of successful representations was the decision of the Minister of Housing and Local Government, early in 1966, to approve the Association as a body to which local authorities can legitimately make contributions on behalf of their members.

The Joint Chairmen of the Association are three members of Parliament drawn from each of the three parliamentary political parties. The Association's Treasurer is the editor of a leading local government journal. Membership is open, on a corporate basis, to all members of English and Welsh local authorities and this entitles individual members to full rights and privileges attaching to personal membership. Members of local authorities in Eire, Northern Ireland, Scotland and the Commonwealth are entitled to associate membership. Subscriptions are fixed by an annually elected Court of Management. The Constitution of the Association also provides for a General Meeting, formation of Branch Associations and election of Officers. The Association of Councillors can play a very useful part in the pending radical reorganisation of local government since it is the only organisation representing the rank and file or "back-bench" councillor.

The Local Government Information Office. It is convenient to conclude with an honourable mention for the Local Government Information

Office, which is sponsored by the four main local authority associations. The Office performs a useful function in disseminating information on behalf of the different classes of local authority. Information or Press Officers of individual local authorities can turn to it for help. Mr. Laurence Evans, Head of the Local Government Information Office, has written[11] that the information officer "is, or should be, the bridge between the local council and their officers and the Press and the public".

A recent example of the work of the Information Office was its collaboration with the *Observer* in order to disprove the myth of corruption in local government. More than a hundred allegations were investigated and only one was found to have the slightest taint of suspicion. An arresting poster, featuring a Chad-like figure peering over a wall, was published by the office in April, 1966, in order to encourage more people to vote in local elections. The caption is "I say! Vote for a share in your council. In town or country it carries out many services for your benfit—with your money. Take an interest in how it is spent. Your opinion *means* local government." The percentage of the electorate voting in the parliamentary general election of 1966 was 75.7. In 1963 the average in county borough council elections was only 41.2 per cent. Local authorities displayed several thousand of the new posters during the 1966 local elections.

Finally, the Local Government Information Office positively encourages local information and public relations officers to advise their councils and chief officers to take press and public into their confidence, especially where they are likely to be affected by the schemes and plans of local authorities.

Local Government Journals. The Official organ of the A.M.C. is the "Municipal and Public Services Review". Other periodicals dealing with urban local government include the "Municipal Journal" and "Municipal Engineering". The C.C.A. publishes the "County Councils Gazette". The R.D.C.A. publishes an excellent monthly journal, the "Rural District Review". The "Parish Councils Review" originally appeared in magazine form as a local venture in Lancashire and was launched as a national journal in 1950; it maintains a consistently high standard to-day.

The oldest journal dealing comprehensively with the subject is the weekly "Local Government Chronicle". A legal weekly, the "Justice of the Peace and Local Government Review" discusses the subject, as its title suggests, but nowadays it is mainly concerned with magisterial law. "Local Government Administration" is the bi-monthly journal of I.L.G.A.

---

1   Other Acts may provide a special procedure, e.g. Water Act, 1945.
2   E.g. the Public Health Act, 1936.
3   *The Municipal Review*, January, 1966.
4   Under the Public Health Act, 1875.

5   Which is not necessarily a local planning authority.
6   *Smith v. East Elloe Rural District Council* [1956] 1 All E.R. 855
7   *Bennett v. Chappell* [1965] 3 All E.R. 130.
8   Herbert Report on Greater London in relation to the late County of Middlesex.
9   Chancellor of the Exchequer 1958–1960 (as Mr. Heathcote-Amory).
10 Following the enactment of the Local Government Act, 1894.
11 *The Local Government Chronicle,* 29th January, 1966 at p. 183.

CHAPTER XIV

CENTRAL CONTROL

Secretary of State for Local Government and Regional Planning. This post was created in October, 1969, the first incumbent being Mr. Anthony Crosland (formerly President of the Board of Trade), a leading and senior member of the Cabinet. The new Secretary of State controls the Minister of Housing and Local Government and the Minister of Transport, both of whom cease to be in the Cabinet. The post of Minister for Planning and Land has been abolished, its functions reverting to M.H.L.G. The detailed responsibilities of the subordinate Ministries will remain broadly as at present, but the new Secretary of State is especially charged with local government reform, responsibility for regional planning councils and boards and with all aspects of environmental pollution.

The new Secretary of State will thus supervise a wide-ranging empire with local government reform as top priority in his in-tray. His responsibilities encompass housing, public health, planning and transport at a time when all these services are in the public eye. The emphasis in local government at present seems to be in slackening central control and it is to be hoped that the Secretary of State will make a powerful contribution in this respect. His responsibilities in relation to regional and economic planning will be considered in Chapter XX.

The appointment of a Secretary of State for Local Government affords an interesting example of an application of the "overlord" system. Formerly, the sinecure offices have been used for this purpose but without great success. The clue to real achievement in this field may well be to give the "overlord" Minister a functional department, with specific tasks to control. It remains to be seen whether M.H.L.G. and the Ministry of Transport remain indefinitely as separate Ministries; the future of the former, at any rate, appears to be uncertain. Having regard to the reconstruction of the Ministry of Defence both the subordinate Ministries may in due course disappear as separate entities. The close connection between town and country planning and transport has at last been recognised, as has the link between local government reform and regional government. The new Secretary of State will be the final arbiter in any dispute between the Ministries of Housing, Transport and Public Building.

The Ministry of Housing and Local Government. The antecedents of this Ministry can be traced back to the early nineteenth century and are closely connected with public health legislation. In 1831 a Central Board of Health was established by the Privy Council to advise the local boards of health in the towns. As we have seen, the Poor Law Commissioners functioned from 1834 to 1847, when they were replaced by a Poor Law Board under a President with a seat in Parliament. In 1848 a General Board of Health was set up but was not very successful, so that ten years later its powers were distributed between the Home Office and the Privy Council.

It was realised during Mr. Gladstone's first Administration that the various powers of central control over local services were too diffuse; accordingly, in 1871 the Local Government Board was established under a parliamentary President. The President of the Local Government Board assimilated responsibility for the poor law, public health and local Acts. With the development of public health, housing and to some extent town and country planning, the President became a powerful Minister outside the Cabinet. In 1919 the Board was abolished and replaced by the Ministry of Health, the Minister having a seat in the Cabinet. The Minister of Health was responsible for poor relief, public health and general supervision of local government, including areas and finance.

In 1943 a separate Ministry of Town and Country Planning was created but this was absorbed in 1951 in a new Ministry of Local Government and Planning, which assumed responsibility for the local government functions hitherto discharged by the Ministry of Health. In the same year, owing to a change of government the new Ministry acquired its present title of "Housing and Local Government". The Minister of Housing and Local Government is responsible for environmental public services, housing, planning, new towns, water supply and until 1969, local government structure, including finance. Many important local government services are controlled by other Ministries (e.g., Education). The Land Commission reports to this Minister and in 1969 reported that it intends to purchase land in areas of housing pressure owing to the failure of local planning authorities to meet Ministry requirements. The Commission proposes to find land independently of the authorities and the Ministry by means of concurrent applications for planning permission and draft C.P.Os. The wide scope of the Ministry of Housing and Local Government can be illustrated by the following statutes introduced by successive Ministers: Rating Act, 1966; Local Government Act, 1966; General Rate Act, 1967; Town and Country Planning Act, 1968; Housing Act, 1969.

The Minister of Housing and Local Government must approve the delegation of "control of development" planning functions to county district councils; he has power to confirm, modify or reject structure or local plans; he has power to hear appeals from decisions of local planning authorities and can order public inquiries to be held in planning matters. The Minister also has very wide default powers and can make a survey and development plan himself if the local authority has failed to do so. He can also order a local planning authority to acquire land for development or to secure its use in accordance with the approved plan. This Minister is also responsible for planning matters in national parks, areas of outstanding natural beauty and surveys of rights of way; he also has certain forestry functions. Again, in the case of housing, if complaint is made to the Minister that an urban housing authority has failed to exercise its functions properly, he may order a local public inquiry to be held, declare the authority to be in default and give it directions on future action. We have already seen that the Minister has power to confirm slum clearance orders after holding a local inquiry.

Again, in the field of public health the Minister has extensive default powers whereby he can order an inquiry into the exercise of their functions by county district councils on the complaint of a county council. The Minister can then make an order and transfer the functions to himself or to the county council, the cost being met by the defaulting authority. The Minister also has power to constitute joint public health boards and port health authorities. In the connected area of water supply, the Minister of Housing and Local Government has very wide powers. He can, for example, constitute a joint water board or joint water committee and vary the limits of supply of water undertakers. M.H.L.G. is responsible for the day to day administration of water supply through local authorities and water undertakings; for licensing abstractors of water; for the appointment of members and financing of the Water Resources Board, whose officers are Crown servants; and for research and publication of information on conservation of water supplies. M.H.L.G. and M.A.F.F. jointly appoint members of the River Authorities constituted under the Water Resources Act, 1963. M.H.L.G. was also responsible for land drainage, prevention of river pollution, control of abstraction and impounding and sewerage but, as noted above, the Secretary of State is now especially charged with responsibility for all aspects of environmental pollution. The Minister, therefore, has wide and detailed powers in relation to local government functions, areas and finance. Although other Ministers are concerned with some local government functions, this Minister deals with all general local government problems and with several important services.

The Ministry of Public Building and Works. This Ministry was created in 1962, its nucleus being the old Ministry of Works which had a romantic past. In olden times it is believed that it was described as the Department of Woods and Forests. The old Ministry was confined to such matters as the preservation of ancient monuments and the maintenance of the royal parks and palaces, which now come within the purview of M.P.B.W. It thus retains responsibility for the provision, repair and maintenance of buildings for government departments; and for the royal palaces and parks and upkeep of ancient monuments. Its main function is to co-ordinate all building for public purposes such as housing. Its Directorate General of Research and Development in 1965 carried out a comprehensive review of research and development work related to the building and civil engineering industries. It has commissioned from the universities a number of research projects on the construction industry and has encouraged the use of the new methods of industrialised building; the grant-in-aid to the National Building Agency is mainly allotted to services given to local authorities in conjunction with the Ministry of Housing and Local Government, to help them in using such methods. The Directorate of Research and Information advises on research policy and specific projects, and investigates problems connected with maintenance of buildings and use of computers in the construction industry; it also deals with training and education for the industry. It has now assumed responsibility for the Building Research Station, whose most persistent problem concerns control of noise.

The Minister of Housing and Local Government was originally to be responsible for making building regulations to replace the building bye-laws.[1] However, in 1964 this responsibility was transferred to the Minister of Public Building and Works. At the same time functions relating to means of escape from fire were transferred to the Home Secretary. [2] A Building Regulations Advisory Committee was set up and reported to the two Ministers. The change of government led to further delay but the Building Regulations, 1965, finally emerged and came into operation in February, 1966. They apply throughout England and Wales except in Inner London and the Ministry has published a useful guide.

Department of Education and Science. In Part I we traced the history of the Education Department from 1839 to 1964 but it remains for us to fill in the recent re-organisation and upgrading of the department. The office of President of the Board of Education lasted from 1899 to 1944, when a Minister of Education with Cabinet rank was appointed. That Minister was responsible for securing the effective execution by local authorities of the national policy of providing a varied and comprehensive national education service. For twenty years the Minister of Education hovered on the brink of the Cabinet, usually being excluded from it in Conservative Administrations. However, in 1964 a Conservative Government appointed a leading member of the Cabinet as Secretary of State for Education and Science and the succeeding Labour Government continued this arrangement.

The Robbins Report on Higher Education in 1963 recommended a much greater expansion of university and higher education and was partly responsible for the reorganisation of the government department. Hitherto the Universities Grants Committee had negotiated direct with the Treasury, which otherwise had no educational responsibilities. The new Department of Education and Science was set up in April, 1964, the Secretary of State being assisted by two Ministers of State, one responsible for primary and secondary schools and the other for higher education and civil science. Higher education in this context includes all types of university; traditional (Oxbridge), red-brick (Keele, Sussex, etc.) and technological. The Minister of State for higher education now meets the University Grants Committee. Some of the former colleges of advanced technology have been designated technological universities (for example, Brunel University, Uxbridge, the University of Surrey, Guildford, and the City University, Islington).

The Secretary of State is responsible for Scottish Universities because they are financed through the Universities Grants Committee. The government decided in 1965 that the demand for university places should be met by expansion of existing universities and that there should be no more new universities at present. In recent years new universities have been constituted in East Anglia (Norwich), Essex (Colchester), Kent (Canterbury), Lancaster, Sussex (Brighton), Warwick and York.

A Council for Scientific Policy advises the Secretary of State on national scientific needs, allocation of resources and scientific manpower. A Science Research Council[3] encourages research in the universities and co-ordinates work on nuclear science, astronomy and space. The Industrial Research and Development Authority,[4] the Natural Environmental Research Council and the Medical and Agricultural Research Councils also report to the Secretary of State. All these scientific responsibilities were transferred to the new Department from the office of the Lord President of the Council.

The Minister of State for primary and secondary education is also very busy. A committee headed by Lady Plowden[5] has reported on primary education in all its aspects and the transition to secondary education. Plowden recommended the opening up of classrooms, a new concept of free activity teaching and greater parental integration in the running of primary schools. Many authorities, notably the I.L.E.A., have adopted these recommendations. In common with several other local education authorities, the I.L.E.A. has abolished the unpopular "eleven-plus" examination and substituted another procedure, based on a "primary school profile" of individual children. In July, 1965, the Secretary of State issued a circular[6] to local education authorities asking them to submit plans for reorganising secondary education on comprehensive lines. It is the government's declared intention to end selection at eleven-plus and to eliminate separation in secondary education. The plans must provide for the integration of voluntary secondary schools into a comprehensive system in one of six main forms that have emerged so far. These include the orthodox comprehensive school with an age-range of

11-18 (the system favoured in Inner London), comprehensive schools combined with sixth-form colleges for pupils over 16 (the Leicester experiment) and a system of middle schools which straddle the primary and secondary age ranges.[7] Statute now provides for making changes in the character, size or situation of county or voluntary schools to enable special age limits to be adopted.

The Secretary of State has powers to approve schemes for divisional administration and to constitute divisional executives; and to approve schemes for "excepted districts" in education administration, as already noted. He also has power to set up Joint Education Boards to administer the service over wider areas. The Secretary of State has very wide powers of control, including default powers, and can make regulations on such matters as maintenance of schools, standards of premises, further education and inspection. The separate departmental inspectorate is another potent instrument of control. The Minister may make an order declaring a local education authority or the governors or managers of schools to be in default and can issue directions to ensure compliance with his wishes. He can prevent the unreasonable exercise of powers by those bodies and can decide disputes between them. The Secretary of State can also hold inquiries, authorise compulsory purchase of land and confirm bye-laws under the Public Libraries and Museums Act, 1964. There are now 3 Ministers of State and an Under-Secretary of State.

Department of Health and Social Security. The Minister of Health was not in the Cabinet[8] from 1951, when local government functions were transferred to the Minister of Housing and Local Government. Since then the Minister of Health had been responsible to Parliament for the general administration of the National Health Service through the Hospital Boards, Hospital Management Committees and Executive Councils. The Minister of Health was also, however, the co-ordinating Minister for those health and welfare services still administered by local authorities. In the welfare field, the Supplementary Benefits Commission gives direct relief to those in need but there are still a number of welfare services administered locally. Proposals for local personal health (including mental health) and welfare services must be made to the Secretary of State, who can approve or modify them or initiate fresh proposals. He has power to settle disputes between authorities and to inspect homes for old people, the disabled and the mentally disordered. As noted in Part I, the Ministry of Health was absorbed into the new Department in November, 1968, under the Secretary of State for Social Services.

The health and welfare services provide a useful and fairly recent illustration of delegation in the county system of local government; and delegation schemes must be approved by the Secretary of State. Again the Social Services Secretary possesses the usual very wide default powers and, in the case of a defaulting county district council, can transfer the functions to the county council. This Minister's wide powers in relation to welfare can be traced back to the arbitrary powers given to the Poor Law Commissioners. Local authorities exercise their welfare functions under the general guidance of the Minister and in accordance with regulations made by him. The former Minister of Health made regulations defining the qualifications of local welfare officers.

The Secretary of State has a considerable measure of control over medical officers of health and public health inspectors employed by local authorities. Thus he has made regulations prescribing their qualifications, duties, mode of appointment and terms as to tenure of office and salaries. In general, if a central grant is payable in respect of the salaries of these officers, they cannot be dismissed without the Minister's consent. Medical officers of health and public health inspectors are mainly concerned with the exercise of housing and public health functions, rather than with the personal health services, but it is convenient for the Secretary of State to remain the controlling Minister. In the case of an outbreak of infectious disease in an area, a medical officer of health must obey any directions of the Minister, who has power to add to the list of diseases considered to be infectious.

The health functions of the Secretary of State impinge most closely on local government. The administration of health services are at present dispersed between the Minister, the hospital boards and committees and local authorities. The implementation of the Seebohm Report may usher in a much more integrated National Health Service, with the enlarged local authorities playing a much greater part.

There is also a link between the activities of the local welfare authorities and the administration of social security benefits which is now the responsibility of the new department. Local welfare departments work closely with area officers of D.H.S.S., the former providing local facilities for the aged (such as meals-on-wheels, home helps, etc.) and the latter the retirement and supplementary pensions.

The new Department's responsibilities for national insurance and sickness benefits also overlaps with local government welfare units in the sense that they are both dealing basically with the same clientele. Moreover some local councillors serve on national insurance and pensions appeals tribunals.

The Ministry of Transport. The Minister of Transport is not only responsible to Parliament for nationalised transport but also for central control of the local highway authorities.

The Minister can delegate repair and maintenance of trunk roads and motorways to local authorities and can resolve disputes between authorities. He may direct that a road shall be or cease to be a trunk road or motorway. Highway and planning powers often overlap and it is sometimes difficult to disentangle the powers of the respective Ministers. Thus the Minister of Housing and Local Government possesses important appellate functions under the street works codes. Normally, the Minister of Transport will retain responsibility for trunk roads and motorways and he has power to construct special roads with limited access and restricted to the use of specified classes of vehicle. Existing roads can be adapted for this purpose, and both the Minister and local highway authorities can make special roads under Ministerial schemes which define the roads and the types of traffic allowed on them.

The Minister of Transport has the usual power to approve delegation schemes, except that the much smaller minimum population figure of 20,000 is taken. The Minister of Transport may be said to share the administration of the Road Traffic Acts with the police but he can designate parking places on highways on the application of a local highway authority.[9] The Ministerial order will normally provide for charges to be made by parking meters.

This Minister considers draft compulsory purchase orders made by local highway authorities for road-widening schemes or other highway purposes. If objections are made, a local public inquiry may be held and the Minister, after considering the inspector's report can confirm, modify or reject the order. The Minister has power to designate Passenger Transport Authorities under the Transport Act, 1968 (see Chapter VII).

Other Departments associated with local government. The Home Office is one of the most important of government departments for local government. It has powers to regulate the machinery of elections and to confirm bye-laws, and the Home Secretary is the Minister responsible for such services as the police, fire protection, civil defence and child care. In all these cases there is a separate Home Office inspectorate; and, as we have seen, the Home Secretary has wide powers, recently strengthened, to order amalgamations of police forces. The arrangements for confirmation of delegation schemes for the child care service are similar to those in respect of health and welfare. Child care functions may be transferred to D.H.S.S. if Seebohm is implemented.

Since 1965 the Welsh Department has assumed responsibility for housing, local government. land use, new towns, rent control, public health, water, civil defence and national parks in Wales and Monmouthshire. Major statutory instruments affecting England and Wales as a whole are made by the Minister of Housing and Local Government in consultation with the Secretary of State for Wales. Functions relating to water, highways, bridges and forestry in Wales have been transferred to the new department.

In conclusion, we may summarise the various forms of Ministerial control over local authorities. Undoubtedly the most potent weapon is the financial one: the government grant ensures that he who pays the piper calls the tune, even if the sanction of reduction of withdrawal is hardly ever used. The role of the district auditor and the necessity for Ministerial sanction of borrowing are also relevant to financial control. Next, the power to make statutory instruments in the shape of rules, regulations or orders which are binding on local authorities is a strong weapon, assisted by circulars issued by Ministers which may be said to be of great persuasive authority since, if the advice tendered is not followed, an order can easily be made. In describing the various services we have seen the very wide default powers available to Ministers, although again they are not often used. Nevertheless it has been known for the powers of a defaulting county district council to have been transferred to the county council, the defaulting authority having been charged with the resulting expenses.

Ministerial confirmation, modification of rejection of bye-laws, orders and schemes made by local authorities constitute another important form of control. Planning decisions, compulsory purchase orders and delegation schemes spring to mind in this connection. In the case of certain services there are powerful inspectorates available to report to their Ministers on any maladministration or inefficiency; education and the police are the leading examples here. Certain officers can be appointed or dismissed only with ministerial approval: this applies to chief education officers, chief constables, chief fire officers, children's officers, medical officers of health[10] and public health inspectors.[10] Finally, the different wording used by various Acts of Parliament in allocating control of a service is instructive.

The Education Act, 1944, provides that the duty of the Secretary of State is to "promote the education of the people . . . *and to secure the effective execution by local authorities, under his control and direction* of the national policy . . .". Very similar wording is used in the Water Act, 1945, and in the Water Resources Act, 1963, and the Ministerial power is reinforced in detail in other sections in all three statutes. A milder form of words is provided by the Children Act, 1948, which provides that local authorities shall perform their functions "under the *general guidance* of the Home Secretary". This formula is also used in the National Assistance Act, 1948, in relation to local welfare authorities and the Minister of Health. Nevertheless both Acts make fairly drastic powers available to the respective Ministers in other sections. Perhaps the high water-mark was reached in the Police Act, 1964, under which the Secretary of State "shall exercise his powers . . . in such manner and to such extent as appears to him to be best calculated to promote the efficiency of the police". The local police authority is not even mentioned and the powers of control available to the Home Secretary under the Act are certainly far-reaching.

1. Public Health Act, 1961.
2. And to the Minister of Labour in the case of factories (now DEP).
3. Partly replacing the Department of Scientific and Industrial Research.
4. Also partly replacing D.S.I.R.
5. Wife of Lord Plowden, another committee chairman.
6. No. 10/65.

7. The Education Act, 1964, could be used for this latter purpose.
8. Except for the period 1962-63.
9. Except in London, where this is the responsibility of the G.L.C.
10. With certain exceptions.

CHAPTER XV

GREATER LONDON

"London, thou art the flower of cities alle . . ."

Historical Introduction. Special problems of organisation and administration have always been present in the metropolis owing to its position as the seat of government and capital of the country. These were accentuated by the great size of London, in terms both of area and population, which in turn necessitated urgent attention being given to sanitation. By 1830 there were eight separate bodies of Commissioners of Sewers for London and these were unified in 1848 into one new body of Commissioners of Sewers for the Metropolis.

In 1834 the parish vestries[1] lost their poor law functions to the new boards of guardians but the special public health problems of London led Parliament to create numerous "select vestries",[2] in some of which the vestrymen were popularly elected if the parish availed itself of adoptive legislation. In some parts of the Metropolis Parliament provided for the creation of district boards governing two or more small parishes. Both the metropolitan vestries and district boards received powers in such matters as highways and sanitation which elsewhere later became the functions of *ad hoc* boards. By the middle of the nineteenth century the metropolitan vestry had become the normal unit of local administration.

However, there was no general control over this great conglomeration of vestries and boards. Accordingly, the Metropolis Management Act of 1855, reorganised the parochial vestries and district boards in London[3] and transferred to them the powers of the former paving commissioners. This Act, a vital landmark in the history of London local government, also set up the Metropolitan Board of Works comprising forty-six members elected by the vestries and district boards. The new Board was responsible for main drainage and bridges throughout the metropolis and also exercised certain improvement powers. In 1866 the Metropolitan Fire Brigade[4] came into existence and was placed under the control of the Metropolitan Board of Works.

The closing years of the nineteenth century witnessed notable local government reforms, not least in London, which were to endure for well over half a century. The Local Government Act, 1888, abolished the Board, replacing it with the London County Council, which came into existence the following year. The L.C.C. differed in material respects from the other county councils created by the Act, since the latter were based on the ancient geographical counties of England and Wales. The L.C.C. was carved out of the urban or metropolitan areas of the counties of Middlesex, Surrey and Kent. Its internal composition was broadly the same as that of the other county councils, with some exceptions. Thus it had a chairman, a vice-chairman, aldermen and councillors, all the latter and one half of the total number of aldermen having been elected triennially. However, the aldermen, although holding office for the usual period of six years, were only one-sixth of the number of councillors.[5] The L.C.C. had power to appoint a deputy chairman and the practice was to offer this position to a leading member of the minority party on the council. The electoral divisions were the parliamentary constituencies, each returning three councillors.

The London Government Act, 1899, took the reorganisation a stage further by abolishing the metropolitan vestries and district boards and replacing them with twenty-eight new metropolitan borough councils. Unlike the borough councils outside London which had been incorporated by Royal Charter, the metropolitan borough councils were purely creatures of statute and did not receive Charters. Each metropolitan borough council annually elected a mayor and triennial elections were held of councillors and one half of the number of aldermen, the latter being one-sixth of the number of councillors. As in the rest of the country, the aldermen were drawn from the councillors or persons qualified to be councillors and, once elected, served for six years, one-half of their number retiring every three years. Thus the aldermanic system, entrenched in the municipal boroughs was extended not only to the new county councils but also throughout London, albeit on a narrower basis.

The L.C.C. was the local authority responsible throughout the area of the old County of London for education, town planning and main drainage,[6] it also administered the personal health, welfare and child care services. There was no delegation of education or of the other personal services to the metropolitan borough councils, but nine[7] administrative divisions controlled from County Hall administered certain local aspects of these services. For example, the education divisions serviced the governing and managing bodies of schools by providing clerks to the governors and managers. Local co-ordination of services could also be effected: for example the divisional education officer would consult the divisional medical officer on the school health service or the area children's officer on problem children. The L.C.C.'s Junior Leaving Examination, popularly known as the "eleven-plus examination", was administered locally in the divisions, which provided Clerks to the Local Advisory or Selection Committees. Maintenance and uniform grants and free travel passes for secondary school children were also obtainable through the divisional offices.

Some planning functions were delegated to the metropolitan borough councils, but there was a special delegation scheme in the case of the City of London. As regards the exercise of local government functions, the City Corporation[8] was more or less in the position of a metropolitan borough with special privileges. The L.C.C. did not control main roads or the police, the metropolitan borough councils having been the local highway authorities for all except major roads.[9] The metropolitan borough councils were responsible in their areas for housing, public health (administration of bye-laws, including those made under the London Building Acts; sewers, sanitation, clean air zones, food and drugs legislation), rating and libraries. Both the L.C.C. and the metropolitan borough councils had concurrent housing powers in relation to slum clearance and the provision of new housing. Thus the main differences between local administration in the County of London and the counties elsewhere were, on the one hand, the concurrent housing powers in London (an ordinary county council having only very limited housing powers for overspill purposes) and, by contrast, the greater responsibilities vested in the metropolitan borough councils for highways. A third major difference was the absence of any provision for delegation in London, except to a limited extent in the field of planning. There was also special legislation for London, notably in the case of public health.

The L.C.C. did not participate in national negotiating machinery and, until 1957, negotiated direct with its Staff Association through a Joint Negotiating Committee. The clerk was appointed to hold his office during the pleasure of the council and, unlike most other county clerks, he was not also clerk of the peace. Other officers and staff were appointed under the general provisions of the 1933 Act. This also applied to the metropolitan borough councils, except that they were required to appoint an adequate number of public health inspectors. The Minister of Health had power to order more appointments, after holding a local inquiry on receipt of representations from the L.C.C. Metropolitan borough councils, in common with the L.C.C., had to appoint finance committees and their accounts were subject to the scrutiny of the district auditor. Every borough council and the City Corporation were represented on the Metropolitan Boroughs Standing Joint Committee, a voluntary co-ordinating body which made representations on matters of common interest to various Ministers and initiated concerted action, for example if legislation was required. There was also a Metropolitan Boroughs' Organisation and Methods Committee[10] and a Metropolitan Boroughs' Libraries Committee whose main task was to control the maintenance of the London Library Catalogue. The new London Boroughs' Committee has established a similar Libraries Committee.

The size and resources of the metropolitan boroughs varied enormously. The largest was Wandsworth, with a population of 347,209; the smallest was Holborn, with a population of 21,596. Islington, Lambeth and Lewisham all had populations of over 220,000; whilst Bethnal Green, Chelsea, Finsbury and Shoreditch all had populations below 50,000, moreover, the county boundary came to be artificial and the time grew ripe for reform.

The Royal Commission. A Royal Commission under the chairmanship of Sir Edwin Herbert[11] was set up in December, 1957, to investigate and report on Local Government in Greater London. Police and water supply were specifically excluded from its terms of reference. The area of Greater London examined was approximately, but not quite, the same as that of the Metropolitan Police District. The Commission took nearly three years over its labours and its Report was finally presented to Parliament by command of the Queen in October, 1960.[12] The Herbert Report repays careful study, since it is a detailed and conscientious document. It should be borne in mind that the area reviewed contains a population of over eight millions and includes the areas of the old counties of London and Middlesex; the former county boroughs of Croydon, East Ham and West Ham; the urban areas of the old counties of Essex, Hertfordshire, Kent and Surrey,[13] and all the county districts within the urban areas of those counties and Middlesex. The area contained two entire counties, three county boroughs and nearly ninety second-tier authorities.

The local government system in the old county of London was, as we have first seen, materially different in several particulars from that obtaining in the rest of the country, and therefore, in the remainder of Greater London. The Royal Commission had to take into account this divergence between the two systems. The Herbert Report, as it is still known, recommended the creation of a Greater London Council for the whole area to administer education, town and country planning, highways, traffic management, main drainage, fire protection, ambulances and refuse disposal. The Report also recommended the establishment of fifty-two Greater London Borough Councils, each administering an area of between 150,000 and 175,000 inhabitants, to replace the three county borough councils and some eighty-odd county district councils. These proposed Greater London Borough Councils would administer the remaining ' personal services": child care, health, and welfare. In addition, they would inherit the administration of housing, public health, rating, libraries and certain roads.

One of the most startling effects of the subsequent implementation of most of the recommendations by the government of the day was the disappearance of the London and Middlesex County Councils. The Herbert Report naturally sparked off considerable controversy, both political and administrative. The L.C.C. had been controlled by the Labour Party since 1934 and the London Labour Party, not unnaturally, objected that the Conservative government's aim would be political if it agreed to the destruction of such an indisputably efficient administrative unit. The Report's recommendations also envisaged disappearance of the three county borough councils, the twenty-eight metropolitan borough councils and all the non-county borough and urban district councils in the area.

Another remarkable recommendation in the Report was that education, surely *the* personal service *par excellence,* should be administered by the giant Greater London Council with an area nearly three times as large as that of the L.C.C., which was, during its life-time, the biggest local authority in the world. The Report postulated a curious division in the responsibility for schools which appeared to be impracticable in the extreme. The Greater London Council was to be the local education authority for the whole area and to own the schools, but the borough councils were to be responsible for their maintenance and repair. This was a strange *volte-face* for a body which had castigated delegation in general, and the scheme operating in Middlesex in particular. The Report also recommended a drastic cut in the number of councillors and aldermen—the G.L.C. was to have 115 councillors elected triennially for each of the parliamentary constituencies in the area. This number was whittled down as various local authorities on the fringe of the area managed to opt out of Greater London.

All the main proposals of the Herbert Report were in due course faithfully implemented by the government of the day, except those dealing with education and the size of the boroughs.

The White Paper and the Report by the Town Clerks. The Government published a White Paper in November, 1961, broadly accepting the recommendations of the Herbert Report, but with some reservations on the size of the boroughs and on education. They opted for larger London boroughs, with a minimum population of 200,000 wherever possible; accordingly, the number of London boroughs was to be reduced.

The most startling deviation from the Report was the proposal to constitute the London borough councils local education authorities. There was, however, one loophole which was eagerly seized upon by the defenders of the splendid London education service: a single education authority was postulated for a central area with a population of the order of two million. The White Paper accepted the Report's conclusions about the distribution of the remaining personal services, highways, housing and planning, except that, in the government's view, the G.L.C. should have some reserve housing powers.

A committee for the protection of London education was formed, including politicians, administrators, parents and teachers. It fought particularly hard for the retention of the London education service in the old County of London. It is believed that battle was joined in the Macmillan Cabinet, from which the then Minister of Education[14] emerged triumphant. At any rate in April, 1962, it was announced that education in the area would be administered by a committee of the G.L.C. for the time being. This was a considerable victory but unfortunately similar arrangements were not made in respect of the children's service. Children deprived of a normal home life do not constitute a powerful pressure group; and the enlightened and disinterested efforts of metropolitan magistrates and probation officers did not prevent the dissolution of the fine L.C.C. Children's Service. It should be mentioned, however, that the new borough councils are discharging their responsibilities in this field with humanity and skill.

The Minister of Housing and Local Government commissioned the Town Clerks of Plymouth, Cheltenham, Oxford and South Shields to make recommendations for the creation of a pattern of boroughs in connection with the reorganisation of London government. The four town clerks held conferences in the area and reported in July, 1962, recommending that there should be thirty-two London boroughs and giving details of their proposed composition and population. The Minister accepted in its entirety the report of the town clerks[15] and these are in fact the thirty-two London boroughs subsequently created. Wandsworth, the largest of the metropolitan boroughs, was split under these proposals; two-thirds of old Wandsworth joined with Battersea to form the new London Borough of Wandsworth, whilst the remaining third joined old Lambeth to constitute the new London Borough of Lambeth. These were the largest groupings, the only others with populations of over 300,000 being those centred on Barnet, Finchley and Hendon; and on Bermondsey, Camberwell and Southwark. On the other hand, there were only two groupings with populations of less than 200,000: those centred on parts of Dagenham and of Barking; and on Barnes, Richmond and Twickenham.

The London Government Act, 1963. Certain parts of Hertfordshire and Surrey originally included in the Review area were excluded from the area administered by the G.L.C. which is known as Greater London. This is defined as the area comprising the London boroughs, the City of London and the Inner and Middle Temples. One hundred councillors[16] and sixteen aldermen were elected in April, 1964, the first general election of councillors for the G.L.C., resulting in a decisive Labour victory. The new council elected a Chairman, Vice-Chairman and Deputy Chairman from its members, the last-named post being offered to a representative of the minority Conservative Party, in accordance with the traditional practice of the L.C.C. In April, 1967, the Conservatives gained control and assumed office at County Hall for the first time since 1934.

The first London borough council elections were held in May 1964, resulting in Labour control of ten of the twelve inner London boroughs, the parties dividing about equally in the control of the outer London boroughs. The first mayors of the new London boroughs were elected in

May, 1965.[17] Responsibility for the administration of relevant functions and certain assets and property vested in the G.L.C. and the L.B.Cs. respectively on 1st April, 1965. The pre-existing authorities in Greater London expired on 31st March, 1965. Thus the old authorities co-existed with the new for the better part of twelve months. The first meetings of the new authorities were held swiftly following the elections in 1964 to enable appointments to be made of chief officers, deputy chief officers and general administrative, professional, technical and clerical staff. In May, 1968, the Conservatives reversed the position in inner London (10:2) and made dramatic gains elsewhere.

The Act enabled the Queen-in-Council to grant charters of incorporation of the inhabitants of a London borough, following representations by the Minister of Housing and Local Government to the Privy Council. This has now been done in each case and in 1964 the Minister made orders naming the boroughs following representations by joint committees of the old authorities. Thus although the London boroughs are statutory creations, they have been granted Royal Charters. The reason for this is that, whereas the old metropolitan boroughs and urban districts in the area were statutory, the county boroughs and non-county boroughs were all incorporated by Charter. It was therefore appropriate to issue Royal Charters to all the new boroughs, whatever the status of their various predecessors-in-title may have been. The expression "Inner London" refers to the old L.C.C. area; "Outer London" means the remainder of Greater London: with ten exceptions, all the boroughs were named after one of the pre-existing units, either the largest or most ancient. The new London boroughs are:—

INNER LONDON

City of Westminster, Camden, Islington, Hackney, Tower Hamlets, Greenwich, Lewisham, Southwark, Lambeth, Wandsworth, Hammersmith, Royal Borough of Kensington and Chelsea.

OUTER LONDON

Formerly Essex

Waltham Forest, Redbridge, Havering, Barking, Newham.

Formerly Kent

Bexley, Bromley.

Formerly Surrey

Croydon, Sutton, Merton, Royal Boroughs of Kingston-upon-Thames, Richmond-upon-Thames[18]

Formerly Middlesex

Hounslow, Hillingdon, Ealing, Brent, Harrow, Barnet, Haringey, Enfield.

On the last day of its existence, the old Metropolitan Borough Council of Battersea passed a resolution urging that the new London Borough of Wandsworth should be re-designated "Wandsworth and Battersea". On the other hand, the East London (former Metropolitan) boroughs of Stepney, Poplar and Bethnal Green are now incorporated in the attractively named London Borough of Tower Hamlets.

Functions of the G.L.C. and L.B.Cs. Education in the former County of London is the responsibility of the Inner London Education Authority, whose members comprise the G.L.C. members for Inner London and representatives from the City Corporation and from each of the twelve Inner London Boroughs. The I.L.E.A. is described in the 1963 Act as a special Committee of the G.L.C. and it has control over the appointment of its officers, except insofar as it is subject to the general rule that the appointment of a chief officer must be approvedd by the Secretary of State. The I.L.E.A. also determines the amount of the G.L.C.'s education precept levied on the rating authorities in Inner London. For these reasons, the I.L.E.A. would appear to be in the position of an *ad hoc* authority for education in Inner London. The G.L.C. has no option but to precept for the amount required by the I.L.E.A., whose independent position is analogous to that of a county police committee.

The twenty Outer London Borough Councils are local education authorities in their own right. This is logical, because many of the Outer London Boroughs have been formed from amalgamations of "excepted districts" in Middlesex and the old metropolitan parts of Essex, Kent and Surrey. There is, therefore, a considerable nucleus of experience in education administration in Outer London.

The remaining personal services of child care, health and welfare are the responsibility of the London Borough Councils; these functions were formerly discharged by the county councils in the area. A London Boroughs Training Committee (Social Services) co-ordinates the training of social workers in the child care, personal health and welfare services; a Director of Training has been appointed. This Committee was set up voluntarily by the London Boroughs and has no statutory authority.

The G.L.C. is the local planning authority for Greater London and is responsible for the preparation of a structure plan for the area but the L.B.C.s must prepare local plans and have certain planning functions.[19] The precise division of responsibility for planning has been determined by Regulations[20] made by the Minister of Housing and Local Government. Except for the reception of applications for planning permission, which remains the function of the borough councils, the G.L.C. is the local planning authority for the three main types of development. With certain exceptions it is the planning authority for areas of Comprehensive Development in Inner London; for certain specified classes of development relating mainly to large buildings; and for certain applications for the extraction of minerals. In addition, the thirty-two

L.B.Cs. and the City Corporation must refer all applications to the G.L.C. which relate to eleven specified classes of development. Much of this is concerned with control of office and industrial development, which, in Greater London, is thus largely the province of the G.L.C., the Minister of Housing and Local Government and the Board of Trade (now Mintech).

Where a London Borough Council consider that an application should be granted for development which is a substantial departure from a development plan they shall refer it to the G.L.C.[21] or to the Minister.[22] Subject to certain criteria, the G.L.C. has power, wheryan application has been referred to it, to give a direction to the L.B.C. if they think that planning permission should be refused or made conditional. The Minister may give similar directions to the local authorities in Greater London where an application has been referred to him.

The G.L.C. has already indicated that, in preparing the new development plan for Greater London, close consultation will be maintained with the L.B.C.s. Government departments, boards and other authorities will also be consulted to ascertain their more important strategic interests. L.B.C.s will also be consulted on the preparation of the development plan map as definite information about the major highway systems and inter-change points becomes available, in order to facilitate the preparation of the local borough plans. In January, 1966, the Minister of Housing and Local Government made an order[23] providing for the form and content of development plans for Greater London.

The Greater London Development Plan was submitted to the Minister in 1968. The Greater London Plan presents the G.L.C.'s main policies and priorities, determines the elements of metropolitan significance and indicates the main strategic developments. In addition, it sets the framework within which the L.B.C.s will be free to prepare their own plans and indicates to other bodies with metropolitan interests matters of crucial importance to be taken into account. In this way the new plan plays a full part in contributing to national and regional policies. The need for flexibility is understood by the G.L.C. which envisages the development of a continuous information system on a common basis of areas and definition, mathematical models for urban planning purposes and economic evaluation methods. Extensive use has been made of the Council's computer and, of course, of the new research and intelligence division.

The L.B.C.s are the local housing authorities or the "primary units for housing"; they therefore have all necessary powers under the Housing Act, 1957-59. However, the G.L.C. also has power to provide new housing accommodation both inside and outside Greater London, but it must in general obtain the consent of the L.B.C. if it wishes to build within the area of that borough. For the time being, until such date as the Minister may appoint, the G.L.C. may exercise certain other housing powers concurrently with the L.B.C.s but it cannot deal with abatement of overcrowding or houses in multiple occupation.[24] Under the London

Government Act, 1963, the G.L.C. housing estates can be transferred by agreement to the L.B.C.s; and M.H.L.G. has power to direct such transfer by order. The first stage of handing over the estates of L.B.C.s has commenced, although some L.B.C.s have refused to agree to the transfer on financial grounds. The G.L.C. maintains a record of need and facilities for the exchange of housing accommodation and the L.B.C.s maintain housing registers. The aim is for the G.L.C.'s central record to be continuously supplied with information from the L.B.C.s. The Ministry of Housing and Local Government reminded all London local authorities of his duty in a circular,[25] thus emphasing the importance attached to such records by the government.

In 1964 the Milner Holland Report disclosed some appalling facts about housing in London and indicated that no policy for housing in London could be formed unless the necessary facts were available. As long ago as 1955 the Central Housing Advisory Committee had recommended to the Minister that residential qualifications for housing should be dispensed with. The Ministry Circular accordingly urged the L.B.C.s to achieve a uniform assessment of residential qualifications and suggested that applicants in one borough should, if necessary, be considered for a house in another. Qualifications to get on an L.B.C.s waiting list are now uniform and such flexibility is invaluable in view of the gross overcrowding in some boroughs. The G.L.C. also operates a "clearing-house" to facilitate exchanges of dwellings between G.L.C. and L.B.C. tenants. Some L.B.C.s have formed groups to carry though large industrialised building projects and the London Boroughs Committee has sponsored a housing consortium. Over half of the London education authorities including the I.L.E.A. have joined the Metropolitan Architectural Consortium for Education.

The L.B.Cs. must enforce certain public health bye-laws made by the G.L.C. The G.L.C. is responsible for the provision and maintenance of main sewers, main drainage and land drainage throughout Greater London. The L.B.C.s are responsible for the provision and maintenance of public sewers other than the main sewers. The indestructibility of some aspects of the old L.C.C. administration is illustrated by the fact that it has proved impossible to dislodge the London Building Acts. Accordingly, the Building Regulations, 1965, which apply to the rest of England and Wales, do not apply to Inner London, which retains its separate building code. The L.B.C.s are responsible for refuse *collection* and other public health matters; the G.L.C. arranges refuse *disposal*.

In the case of highways, there is a new classification of "metropolitan roads",[26] for which the G.L.C. is responsible. This is closely linked with traffic engineering and management and the G.L.C. has a Department of Highways and Transportation. The G.L.C. has completed its first motorways, the Western Avenue Extension and the first section of the Western Cross route, which is part of the future London motorway "box"; a grant of £20 millions has been made by the Minister of

Transport.

Opposition is growing to the current proposals for motorway boxes on both sides of the river; in addition, the Archway Road (A1–M1 spur) road widening scheme has run into much local opposition channelled by the Archway Road Campaign. In South London the inhabitants of Eltham are threatened with a motorway box. The destruction of good housing accommodation and consequential displacement of residents seem too high a price to pay for smooth traffic flow, whose increased speed brings danger to young and old alike.

The L.B.C.s are responsible for the maintenance of "non-metropolitan' roads, in other words all highways except those for which the Minister of Transport is responsible.[27] The G.L.C. has a general duty in relation to road traffic and has powers to make traffic regulation orders and experimental traffic schemes, and to provide parking accomodation[28] and traffic signs. Thus the Christmas shopping parking arrangements for central London and restrictions on off-street parking now emanate from the G.L.C. The G.L.C. is now responsible for making schemes for[29] pedestrian crossings on all roads in its area other than the trunk roads.

The G.L.C. is responsible for ambulances and the London Fire Brigade. It precepts upon the L.B.C.s, which are the local rating and library authorities and the main civil defence authorities. The accounts for both the G.L.C. and the L.B.C.s are subject to district audit. The London Boroughs Committee has replaced the Metropolitan Boroughs Standing Joint Committee, and the London Boroughs Management Services Unit has replaced the Metropolitan Boroughs Organisation and Methods Committee.

In November, 1965, the G.L.C. appointed a director of intelligence in the department of the clerk to the council to head its research and information division. The Act broke new ground here and the aim is to collate information on Greater London and to make it available to local authorities, government departments and the public. Moreover, Ministers concerned with local government may require the G.L.C. to provide them with relevant information. The creation of such an organisation was postulated in the Herbert Report and it should prove extremely useful and beneficial to all concerned.

In May, 1965, the Greater London Whitley Council for Local Authorities[30] Administrative, Professional, Technical and Clerical Services was constituted. Following the reorganisation of local government in Greater London, this broadly replaced the London District Council, the Middlesex District Whitley Council, the North Metropolitan Joint Council and the South Metropolitan District Council. The Council is a constituent member of the National Joint Council for Local Authorities' Administrative, Professional, Technical and Clerical Services. The Greater London Council Staff Association broadly replaced the L.C.C. Staff Association. Some G.L.C. officers and most of the officers of the L.B.C.s belong to N.A.L.G.O.; some belong to N.U.P.E.

The new authorities in action. The reorganisation of local government in Greater London was a great constitutional experiment. At the time of writing the new authorities have been exercising their functions for 4 years and some illustrations of their achievements follow.

Inner London. The I.L.E.A. during the first year of its existence abolished its Junior Leaving Examination (the "eleven-plus exam") and replaced it by a system of free parental choice. During each child's last year at primary school a "profile" of his or her work is compiled from gradings of the Head and the results of verbal reasoning tests. Overall assessments of standards are checked centrally against tests taken in all schools. The parent chooses a school for his offspring in consultation with the primary school Head and the profiles are available to secondary Heads. In 1965, the first year of the new system, 85 per cent of children went to schools of their parents' first choice, 12 per cent went to second choice schools and only 3 per cent were disappointed.

The success of the scheme will probably greatly ease the Inner London transition to fully comprehensive education since school neighbourhood zones or catchment areas should not be necessary. Parental choice can range over single-sex and co-educational schools, large or medium sized schools, "aided" or "County" schools. Other local education authorities are seeking detailed information from the I.L.E.A., which emphasises the parent-teacher relationship and the traditions, inherited from the L.C.C., of trying to meet parental wishes. At present the scheme embraces direct-grant, aided and maintained grammar schools; and comprehensive schools. But even when the authority's area is fully comprehensive some schools will have different specialities, such as technology, and others will have an academic bias.

Subsidies are available from the Exchequer under the government's plan to render extra assistance to cities with exceptional housing needs and slum clearance problems whose local authorities have already instigated large and costly housing programmes. These include Inner London and its twelve L.B.C.s, Birmingham, Leeds and Manchester. Authorities building houses for overspill families from these cities qualify for the extra grant. The housing problem of Inner London is helped by the new town at Milton Keynes, Buckinghamshire and the expansion of Ispwich, Northampton and Peterborough. The position is strengthened by the Local Government (Social Needs) Act, 1969.

Islington. The Islington L.B.C. Social Services and Health Committee have set up a separate service for a group of about 130 deaf and dumb in the borough as part of the welfare arrangements for the handicapped. This number is more than was known to the voluntary society which acted as agent for the L.C.C. in this field until 1965. Islington's chief welfare officer has to rely on doctors, almoners, clergy and neighbours of the handicapped for information and on house to house convassing. There is a serious shortage of trained social workers which could be alleviated by joint action by the London Boroughs Training Committee (Social Services) and the College of Deaf Welfare and Social Studies in Haringey, on the Islington border. Islington has called in a firm of management consultants and wide-reaching reorganisation of the borough's administration is expected.

Islington has also been prominent in its drive on slum clearance. The G.L.C. and the L.B.C., in full co-operation, are in the process of attacking slum clearance in Islington by means of a joint scheme under which the two local authorities are pooling their resources and expertise. The G.L.C. assumes responsibility, under the scheme, for substandard tenement blocks in the borough, the so-called "twilight areas". Although demolition is not likely to take place for some years, as soon as the building become council property there will be an adjustment of rents and execution of repairs and minor improvements. The two authorities were also concerned in the redevelopment of the Packington Estate in Islington. The Minister decided, after holding a public inquiry in 1965, that this old Victorian estate should be redeveloped rather than rehabilitated. He called for a new scheme before making his decision and was criticised for not holding another inquiry. The net result was that urgently needed slum clearance went ahead after six years delay.[31]

Lambeth. Lambeth L.B.C. is just embarking upon an imaginative scheme for the redevelopment of Brixton Town Centre in the middle of the borough at an estimated cost of £47m. Brixton has a population of some 4,000 and is one of the seven most import shopping centres in London. It has two railway stations and is served by numerous bus routes; the current construction of the Victoria Line extension to Brixton, due for completion in 1971, and the G.L.C.'s proposed Ring way motorway have been taken into account. The aim is to eradicate pedestrian/traffic conflict and to replace obsolete buildings and layout. 61 acres of the town centre are programmed for redevelopment by 1987. The proposals for the new town centre include segregation of traffic and pedestrians by means of upper level pedestrian walkways; a transport interchange station; a car centre for the motor trade; thirty storey residential tower blocks and hostel accommodation for students to the north; realignment of the shopping centre; offices, an hotel, a park, an art centre, a new central library, swimming baths and sports centre, a College of Further Education and multi-storey car parks.

Lambeth L.B.C. in 1969 approved a pilot scheme to provide a "family visiting service" or "local case-work" service in a selected area office serving a population of about 30,000. The introduction of the pilot scheme was influenced by the Seebohm Report but is of more limited scope. The social worker element of the area team comprises field workers from the Health, Welfare, Childrens and Housing Departments organised in small mixed teams under the leadership of a social work co-ordinator. The services provided include health visiting; mental health, home help; child care; visiting of blind, handicapped and aged persons; preliminary investigation of applications for admission to old people's homes, temporary accommodation and prevention of eviction; preliminary recommendation for priority rehousing; and housing welfare.

Hounslow. In April, 1966, the London Borough of Hounslow announced an imaginative plan to revitalise Brentford, the former county town of Middlesex and one of the oldest towns in Britain. Under the plan Brentford, much of which is derelict or decaying, will become an attractive town, making far greater use of its Thames-side position. The proposals, involving about 400 acres south of the Great West Road, include ambitious housing developments, a "town quay", a footbridge over the Thames to link with Kew Gardens, a boating lake, an educational and cultural centre and a riverside walk to the World Garden Centre at Syon Park. The estimated cost is about £45 millions and it will take about twenty years or more to implement the scheme; the large scale housing development, however, has started, the first stage to be complete in 1970. Consultation has taken place between the local authority and interested bodies such as the four local preservationist societies. Public reaction and comment is a key feature in the adoption of the blue-print for "New Brentford" and the proposals were explained and illustrated in detail at a town's meeting of the local inhabitants.

Tower Hamlets. An ambitious scheme in the heart of London's dockland has been initiated by Tower Hamlets L.B.C. which will probably be the most important single contribution to the enormous housing problem in this area. It relates to complete redevelopment of the St. Katharine and London Dock area in association with the G.L.C. and the City Corporation. In July, 1968, the L.B.C. considered reports from its Town Planning and Housing (Building and Development) Committees. The L.B.C. approached the matter on the basis of the following sound planning principles:--

> (a) That St. Katharine Docks site, which lies immediately to the east of Tower Bridge and the Tower of London forms part of a larger area where major land use changes can be expected, and the development of St. Katharine Docks should, therefore, be regarded as the Western Gateway to the new "East End".
> (b) That it was recognised in the interests of a balanced community that some private development, whether by housing association or private developers, must be permitted.

Negotiations are proceeding with the P.L.A. for acquisition of the site and 75 per cent of the land allocated for residential use in London Docks will be under the control of Tower Hamlets L.B.C., whose urgent need is to have cleared sites available to rehouse families from the numerous sub-standard tenement blocks in the borough. The G.L.C. will allow private development in the 25 acres of the St. Katharine Dock area, whilst the L.B.C. will develop some 70 acres in the London Dock area. In the former area a yachting marina, hotel and private houses are to be constructed but there will be at least 300 council dwellings, to be divided between G.L.C. and Tower Hamlets. Thus an admirable scheme comprising a partnership between local government and private enterprise in under way. Emphasis in the London Dock area, under the direct control of the L.B.C., will be on urgent rehousing following slum clearance, bringing vast improvement to a historic locality.

L.B.C. Co-operation. The thirty-two L.B.C.s have adopted a common code for co-operation with and helping London charitable bodies. Homes and hostels inherited from the county councils are being sensibly shared pending complete provision by each L.B.C.

Following the eventual removal of Covent Garden Market to Battersea, it will be necessary to redevelop the site and a consortium has been formed by the G.L.C. and Camden and Westminster L.B.C.s.

London Transport The Transport (London) Act, 1969, imposes a general duty on the G.L.C. to develop policies and to encourage, organise and carry out measures to promote the provision of integrated, efficient and economic transport in Greater London. To this end the G.L.C. must prepare plans relating to transport in Greater London and send copies to the Minister after consultation with him, B.R.B., L.T.E. and affected local authorities.

The Act provides for the constitution of a London Transport Executive comprising a chairman appointed by the Council and not less than four nor more then ten other members appointed by the Council after consultation with the chairman. All members must be appointed from persons with wide experience and capacity in transport, industry, commerce or finance, administration, applied science or the organisation of workers. L.T.E. has power to pay its members salaries, fees and allowances to be determined by the G.L.C. Provision is also made for pension rights and compensation for loss of office. Powers are conferred directly on the L.T.E. to whom the undertaking of the L.T.B. is to be transferred.

The L.T.E., B.R.B. and National Bus Company must co-operate for the purpose of co-ordinating and providing effective passenger transport services. L.T.E. must promote and utilise research and the G.L.C. may give it directions on the exercise of such function. L.T.E. is given wide powers to carry passengers by road, rail and water; it must prepare an annual statement of audited accounts and an annual report to the G.L.C., copy to the Minister. G.L.C. has power to give general directions to the L.T.E. on financial matters, including estimates, proposals for substantial outlay on capital account and the general level and structure of fares (to be charged to bus and rail passengers), which must be published if G.L.C. so direct. Provision is made for consulation on fares between G.L.C. and local authorities, which must be informed in advance of any proposed change of substance. G.L.C. is empowered to review the L.T.E.'s organisation and to give relevant directions. G.L.C. must set up a users' consultative body.

The Act provides for notification by B.R.B. to G.L.C. of proposed railway closures and for a procedure enabling G.L.C. to protest to the Minister. The Act removes from the Transport Tribunal control over passenger fares in London. The transfer of responsibility to G.L.C. took place on 1st January 1970.

G.L.C. The G.L.C., in association with the L.B.C.s of Bexley and Greenwich, is studying a route for a new Thames tunnel linking north and south circular roads downstream from the Blackwall Tunnel. At the same time, a new town of 60,000 people is being planned for Erith Marshes to be call Thamesmead, by the G.L.C.s Thamesmead Committee. A strong form of development is envisaged, with higher density limbs embracing the lower density residential areas. The new town will be a "river orientated" community. The tunnel is one of the G.L.C.'s strategic road proposals and would benefit the new town by providing access to employment across the river in the London Boroughs of Barking and Newham. The development will probably be completed by 1980.

The City of London. The City of London Corporation, which is a body corporate by prescription or custom, remains unreformed and has done rather well out of the reorganisation, since it has acquired more functions. The Lord Mayor is Admiral of the Port of London and Lord Lieutenant of the City. The Court of Common Hall comprises the Lord Mayor, sheriffs, aldermen and freemen of the City. As the City of London is also technically a separate county, Common Hall enjoys the privilege of annually electing the two City sheriffs. It also nominates two senior alldermen for the election of one as Lord Mayor by the Court of Aldermen, which also elects the Recorder of the City of London. Aldermen of the City of London are elected for life and *ex officio* can sit alone as justices of the peace. Nowhere else in the country can lay justices sit alone.

The Court of Common Council is the real governing body of the City Corporation and comprises the Lord Mayor, twenty-six aldermen and 159 common councillors, who can perhaps best be described as "uncommon councillors". The Common Council controls the property of the Corporation and maintains Tower, London, Southwark, and Blackfriars Bridges over the Thames. In 1965 its Estates Committee approved a plan to renovate London Bridge[32] at a cost exceeding £2 million; this expenditure will be met from the Committee's funds and none of it will therefore be borne by the general taxpayer or ratepayer. The Common Council retains the functions formerly discharged in common with the metropolitan borough councils: housing, public health, highways, rating and libraries. In addition, it remains the port health authority for the Port of London as well as sanitary authority for the City. Under the new dispensation, the Common Council is responsible for child care, personal health and welfare services: and for non-metropolitan roads. This is because, under the 1963 Act, whilst the internal composition and structure of the City Corporation are untouched, it exercises all the functions of a L.B.C.

There is a close link between the City Corporation and the ancient City livery companies, such as the Mercers, the Haberdashers, the Brewers and the Apothecaries. Some of the liverymen of the City companies are also free of the City.[33] As Sir William Hart, the distinguished former Clerk of the G.L.C., says in his book,[34] the internal organisation of the Corporation "provides a clear illustration of the extent to which trading guilds in the Middle Ages had become identified with the local government of the towns in which they existed . . . The City Corporation remain a picturesque and honourable relic of a former state of society, and is important not so much because of its local government activities as of its charitable work, the positions of high dignity which it can offer its members and the honourable hospitality it can give to distinguished visitors from other countries."

The ancient traditions of the City Corporation are reflected to some extent in the titles of its chief officers. Whilst it has a town clerk (itself an appellation of no mean ancestry), there are also a City Solicitor and Controller, a City Chamberlain (who performs the office of a treasurer) and a City Remembrancer. Although the City Corporation is not a local education authority it maintains the City of London schools; and many of the numerous London voluntary aided schools furnish a working partnership between the City Companies, who provide the governing bodies and much of the cash required, and the local education authority.[35] All these schools are now located outside the City of London with one exception. The governors of voluntary aided schools receive a departmental grant of 80 per cent of their proportion of the cost of alterations and repairs. At the same time, the City Corporation keeps up to date, for example in its participation in the imaginative Barbican housing development scheme.

Special *ad hoc* authorities for London. We have already seen that the Home Secretary, acting through a Commissioner of Police, is the police authority in the Metropolitan Police District; and that there is a separate police force in the City of London, for which the City Corporation is responsible. These arrangements differ substantially from those obtaining in the rest of the country in respect of police forces. The Royal Commission did not examine police functions in Greater London, nor was the metropolitan administration of the police disturbed by the Police Act, 1964.

The Metropolitan Water Board was constituted under the Metropolis Water Act, 1902, to administer the supply and distribution of water in a large area of what is now Greater London.[36] The Board is a body corporate comprising a Chairman, a Vice-Chairman and representatives of all the local authorities in its area and of the Thames and Lea Conservancy Boards. The Metropolitan Water Board is a highly efficient undertaking and has even managed, on occasion, to *reduce* the water rate one or twice since the war. The necessary adjustments in its representation were made under the London Government Act, which had the effect of more than halving its membership. The Board includes among its chief officers a Chief Engineer, a Chief Executive, a Comptroller, a Solicitor and a Surveyor.

The Port of London Authority was created in 1909[37] and controls the Port of London, reaching to Teddington Lock up the river Thames. Its members are partly elected by users of the port and partly appointed by the Navy Defence Board, the Minister of Transport, Trinity House, the Greater London Council and the City Corporation. London River is controlled by the Conservators of the River Thames above Teddington Lock. The P.L.A. has its own police but there is also a river police division of the Metropolitan Police. The Thames-side Consultative Committee of officers conprises G.L.C. planning and highways officers, planning officers of the sixteen London Boroughs past which the Thames flows, representatives of the Thames Advisory Committee of the London Tourist Board, commerical interests, the P.L.A. and the Thames Conservancy. After consultation with the London Boroughs Committee, there was constituted a committee of three G.L.C. members and a representative from each of the sixteen riparian boroughs. The Thames-side Consultative Committee of officers reports to this Committee and its objects include preservation and improvement of the docks and riverside trade and of the amenities of the river.

We have already traced the descent of the London Transport Board from the London Passenger Transport Board *via* the London Transport Executive and back to full circle.

A Covent Garden Market Authority was established in 1962 and a Lea Valley Regional Park Authority has been constituted by statute.

Rent officers and Rent Assessment Committees. The Rent Act, 1965,[38] gave security of tenure to the tenants of all dwelling-houses with a value of £400 or less in Greater London.[39] In general, a landlord cannot evict a tenant without first obtaining an order from the local county court. These provisions are of great social significance and, following the disclosures in the Milner Holland Report, penalties are provided for harrassment of tenants. However, the security of tenure afforded by the Act does not greatly affect local government, which is indirectly concerned with the rent assessment provisions.

Rent officers and Rent Assessment Committees began to function in Greater London in January, 1966. The functions of the rent officers and Rent Assessment Committees relate solely to the regulation of fair rents of unfurnished accommodation in dwelling-houses with a rateable value of £400 or less.[40] All except personal circumstances are to be taken into account in determining fair rents; thus the age, character, locality and state of repair of a dwelling-house are all relevant. Scarcity value is to be disregarded, so that the number of persons seeking accommodation in a particular neighbourhood is to be ignored. The town clerks of the thirty-two L.B.C.s have carried out their statutory duty, cast upon them individually, to appoint rent officers, who cannot be dismissed without the consent of the Minister of Housing and Local Government. The Treasury pays the salaries of rent officers and the expenses of committee members. Thus, although rent officers were appointed by the town clerks, they are not local government officers. The rent officers are of a high calibre and some are former local government officers; their efficiency and integrity have been commended in Parliament.

Applications to rent officers fall into two categories:—
    (a) to fix a fair rent by means of registration;
    (b) to issue a certificate of fair rent.

Applications to fix a fair rent may be made by a landlord, by a tenant, or jointly. The certificate procedure is useful where conversion of an old house into flats or a new block of flats to let is envisaged. The rent officers have no power to inspect premises or to compel answers, since the essence of their work is informality.

An applicant must first go to the rent office and can then serve a notice of objection which the officer must forward to the Rent Assessment Committee. Committees have been appointed by the Minister from panels of lawyers, valuers and laymen; and chairman have been designated by the Lord Chancellor. There are at present three members of each committee, including a layman. Hearings are in public and parties can appear in person or be represented. The Rent officer must send a copy of his report to the committee. Rules of Procedure have been agreed with the Council on Tribunals. Rent Assessment Committee decisions are announced in public and if possible, on the day of the hearing. No appeal lies to the High Court on a point of law but decisions can be reviewed by *certiorari* or *mandamus* if an error of law or excess of jurisdiction is alleged.

The President visits the committees regularly in order to co-ordinate procedure and regular meetings are held of committee members, who are expected to serve anywhere in some twenty different places in Greater London. Each committee has a clerk who, like a clerk to the justices, must not retire with the members when they reach their decision. Rent officers and Rent Committees are completely independent of the Ministry of Housing and Local Government. There is no power to instruct Rent officers who must, however, take note of committee decisions. The President has asked the committees to give reasons for their decisions, which must be recorded in writing. This accords with the recommendations of the Franks Report and the subsequent legislative and administrative action. The first Rent Assessment Committee meetings were held in London in March, 1966. Mobile units of the Ministry have toured Greater London with leaflets, books and films with the object of publicising the rights of tenants and landlords under the Act.

It has been considered appropriate to describe this aspect of the operation of the Rent Act in Greater London at this juncture. It should be emphasised, however, that the new Rent Act applies to the country as a whole. Accordingly, rent officers and Rent Assessment Committees have now been appointed in other areas of the country, including Birmingham, Bristol, Manchester, Yorkshire, Scotland and Wales.

1. Based on ecclesiastical divisions.
2. As opposed to "open vestries".
3. In the same area of the old county of London which was subsequently administered by the L.C.C. from 1889 to 1965.
4. Renamed the London Fire Brigade in 1904.
5. Instead of a third, as elsewhere.
6. The main drainage area was larger than the old county.
7. Originally twelve (the I.L.E.A. now has ten education divisions).
8. The history and present position of the City of London Corporation are traced below (pp. 193-194).
9. Which are the responsibility of the Minister of Transport.
10. Now replaced by the London Boroughs Management Services Unit.
11. Now Lord Tangley.
12. Cmd. 1164.
13. Unlike the old counties of London and Middlesex, these counties still exist but are now smaller.
14. Lord Eccles (at the time Sir David Eccles).
15. London Government: the London Boroughs.
16. One for each parliamentary constituency in the area.
17. A chairman was elected in each case for the first year.
18. Formerly partly in Middlesex.
19. The "development plan" terminology is used in the following section as the G.L.C. development plan was in fact recently approved.
20. Town and Country Planning (Local Planning Authorities in Greater London) Regulations, 1965 (S.I. 1965, No. 679).
21. If the inconsistency is with the Greater London Plan.
22. If the inconsistency is with the Borough Plan.
23. The Town and Country Planning (Development Plans for Greater London) Regulations, 1966 (S.I. 1966, No.48).
24. The Greater London Council (Housing Powers) Order, 1965 (S.I. 1965, No. 835).
25. No. 22/65.
26. These now include roads classified as principal roads under the Local Government Act, 1966.
27. I.e. trunk roads and motorways.
28. The L.B.C.'s have concurrent powers.
29. London (Transport) Act 1969.

30. See Chapter XVIII.
31. See article by the author in Journal of Planning and Property Law, April, 1966.
32. The old London Bridge is now deep in the heart of Texas.
33. I.e. Freemen.
34. Local Government Law and Administration (*Butterworths,* 8th ed. at pp. 270).
35. For 60 years the L.C.C., now the I.L.E.A.
36. The area was larger than that of the old County of London.
37. Under the Port of London Authority Act, 1908.
38. Largely consolidated in the Rent Act, 1968.
39. And £200 or less elsewhere.
40. With certain limited exceptions.

CHAPTER XVI

REORGANISATION OF AREAS AND AUTHORITIES

Creation of Municipal Boroughs. An urban district council or rural district council may petition the Queen-in-Council for a charter of incorporation. It may seem strange that a rural district council should have these powers but it is possible, within a generation or two, for the character of an area to change. It is some seventy-five years since the great reforming local government legislation was enacted towards the end of the nineteenth century, and it is now regarded as having served its purpose. Why should a district council seek municipal borough status anyway? Designation as a municipal borough does not result in any accretion of functions[1] but it is largely a matter of status. A borough has a mayor instead of a chairman, aldermen as well as councillors, a town clerk instead of a clerk; above all, it has a Royal Charter. Moreover, there is always the possibility of going on to achieve county borough status and real independence in the local government context with the right to exercise all the functions of local government. Except as the result of a statutory review, it is not possible for the district council caterpillar to emerge as a county borough butterfly without passing through the chrysalis stage of a municipal or non-county borough.

The first step is for a resolution to be passed at a specially convened meeting of the district council. The resolution to present the petition must be confirmed at another special meeting at least a month later. The petition is referred to a Committee of the Privy Council and the promoting district council must give notice of it to the Minister of Housing and Local Government and to the county council. The Privy Council normally directs that Minister to hold a local inquiry and the inspector must investigate the statements contained in the petition. He must report upon such matters as the character of the district, the condition and expenses of its local government and the possible advantage or disadvantage that might accrue from the establishment of municipal government.

The Privy Council Committee will consider the inspector's report and any representations from the Minister and the county council and may have regard to historical traditions. The Committee advertises in the *London Gazette* the time when it will consider the petition and, if it is favourably impressed, will then require submission of a draft charter and draft scheme. The draft charter provides for the number of electoral wards and councillors, the date of the first meeting of the new council; the election of aldermen; and the dates of retirement of the mayor, aldermen and councillors. The draft charter is sent to the Privy Council, which forwards it to the Ministry of Housing and Local Government and other interested government departments such as the Home Office. Any modifications suggested by the Ministries are notified to the petitioners. The draft scheme deals with administrative matters such as dissolution of the district council, bye-laws, transfer of property and compensation of officers. After its submission, the Committee inserts a notice in the *London Gazette* and in the local press stating where the draft scheme can be inspected, and that representations may be received within a month. The draft is then sent to the government departments.

After taking account of any objections, the Committee settles the scheme and again publishes press notices as to inspection. A petition may object to the scheme but if none are received or if those lodged are withdrawn, the scheme is submitted for confirmation by Order-in-Council. But if a public body or a twentieth of the local government electors petition against the scheme within a month of publication of the notice, confirmation by Parliament is necessary. The Privy Council Committee may alter the scheme before introduction of the Confirmation Bill. Petitioners may oppose the Bill in Select Committee in either House, since it is treated as a local Bill.

It is in this way that a new borough may be created by the Crown, on the advice of the Privy Council, by the grant of a Charter incorporating the inhabitants of the area. The new corporate body comprises the inhabitants at large, usually depicted in the Charter as the Mayor, aldermen and burgesses of the borough. Although this procedure has been little used in recent years, it is still available to urban district and rural district councils, despite the recent upheavals in local government reorganisation to which we shall shortly turn.

Alterations Possible under the 1933 Act. The electoral areas in counties are called electoral divisions, each returning one member. The Home Secretary can alter divisional boundaries and the numbers of divisions and councillors in counties, at the instance of a county council or of a district council. If a district council petitions the Home Secretary on such matters he has a discretionary power to hold a local inquiry. Representations will first have been made by the aggrieved district council, which must issue a press notice and send copies to the county council and to other district councils in the administrative county. Certain criteria must be observed in the constitution of electoral divisions. Thus the populations of each division should be approximately equal, due regard being paid to area, a proper representation of both urban and rural population, their distribution and pursuits, and the last published census and evidence of any considerable change since then.

Certain changes in the organisation of boroughs may be effected by Order-in-Council, for example, division of the borough into wards, alteration of ward boundaries, increase or decrease in the number of borough councillors. Such alterations may necessitate ordering a fresh election.[2] Again, the procedure is initiated by petition to the Privy Council preceded by a resolution of the borough council and notice in the local press. An Order-in-Council can be made without any preliminaries to divide a borough into wards; this is rare nowadays, as small boroughs are fast disappearing. In all other cases, the petition is referred to the Home Secretary, who appoints a commission to hold local inquiries and to prepare a scheme. The Privy Council approves, modifies or rejects the scheme; if approved, it is publicised in the usual way.

The county council is responsible for dividing urban districts into wards, altering the number and boundaries of such wards, and altering the number of councillors. The county council has a discretionary power to hold a local inquiry and if it does so must give notice in the local press and to the usual government departments. The county council may then prepare a draft order and confirm it six weeks later: during this period representations may be made. An aggrieved urban district council may move the Home Secretary to make an order after hearing the county council's case against it where the district has taken the initiative.

The county council has even wider powers in the rural districts, where the electoral area is usually based on the rural parish.[3] A county council may by order fix or alter the number of councillors to be elected in each case, may divide a parish into wards, may determine the number of councillors for each ward, may alter ward boundaries and may combine parishes for electoral purposes.

The 1933 Act also contains provisions for individual alterations of areas which are still at present available. The areas of counties may be changed by altering their boundaries, by uniting one county with another or by dividing a county into two or more separate counties. The areas of county boroughs may be changed by altering their boundaries, by uniting a county borough with another or with a non-county borough or by including an urban district within a county borough. In both cases the local authority must make a proposal to the Minister, who may unite a county with a county borough. There are the usual provisions for the giving of public notice and the holding of local public inquiries.

In the case of county districts, a new non-county borough can be created only by amalgamation of an existing one with one or more county districts.[4] A new urban or rural district may be created by amalgamation of existing units. There is no power to abolish a borough under the 1933 Act, which does, however, enable an urban district or rural district to be liquidated. The county council has a discretionary power to hold a local inquiry and there is provision for advertisement of the draft order and presentation of petitions to the Minister, who may confirm modify or reject the order after a public local inquiry if a petition of objection has been lodged. Otherwise, the county council or a county district council may demand an inquiry and the latter authority, if the county council is inactive, can seek to move the Minister to make an order by making representations to him. A county council may make an order for submission to the Minister providing for alteration of parish boundaries, abolition of parishes or constitution of new parishes.

The Local Government Act, 1958. This important statute recast local government finance, as we have seen, and made new provisions for the alteration of areas. Although its provisions have been overtaken by events, it is necessary to give a brief account of its provisions on areas in order to try and understand the present position. The Act provided for a review of the organisation of local government in England and Wales, excluding the metropolitan area,[5] by two Local Government Commissions, one for England and one for Wales. Five special review areas were constituted for the large conurbations outside Greater London, itself the largest conurbation of them all. Conurbations are large areas of more or less continuous urban development, containing a substantial number of local authorities. This does not mean that no blade of grass is visible in a conurbation but, on the other hand, areas of outstanding natural beauty are unlikely to be found in one. The five conurbations outside Greater London are Merseyside, South-East Lancashire, Tyneside, the West Midlands and West Yorkshire.

In areas of both general and special review the Local Government Commission could recommend the alteration of the area of a county or county borough, the constitution or abolition of a county or county borough and the conversion of a county borough into a non-county borough. This latter power was considered by county boroughs to be a fate worse than death and loud were the protests at such threats during the seven-and-a-half years of the Commission's existence. In areas of special review the Commission could make certain other recommendations on the organisation of county districts; it could suggest the creation of a continuous county, that is, a county with no county boroughs situated within its borders, in which case it could propose a redistribution of functions. Little advantage was taken of this radical departure, however. In fact, the Commissions could not recommend the creation of any new class or type of local authority. Their functions were limited to juggling with pre-existing authorities most of which were created in 1888 or in 1894 and it was not surprising that by 1966 they had so many balls of different colours in the air that the Minister decided to start again from scratch.

The Commissions had a general duty of consultation with local, public and voluntary bodies. The 1958 Act laid down an elaborate procedure for preparation and formulation of proposals, conferences with local authorities, public notices, public inspection, public inquiries and so forth. Eventually the Minister of Housing and Local Government, if he had the strength and patience, could make an order[6] giving effect to or modifying the proposals. His modifications could convert one or more non-county boroughs or urban districts into a county borough, or extend the area of a county borough, provided that the local authorities concerned had sought the change and the matter was in issue at the public inquiry.

Prior to 1958 there had been much discussion on the correct minimum population for a county borough. 125,000 was the favourite at one time but Parliament finally settled on 100,000. The Act provided, somewhat curiously, that a population of 100,000 should be sufficient to constitute a presumption that a local authority could discharge the functions of a county borough council. The 1958 Act fixed a population bar of 100,000 for the promotion of a local Bill for county borough status. This could not in any event be done until 1973, nor could a local Bill be promoted to create or alter the status of any local authority before that date. Under the doctrine of the sovereignty of Parliament, a later Parliament need not be bound by this provision.

Finally, the Act enabled county councils to undertake limited "County reviews". With one exception, these were limited to juggling with their county districts and parishes. However, they could also recommend the inclusion of a small non-county borough in the surrounding rural district to form a rural borough. A rural borough council has only the functions of a parish council. It retains its Mayor, Charter, town clerk and mace, but its aldermen disappear. The Minister was empowered to fix the number of councillors between a range of five and twenty-one; as in the case of parish councils, casual vacancies are filled by co-option. The county reviews were to start after the Commissions had reviewed an area—but in fact only three[7] got off the mark. There were the usual provisions for consultation, public notice, public inquiry and, eventually, ministerial order. It is noteworthy that the rural borough council was the only new local government unit postulated by the 1958 Act; it was invented to deal with the small, ancient, non-county borough which was no longer really an urban area.[8]

The Royal Commissions and actions taken under the 1958 Act. The membership and terms of reference of the Royal Commissions on Local Government in England and Scotland were announced in May, 1966. Sir John Maud, Chairman of the Committee on Management in Local Government, was the Chairman of the English Commission. The Chairman of the Scottish Commission was Lord Wheatley, a former Solicitor-General and Lord Advocate; and this Commission included three Members of Parliament.

The terms of reference of the English Commission were:—

"To consider the structure of Local Government in England, outside Greater London, in relation to its existing functions; and to make recommendations for authorities and boundaries, and for functions and their division, having regard to the size and character of areas in which these can be most effectively exercised and the need to sustain a viable system of local democracy."

The terms of reference of the Scottish Commission were similar. Research units were made available and the Commissions considered such matters as regionalism and local government finance.

Some orders had been made under the 1958 Act by Conservative Ministers of Housing and Local Government. For example, orders were made designating Luton and Ilford as county boroughs; whilst the former county boroughs of Worcester and Burton-on-Trent lost this status and were demoted to non-county boroughs because their populations were well below 100,000. On the other hand, the Commission's proposal to merge Rutland, the smallest county, with Leicestershire was fought locally "to the last rut" and the then Minister of Housing and Local Government, Sir Keith Joseph, declined to make the necessary order. The Commission's recommendation to merge into one large administrative county the fen counties of Cambridgeshire, Huntingdonshire, the Isle of Ely and the Soke of Peterborough was also not implemented by the Conservative Government.

The Minister did, however, create two new counties out of the four, but the city of Cambridge failed to stake its claim successfully to county borough status, despite its population of some 90,000 and its separate police force.[9] The reason is thought to be that the new county of Cambridgeshire and Ely would not have been a viable unit if it had sustained an initial loss of so much rateable value. The better solution might have been to amalgamate the four county units and grant county borough status to Cambridge. Similar reasons prevented the creation of new county boroughs in Middlesex for many years before the appointment of the Royal Commission of Greater London.

The West Midlands Order, 1965,[10] largely implemented the Commission's recommendations by an extension of the county borough system to that area. Thus the order extended the areas of the county boroughs of Dudley, Walsall, West Bromwich and Wolverhampton, created a new county borough of Warley and abolished the county borough of Smethwick.

As a result of the Minister's approval of the Shropshire county review, the small town of Much Wenlock became in April, 1966, the first rural borough. The town received its Charter, which it will retain, in 1468 and is now included in the rural district of Bridgnorth; its population is fifteen thousand. It will also retain its mayor and town clerk but its functions will be those of a parish council. The Local Government (Termination of Review) Act, 1967, finally wound up the Commission.

Scotland. In 1963 a Steering Committee of members and a working party of officials was set up to consider the structure of Scottish local government following publication of a White Paper, which suggested a minimum population of forty thousand for the smaller authorities. A report was published the following year suggesting a two-tier system. Scottish county councils administer most functions in the landward or rural areas, with some delegation to district councils; they also exercise some functions on behalf of the burghs. The four large cities are the equivalent of English county boroughs and therefore exercise all local government functions. The larger burghs administer most functions except education and valuation for rating. County councils and the councils of both large and small burghs are responsible for housing, rate collection, general sanitation, sewage, refuse disposal and aspects of street lighting. District councils, in addition to any matters delegated to them by county councils, administer as of right certain minor functions. The latter include provision of allotments, cattle grids, bus shelters, caravan sites, entertainment and the encouragement of social and physical recreation. There are thus 430 local authorities with executive powers; councils of cities, large and small burghs, county councils and district councils.

The Royal Commission on Local Government in Scotland reported in September, 1969 (the Wheatley Report). It recommended the establishment of a two tier structure with seven regional and 37 district authorities. Regional authorities should be responsible for major planning, industrial development, roads, water, sewerage, personal social services including education, housing, police, fire, civil defence and refuse disposal. The seven strong regional authorities could also administer new services, including the N.H.S., if necessary. The functions of the district authorities would include local planning and assistance to industry, housing improvement, environmental health, libraries, museums and art galleries.

The Wheatley Report is opposed to the transfer of education to central government and recommends that local authorities should raise a larger proportion of the cost by means of rates. Control of local education authorities by the Secretary of State should be examined and simplified. The Report opts for a two-tier system as more flexible than the rigid unitary system of all purpose authorities postulated by Redcliffe Maud. It also proposes that substantial salaries should be paid to the ordinary councillor, with special allowances for those with added responsibilities; devolution and delegation are also advocated. A two-tier system for Scotland would be wholly admirable, as are the Report's proposals on education and on payment of councillors. Finally, the Commission state that community councils might be provided at the most local level.

Wales. The local government system in Wales is based on the same pattern of authorities as in England. The Local Government Commission for Wales recommended the reduction of the thirteen Welsh counties to seven,[11] but the then Minister of Housing and Local Government, after pondering the report, decided to let well alone and to make no order, retaining the thirteen counties. There were no special review areas for conurbations in Wales so that the entire principality could be examined as a whole. Recent Conservative Prime Ministers have designated a leading member of the Cabinet as Minister for Welsh Affairs, usually the Home Secretary or the Minister of Housing and Local Government. The Labour Government formed in 1964 included a Secretary of State for Wales who had produced a White Paper on local government reorganisation in Wales.

The Welsh White Paper, published in 1967, proposed the retention of the two-tier system but the creation of a regional authority and five counties. The Secretary of State has announced that there will be six Welsh counties[12] instead of thirteen and three county boroughs instead of four. District Councils are to be amalgamated within the existing structure. Joint police authorities will continue and the new county councils will have the usual county functions. Following pressure from the local authority associations the Secretary of State appears to have agreed that district councils will be the rating authorities, not the county councils as originally proposed. A Welsh Council has been appointed by the Secretary of State, with advisory functions; it formulates development proposals and encourages local authority co-operation. Pressure is mounting for this Council to be directly elected and to have wider powers.

A very thorough survey of Welsh housing has been undertaken by the Department and local authorities will have wider powers following the Housing Act, 1969. A Welsh Staff Commission is to be set up under legislation. Professor Ivor Gowan thinks that the Welsh Council should administer education, planning, main roads, police, fire and water supply. The Welsh Office now has a new division dealing with reorganisation.

Legislation is expected in the next session of Parliament, in which case elections for the new authorities would take place in 1971 with a probable vesting date in 1972. These dates are the earliest possible and they may be considerably delayed in case of a general election or for other extraneous reasons. It is thought that legislation on Wales may be affected by the Maud Report.

The Future Pattern. What, then, is the future pattern of local government in Britain?

Undoubtedly the modern trend is towards larger authorities, in the search for viability and efficiency. A broad division can be made, so that impersonal services which need planning over a wide area are discharged by very large authorities, whilst the personal services remain the responsibility of smaller authorities. However, the problem is not as simple as that, because some functions contain both elements and there are different requirements for urban and for rural areas.

To take the conurbations first, the so-called areas of special review under the 1958 Act, it may well be that London has set the pace for the rest of the country, as befits the capital city. The alternatives appear to be a large continuous county with broad responsibility for police, town and country planning, highways and traffic management, main drainage, refuse disposal, ambulances and civil defence; or much larger county boroughs responsible for all services: it should be borne in mind that the City of Birmingham, with a population of over a million, is a county borough.

Within the continuous county there should also be ''most-purpose' authorities administering the personal services of education, libraries, child care, health, welfare and housing. These would be municipal corporations upon which the continuous county would precept for a rate. If Greater London is to be taken as a guide, the continuous county could have a population range of up to ten millions. The average population of a London Borough is about 250,000 and this might be taken as the criterion for the second-tier authorities. If this solution is preferred to an extension of the county borough system, it would have the advantage that all boroughs could have the same status. Using the pattern of the London Government Act they would all be statutory and, where necessary, new charters of incorporation could be granted by the Crown. Some aspects of planning could be discharged by the borough councils, which would continue to be public health authorities. It should be recalled that for more than twenty years many district councils with populations of 60,000 or more have been exercising delegated planning functions, in some cases quite successfully; granted that they should be larger, a borough council of the size envisaged could quite competently deal with most planning applications lodged in its area.

Outside the conurbations the county council system could probably continue as the basis of rural local government. Larger counties would have to be created. It would possibly no longer be necessary for Suffolk and Sussex to be divided, whilst a county of the size of Rutland could hardly survive in the modern era, despite the brave fight it put up.

On the second tier of the county system the existing plethora of authorities could surely be simplified and streamlined. There would be no necessity for non-county boroughs and rural boroughs, since the former could be absorbed into districts (together with the urban and rural districts) and the latter could be recognised as parish councils, which they really are. Cognizance should naturally be taken of local variations but a rough population guide could be 500,000 for counties, 100,000 for districts and 1,000 for parishes.

The structure of local government which emerged in late Victorian England has hardly been tampered with in the twentieth century. On the other hand, Parliament has loaded the archaic structure with function upon function so that it is in danger of breaking down in the jet and computer age.

Nevertheless, it is fitting to pay tribute to the members and officers of local authorities up and down the country who, in spite of enormous difficulties which are not of their making, have some tremendous achievements to their credit. Leading examples of municipal enterprise are the Birmingham Municipal Bank and the local telephone service operated by the Kingston-upon-Hull Corporation.[13] Many local authorities have played a leading part in the promotion of new universities, the key men having frequently been their town clerks or clerks.

Nor should it be forgotten that local government is an inherent part of the British system of free elections. With the advent of regional government, it is vital that local authorities should continue to represent the people on a elective basis. The problems of size, efficiency and contact with the electorate do not all lead to the same solutions. It is important that local authorities administering the personal services should not be too remote from the people; at the same time they should not be too small to be effective. There is a case for the retention of rural parishes in the counties; and there is a school of thought which advocates the creation, or re-emergence, of urban parishes.

Many other problems remain, apart from those connected with organisation and structure. Perhaps Parliament could at last be persuaded to abolish the aldermanic system and to pay councillors a realistic salary. Tradition dies hard in this country. It is only comparatively recently that the concept of the professional paid politician has been accepted at Westminster.

Payment of councillors would probably attract younger people to become candidates at local elections. Much is said and written today about the declining quality of councillors. There may be an element of truth in this, but the real problem is that membership of local authorities is too often confined to retired persons, housewives and those with private means, a rapidly dwindling class of the community. They may be, and often are, excellent people but they are hardly representative of the whole range of the population. Except in London and in some of the larger cities, the officers alone provide professional expertise.

A careful but radical reform of local government could result in a first class service. On the whole, local government has served this country well and new forms of organisation and machinery would enable it to continue to do so.

The present system of local government will probably remain with us at least until 1975, so that it is thought that students may find the accompanying simple diagrams useful.

COUNTY SYSTEM

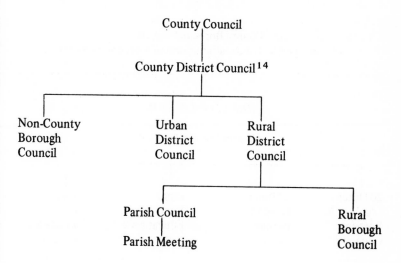

County Council

County District Council [14]

Non-County Borough Council

Urban District Council

Rural District Council

Parish Council

Parish Meeting

Rural Borough Council

UNITARY SYSTEM

County Borough Council
(An independent, autonomous unit of local government)

GREATER LONDON

Greater London Council

20 Outer London Borough Councils[1][5]	12 Inner London Borough Councils	Inner London Education Authority	City Of London Corporation

---

1. Except that, in the case of a rural district council, highway functions might be acquired for the first time.
2. This is the reason for occasional local elections being held "out of season".
3. Or a combination of parishes or the ward of a parish.
4. Apart from the method of incorporation by Royal Charter.
5. Owing to the existence of the Royal Commission on Local Government in Greater London, 1957–60.
6. Which had to be laid before Parliament with the Commission's report.
7. Shropshire, Cornwall and Worcestershire.
8. E.g. Tenterden, Kent.
9. Still retained initially by the Police Act, 1964, as in the case of Peterborough.
10. S.I. 1965 No. 2139.
11. The initial proposal was that there should be five.
12. Gwyned, Clwyd, Cardiganshire, Pembrokeshire, Glamorgan, Gwent.
13. Operated at much lower cost than that of the G.P.O.
14. N.B. This is a generic name for non-county borough, urban, and rural district councils.
15. Local education authorities.

CHAPTER XVII

REPORT OF THE ROYAL COMMISSION ON LOCAL GOVERNMENT IN ENGLAND, JUNE, 1969

The famous Redcliffe–Maud Report, for which the local government world waited with bated breath for so long (or did it?) appeared at last in June, 1969, some fifteen months behind schedule. At least it rejected the clamour of government departments for city regions but it was not unanimous and Mr. Senior produced a voluminous dissenting report of his own.

The main recommendation of the majority Report is that England (outside Greater London) should be divided into 61 new local government areas. In 58 of these areas a single unitary authority should be responsible for all services. They would therefore be analagous to existing county boroughs on a functional basis, although much larger in area. Many of the existing county areas would survive on this basis, although some would be divided and some, like Rutland, would disappear.

In the three very large metropolitan areas around the Birmingham, Liverpool and Manchester conurbations responsibility for local government services should be divided between a main metropolitan authority and several metropolitan district authorities (do we here discern the marriage of Herbert and Maud, with nuptial celebrations under the Greenwood tree?) The key functions of the main authorities would be planning, transportation and major development, whilst the districts (seven in Birmingham, four in Liverpool, nine in Manchester) would administer education, personal social services, health and housing. Terminology might be important: I would suggest Greater Birmingham Council, Birmingham Borough Councils, etc. on the London pattern. It is good to see that, at least in these areas, the personal services including education have been included in the second-tier.

Local Councils should be constituted within the 58 unitary areas and wherever they are needed in the metropolitan areas. They would succeed existing county boroughs, borough, urban and rural district and parish councils and their aim should be to represent and communicate the wishes of cities, towns and villages. Their only duty would be to represent local opinion but they would have the right to be consulted on matters of local interest. They will have powers to spend money for the benefit of their inhabitants on such items as village greens, parks, fairs, community centres, concert halls and theatres. In unitary areas it is envisaged that they should participate in such matters as house building and improvement, planning and highways. This would seem to be essential as otherwise the Lord Mayor of Bristol, for example, would hardly relish having merely the powers of a parish council chairman. Such participation, it is suggested, could be achieved in the housing field by unitary authorities inviting local councils to appoint committees to work with their area officers. In case of disagreement, of course, the unitary council prevails. Building, renovation, conservation and preservation of housing on a small scale could also be the function of local councils. They should also have the power to nominate for school governing and managing bodies and for house committees for old peoples s and children's homes. This is all very well but, as the Report emphasises, the only *duty* of local councils will be to voice local opinion. How will councillors of calibre emerge in these circumstances?

The whole of England, including Greater London, should be grouped into eight Provinces, each with a provincial council elected by the unitary and metropolitan authorities with provision for co-opted members. Their key function would be to settle the provincial strategy and planning framework. They would replace the present regional economic planning boards, whose demise would hardly be a great loss, and "collaborate with the central government in the economic and social development of each province". The provincial councils, unlike the unitary, metropolitan and local councils would not be directly elected by the people and this is to be deplored. They would be regional planning boards writ large and they would not appear to have any greater potential for effectiveness.

Mr. Derek Senior in his memorandum of Dissent (Volume II of the Report) postulates 35 directly elected regional authorities responsible for planning, highways, water supply, sewerage, refuse disposal, etc; and 148 directly elected districts responsible for personal social services, housing management, consumer protection, etc. In four areas the same authority would exercise both regional and district responsibilities. Mr. Senior recommends delegation of personal and local aspects of a regional authority's functions to district officers; and concentration of responsibility for the wider aspects of district functions in a joint organisation of districts. His two levels of administrative local government would be complemented by directly elected common councils at "grass roots" level representing existing parishes and small towns; and by five appointed provincial councils nominated by the regions.

Mr. Senior's common councils would be similar to the local councils adumbrated by the majority report. Again, he says that the provincial councils would be responsible for long term strategic planning. He recommends that the district councils should be financed by rate revenues and urges examination of the possibility of transferring motor taxation to regional authorities. If that is not feasible, he goes on to make the debatable suggestion that the whole of the education service should be taken out of local government. Mr. Senior also recommends that local government should cease to administer advanced higher education and national parks but that it should acquire responsibility for all branches of the health service, all roads other than national motorways, the management through executives (presumably on the model of the London Transport and Passenger Transport Executives) of all ports and airports outside the London Metropolitan Region and for the discharge of all functions of river authorities subject to national direction of water conservation policy.

Taking Maud and Senior together (Senior is, I suppose, Maud Senior or Junior) their most unpopular proposition seems to be that for the consitution of provincial councils. In neither scheme would they be elected nor would they have any executive powers. They would not be local government, they would not constitute a proper devolution of power with provincial Prime Ministers as postulated by Macintosh, they would not even be effective or viable agents of the central government (even if that was considered desirable).

The regional economic planning boards and councils already established have not been a startling success, to say the least. The Maud Provincial Councils would be mainly responsible for producing strategic plans for their areas. If established, they would encourage an English nationalism to develop on the Scottish and Welsh patterns.

Turning to the next tier, or the first tier proper on the local government scale, the Majority Report's proposals are the more attractive; Mr. Senior's regions would be too large and too remote from the people. On the other hand, his arrangements for the second tier are more attractive. It is indeed a trifle odd that Maud postulates unitary authorities everywhere except in the four conurbations since, outside the very large cities, the divided system of local government is so well entrenched. The Greater London reorganisation has worked well and it is logical that this pattern should be extended to Birmingham Liverpool and Manchester. Perhaps Newcastle-on-Tyne and its environs should also be added to the list of metropolitan authorities; this presumably would have been the view of at least one leading member of the Royal Commission. If a solution is right is should be imposed and any necessary unscrambling should be undertaken. In the North an enlarged county borough of Tees-side was recently created, one of the last major reconstructions under the 1958 legislation.

Turning to the local or common councils the Royal Commission have gallantly attempted to provide something for the smaller, local communities but they have failed. For this reason, Mr. Senior's second tier is to be preferred because his common councils will be confined to very small towns and parishes and the services and duties allocated to them on such a basis are just about right. If the Majority Report is implemented, with nothing between the unitary and local councils (except in the four large cities), many historic chartered towns and cities will be reduced virtually to the status of parish councils. Nor is this merely a matter of sentiment. The local personal services, including and especially including education, should be administered on as local a level as possible commensurate with viability and efficiency. Here Mr. Senior scores with his 148 directly elected district authorities although it can be argued that the number should be greater, say 200 although there is no magic in a particular number, as Professor Robson has observed in another connection. The important proviso is that his personal social services should include education. Primary and secondary education should in no circumstances be transferred to the tender mercies of the central government. There is a case for transfer of advanced higher education, the former colleges of advanced technology having graduated from technical colleges under local control to autonomous technological universities. The U.G.C. has improved its position in this regard since it now negotiates with the milder D.E.S. rather than with the more rapacious Treasury.

Finally, what are the prospects for implementation of the Maud Report, in whole or in part, Maud or Senior? The Prime Minister has announced in the Commons that the government accepts the report in principle. Virtually no alterations in the boundaries of parliamentary constituencies are to be made outside Greater London until local government in the rest of England and Wales has been reorganised on the basis of the Maud Report. That is the Labour Government's intention, although the Conservative Opposition alleges that the motive is to delay alteration in the boundaries because such delay would give electoral benefit to the party in power. Consultations between the Secretary of State and the local authority associations and other interested parties are due to be completed by the end of October, 1969. They will be followed in due course by the publication of a White Paper and, subsequently, a Local Government Reform Bill. It may be that the legislation will be available for comment and instruction when the third or fourth edition of this book needs to be prepared.

The Skeffington Report. The Skeffington Report on "People and Planning" was published in July, 1969, as an illustrated booklet. It has been welcomed by the Minister of Housing and Local Government and by the Secretaries of State for Scotland and Wales. Copies have been sent to all local planning authorities and joint planning boards.

The Report's three main recommendations are:

   (i) Local planning authorities should use all the mass communications media to keep people continuously informed of their intentions

   (ii) Local organisations should be encouraged to create forums to

act as testing grounds for planning proposals
(iii)Community development officers should be appointed to keep in touch with local opinion.

The Committee felt that proper publicity was vital and that therefore the local press should be encouraged to report and comment on planning matters. The national press might take an interest in structure plans under the 1968 Act, especially if groups of adjacent authorities collaborated to produce relevant proposals. The local authority member should lead a team of officers in visits to his ward. Planning officers should be in touch with the public through local groups, canvassing opinion before going to committee. Thus the secrecy hitherto attaching to committee reports would disappear.

The Report makes many other proposals, including greater use of local broadcasting and the need for residents to be given a greater voice in traffic plans required from local authorities by the Minister of Transport. There is considerable overlap between highways and planning functions but it is probably true to say that localities can become more incensed over new roads proposals than on any other single matter. So-called traffic engineering can engender a desperate feeling of bureaucracy rampant, riding roughshod over the rights of local citizens, including their children and elderly relatives. Urban and rural areas suffer alike in this respect, unfashionable as it is to attempt to distinguish between town and country nowadays. The march of progress is such that traffic experts now allege that pedestrian crossings are no longer safe.

Finally, the Report urges planning and education officers to ensure that school children understand the rudiments of planning. The subject should be included in the liberal studies of technical colleges which should provide courses for adults. The Ministries involved should produce information in the shape of booklets and pamphlets. The Report should also be of considerable interest to the Minister without Portfolio responsible, *inter alia* for encouragement of the participation of the individual in the decision-making processes of democracy. The Report has to some extent been anticipated by the Town and Country Planning Act, 1968, which enshrines the principle of early participation in planning matters in the law.

CHAPTER XVIII

PERSONNEL POLICY

The Civil Service. The Civil Service Commission was established in 1855 and the principle of entry by open competitive examination dates back to 1870. The Commissioners are appointed by the Queen-in-Council and are completely independent of political control. Following publication of the Fulton Report, a new Civil Service Department was created in 1968. Management of the Civil Service, pay, conditions of service and approval of competition regulations were transferred to the Minister for the Civil Service (the Prime Minister). The Lord Privy Seal assists in the day to day running of the Department and the Paymaster General[1] is also concerned with it. Thus the management of the Civil Service has been separated from the Treasury and has been brought under the direct control of the Prime Minister, who is of course, First Lord of the Treasury. The functions of the new Department comprise:—

(a) Personnel Management, including selection, recruitment, training, promotion, welfare and security.

(b) Development of managerial skills, general oversight of departments and machinery of government, working conditions, common services (O. and M., computers, O.R.).

(c) Supervision of departmental administrative expenditure and manpower requirements.

(d) Control of rates of pay, expenses, allowances and co-ordination of government pay policy in the public services.

(e) Superannuation policy and pensions.

Before we leave the organisation of the Department and turn to recruitment, let us note that it now comprises two machinery of Government Divisions, a Management Services (Department) Division, a Recruitment Planning Division, four Personnel Management Divisions, an expenditure and manpower Division, a Pay Division and an expanded Education and Training Division.

The Civil Service Commissioners have been integrated with the Department and the First Commissioner is now also Deputy Secretary of the Department. He is responsible for recruitment policy as well as actual recruitment and a new post of Second Civil Service Commissioner has been created. The Department itself is staffed by a combination of permanent cadre and staff on loan, including specialists.

The Civil Service Commissioners derive their independence from the Civil Service Order in Council 1956 and are appointed by Order-in-Council. This procedure continues in the post-Fulton era so that the selection of recruits is independent of any form of Ministerial control. The Civil Service Order in Council 1964 requires the Civil Service Selection Board to select personnel for permanent posts in the Home Civil Service and the Diplomatic Service.

A new Civil Service College is to be established in 1970 and the Department envisages a residential centre in London developed initially around the existing training centres at Regent's Park; and two residential centres, one of which is at the old Civil Defence College at Sunningdale. The best non-specialist graduates and of the 18 year old intake should receive a year's training, including management. (The establishment of a "training" or "cadet" grade for graduate entrants is being considered). The remainder would have specialised courses in O. and M., A.D.P. and Middle Management; some specialists would also attend the latter courses. Use will be made of external courses at universities and business schools; there will be a senior "Staff College" course for top management. The Centre for Administrative Studies will provide a five month course on economic and Social administration followed by specialised shorter courses. Vast increases in management courses at all levels are planned.

The Department's responsibilities for central personnel management connote the use of central management committees for professional groups. Thus the Management Committee for Lawyers was considered the best method of organising the legal work of the Service and the career management of legal staff. Fulton proposals about greater specialisation of Administrative and Executive staff are being considered in the light of the recommendation of a broad division between social administrators and financial, economic and industrial administrators. The aim will be to move administrative staff less frequently.

There is normally an annual examination of about 90,000 candidates for 20–30,000 posts. There are many small specialised classes for which open competitions must be held, and in an average year more than 300 competitions will be held. There used to be two methods of selection for the Administrative Class, the Diplomatic Service and Special Departmental Classes.[2] Under Method I there was a qualifying examination followed by interviews and written examination in academic subjects at honours degree level. Method II requires candidates to obtain a degree or diploma in technology with first or second-class honours: they then sit a qualifying examination, after which they may be selected for group tests and interviews at the Civil Service Selection Board and subsequently for interviews at the Final Selection Board. At least half the Administrative Class vacancies and about three-quarters of the Diplomatic Service vacancies were normally filled by Method II. First-class honours graduates were exempt from the qualifying examination under Method I and may be exempt from the examination in academic subjects under Method II. The age limits for the competition are at least 20 and under 28[3] on a prescribed date. The Commission does not set the papers or mark scripts, but utilises the service of outside examiners drawn from universities and schools. Members of interview boards are drawn from retired civil servants, the professional classes, academics, industrialists, trade unionists and others. Following a recommendation of the Fulton Report, Method I will be discontinued in 1970. Method II will thus be the sole process for Administrative Grade Selection. The general rules and regulations governing the conduct of competitions and the conditions for issuing certificates of qualification are made by the Commissioners who are then solely responsible for declaring which candidates are successful in the various competitions.

The Fulton Report recommendations that classes within the Civil Service should be abolished and that there should be a unified grading structure have been accepted by the Government but implementation of these reforms will take some time.

In its booklet, *Civil Service Posts for Graduates*[4] the Civil Service Commission make three broad divisions:—

1. The General Classes

    (a) The Administrative Class, which is concerned with policy, organisation and management (3,625 members[5]).

    (b) The Executive Class, which is concerned with detailed organisation and control and provides most of the highly trained semi-professional staff, such as auditors (84,000 members).

    (c) The Clerical Class, which deals with general clerical duties such as routine correspondence (136,000 members).

    (d) Miscellaneous general classes, including typists, machine operators, filing clerks and messengers (130,000 members).

2. The Professional, Scientific and Technical Classes

These include architects, doctors, engineers, lawyers, accountants, chief scientific advisers, physicists, chemists, biologists and laboratory assistants. Each class has its own structure and career prospects are not limited to the posts available in a single department.

3. Departmental Classes

These include Inspectors of Taxes, Economists and Statisticians, whose recruitment is on the same basis as that of the Administrative Class. They also include the National Agricultural Advisory Service of the Ministry of Agriculture; the Forest Officers of the Forestry Commission; and the small Home Office inspectorate appointed under the Cruelty to Animals Acts, which is in urgent need of expansion.

Except for a few small departments which are entirely staffed by specialists[6] the control, organisation and management of Civil Servants is the responsibility of the Administrative Class. Under the system of recruitment by open advertisement and competition already described, impartial selection on merit is strictly observed and patronage does not exist. Recruitment to the Executive Class is limited to candidates aged at least 17½ and under 28. Selection in open competitions is by interview of certain candidates with university degrees or with G.C.E. passes in English language and four other acceptable subjects, two of which must be at the Advanced Level and taken in the same examination. Competitions for the Executive Class are held twice a year. There are stringent nationality provisions for entry to the Civil Service, with certain limited exceptions to the requirement of British citizenship. Character referees are invariably required and, in some cases, referees on qualification for the post.

No-one may be employed in the Civil Service on work vital to the security of the State if he is or has recently been a member of the British Communist Party or of a Fascist organisation; or if, in such a way as to raise legitimate doubts about his reliability, he is or has recently been sympathetic to Communism or Fascism, or associates with Communists or Fascists or their sympathisers, or is susceptible to Communist or Fascist pressure. Certain departments and certain posts in other departments are not open to persons who are thought to fall within these categories.

In order to ensure the reliability of persons to be employed in exceptionally secret work, departments make special inquiries known as positive vetting. These entail completion of a security questionnaire and back ground inquiries by special investigating officers which include revelation of any character defects which might be a potential risk to security.

The Commissioners cannot enter into correspondence with candidates about security enquiries, which are the responsibility of the Minister in charge of the relevant department. These security requirements emanate from recommendations by a Conference of Privy Councillors appointed to examine the security services in 1955. Once a person is working in the Civil Service, if the security services sustain allegations of political unreliability against him, he may be transferred to other work or even dismissed. The Civil Servant can first appeal to three advisers before the Minister takes a final decision. The reason for these requirements is that persons owing allegiance to totalitarian doctrine cannot be expected to be loyal to the Crown.

All permanent civil servants are liable for service anywhere in the U.K.

or overseas but in practice extensive overseas service is usually required only in departments with major overseas responsibilities. There is a non-contributory pension scheme and a compulsory contributory scheme for widows' and children's pensions; an established civil servant receives on retirement both a pension and a gratuity.

Staff Associations and Whitley Councils in the Civil Service. Civil Servants are encouraged to belong to their appropriate associations in order to foster good staff relations and to promote effective negotiations on conditions of service. Those associations which have a right to negotiate on behalf of their members are known as recognised associations. National recognition is granted by the Treasury as employer and enables an association to participate in negotiations, agreements and arbitrations affecting staff in more than one department. Where representation of a group of staff cannot be confined to one association, there may be joint recognition. There are also departmentally recognised associations representing general service grades. Recognised associations preceded the Whitley Councils and are still active on behalf of their members, particularly in relation to grievances of individual civil servants. Civil service staff associations may apply[7] for registration as trade unions and may affiliate to the Trades Union Congress or to a political party.

THE MAJOR NATIONALLY RECOGNISED ASSOCIATIONS

Association of First Division Civil Servants;
Society of Civil Servants;
Institution of Professional Civil Servants;
Federation of Civil Service Professional and Technical Staffs;
Civil Service Alliance;
Civil Service Legal Society;
Civil Service Union;
Society of Technical Civil Servants.

N.B. The Civil Service Alliance is a federation comprising:--

The D.E.P. Staff Association;
The Inland Revenue Staff Federation;
The Ministry of Labour Staff Association;
The County Court Officers' Association

The G.P.O. has the Union of Post Office Workers and the Post Office Engineering Union.

The Civil Service National Whitley Council was set up in 1919, and this was followed by the establishment of departmental Whitley Councils. The official side was originally appointed by the Cabinet and for a time[8] included three M.P.s; nowadays its members are selected by the Civil

Service Department from serving civil servants who are usually heads of departments. A departmental official side contains senior serving officers in the department, including the establishment officer. The staff side of the National Council is appointed annually by the major groups of staff associations, and has regular monthly meetings. A substantial proportion of their members tend to be full-time staff association officials. Civil servants predominate on departmental staff sides, whose members are drawn from the relevant associations.

The main business of the National Whitley Council is carried out in committees and relates to all matters affecting conditions of service. In practice, however, the pay and grading of the higher posts are not dealt with by Whitley machinery.

Cabinet authority lies behind the official side of the National Council on all major matters; similarly, ministerial authority lurks behind departmental official sides. The Civil Service National Whitley Council Arbitration Agreement of 1925, as subsequently modified,[9] provides for reference to the Civil Service Arbitration Tribunal in case of disagreement between the two sides. Certain matters such as superannuation are excluded from the arbitration procedure, which does not of course apply to individual cases. Arbitration claims are submitted to the Tribunal through the D.E.P.[10] The Government is a party to all arbitration claims; the hearing is in public and the procedure informal. If the members of the Tribunal disagree, the Chairman may make an "umpire's award". The government will give effect to the awards of the Tribunal "subject to the overriding authority of Parliament".[11] The constitutional sovereignty of Parliament is thus preserved; the government would not *propose* to Parliament the rejection of an award. The Prices and Incomes Board recommended that the Government and the National Staff Side of the Civil Service Whitley Council should invite the Standing Advisory Committee on salaries for Higher Civil Service grades to take account of the White Paper on Prices and Incomes.

The Official and Staff Sides meet in a special Joint Committee of the National Whitley Council whose task is to examine the reform of the Civil Service, taking into account the Fulton Report. In accordance with a Fulton recommendation, the Head of the Civil Service is now assisted by a Senior Appointments Committee in putting forward names to the Prime Minister for top-level appointments. It comprises Permanent Secretaries and senior professional officers and has a series of panels for different categories of appointment.

Management Services in the Civil Service. In 1919 a few "Treasury Investigating Officers" were appointed to advise departments on the use of office machinery. During the war their numbers were substantially increased, and an "Organisation and Methods Division" was created. Teams of Treasury officers were assigned from the Division to specific investigations in Government departments. The large departments began to establish their own O. and M. branches, the Treasury providing guidance and co-ordination and, in the case of smaller departments, an advisory service. The O. and M. Division was fully integrated with the Treasury machine and placed under an Under-Secretary.

O. and M. Branches review organisation, procedures and methods of work and advise on improvements. In most departments the work is done by a central unit under an Assistant Secretary responsible to the Establishment Officer. In some cases the introduction of automatic data processing and its concomitant systems analysts and programmers has altered the pattern.

The Management Services (Development) Division advises departments of the use of office machinery and equipment and A.D.P. projects; it is assisted by the Technical Support Unit consisting of qualified engineers. A.D.P. systems are used for calculation of pay, pensions, statistics and farming subsidies; the Inland Revenue use A.D.P. for assessment and collection of P.A.Y.E. income tax. The division organises training courses in general O. and M. work and in systems analysis and programming for A.D.P. It also disseminates information on O. and M. work, maintains a library and produces the quarterly O. and M. Bulletin.

A specific course of action has been devised for the development and reorganisation of management services. A service-wide study of management services organisations is currently examining such subjects as the relationship with Personnel management; efficiency audits; computer planning, management careers and training; and the link between O.R. and other management services such as advice on computers and O. and M. review of possible areas for hiving off is under way and accountable management is being encouraged throughout the Service. The C.S.D. is also concerned with the difficult question of parallel and integrated hierarchies; it is also aiming at a high standard of working environment. Planning units to carry out the policy planning funcion and senior policy advisers may eventually be introduced.

Local Government. Local government negotiating machinery has already been described in Chapter X *(p. 106, ante)*. It will be recalled that the National Joint Council for Local Authorities' Administrative, Professional, Technical and Clerical Services considers salaries, wages and conditions of service; and that N.A.L.G.O. is the main staff association concerned. The extension in the application of "Whitley" machinery has been most marked in recent years, so that practically all local authority staff are within the scope of national or regional negotiating machinery. Individual local authorities are represented on the provincial councils of the main negotiating bodies. Each local authority has an establishment committee charged with the duty of dealing with all questions relating to the number, pay, promotion, superannuation and conditions of service of staff.[1][2] Establishment committees of some of the larger authorities have delegated powers to deal with all staffing questions of employees whose salaries do not exceed a prescribed maximum.

MAIN NEGOTIATING BODIES

Joint Negotiating Committee for Chief Officers;
National Joint Council for Local Authorities' Administrative, Professional and Technical Services:
Burnham Committee for Teachers;[13]
Joint Negotiating Committee for Inspectors, Organisers and Advisory Officers;[14]
Whitley Councils for the Health Services;
National Joint Council for Local Authorities' Fire Brigades;
National Joint Council for County Council Roadmen;
National Joint Council for Local Authorities' Services (Manual Workers);
Joint Negotiating Committees for Local Authorities Services.[15]

One of the most progressive authorities in staffing matters is Surrey County Council, whose Establishment Committee has for some thirty years had a special sub-committee known as the Staffing Board. The Board deals with such matters as conditions of service of all administrative and clerical staff, recruitment, post-entry training and internal promotion. In 1956 the committee adopted the Board's proposal to grant higher commencing salaries to junior entrants, in recognition of educational attainment by way of passes in the G.C.E. Examinations. Many of the larger authorities operate similar schemes. An attractive recruitment brochure, *Local Government in Surrey*, is distributed periodically to schools and libraries in the county and neatly contains an application for entry to the service in Surrey. In common with many other local authorities, Surrey County Council provides induction courses for junior entrants held during office hours, grants day release for study purposes, gives grants towards the cost of qualifying examinations, provides evening classes and arranges refresher and post-entry courses for senior staff.

Surrey County Council also recruits a number of university graduates to its administrative staff. The course of training for junior entrants provides lectures by chief and senior officers upon different aspects of the council's service. Under the day release scheme junior entrants receive paid leave once a week during term time in order to attend day-time courses of study provided by the county council as local education authority. Advanced training courses on staff college lines have been held periodically for more senior officers. Courses at the Administrative Staff College at Henley-on-Thames are available to civil servants and local government officers sponsored by their employing departments and authorities. Surrey also has a Joint Staff Committee upon which sit representatives of the council, the officers and the County Officers Branch of N.A.L.G.O. in accordance with the model scheme approved by the N.J.C.

N.A.L.G.O. has an Education Department which offers excellent facilities for post-entry training. It also provides correspondence tuition for the various examinations at low cost, scholarships and loans for study purposes, a library of text-books which may be borrowed at a small fee and lectures and courses at week-end and summer schools in England and abroad.

Clerical and administrative officers can qualify themselves for promotion by passing the examinations of the Local Government Training Board. These include papers in such subjects as Central and Local Government, Public Administration and the Social Services. The L.G.T.B. has an Examinations Committee, including a town clerk and three professors, to devise and manage its examinations and generally to advise the Board. There is an elementary Clerical Division Examination and a more advanced Administrative Examination, with Intermediate and Final sections, which forms the basis of the Diploma in Municipal Administration.

In 1957 the L.G.E.B.[16], in collaboration with the Royal Institute of Public Administration, sponsored the Diploma in Government Administration. This is an academic qualification, of the standard of a university pass degree, specially devised for civil servants. This Diploma provides an opportunity for those who have already entered the highest classes of the Civil Service to undertake a systematic course of study. It provides a convenient facility for higher study for non-graduates and includes subjects likely to be of particular interest to civil servants. Part-time study for the Diploma can be spread over two or three years. Similar advantages are afforded to local government officers by the Diploma in Municipal Administration.

Examinations are available to specialist officers, for example the Diploma in Housing Management of the Housing Management Examinations Board. This Board was sponsored by the Institute of Housing and the Society of Housing Managers. The new Diploma replaced the examinations of the Institute of Housing and the Housing Managers Certificate of the Royal Institution of Chartered Surveyors. Correspondence tuition is provided by the N.A.L.G.O. Correspondence Institute for these diplomas and for numerous other local government examinations.

The Local Government Training Board. The Mallaby Report did not advocate establishment of a unified local government service, nor a local government staff commission nor regional commissions. They recommended that the local authority associations set up a Central Staffing Organisation.

The Local Government Training Board was set up in January 1968 and operates a Levy/grant scheme on a voluntary basis similar to those of the statutory industrial training boards. The Levy in 1970/71 is to be based on the number of staff employed rather than on the present basis of population and rates have been agreed with the Associations and G.L.C. Returns giving the number of staff on the payroll will remedy the lack of adequate statistics on local government manpower. It aims to redistribute 75 per cent of approved training costs and to make 100 per cent grants for particular items. L.G.T.B. excludes from its grants scheme local government employees within the scope of an I.T.B.

The Board has incorporated the old Local Government Examinations Board. Its aims are to increase efficiency by ensuring that sufficient training of the right quality is given to staff and employees; and to ensure that the cost of training is evenly and fairly spread amongst all local authorities. Local authorities are estimated to be spending £7m. annually on training staff (an average expenditure per head of £7). This year's levy is £2m., next year's will be £3½m. 1,030 out of 1,434 authorities have paid the levy. The activities of local authorities are exempted from levy of some of the statutory I.T.Bs. The House of Lords has held in a recent decision[17] that insofar as the relevant Order specified non-industrial and non-commercial activities as part of the activities of the hotel and catering industry, the Order was *ultra vires*, having regard to the ordinary or natural meaning of 'industry or commerce''. This particular order did not specifically exempt the activities of local authorities. It would appear that the whole of the school meals service is now out of scope of the I.T.B. The local authority associations have taken up the question of the exclusions with D.E.P., especially those relating to Catering and Construction Workers.

The Board encourages research in collaboration with such bodies as the Institute of Local Government Studies, Birmingham University, the Royal Institute of Public Administration, L.A.M.S.A.C. and the London Boroughs Management Services Committee. The Board sponsors training in modern management techniques, such as "management by objectives" and in specialist education, fire and ambulance services.

The new O.N.C. in Public Administration was sponsored by the Department of Education and Science and if appropriate credits are obtained this will give full or partial exemption from the Intermediate D.M.A. This development follows the recent introduction of a new O.N.C. in Business Studies. L.G.T.B. is considering the future development of the D.M.A. in the light of this innovation.

Greater London Council. The G.L.C. has continued the former L.C.Cs. separate system of recruitment of its major establishment by open competitive examination at an academic level. A detailed professional and technical training scheme encourages young people to enter the service by providing firstclass training for those professions where it is difficult to find qualified staff by direct recruitment. The impact of the Industrial

Training Act, 1964, is also taken into account since training standards of I.T.B.s have repercussions on other fields of employment. The non-statutory L.G.T.B. now collaborates closely with the G.L.C. as its biggest "client". The G.L.C. also arranges recruitment training schemes, sponsoring of staff as students for full, part-time or short courses and reciprocal arrangements for exchange of staff with other employers.

The G.L.C. does not participate in national negotiating machinery, the G.L.C./I.L.E.A. Whitley Council for A.P.T.C. Staff being independent. The Staff side comprises eight representatives of the G.L.C. Staff Association, one representative of N.A.L.G.O. and one representative of the T.U.N.J.C. It should be noted that the Greater London District Whitley Council for Local Authorities A.P.T.C. Services is subordinate to the national machinery and deals mainly with staff in the London Boroughs. The G.L.C./I.L.E.A. Whitley Council referred to above is quite a distinct organisation.

Organisation and Methods and Work Study in Local Government. Leading specialists in this field are: S.J. Noel-Brown and Co. Ltd., Consultants to Industry, Hospitals and Local Government, the only firm of management consultants to give evidence to the local commission.

The managing director in a BBC broadcast said:-
"An organisation and methods survey really means an investigation of every administrative function. It means reviewing every single person's work; every bit of paper; every form; every letter; all the minutes and agenda that are prepared; the committee procedure; every file, book, register; in fact, every record and every action or function taken by the administration."

The former chairman of the finance committee of the old metropolitan borough council of Wandsworth has testified that the council paid a £9,000 consultancy fee. As a result of the review, savings of about £20,000 were effected in the first year, £30,000 in the second year and £40,000 in the third and every subsequent year. This was a good bargain by any standards.

A description of the O. and M. Consultant in local government is given in the company's brochure, *Management Matters.* From this it emerges that regular reviews are especially necessary in local government, because of the need to secure the best possible return for public money, the scale and complexity of the services, the absence of the profit motive and the distrust of ratepayers. The general manpower shortage is also clearly relevant. An experienced team qualified in both local government and O. and M. techniques can quickly produce valuable ideas for greater efficiency and economy. The firm's normal terms of reference are to carry out an investigation and survey of (all) the departments of the local authority. This includes a detailed investigation of the methods and necessity for the services normally performed by every member of the administrative staff. This connotes an examination of all procedures, records, office equipment and paperwork to eliminate unnecessary work, and an appraisal of the administrative organisation section by section, department by department and as a complete administrative team.

The first stage is consultation with chief officers who furnish any background information required.[18] Individual consultants are then allocated to each department and individual officers are questioned about their work, detailed notes being made and checked. The purpose is purely to establish existing procedures and no criticism is implied. Consultants also seek permission to attend meetings of the council and its committees. Each consultant prepares a report and subsequently a draft report is presented to the chief officer concerned. A final report is then prepared and submitted to the council with details of recommendations and their financial effects. The report can usually be implemented by the authority but the consultants will check progress without further fee if requested to do so. Reviews cover such matters as committee procedure and preparation of agenda, reports and minutes; purchase of stores; organisation of transport; and costing and financial control.

Messrs. Noel-Brown broadly define work study as the systematic, objective and critical examination of any given work situation directed towards increasing the efficiency of that work. The techniques are very similar to those used in O. and M. and the present division appears to be that O. and M. techniques are applied to administrative and clerical organisations and work study techniques are applied to manual operations. Work study promotes economy and efficiency and has a vital role to play in times of labour shortage, as in the present day. It does not necessarily involve bonus incentive schemes, but work study analysis should first be undertaken if their introduction is envisaged. Work study can be as effective in local government and the hospital service as it has been in industry. The company's terms of reference for work study are to carry out an investigation and survey of the work undertaken by all the manual workers employed by the council. Such surveys include investigation of the administration, management, supervision, methods and equipment, the application and necessity of the work and work study or time and motion study where deemed necessary. Reports are submitted incorporating recommendations to achieve economies, simplification and greater productivity. The procedure is very similar to that for an O. and M. review, culminating in a final report to the council. The firm now have an alternative method of procedure for reporting upon and implementing proposals arising from an O. and M. survey of staff procedures and duties. They work through an officers' "steering committee" comprising the chief officer or a senior representative of each department. The steering committee is normally empowered by the Council to implement proposals which do not affect Council policy or its relations with the public; staff conditions of service; or supplementary expenditure in excess of estimates. Proposals affecting Council policy are made the subject of "interim reports" to the Council before they are implemented. At the conclusion of the assignment a report is prepared summarising the results. This alternative is preferred as, in addition to relieving members of the need to discuss minor matters, it fosters greater interest and enthusiasm for the survey amongst the staff, gives greater scope for dealing with the organisation as a whole and accelerates implementation of the improvements resulting from the survey. It does, however, involve additional consultant time because when implementing agreed proposals consultant staff tend to become closely involved in the day to day working of departments. Members' and officers' time, however, is saved.

Messrs. Noel-Brown also have an Appointments Division which deals with staff selection for local government. The aim is to cut advertising costs by means of specially drafted advertisements in selected daily and weekly newspapers as well as in trade and professional journals. Large display advertisements containing numerous appointments give an added impact. A panel of experts draws up a short list of candidates and submits a report on each for final selection by the local authority, which may sometimes invite the consultant to be present at the interview. In this way an attempt is made to appoint a candidate of the required calibre.

Local government now has many successful internal O. and M. units. Leading examples are the Management Services teams operating in London (London Boroughs Management Service Committee) and Coventry; and the team drawn from the co-operating authorities of Berkshire and Oxfordshire County Councils and the County Borough Council of Reading.

The Newcastle Experiment. The appointment of a "principal city officer with town clerk" in the city and county borough of Newcastle-upon-Tyne is an important development in personnel policy at the highest level. An account of the factors culminating in this appointment is given in an article[19] by Mr. T. Dan Smith, former leader of the City Council and now Chairman of the Northern Regional Economic Planning Council.

Following the election of a Labour majority on the city council in 1958, Mr. Smith realised the urgent need for modernisation of the structure of local government. This was brought home to him by the critical housing situation in the city "with a waiting list of nearly 10,000 families and not a single acre of land on which to build within the city boundaries". In these circumstances, a detailed five-year plan for housing and slum clearance was produced and explained to crowded public meetings. The nub of the plan was that slum clearance was the priority and only people from the clearance areas were to be rehoused during the first three years to enable the cleared land to be available for building. People on the housing waiting list had to be patient. Slum dwellers were moved into the last remaining houses under construction, as they were completed The plan was broken down to include all the slum areas in the city and was published in three-monthly cycles.

After the first six months, the local populace realised that the plan was working. The public meetings continued and people living in slum property and those on the waiting list were told when they would be housed. The five-year plan was an unqualified success and the former Labour Leader of the City Council pays generous tribute to Mr. Henry Brooke (as he then was) the Conservative Minister of Housing and Local Government,[20] and his staff.

The success of the Newcastle housing plan demonstrated the need for a separate planning department. Initially, there was strong opposition from councillors and officers, as there has been in some London boroughs, but Mr. Smith won over his colleagues. The way was paved by organising support for a new multi-level city through continuous meetings between councillors, professional bodies and individual businessmen. The importance of the landscape architect and sculptor was also canvassed and a sculpture competition organised.

In 1961 Newcastle-upon-Tyne became one of the first cities in Britain to appoint a planning officer to head an independent planning department. As a regional capital it has planning responsibilities far beyond its local government boundaries.

Mr. Smith became Leader of the City Council in 1960 and at once turned his attention to what he describes as "that bulwark of local government reaction, the Committee". The co-ordination of planning, education, housing, health and other services necessitated a new look. Official recognition was given to the leader of the council and the leader of the opposition and both were given an office and secretarial assistance. A city cabinet was then formed, comprising nine senior members of the party in power. This "policy advisory Committee" was serviced by the officers, as the city council adopted the recommendation. These reforms led to the production of a comprehensive development plan for Newcastle as a regional capital and pointed to the urgent need to streamline the administrative and financial planning structure. This led to the decision to appoint a city manager following the retirement of the town clerk and he was envisaged as the senior officer of the corporation reporting to a special management committee of the council. We have already seen (p. 114, ante) that the officer appointed has submitted his proposals for committee reorganisation. Mr. Smith's "special management committee" would appear to approximate to the "resources planning committee".

The method of selection used in connection with this appointment is interesting, as it bears a close affinity to the methods of the consultants already described. A special committee was set up and a consultant psychologist interviewed every member and several of the chief officers of the corporation. A job description emerged which was adopted by the committee; the designation of "town clerk" was included in the title. The job description said that the person appointed would be expected to develop the post and that a completely new job description might be drafted after a year. The requirements were: a man of university standard, top I.Q. rating, professional qualifications and a record of achievement. The maximum salary offered was £10,000 a year. There were written tests, group discussions, two interviews and a written problem. Mr. Frank Harris, a production planning executive with Ford of Dagenham, was the unanimous choice of the consultant and the committee and he took up the appointment in August, 1965. Mr. Harris sees himself as a managing director responsible to a board; he has a background of commercial and industrial experience. Mr. Smith believes that in this way local democracy can be made efficient: let us hope that he is right. In 1969 Mr. Harris resigned his appointment in order to return to industry.

The emergence of the city manager type of appointment may well erode the virtual monopoly of the Law Society in this field. At present the majority of town clerks are solicitors, as are a substantial majority of clerks of county and district councils. In March, 1966, Oxford City Council appointed the former county treasurer of Cumberland as town clerk. Legal qualifications were not stipulated as essential in recent advertisements for the town clerkship of Leicester or the county clerkship of West Sussex, and as already noted (p. 113, *ante*), Basildon Urban District Council appointed its former clerk as town manager. With the general trend towards larger authorities it may well be possible to have a principal city officer with mainly administrative rather then legal qualifications. The bigger authorities usually have a separate legal department under a solicitor or, exceptionally, a barrister.

Since 1968 an increasing number of local authorities have called in management consultants to streamline administration and committee structure. Haringey L.B.C., for example, has appointed a chief executive officer and new-style Directors of Education: Health and Welfare; and Technical Services. Similarly, Islington L.B.C. has appointed its existing town clerk as chief executive and town clerk, responsible for the effective execution of policy throughout the council's departments. The traditional functions of a town clerk's department will be carried out by a director of legal and administrative services and supporting staff. The committee structure in Islington has been revised and there is a Special Reorganisation Committee as well as a resources planning committee and a secretariat for members. Islington is to have a Director of Development to control physical planning and development. The Director of Development will control the work of the Borough Engineer and Surveyor, the Borough Architect, the Planning Officer, the Borough Valuer, the Housing Manager and the Cleansing Superintendent. A Director of Social Services will be responsible for child care, welfare and selected social services and supporting facilities from the public health department. This organisation will be reviewed following implementation of the Seebohm Report. A Director of Public Health will control medical and nursing services and the public health inspectorate.[21] All deputy chief officers are to have functional responsibilities. Lambeth L.B.C. has just appointed a new style chief executive officer, thus following in the footsteps of its sister borough Wandsworth. Another welcome development is that an increasing number of local authorities, especially in Greater London, employ well-qualified Public Relations and Press Officers.

The Nationalised Industries

Coal. The National Coal Board has an Administrative Assistant Training Scheme which is briefly mentioned in its leaflet on *Careers in Coal* and described in detail in its pamphlet on *The Arts Graduate in the Coal Industry*. The industry has an annual turnover of £900 million and provides great opportunities for men without technical qualifications who have the necessary ability. The Scheme is open to people within the industry as well as arts and other graduates with good honours degrees. The applicants must be men under 28 who have completed a full-time course of at least three years at a university or are due to complete it within a year. A preliminary selection is made after an interview with a representative of the Board. A final selection board is held at London on "group selection" lines.

Entrants are trained for about two years in one of the areas or at national headquarters.[22] The training is designed to give a broad conspectus of the Board's activities and organisation and to instil administrative expertise. Those appointed to areas are sent to London for about six months, whilst those attached to headquarters have a similar spell in a coalfield. By the end of his training an Administrative Assistant should have a birds'-eye-view of the industry, from the day to day running of a colliery to the formation of policy at the Board's headquarters. In the early stages trainees spend some time at a colliery learning about mining operations and all aspects of colliery organisation; they also make short visits to some of the main departments at Area Headquarters. Afterwards, trainees spend longer periods in selected departments working under the supervision of heads of branches in order or learn, by participation, the basic principles of administration. Each trainee is assigned for the whole of his time in the scheme to a supervisor who arranges his programme and helps him to choose his eventual field of activity within the industry. His programme, in the second year especially, is directed to providing more experience appropriate to that field and he usually spends the concluding months in the department where he hopes to obtain his first post.

There are opportunities for administrative assistants in the non-technical departments: these deal with marketing, purchasing and stores, finance, industrial relations, staff and secretarial services. There are also opportunities for graduate scientists in the coal industry to take part in mining research, coal research, operational research and in work relating to marketing technical services and computer centres. The Board also has an Industrial Relations Training Scheme for men with experience in the mining industry to equip themselves for work in the Industrial Relations Department. The Board has a National Apprenticeship Scheme for Engineering Draughtsmen culminating in a N.C.B. Certificate of Apprenticeship; and it offers annually a number of university scholarships in mining, mechanical, electrical and chemical engineering as well as science and general scholarships. The N.C.B. Engineering Training Scheme covers mining, electrical, mechanical and coal preparation engineering; and workshop managers. In addition, there are career prospects for civil engineers and graduate scientists; and in marketing, research and development, scientific control, operational research, computer services. The Engineering Craft Apprenticeship, which is now a four-year training scheme, provides the industry with skilled fitters and electricians.

Joint consultation takes place at colliery, area and national levels. Management and trade unions are represented on colliery committees and on area and national councils where such matters as safety, health and welfare are discussed. Wages and terms of service are negotiated through the industry's conciliation and consultation machinery.

Gas. Training is carried out by the Area Gas Boards each of which has a training centre where a full range of training activities is carried out to meet identified recruitment and training needs (e.g. craft and student apprenticeship, pupillage schemes). They offer generous further education facilities to their employees and have set up their own training centres, each will a staff of training officers and instructors. In addition, management development and training is now receiving considerable attention and resources. A Gas Industry Training Board was set up in 1965, its first levy grant year being 1966/67. The Board makes recommendations on all vital aspects of training in the gas industry and bases its grant scheme on training carried out in accordance with such recommendations, as well as initiating work on training standards.

The Area Boards also provide training by means of student apprenticeships in gas, civil, mechanical or chemical engineering and in chemistry. There are also careers in industrial or chemical research. The gas industry sells a great variety of equipment and is responsible for the installation and maintenance of gas appliances. Area Board training centres provide for the training of gas industry representatives, sales, fitting and service staff. Special courses are arranged for sales and service managers and for specialists.[23] Sales staff are encouraged to obtain suitable sales qualifications through Area Board education schemes. Home service advisers give demonstrations and advice to the public on gas appliances such as cookers and washing machines. Before appointment they must have a recognised domestic science diploma and on joining the industry they receive further training.

Most administrative and clerical training is given on the job by supervisors in the gas industry but courses are arranged for specialists such as telephone inquiry clerks. Trainees in professional accountancy or administration may be sponsored either by day release or correspondence course to study at technical colleges and are given generous grants. Many of the office staff are sent on courses run by other organisations in order to keep abreast of such developments as mechanised accounting and O. and M. Young employees may attend day or evening courses in shorthand and typing.

Many courses are held for the training of foremenand supervisors, including Training Within Industry programmes and residential courses. Gas industry managers are trained in mainly residential courses run by Area Boards, the Gas Council, local education authorities, universities and the Administrative Staff College.

Area Boards arrange induction courses for new employees and send many of them on numerous courses provided by manufacturers and professional bodies. All Area Boards provide facilities for staff wishing to improve their education by payment of course and examination fees and granting leave to sit for examinations. Young employees may be released for one day a week to attend classes at local colleges.

Vacancies for administrative staff are widely advertised within the industry but some administrative staff are recruited from outside, particularly where special qualifications, such as a university degree, are required. The Secretary's Department in an Area Board is normally divided into sections dealing with administration, education and training establishments, estates and wayleaves, insurance, legal matters, public relations and welfare. The general pattern is repeated at Sub-Area Headquarters, where wayleave officers work in close co-operation with the engineering staff in the planning department and have the task of obtaining consents from landowners for the construction of supply lines across their property. Below the Sub-Area is the District, where the District Senior Clerk is responsible for clerical services.

Electricity. A large number of clerical and administrative staff are employed at C.E.G.B. Headquarters, at Region H.Q., and in the offices of the four Project Groups. Each power station is in the charge of a station superintendent, under whom a Station Clerk is responsible for clerical and administrative services.

Selected employees are encouraged to undertake a planned course of training, lasting perhaps four years, during which they are given time off for study. Trainees are expected to obtain the professional qualifications of a secretarial or administrative body.[24] Secretarial traineeships are open to members of the clerical staff who already hold a good G.C.E. and have obtained either exemption from the preliminary examination or a National Certificate in Business Studies. Trainees may transfer temporarily from a Board to a Region, or vice versa, and are given wide experience in a variety of offices and duties.

Many posts of senior administrators and non-technical managers are filled by arts graduates, who are normally recruited to fill specific posts. Some Boards and Regions, however, recruit graduates, particularly to the

Secretarial and Accountancy Training Schemes. A number of arts graduates have been recruited as administrative trainees at the H.Qs. of both the Electricity Council and the C.E.G.B. Trainee accountants are given study leave and an "Accountants-in-Training Scheme" enables more mature officers to obtain appropriate professional qualifications.

Service Centre Assistants are recruited from junior clerical staff, school-leavers[25] those with retail trading experience outside the industry and skilled electricians. Trainee demonstrators are recruited from school-leavers aged 16 to 18 and Service Centre Assistants, and from domestic science colleges, and other departments or industries. There are Service Centre Supervisors in the larger Service Centres, drawn from the ranks of the assistants. Other sales and service staff include housecraft advisers, sales representatives, commercial assistants and district commercial officers.

Younger employees are eligible under the Educational Incentives Scheme for part-time release to attend approved courses, usually for one day a week. Older workers are given the same facilities if they have made substantial progress through evening study.

All employees following an approved course are reimbursed the whole of their tuition and examination fees and grants may be made towards the cost of books and travelling expenses. Approved courses include the Diploma in Public Administration and the Ordinary and Higher National Certificate in Business Studies. Those who left school before taking their G.C.E. may work for it in suitable subjects or may study for a Certificate in Office Studies or for an R.S.A. Certificate.

Residential training courses are provided by the Electricity Council at Horsley Towers[26] and by the C.E.G.B. at Electricity Hall[27] on selection methods, wayleaves and staff supervision. Management training is provided by executive development courses, at which a mixed group of engineers and administrative staff spend three weeks studying problems outside their daily work. The industry also makes use of many outside training courses such as those at the Administrative Staff College.

Under the Electricity Supply Scholarship Scheme, annual scholarships are awarded to enable selected employees to spend up to three years full-time at a university reading for a degree.

The Chairman of the Electricity Council, Sir Norman Elliott, is also Chairman of the National Joint Advisory Council of the Electricity Supply Industry, which comprises over sixty members representing the Electricity Council, the Area Boards, the ten trade unions and the industry's local advisory committees. The twelve District Joint Advisory Councils each cover one Area Board and those units of C.E.G.B. in the same geographical area. They include representatives of the Area Board, the C.E.G.B., the trade unions and the 488 Local Advisory Committees. The latter consist of representatives nominated by local management and elected by employees, and the L.A.C.s cover local units such as a power station, a transmission district, a research laboratory, a project group, a distribution district of an Area Board or a headquarters office.

In 1965 a separate Industrial Training Board was established for the electricity supply industry.

Engineers work in all parts of the industry, on generation, transmission, and distribution. Physicists, chemists, metallurgists and other scientists are employed by the C.E.G.B. on a wide variety of work including research and development. The Electricity Council's illustrated booklets give an excellent account of the industry, describing qualifications and training, prospects and promotion.

Draughtsmen and craftsmen are employed both by the Boards and by C.E.G.B. There are graduate and diploma trainees, student apprentices and craft apprentices. Electricity Council pamphlets[28] on *Training and Advanced Study Courses for Engineers, Engineering Training for "O" Level School Leavers* and *Salesmanship Training* describe those careers in electricity supply. The Council even provides a correspondence tuition course in "Power System Protection". All in all, the electricity supply industry appears to have the most enlightened education and training arrangements.

The Industrial Training Boards: Engineering. From its inception E.I.T.B. imposed a levy of 2.5 per cent on all emoluments paid by engineering employers during a particular financial year, with an exception for very small employers whose emoluments were less than £5,000. In 1968 the Board concluded that the small firms had very different training needs from the larger and that a levy of 1 per cent should be charged on emoluments between £5,000 and £15,000. This change was approved by the Secretary of State and incorporated in a revised levy order. The effect was to reduce the levy on very small firms to a level more closely related to their training needs; and larger firms obtained a small reduction. In the 1969/70 levy year there will be total exemption of the first £7,500 of emoluments, the levy on emoluments between £7,501 and £17,500 will be one per cent and the standard rate of 2.5 per cent will be charged on emoluments over £17,500. The Foundry Industry Training Committee is a statutory committee of E.I.T.B. responsible for separate establishments in which foundry work, diecasting or patternmaking is the main activity. F.I.T.C. charges the full levy of 2.5 per cent of all emoluments above the lower exemption limit.

The obverse side of the coin is the grant scheme. E.I.T.B. pays a general grant as a percentage of levy; specific grants for first year craft and technician training and supplementary grants are paid in full, regardless of rate of levy, thus providing a powerful incentive for very small firms with a marginal training need. The Board's Annual Report for 1968 indicates an overall improvement of 15 per cent in the quantity and quality of training and points to greatly improved training systems in small and medium firms. The levy/grant scheme is a powerful factor in encouraging improvement of performance. The Report covers Operator, Craft,

Supervisor and Management Training, Training of Computer Staff, Technologist and Technician Training and Group Training Schemes (which assist small firms).

The E.I.T.B. has its own Staff Training Division at Watford providing training and instruction for the Board's administrative and clerical staff. Standard features include introductory courses for clerical and executive staff and Training Within Industry courses for office supervisors. New courses introduced in 1968/69 covered the subject matter of clerical duties, training clerks, grant editing, computer appreciation, middle management and introduction to the industry. In addition senior administrative staff have enjoyed staff appraisal and promotion board conferences as well as management seminars and instruction in visual aids. The centre is pleasantly situated and well equipped with many of the new visual aids available there now being used by senior officers of the Board when lecturing to new entrants. In view of their daily work dealing with companies, visits to Companies House (London) have been arranged for administrative and executive staff, as well as to the D.E.P. to other government departments, to other I.T.B.s and to a number of industrial and commercial organisations.

1. Since October, 1969, one of the Ministers without Portfolio.
2. E.g. H.M. Inspectors of Taxes in the Inland Revenue and Assistant Postal Controllers in the Post Office.
3. Twenty-seven for the Diplomatic Service; twenty-four for Clerkships in the House of Commons.
4. Civil Service Commission, 1969.
5. E.g. museums and the Government Actuary's department.
6. Including the Diplomatic Service.
7. To the Chief Registrar of Friendly Societies.
8. 1922–30.
9. In 1936, 1939, 1947, 1951, 1952, 1955, 1959, and 1964.
10. Industrial Relations Department.
11. Treasury Circular of 1925.
12. With certain exceptions, e.g. teachers, firemen and roadmen.
13. As constituted under the Remuneration of Teachers Act, 1965.
14. The Soulbury Committee.
15. E.g. engineering craftsmen.
16. Now incorporated in the L.G.T.B.
17. Hotel and Catering I.T.B. v. Automobile Proprietaries Ltd. (T.L.R. 13.5.69).
18. E.g. Standing Orders, Abstracts of Accounts.
19. Local Government in Newcastle-upon-Tyne: the background to some recent developments. (*Public Administration*, Winter, 1965, Vol. 43).
20. 1957–62. He was given a Life Peerage in the 1966 Dissolution Honours List.
21. Which has important housing functions.
22. Training for business management (the Administration Assistant Schemes 1969).
23. E.g. in central heating or clean air.
24. E.g. the Chartered Institute of Secretaries, the Corporation of Secretaries or the British Institute of Management.
25. Preferably those with a G.C.E. in English, Mathematics or a Science.
26. Near Leatherhead, Surrey.
27. Buxton, Derbyshire.
28. Obtained from the Electricity Council, 30 Millbank, London, S.W.1.

PART III: SOME PROBLEMS OF PUBLIC ADMINISTRATION

CHAPTER XIX

CONTROL OF EXPENDITURE

Introductory, We have already seen that there is parliamentary control of expenditure through Select Committees of the House of Commons, notably the Select Committee on Estimates and the Public Accounts Committee. Although the Select Committee on Nationalised Industries can examine the annual report and accounts of a public corporation, the relevant Minister has rather greater powers, particularly in relation to the issue of mandatory directions. Borrowing by a public corporation and the financing of capital expenditure are subject to the consent of the Minister as well as to that of the Treasury. The main concern of the Treasury is with the level of investment and the investment programmes of the public corporations are reviewed annually.

We have also traced (pp. 146-155, *ante)* the considerable control exercised by the central government departments over local authorities through the grants system and the requirement of loan sanction for numerous projects. The system of district audit is also a serious check or control on local government expenditure. Control through the grant system may be said to be parliamentary as well as ministerial, as a Rate Support Order must be approved by Parliament. In the final analysis control of both central and local government expenditure lies with the electorate. The Treasury's function in this respect is performed, in a somewhat different way, by the finance committee in local government. The desirability of controlling public expenditure in the national interest and of receiving value for money is recognised on all sides and there has in fact been an annual survey of public sector expenditure since 1961, in accordance with the recommendations of the Plowden Committee on Public Expenditure.[1] Our system connotes the drafting and collating of estimates by professional experts, followed by the authorisation of the expenditure by the elected representatives of the people. The finances of the public corporations do not conform to this simple pattern, since parliamentary control is more tenuous in that field.

Public Expenditure. The Chancellor of the Exchequer presented to Parliament in February, 1969, a White Paper on Public Expenditure 1968–69 to 1970–71.[2] He estimated that aggregate expenditure for 1968/69 would be £15,870 million as against an aggregate of £15,165 million for 1967/68, an increase in real terms of 4.6 per cent. For 1969/70 the increase in public expenditure over 1968/69 would be held to 1 per cent in real terms. The total estimate for 1969/70 was £16,435 million, including £75 million for contingencies, an increase of approximately one per cent.

The net total of the supply Estimates for 1969–70 was £11,571 millon, an increase of 7.9 per cent. About a quarter of Supply Expenditure is not public expenditure (e.g. grants and net lending to local authorities and public corporations, transactions within central government). Public expenditure includes a number of large items which are not voted annually by the House of Commons (e.g. outgoings of National Insurance Funds, local government expenditure, capital expenditure of public corporations other than nationalised industries). Thus the total and composition of public and supply expenditure are different. The estimated increase in public expenditure in 1969/70 in real terms was the planned figure of one per cent.

Capital expenditure by the nationalised industries, B.B.C. I.T.A. and Covent Garden Market Authority in 1968/69 was about six per cent at constant prices below the level expected and this should continue in 1969/70, although it is expected to rise again in 1970/71.

A copy of the Financial Statement and Budget Report 1969–70 laid before the House of Commons when opening the Budget in April, 1969 is published by H.M.S.O.[3] Part I deals with the Economic Background to the Budget and includes useful tables on forecasts, balance of payments trends, etc. The outlook to mid–1970 indicates that the volume of public authorities' current expenditure should rise by over one per cent; most of this is likely to be in local authorities' expenditure. Increases in both public and private sector investment are anticipated. An increase in total final expenditure of nearly three per cent is implied. A substantial improvement in the balance of payments position is forecast, coupled with improvements in the visible trade balance, net invisible earnings, net outflow of long–term capital and balance of current and long–term capital movements. Part II deals with Public Sector transactions. The public sector accounts cover the current and capital transactions of the central government (including the Consolidated and National Loans Funds, the National Insurance Funds and all other central government funds and accounts) and of local authorities, together with the transactions of the nationalised industries and other public corporations on appropriation and capital accounts.

The announced target for public expenditure in 1969–70 is a one per cent increase over the estimate for 1968–69. This implies a total of £16,440 million on the basis of the 1968–69 estimate. Part III is purely

TABLE 1*

PUBLIC EXPENDITURE [1] BY FUNCTION, 1967-68 AND 1968-69

£ million

	1967-68 Provisional Outturn[2] at 1967-68 Outturn prices	1968-69 Estimated Outturn at 1968-69 Outturn prices
Defence Budget	2,231	2,268
Other Military Defence	198	169
Overseas Aid	205	215
Other Overseas Services	127	127
Roads and Public Lighting	528	600
Transport	256	261
Technological Services	177	225
Other Assistance to Employment and Industry	631	834
Research Councils, etc.	76	86
Agriculture, Fisheries and Forestry	373	381
Housing	1,055	1,090
Local Environmental Services	761	816
Law and Order[3]	513	565
Arts	15	16
Education[4]	2,123	2,295
Health and Welfare[5]	1,662	1,785
Social Security	2,906	3,313
Financial Administration	187	211
Common Services	145	169
Other expenditure	411	444
Total	14,580	15,870
At 1968-69 Outturn prices	15,165	15,870

1 Excludes capital expenditure by the nationalised industries, the broadcasting authorities and Covent Garden Market Authority, and debt interest.
2 As in the Treasury Analysis of Public Expenditure in "National Income and Expenditure, 1968".
3 Includes Child Care.
4 Includes Local Libraries and Museums.
5 Includes Welfare Foods.

* Tables 1 to 3 are Crown Copyright, and are reproduced from Cmnd. 3936, February, 1969 by kind permission of Her Majesty's Stationery Office.

TABLE 2

PUBLIC EXPENDITURE[1] BY FUNCTION, 1968-69 TO 1970-71: ESTIMATED EXPENDITURE[2]

£ million
at 1969-70 Estimates prices

	1968-69 Cmnd. 3515 estimate	1969-70	1970-71
Defence Budget	2,390	2,266	2,281
Other Military Defence	332	125	35
Overseas Aid	235	227	235
Other Overseas Services	135	120	128
Roads and Public Lighting	622	608	698
Transport.....................	263	251	242
Technological Services	236	246	232
Other Assistance to Employment and Industry	806	821	856
Research Councils, etc.	90	97	105
Agriculture, Fisheries and Forestry[3] .	424	396	400
Housing......................	1,125	1,090	1,126
Local Environmental Services	829	878	887
Law and Order[4]	572	603	658
Arts	16	18	20
Education[5]	2,280	2,385	2,474
Health and Welfare[6]	1,825	1,876	1,958
Social Security[7]	3,262	3,438	3,528
Financial Administration	211	226	218
Common Services	168	195	209
Other expenditure	456	494	471
Contingency Reserve		75	165
Total	**16,277[8]**	**16,435**	**16,926**

1 Excludes capital expenditure by the nationalised industries, the broadcasting authorities and Covent Garden Market Authority, and debt interest.
2 In this table Selective Employment Tax paid by local authorities has been allocated to the individual services. In Cmnd. 3515 this expenditure was included under "Other expenditure".
3 Excludes the effect of the Farm Price Review for 1969 and later years, which will be provided for from the Contingency Reserve.
4 Includes Child Care.
5 Includes Local Libraries and Museums.
6 Includes Welfare Foods.
7 The figures for 1969-70 and 1970-71 have been estimated on the basis of existing rates of benefits.
8 This total corresponds to that of £15,078 million in the table in Cmnd. 3515, plus £31 million for the estimated cost of the 1968 Farm Price Review as given in the Financial Statement, 1968-69 (H.C. 151), revalued from 1967 Survey prices, as used in Cmnd. 3515, to 1969-70 Estimates prices.

TABLE 3

PUBLIC EXPENDITURE,[1] 1968-69 AND 1969-70
RECONCILIATION WITH SUPPLY ESTIMATES

£ million

	1968-69 Estimates, at 1968-69 Estimates prices	1969-70 Estimates, at 1969-70 Estimates prices
Supply Estimates (net Vote)	10,725[2]	11,571 (Increase over 1968-69 7.9 per cent)
Less		
Grants and net lending to local authorities and public corporations[3]	-2,070	-2,287
Transactions within central government[4]	-404	-614
Items treated as part of revenue and net borrowing[5]	-407	-498
Public Expenditure element in Supply Estimates	7,844	8,172
Other central government:		
National Insurance Funds	2,399	2,524
Other[6]	340	350
Local authorities	4,840	5,120
Public corporations (mainly New Towns)	201	194
Contingency Reserve	–	75
Total Public Expenditure . . . . (Financial Statement, 1968-69–H.C. 151)	15,624	16,435
Add		
Difference between the Financial Statement, 1968-69 (H.C. 151) and Cmnd. 3515[7]	44	–
Total Public Expenditure (Cmnd. 3515)	15,668[8]	–

	at 1969-70 Estimates prices	at 1969-70 Estimates prices
Total Public Expenditure (Cmnd. 3515) expressed at 1969-70 Estimates prices	16,277	16,435 (Increase over 1968-69 1 per cent)

1 Excluding capital expenditure by the nationalised industries, the broadcasting authorities and Covent Garden Market Authority, and debt interest.
2 1968 Budget Estimates.
3 Mainly Rate Support Grant and other current grants to local authorities.
4 Including grant to National Insurance Funds.
5 A net figure comprising Vote payments not entering into public expenditure (*e.g.*, refunds of Selective Employment Tax) offset by sums appropriated in aid of Votes but not deductible from public expenditure (*e.g.*, National Health Service contributions).
6 Including expenditure from the National Loans Fund and by the Northern Ireland central government.
7 Between 16th January, 1968, when Cmnd. 3515 was published, and the Financial Statement, 1968-69 (H.C. 151) of 19th March, 1968, there were net reductions in various public expenditure programmes amounting to £44 million.
8 This total corresponds to that of £15,078 million in the table in Cmnd. 3515, plus £31 million for the estimated cost of the 1968 Farm Price Review as given in the Financial Statement, 1968-69 (H.C. 151), revalued from 1967 Survey prices, as used in Cmnd. 3515, to 1968-69 Estimates prices.

statistical and comprises central government transactions.

A Green Paper on Public Expenditure: A New Presentation was presented to Parliament by the Chancellor of the Exchequer in April, 1969.[4] The Government has submitted the proposed changes to the Select Committee on Procedure. Five changes are proposed:-

(i) to show regularly every year figures for the year preceding publication, the year of publication (year 1) and each of the four following years (years 2 to 5). Year 3 would be the crucial year for making substantial changes without causing disruption and for rolling plans forward. The figures for years 4 and 5 will represent projections of cost, not decisions;

(ii) to bring capital expenditure of the nationalised industries into the public expenditure review;

(iii) to present projections of all receipts from taxation, contributions and charges and of all other receipts accruing to the public sector, including the estimated gross trading surpluses of the nationalised industries and other public enterprises;

(iv) to distinguish between expenditure and receipts on:

(A) direct use of resources (e.g. goods and services)

(B) transfers (e.g. rates and taxes)

(C) Assets (e.g. net purchases of land, taxes on capital)

(v) to include in the total of outlays an allowance (the "relative price effect") for the probable change in the real cost of public sector purchases (especially labour).

The Government propose that the new form of presentation should be used in an annual White Paper to be laid before Parliament subject to the views of the Select Committee on Procedure.[5] It is suggested that the Vote on Account is an unsatisfactory procedure and at times misleading and the Government propose to replace it by a clause in the Appropriation Bill enabling it to spend in the period before the end of the financial year and before the next Appropriation Act a stated proportion of the sums voted for the current year. The Government propose that the new procedure should be made the subject of a special Bill in the first year to enable Parliament to debate the matter fully.

The First Report from the Select Committee on Procedure, 1968/69 has accepted many of these recommendations. The effect would be to enable Parliament to decide the best use of the national resources for years ahead and would break the century old tradition of restricting the function of Parliament in this connection to mere auditing of accounts and approval of expenditure. The aim is to achieve the more efficient planning and management of public spending. The Estimates Committee should be replaced by a Select Committee on Expenditure whose functions would be:-

(i) to discuss strategy and policies of expenditure set out in projections several years ahead;

(ii) to examine means of implementation and execution of policies, including new managerial methods; and

(iii) to look back on results and value for money obtained on the basis of annual departmental accounts and ancillary information.

The Report recommends publication of forecasts of movements of prices and earnings for three years ahead. The forecasts, real costs in terms of resources and assumptions behind the choice of alternatives should be made available to the House of Commons. The annual estimates are not discussed in the Commons in sufficient detail at present. The Treasury should review the basis on which the estimates are prepared and present them in functional form. The Report welcomes the decision to publish an annual White Paper on planned public spending over five years. The new Select Committee on Expenditure should have sub–committees for industry, technology, manpower and employment; power, transport and communications; trade and agriculture; education, science and the arts; housing, health and welfare; law, order and public safety; defence; and external affairs. A general sub- committee would report on progress to Parliament.

The Civil Estimates for 1969–70 for the year ending 31st March, 1970 were ordered by the House of Commons to be printed (19th February, 1969)[6] Class VI relates to Local Government, Housing and Social Services and encompasses the following:-

Minister of Housing and Local Government, Scottish
Development Department, Welsh Office; Housing; Rate
Support Grants to Local Revenues; Land Commission:
Department of Health and Social Security: National
Health Service: Health & Welfare Services: National
Insurance: Family Allowances: Non--Contributory
Benefits: War Pensions, and Social Work, Scotland.

In "The Task ahead—Economic Assessment of 1972"[7] Chapter V is entitled "Public Expenditure". Following devaluation the rate of public expenditure was reduced by £300 million in 1968/69 and by over £400 million in 1969/70. The Chapter examines Defence, Education and Health. The cumulative effect of the Defence Review begun in 1965 (Statement on Defence Estimates, 1966[8]; Supplementary Statement on Defence Estimates, 1968[9]) will result in a total contraction of service and civilian employees of nearly one—quarter by 1973/74. Defence expenditure will be reduced from the 1968/69 total of £2,276 million to a level forecast for 1972/73 at a little over £2,000 million at 1968 prices. This implies that the proportion of the total output devoted to defence will be reduced from about 7 per cent, as in the original 1964 programme, to below 5 per cent in 1972/73. A cut of over £30 million will be made in the defence research and development programme for 1970/71; it will affect development projects as well as research in Government establishments and in industry, and will free qualified engineers, scientists and technicians, as well as other resources, for civil work. The United Kingdom's local defence expenditure in areas other than Germany will be cut by one–third by 1970–71, and by a further third in 1972/73 compared with the 1967 rate of expenditure.

Education. The numbers in maintained primary schools will rise by 4.95 per cent in 1968/69 to 5.7 m. in 1970/71; in secondary schools by 6.1 per cent to 3.3 m; and in higher education by 7.5 per cent to over 450,000. Larger age–groups and greater numbers remaining voluntarily at school increase the pressure. A special programme of school building costing £105 million is planned to meet the demand for places following the raising of the statutory school age in 1973 and will be spread over the three preceding years. The allocation of extra resources in 1967/69 for school building in socially deprived areas has been supplemented by the provision of more nursery education under the Urban Programme, 1968. The total number of teachers in England and Wales is expected to increase from 317,000 in 1968 to 365,000 in 1971. It is envisaged that education in the public sector, including universities, will employ nearly one million in Great Britain by 1970/71; this includes ancillary staff.

Health. Between 1967 and 1972 the total population is forecast to increase by 2.6 per cent, persons over 65 by 8.4 per cent and children under ten by 4.7 per cent. It is expected that fifteen per cent more patients will be treated in 1972. Other factors include replacement and modernisation of old hospitals, growing demand for health centres and increased pharmaceutical services. The health and welfare services employ the full–time equivalent of about 820,000 people and the average annual increase has been over three per cent.

National Board for Prices and Incomes. In November, 1964, the Labour Government began negotations with management and trades unions to reach agreement on a policy to tackle the problems of inflationary price and wage rises and a slow rate of growth in productivity. In the following month the three parties to these negotiations issued the "Joint Statement of Intent on Productivity, Prices and Incomes". A White Paper published in February, 1965, "Machinery of Prices and Incomes Policy" embodied an agreement on the composition and functions of the National Board for Prices and Incomes. A second White Paper, "Prices and Incomes Policy" appeared in April, 1965. In the same month, the National Board was established as a Royal Commission to examine particular cases of price and income behaviour referred to it by the Government. The Board advises whether these cases accord with the national interest as defined by the Government after consultation with management and unions.

Mr. George Brown, First Secretary of State, appointed Mr. Aubrey Jones, a former Conservative M.P., as the first Chairman of the Board. In a speech at Oxford in December, 1965, Mr. Jones offered some reflections on Prices and Incomes Policy after the first six months. He said that the main factor governing the formulation of a wage claim was comparison with everybody else. A standard has to be determined as the result of a "social agreement" between government and representative organisations of employers and workers. At the same time there must be variation around the standard. Recent governments in their incomes policies have selected a standard related to the expected rate of increase in output per man hour over the following few years. The figure under the last Conservative Administration was initially 2 to 2½ per cent, later raised to 3 to 3½ per cent, which had been maintained by succeeding Labour Governments. There must be flexibility because of the need for differentiation to encourage efficiency.

An incomes policy must attempt to promote equality and differentiation at the same time. Mr. Jones referred to the development of productivity agreements, whereby workers agree to more flexible working arrangements in exchange for generous increases in remuneration, in some cases up to 25 per cent. Such increases are received in exchange for the abandonment of restrictive practices and this reacts on the white--collar workers, who have no restrictive practices with which to negotiate but see their differentials disappearing. This problem arose in 1965 in the electricity supply industry, in which the administrative and clerical staff were convinced that they had received less than fair and reasonable treatment having regard to settlements agreed for other categories of employees. In this case the Board was able to make certain recommendations aimed at reducing this sense of disturbance. The spread of productivity agreements requires an incomes policy which encourages a limited amount of differentiation.

Greater productivity resulting from differentiation should be reflected in reduced prices, so that productivity benefits the consumer as well as the wage-earner. According to Mr. Jones, this idea is foreign to the manufacturer and trade union leader alike, and "one of the great unaccomplished tasks of the Board is to propagate this strange conception." Consumer protection is thus the province of the Prices and Incomes Board, which is trying to strengthen the consumers' movement. The Board's function is concerned with systems and changes of systems, for example its task may be to examine the wage structure of a particular industry. This is to be distinguished from the essentially "peace-keeping" function of the arbitrator, working within narrow limits. There must be erected a body of conventions or moral restraints so that workers would not strike in vital industries such as electricity or printing, because the effect of such a strike would be to hold the community to ransom. An incomes policy has an important part to play in establishing the requisite moral restraints.

The Board has two Joint Vice-Chairmen, two other full-time members and four part-time members. In its early days it issued reports on road haulage; the prices of bread and flour, soap and detergents; tariffs charged by the London Electricity Board, the Scottish Gas Board, the South-Western Gas Board and the Wales Gas Board; the pay of bank staffs and of clerical and administrative workers in the electricity supply industry; wages, costs and prices in general printing and provincial newspapers; pay and conditions of certain grades of British Railways staff; wages in the bakery industry; pay of the Armed Forces and the Higher Civil Service; the proposal of the National Coal Board to raise coal prices; the price of beer; the pay of Scottish teachers; busmen's pay; and the pay of industrial workers employed by the Government. The Standing Advisory Committee on the Pay of the Higher Civil Service had recommended an increase of 6 per cent and the Board found this to be within the standard laid down in the White Paper on Prices and Incomes Policy. The only exception was the increase proposed for Assistant Secretaries and this was justifiable in order to maintain differentials.

More recently the Board has issued reports on the pay and conditions of manual workers in local authorities, the National Health Service, Gas and Water Supply; Fire Service Pay; the Pay of Chief and Senior Officers in the Local Government Service and the G.L.C.; Local Authority Housing Rents; and the Pay of Municipal Dustmen. In January, 1969, the Board published "100 P.I.B. Reports Summarised", an extremely useful reference book. The subjects covered by the Board's first 112 Reports included 43 on Prices, 58 on Pay, 8 on both subjects and 3 general reports.

The Board comprises five full-time members and ten part-time members. The present Chairman, Mr. Aubrey Jones, has indicated his intention to resign in the spring of 1970 to take up an appointment with I.P.C. It is expected that his successor will be one of the Deputy Chairmen, probably Lord Peddie. Overall responsibility for prices and incomes was transferred from the D.E.A. to the D.E.P. in April, 1969. The Board's Annual General Report is thus submitted to the Secretary of State for Employment and Productivity.

The Board's fourth General Report (July 1968 to July 1969) published on 29th July, 1969, makes some interesting points. For example, a productivity, prices and incomes policy is not a substitute for, but a necessary complement to, a fiscal and monetary policy. Perhaps the Board's most interesting and controversial view relates to prices which rose less than expected in 1968, according to the Report. The increase in earnings in 1968, the Board opines, was partly in response to price increases expected after devaluation. The number of new references to the Board has declined, the decrease in price references being more marked than in incomes references. The most important development by the Board in the field of prices was the conduct of efficiency studies in relation to the nationalised industries.

As regards incomes the Board seeks to rationalise determination of pay in the public sector in order to minimise "leap–frogging" or "pace–setting". In the private sector national settlements at industry level continue to play their part. At company or plant level there is a case for looking at the pay system of individual firms as wage inflation often arises because one group of employees feels that it is harshly treated in comparison with others. Despite its dangers, the Board considers that its work should be complemented by a fuller reference to the question of comparability.

A review of the functions and structure of the Board, the Commission on Industrial Relations, the Monopolies Commission and the Registry of Restrictive Trade Agreements is expected at the end of October, 1969.

Selective Employment Tax. The Chancellor of the Exchequer in his Budget Speech in May, 1966, announced that a new selective employment tax would be imposed on employers of labour. Provision is made for the collection of this tax in the Finance Act, 1966 and in the Selective Employment Payments Act, 1966 implementing the proposals in the White Paper on "Selective Employment Tax"[10]. From July, 1969[11] employers were liable to pay the following selective employment tax:–

    (a) 48s. for each man over 18;
    (b) 24s. for each woman over 18;
    (c) 24s. for each boy under 18; and
    (d) 16s. for each girl under 18.

	Full–time employees s. d.	Part–time employees s. d.
Men	85 3	70 6
Women	42 9	35 3
Boys under 18	42 9	35 3
Girls under 18	28 0	23 3

The tax is collected together with employers' insurance contributions and paid into the Exchequer. Selective employment *premiums* will be paid to employers who have paid selective employment tax in respect of establishments where:–

    (a) manufacturing activities or relevant scientific research is carried on: and
    (b) more than half the employees are normally concerned with such activities.

The rate of premium payable by the D.E.P. to the employer for each contribution well will be a refund of tax plus:–

    (a) 7s.6d. for each man over 18;
    (b) 3s.9d. for each woman over 18;

(c) 3s. 9d. for each boy under 18; and
(d) 2s. 6d. for each girl under 18.

Premiums are not be payable to local authorities or to certain other public bodies. The tax is *refunded* to employers in the fishing, mining, quarrying, transport and communication industries; and to employers in agriculture, horticulture and forestry and to certain research establishments. Refunds will also be made to certain public corporations including the coal, gas, electricity and air boards; and there will be power to make relevant payments to local authorities and charities.

Registers of qualifying establishments and charities have been compiled by the appropriate Ministers[12] but no business will be registered except on the application of an employer, who must keep appropriate records. Questions on registration and amounts payable may be determined by the industrial tribunals constituted under the Industrial Training Act, 1964. These tribunals now deal, therefore, with appeals against industrial training levies under that Act; redundancy payment appeals under the Redundancy Payments Act, 1965; and selective employment tax appeals.

It has been calculated that the "payroll tax" is in effect a tax on London and that it will bear adversely on South West England and Ulster. It may well be a move away from personal taxation towards a tax on production costs. Meanwhile the concept of a value-added tax on the French model is being considered in certain quarters notably the Conservative Party. V.A.T. is an indirect tax on costs and in France it is paid in stages as value is added to a product.

1. Cmnd 1432 (July, 1961).
2. Cmnd. 3936, H.M.S.O. 1/3d.
3. Price 6/6d.
5. Which is currently examining procedure for handling the Defence Votes by means of "output budgeting".
6. H.M.S.O. 13/6d. net – H.C. 136 – VI.
7. D.E.A.: H.M.S.O. 10/6d. net.
8. Cmnd. 2901.
9. Cmnd. 3701.
10, Cmd. 2986.
11. Thus almost doubling the original rates.
12. Secretary of State for Employment and Productivity, Minister of Agriculture, Secretary of State for Scotland, Minister of Housing and Local Government.

CHAPTER XX

ECONOMIC PLANNING AND REGIONAL GOVERNMENT

Introductory. The first attempt at regional government was initiated by Cromwell, following a Royalist rising at Salisbury in 1655, when the judges on circuit were seized and threatened with hanging. Cromwell then divided England into eleven military districts, each under the command of a Major-General. This military rule, coupled with puritanical suppression of virtually all public entertainments, was extremely unpopular and lasted for little more than a year. The second Parliament of the Protectorate voted Cromwell a large sum in exchange for the removal of the Major-Generals. With the ensuing restoration of the monarchy in 1660, no further attempts at regional government were made until modern times. The justices of the peace and the chartered boroughs remained responsible for local administration until the emergence of the nineteenth century system of local government.

The twentieth century saw an untidy, mushroom growth of regional offices of government departments. A landmark in regional development was the enactment of the Special Areas (Development and Improvement) Act, 1934, which was the first measure to affect the geographical distribution of industry. Two Commissioners, one for England and Wales and one for Scotland, were appointed under the Act, with wide powers to facilitate the economic development and social improvement of designated areas.

The Report of the Royal Commission on the Industrial Population, 1940, indicated that a regional system of administration would materially assist the better planning of industrial growth. This Report recommended the creation of a central authority to regulate the location of industry and a minority Report advocated the establishment for this purpose of a new government department, which would set up divisional or regional boards to aid industrial location.

During the second world war Regional Commissioners were appointed in ten English regions, and in Scotland and Wales, with wide powers to co-ordinate the work of local authorities in the organisation of civil defence. In practice, little use was made of the emergency powers and much was achieved by consultation and persuasion. The Commissioners assumed responsibility for the National Fire Service, the administration of which was returned to local government after the war by the Fire Services Act, 1947. However, county councils and county borough councils became the local fire protection authorities, whereas before the war the service was administered by the smaller authorities.

There was also regional control of production, the building industry and the allocation of road vehicles during the war. In 1940 Regional Boards were appointed to deal with problems of industrial production and output. They comprised regional officers of the main economic departments and three representatives from both sides of industry. These Boards had executive functions and included members who were not Civil Servants.

The Regional Commissioners were disbanded in 1945 and regional control was in general discontinued. The Regional Production Boards were translated into Advisory Regional Boards for Industry. Even the Special Areas Commissioners vanished, the Board of Trade assuming responsibility for distribution of industry. However, during the last ten years numerous studies of regions of the Kingdom have been published. These studies have stressed economic aspects of regional policy and the need for co-ordination of housing and physical services, as well as the projection of economic growth. In this connection, an effective partnership between central and local government is absolutely essential.

Meanwhile, in October, 1963, the President of the Board of Trade[1] had been designated Secretary of State for Industry, Trade and Regional Development. Studies of Britain's economic development as a whole had been made between 1962 and 1964 by the National Economic Development Council. In 1962 a Scottish Development Department was established within the Scottish Office to perform social and economic functions. In 1963 important policy statements on development in central Scotland and north-east England presaged "growth areas" selected for special government aid. At the same time improved communications, social investment[2] and encouragement of the arts were stressed. A special committee had reported on Northern Ireland's economic problems to the governments of the United Kingdom and Northern Ireland.[3] A study of South-East England was published in 1964. Detailed studies of the North-West and the West Midlands were also initiated at this time.

All the three main political parties are in favour of a measure of regionalism. In December, 1963, Sir Keith Joseph, then Minister of Housing and Local Government in a Conservative Administration[4] said that the government's view was that machinery at regional level should be achieved by strengthening central government in the regions and by making it more region conscious. In February, 1964, Mr. Harold Wilson, then Leader of the Opposition, said that regional regeneration and urban renewal would require a courageous degree of administrative decentralisation and that all the major Ministries concerned would have high-ranking regional officers to whom maximum authority must be delegated, subject only to the ultimate control by Ministers and by Parliament. At about the same time Mr. Michael Stewart, the present Foreign Secretary, was suggesting that major planning decisions would have to be taken nationally and would be administered by regional organisations of the central government.

The views of the recent Conservative Government have been expressed by Sir Keith Joseph,[5] who emphasised that Government's strong adherence to the concept of regionalism. Regional policies of central government ought to be made and carried out by a partnership between central government and reorganised local government. Sir Keith favoured regional plans and regional development but not necessarily regional government in the sense of regional representative councils. The Conservatives aimed at strong regional arms of central government and a more effective local government, based on the limited reforms possible under the Local Government Act, 1958. The outgoing Conservative Administration had, somewhat belatedly, recognised the special problems of the North-East by allocating responsibility for the development of that region to a senior Cabinet Minister.[6] This was due to the fact that problems of unemployment and location of industry were more acute in this area.

The Liberal Party, in a report published in April, 1966, entitled *Federalism—a Study in Devolution and Decentralisation,* postulated a federal structure of regional government with directly elected regional councils. The power to promote local bills would be transferred to the new councils. The Liberals proposed that the regional councillors should be paid and that the councils, which would replace the existing regional planning boards, would become Regional Planning Research Units. They would have far-reaching responsibilities for town and country planning, transport, health, police, fire, ambulances, civil defence and even education, although in the latter case local authorities would retain certain functions. The main departments would be controlled by a regional Minister and their policies would be approved by specialist committees.

Department of Local Government and Regional Planning. A Secretary of State for Local Government and Regional Planning was appointed in October, 1969, and we are here concerned with his regional planning functions. The Department of Economic Affairs, created in 1964, ceased to exist, its functions being shared between the new Department and the expanded Ministry of Technology (see Chapter XXI). The new Secretary of State is responsible for the regional economic planning boards and their staffs and this is logical, since they have become increasingly concerned with transport, social and environmental problems. It will be recalled that the new Department controls the Ministries of Transport and of Housing and Local Government and that it is especially charged with the problems of environmental pollution. The new Department has thus inherited the regional planning functions of the D.E.A. On the other hand, the D.E.A.'s former responsibility for regional economic development has been transferred to the enlarged Ministry of Technology.

The connection between regional planning and local government reform is obvious, as is that between land-use planning and transport. Technology controls regional industrial planning but the Department of Regional Planning is responsible for environmental planning. Consequently, the political voice of the regions will be heard through the new Department. An account of the regional planning boards and councils follows.

The National Economic Development Council. Until 1962 the Treasury's Economic Planning Board and the National Production Advisory Council for Industry were the main bodies whose function it was to advise the Government on economic planning and growth. The T.U.C. agreed to join the National Economic Development Council, having been assured by the then Chancellor of the Exchequer[7] that the Council would be consulted before the formulation of national economic policy. The Federation of British Industry and the British Employers' Confederation[8] also supported the project.

N.E.D.C. was formed in 1962 with the Chancellor of the Exchequer as Chairman. Its other members comprised the President of the Board of Trade, the Minister of Labour, six T.U.C. representatives, six employers, two chairman of public corporation[9] two independent members and a Director-General. The Council has been reconstituted with the Premier as Chairman and it now includes the Minister of Technology and the Chairman of the National Board for Prices and Incomes; and the Confederation of British Industry provides the management representatives. "Neddy's" terms of reference are to seek agreement on ways of improving economic performance in the U.K. It is thus particularly concerned with plans for the future in both sectors of industry and seeks to overcome obstacles to quicker growth. The staff was drawn partly from the Civil Service and partly from industry and elsewhere.

Economic Development Committees were formed in 1963, with representatives of management, trade unions and relevant government departments sitting with members of the National Economic Development Office. These 'little Neddies", of which there are now about twenty, examine the performance, prospects and plans of individual industries and consider methods of improving competitiveness and efficiency.

The chairmen and a few of the members of the E.D.C.s are independent and the N.E.D. office in each case provides a senior member and a secretary. D.E.A. industrial advisers also sat on the E.D.C.s; and the Chief Industrial adviser of D.E.A. and the Industrial Director of the N.E.D. office were joint chairmen of a steering committee which co-ordinated relations between government departments and the E.D.C.s. The National Plan was prepared by the D.E.A. in collaboration with N.E.D.C. The Council followed up its original general work on policies by examining progress in management training and by studies of investment incentives; it also did work on policies for particular industries. A major development has been the greatly increased emphasis on the "little Neddies" as a means of stimulating modernisation and change in industry. Since the demise of D.E.A., N.E.D.C. has reported direct to the Cabinet office.

Regional Planning Boards and Councils. The two main aims are to provide for a full and balanced development of the country's economic and social resources; and to ensure that the regional implications of growth are clearly understood and taken into account in the planning of land use, of developments[10] and of services.

The economic planning councils are concerned with broad strategy on regional development and the best use of the region's resources. Their principal function is to help in the formulation of regional plans and to advise on their implementation; they have no executive powers. The councils do not trench upon the existing powers and responsibilities of Ministers or local authorities. They normally prepare draft plans for the regions and co-ordinate the work of government departments in implementing the final plans.

England has been divided into eight regions:—Northern, North-West, Yorkshire and Humberside, East Midlands, West Midlands, South-West, East Anglia and the South-East. Separate economic planning boards and councils have been established in Scotland and Wales by the respective Secretaries of State. In Scotland, the Chairman of the Board is an officer of the Scottish Office, and in Wales he is an officer of the Welsh Office. In both countries D.L.G.R.P. is represented on the board by a senior official. The economic planning boards comprise senior regional officers of the departments concerned with economic planning (that is, Civil Servants). In England, the Chairman is an Under-Secretary of the D.L.G.R.P. The boards meet regularly every month; contact is maintained with the nationalised industries through the responsible departments.

The members of the economic planning councils have been appointed as individuals, and not as delegates or representatives of particular interests. Most have some twenty-five part-time members including people experienced in the fields of agriculture, commerce, industry, social service, trade unions, local government and the universitites. In Scotland and Wales, the Chairman of the Council is a Minister. The councils meet monthly and have appointed sub-committees on such matters as communications, land use, industrial structure and labour mobility. The chairmen of the regional board and council attend each other's meetings and the Planning Board Secretariat also services the council.

The new boards and councils have the tasks of assessing the economic potential of each region and the social and other measures necessary to realise that potential. They must also ensure that full weight is given to the regional significance of national policies. They have already given advice on such matters as the proposals of the National Ports Council for the development of major ports, the long-term road programme and the regional implications of proposed railway closures. The councils can also encourage local authorities and voluntary bodies to adopt a regional approach to common problems. The board can improve administration in the regions by strengthening co-operation between departments and reducing delays.

D.L.G.R.P. has specialists in regional questions in its Planning Division, who can advise the boards and their research staff. It also has research staff in each region, working closely with regional research staff of other departments.

In some of the planning areas, development councils are in active existence, receiving grants from local authorities and industry. The Government envisage the continuation of such councils alongside the new regional machinery. Government grants will continue to aid the valuable publicity work of the Scottish Council and the North-East Development Council. The chairmen of the Regional Economic Planning Councils are urgently examining the transport needs of their regions and conducting pilot studies of particular problems of integration, in accordance with the Government's policy.

Planning Regions

NORTHERN
> Cumberland, Durham, North Riding of Yorkshire, Northumberland, Westmorland.
> Regional Capital: Newcastle-upon-Tyne.

NORTH-WEST
> Cheshire, Lancashire, High Peak District of Derbyshire.
> Regional Capital: Manchester.

YORKSHIRE AND HUMBERSIDE
> East and West Ridings of Yorkshire, Lindsey (a Part of Lincolnshire). City of York.
> Regional Capital: Leeds.

EAST MIDLANDS
> Derbyshire,[11] Leicestershire, Holland-with-Boston and Kesteven (Parts of Lincolnshire), Northamptonshire, Nottinghamshire, Rutland, City of Lincoln.
> Regional Capital: Nottingham.

WEST MIDLANDS
> Herefordshire,   Shropshire,   Staffordshire,   Warwickshire,

Worcestershire, City of Birmingham.

Regional Capital: Birmingham.

SOUTH-WEST

Cornwall (including the Isles of Scilly), Devon, Dorset, Gloucestershire, Somerset and Wiltshire.

Regional Capital: Bristol.

SOUTH-EAST

Greater London, Bedfordshire, Berkshire, Buckinghamshire, Essex, Hampshire, Isle of Wight, Hertfordshire, Kent, Oxfordshire, Surrey, East and West Sussex.

Regional Capital: London.

EAST ANGLIA

Cambridgeshire and the Isle of Ely, Huntingdon and Peterborough, Norfolk, East and West Suffolk.

Regional Capital: Norwich.

The South-East. The South-East Study, 1961–1981, and a White Paper on South-East England[1] [2] were published in March, 1964. The study was a comprehensive examination of the housing and land use problems of Greater London and the South-East. It provided a basis for discussion with local planning authorities on the necessary provision for growth and movements of population in the area south-east of a line from the Wash to Dorset. It considered that the population of the area would increase during the twenty years by 3½ million.

The present level of population in Greater London of about eight million was thought unlikely to change much, so that the whole of the increase would have to be accommodated outside that area. Provision for about two-thirds (some 2–2½ million) was envisaged through land allocations in development plans, followed by ordinary development. Such allocations would mainly provide for the natural increase of the local population, for "commuter overspill" from the conurbation and for migrants for retirement. Further, provision should be made for nearly 1½ million to be accommodated in planned expansion schemes. A quarter of a million would be within the capacity of existing new towns and current town expansion scheme, the remainder would have to be housed in a second generation of new and expanded towns larger than the first set and further from London. New cities were postulated in the vicinity of Southampton-Portsmouth, Bletchley and Newbury. Six major expansions were proposed– of Stansted, Ashford (Kent), Ipswich, Northampton, Peterborough and Swindon.[13] Growth beyond present targets at existing new towns such as Harlow and Stevenage was envisaged. The main criteria for selection were prospects of rapid, sound and prosperous growth and ability to attract commerce and offices from London.

No sudden decrease in the development of new employment was

expected; and many would be attracted to the area from other regions and from abroad to work in offices and in the manufacturing and service industries. A continuing annual increase of about 20,000 was foreseen in central London employment. New office centres on the periphery should be provided for central London firms willing to move. An estimated 400,000 workers would move to homes beyond the Green Belt and commute to central London. Land allocations for housing should be aligned with railway capacities and thus would involve considerable capital expenditure on both British Railways and London Transport.

A limited amount of land could reasonably be found for housing in the Green Belt: this policy has been increasingly pursued during the last five years. The White Paper broadly accepted the South-East Study's assessment of the problems. It stated that the Government, by controlling public investment and industrial building and by phasing the release of land for the planned schemes, would ensure that development in the South-East was carried out without prejudice to growth in other regions. The principal instruments for diverting office employment from London would be the Location of Offices Bureau and the Government's own decentralisation policy. Considerable success has attended their efforts, aided by a reduction of employment in factories owing to automation. A growth of nearly two million was expected in the outer Metropolitan region in sites allocated by the planning authorities. This would tend to be somewhat sporadic and a more coherent development is necessary in this region. Building across the Green Belt on chosen sites has been suggested, coupled with the creation of large and permanent parks elsewhere.[14] Any such proposals would have to be linked with the new Greater London Development Plan.

The area of the South-East Study has been divided by the Government into two economic planning regions: East Anglia and the South-East.

The region is the largest in England, both as to area and population. The regional council meets every two months but its committees meet more frequently. Universities in the area[15] may well be asked to help with demographic and sociological research. A committee on planning strategy considers the distribution of housing and industry in the light of the likely growth of population and employment. A communications committee deals with transport strategy and such matters as investment in roads, passenger railway closure proposals and travel to central London. An amenities committee reports on proposals to extend the green belt, on parks and the growth of the holiday trade.

In 1967 the South-East E.P.C. published "A Strategy for the South-East". The region's population is likely to grow by about 2 million between 1964 and 1981. There is evidence of continued growth in the employment field. Great efforts are required to reduce employment pressures and congestion in London and to persuade employers to move out. Industrial and employment growth should not be unduly restricted outside London, in view of the region's most important contribution to national prosperity.

In 1967 the average rate of unemployment was 1.6 per cent. There will be a significant change in the labour supply position owing to slow growth in the region's working age population; this will pose difficulties in ensuring that sufficient industry is available to move to the new and expanding towns. A special problem is the physical expansion of Greater London which will necessitate finding accommodation outside London for a million people by 1981; failure to do so will have adverse repercussions on London housing and major redevelopment.

Since 1964 eight new towns have been created beyond the Metropolitan Green Belt and "overspill" agreements made with expanding towns in and outside the region, largely to provide for people from London. Since 1965 the Government have approved the development of a new town at Milton Keynes and expansions of Northampton, Peterborough and Ipswich; there is a proposal for a major development in South Hampshire.

Recent developments in the other Regions. In 1961 the Toothill Report recommended that a new Scottish Department should be created, whose functions would include the Secretary of State's responsibility for the general oversight of the economy and his statutory powers relating to town and country planning, roads, electricity and water in Scotland. In 1962 the Scottish Development Department was established to administer these statutory functions relating to physical services; and the same year saw the creation of the Scottish Development Groups, which included senior representatives of all government departments concerned with economic development in Scotland. Meanwhile, N.E.D.C. was also playing its part by emphasising the positive aspects of regional development, including public investment as well as incentives for the expansion of private industry. In this way regional imbalance could be corrected and labour fully used. Growth zones were created in Central Scotland and North-East England and no parts of the zones were to be removed from the list until there was strong evidence of genuine improvement in regional employment. Public investment in housing, roads and other services was encouraged and, in the North-East, the co-ordination of government administrative machinery. The Scottish Development Group formed the nucleus of the Scottish Economic Planning Board, under a Chairman appointed by the Secretary of State and including representatives of the economic planning departments.

The first results of the series of industrial studies commissioned by the Scottish Economic Planning Council indicate good prospects of continued growth in the domestic electrical appliance and business machine industries in Scotland. The Council has made a special inquiry into the movement of professional, scientific and technical staff employed in all Scottish manufacturing establishments with 500 workers or more. This survey established that in 1964–65 the movement into Scottish industry of professional and higher grade staff had shown an encouragingly substantial upward turn and slightly exceeded the outward movement to other parts of Britain. A high rate of public investment in Central Scotland and North-East England will continue, thus reinforcing the regional economic plan. Studies are also being undertaken of the economic problems of the Highlands and the rest of Scotland. In 1969 Parliament set up a Select Committee on Scottish Affairs, which is examining the way in which Scotland's economic plans are prepared and its levels of public spending determined.

A survey of the prospects in Wales during the next twenty years is in hand and economic planning machinery has been set up. The Chairman of the Welsh Economic Planning Board and the members of the Welsh Economic Planning Council were appointed by the Secretary of State for Wales. The Council's mid-Wales panel has met the consultants studying the possibility of a new town for mid-Wales and has discussed the project with representatives of the West Midlands Council and Board. The Northern Ireland Government has set up an Economic Council and that Government is represented at meetings[16] of the chairman of the Economic Planning Boards. The Government periodically consults the Councils on specific policy issues relevant to regional distribution of population, economic activity and physical resources. This has been done in connection with future policy for the development of major ports and the question of industrial de-rating in Scotland.

Unemployment is a good example of a special problem which exists in some regions and it has for decades been consistently above the national average in Scotland and the North. At the end of 1964 the national average rate of unemployment for Great Britain was 1.5 per cent. The rates in London, the South-East and the Midlands were 1 per cent or less but the percentages for Scotland, the North and Wales were 3.4, 3 and 2.7 per cent respectively. There are also pockets of much higher unemployment in these three regions and in the South-West. High levels of unemployment result in a slower rate of economic growth, uneconomic use of manpower and drift of population to the South. Moreover, in the "booming" areas there are such repercussions as pressure on incomes, prices and the balance of payments caused by "overheating"; and congestion, housing shortage and overcrowding resulting from the population drift. The new boards and councils have a vital part to play in reversing these trends and most of them have already indicated an awareness of the problems.

The Chairman of the Northern Economic Planning Council is Mr. T. Dan Smith, the former leader of the City Council at Newcastle-upon-Tyne, who has called for a radical reform of local government[17] and a modification of regional planning machinery to produce one large organisation capable of providing at regional level a critical path analysis of public expenditure. The Northern Economic

Planning Council Working Group has forecast a substantial increase in demand for workers in certain skilled engineering and construction occupations, particularly in engineering and electrical goods. It has also emphasised the need to ensure adequate training for which material assistance is provided by the Industrial Training Boards. Mr. Smith has also urged the development of Manchester airport as the North's main centre for international flights.

Throughout its industrial history the region has been heavily dependent on coalmining, shipbuilding, iron and steel production and heavy engineering. Since 1962 over 180 manufacturing firms new to the region have set up factories in the North or made the decision to do so. In 1966 virtually the whole region was made a Development Area and in 1967 "Special Development Area" status was accorded to 22 Employment Exchanges likely to be severely affected by pit closures. In 1967 the unemployment rate in the North was 4 per cent. Five new towns have been designated—Aycliffe, Peterlee, Washington, Cramlington and Killingworth. Progress is being made with reclamation of derelict land.

In 1967 the Chancellor of the Duchy of Lancaster assumed special responsibility for Northern regional matters but this arrangement ended in 1969 on the formation of D.L.G.R.P.

An interesting contribution to the regional debate has been made by one of England's largest local authorities, West Riding County Council, in *A growth policy for the North,* issued as part of the county development plan's second review.[18] Despite the existence of the new planning machinery, the county council contend that the sixteen local planning authorities in the region should promote forward regional policies through a joint standing conference. The Yorkshire and Humberside region contains one-tenth of the land mass and population of England and Wales. The Humber is the confluence of five inland waterways and is the sea outlet for the river basin of the Ouse and Trent. Humberside is the only deep-water estuary in England still largely undeveloped and has great potential for further industrial and commercial development. With improved accessibility, the Humber ports could serve a large hinterland; moreover, they face the Continent, Britain's fastest growing foreign market. The completion of the motorway system and the projected building of two oil refineries should boost the region's economy, as would cheap supplies of North Sea natural gas, if they become available; and the possibility of a new power station.

Other developments include construction of the largest gas-producing plant in the country[19] and plans by the National Coal Board resulting in the creation[20] of the largest bulk-handling coal port in Western Europe. The three northern regions provide an enormous proportion of the country's wealth and much unspoilt countryside. They should, together with Scotland, clarify their aims and priorities and "evolve the concept of a dynamic, renewed North". Problems to be overcome include population loss and over-dependence on the basic industries of coal, steel and textiles.

t

There should be a more flexible outlook on strategic planning and location of industry and housing. There is also subsidence in the coalmining zone, which is slowly moving from west to east, towards the greatest growth potential for surface development. Airport facilities are inadequate and there is too much waste and pollution of water. The Report stresses the need to renew the outworn building fabric in town and country and to transform the landscape. One aim of the proposals would be to create a new Humber-Mersey axis as an effective counter to the London-Birmingham axis.

Meanwhile, the Yorkshire and Humberside Economic Planning Council had already formed a Group to consider the economic development of Humberside, including both banks of the river. Another Group has been established to consider environmental problems in the region. The Universities of Hull, Leeds and York have been invited to participate in setting up an Academic Advisory Committee. The West Riding County Council has also suggested that representatives of the three Northern Economic Planning Councils should meet to co-ordinate their capital expenditure. This would be a plan for 15 million people and such co-operation would provide the North with a coherent investment programme.

The E.P.C. published its Review of Yorkshire and Humberside in 1966 and in 1968 suggested a planning strategy for maintaining future employment in the Yorkshire coalmining areas up to 1975. The Humberside Feasibility Study was published in 1969 and recommended the early completion of a Humber Bridge (which would be the longest in the country) to facilitate the extension of the two sides of the Humber into a single economic area. Humberside is included in a study of proposed Maritime Industrial Development Areas.

Cash grants for industry. Under the Industrial Development Act, 1966, cash grants for new capital investment in selected industries replaced investment allowances. The general rate was 20 per cent (40 per cent in new development areas in Scotland, Wales, the North, Merseyside and parts of South-West England). A special building grant is available to encourage businesses to settle in the more remote areas. The Board of Trade retains control through the issue of industrial development certificates[21] and administers the grants. The annual cost is about £250 m. The public corporations are largely excluded because the government already controls their investment programmes. Manufacturing and extractive[22] industries mainly benefit and computers qualify for grant. Separate legislation provides for agriculture, fisheries and ports in Northern Ireland.

The Government's aim is to channel funds into productive investment and to encourage exports; the grant system is also relatively simple. It is more generous to manufacturers than they expected. The scheme does not apply to the distributive and service industries, which account for about a third of British investment. The certain knowledge that a substantial proportion of their outlay will return within 18 months should encourage the more adventurous industrialists.

The Hunt Report and the Intermediate Areas. Regional employment premiums of 30/- a week were introduced in development areas in 1967.[23] A committee under Sir Joseph Hunt was appointed to study in depth the problems of areas intermediate between development areas and the more prosperous regions. The main recommendations of the Hunt Report were:—

(i) The whole of the Yorkshire and Humberside and North West Regions should qualify for a new 25 per cent building grant, training grants and direct training help.

(ii) Government estates, factory building, investment and link roads should be made available in selected growth zones within these regions.

(iii) There should be an 85 per cent grant for derelict land clearance in the two regions.

(iv) The industrial development certificate control should be relaxed generally by raising the exemption to 10,000 sq. ft. (not accepted by the Government).

(v) The Merseyside development area should be incorporated in the new North West intermediate area (this was not accepted by the Government).

The Government also rejected the general building grant idea and made certain limited proposals for parts of Humberside, the North West and elsewhere (e.g. S.E. Wales, the Yorkshire Coalfield, Plymouth). These include seeking powers under the Local Employment Acts for:—

(i) grants at 25 per cent of factory building costs
(ii) government built factories
(iii) development area training grants, etc.

These main proposals would be complemented by assistance in transfer of key workers, new housing, expenditure on roads and derelict land clearance for schemes certified by the Board of Trade[24] (which would continue to operate i.d.c. control so as to give development and intermediate areas general priority).

The Industrial Reorganisation Corporation. The special function of the Industrial Reorganisation Corporation is to search for opportunities to promote rationalisation schemes which could yield substantial benefits to the national economy, especially in terms of increased exports and more rapid technological advance. The Corporation has power to initiate and finance industrial mergers and rationalisation and to draw up to £150 million from the Exchequer. It does not, however, retain ownership of the new or reorganised enterprises but withdraws its capital as soon as possible and moves on to further schemes so that the same funds can be used repeatedly.

The Industrial Reorganisation Corporation Act, 1966, enables I.R.C., for the purpose of promoting industrial efficiency and profitability and the national economy in whole or in part, to:—

(a) promote or assist the reorganisation or development of any industry or
(b) if requested by the Secretary of State, to establish or develop any industrial enterprise.

The Corporation seeks the fullest co-operation from industry and finance houses and, whenever possible, its schemes would be implemented either through the normal machinery of the market or in close collaboration with the market. It can acquire a stake in the ownership of the new groupings or enterprises thereby created. Priority is given to rationalisation and modernisation schemes offering good prospects of early returns in terms of increased exports or reduced import requirements. Advice is sought from industry and the City, from government departments and the Economic Development Committees. The Corporation acts as a catalyst, help companies to evolve practical schemes, providing expert services and paying particular attention to the management needs of new groupings.

The Corporation is empowered to hold physical assets in order to purchase machines and make them available to new groupings, for example by leasing the machines. The Corporation might provide capital for new projects or expansions of special importance to the economy for example, expansion of research, development and design facilities, investment in new plant, especially cost-saving machinery of modern design. The Corporation co-operates with the Ministry of Technology, and the National Research Development Corporation; and with the Ministry of Housing and Local Government in matters affecting the construction industry. Mergers resulting from schemes sponsored by the Corporation would not be referred to the Monopolies Commission, as the government does not wish to hold back mergers which are in the national interest. Many of the schemes would result in mergers within the scope of the Monopolies and Mergers Act, 1965.

The Minister of Technology is the Minister responsible for the Industrial Reorganisation Corporation. The first chairman of the Corporation was Sir Frank Kearton, Chairman of Courtaulds, an industrial leader of renown.[25] In its day to day work, the Corporation works very closely with the Ministry of Technology and the Board of Trade.

Some light is thrown on I.R.C. activities by its Annual Report and Accounts for 1968/69. The Board members seek to improve the structure of our industries and, whilst size in itself is no solution, it can provide the essential base for large scale effort required for prosperity. The Report points to the need to improve the quality of management and to improve our system of industrial relations. The I.R.C. sees its main task as improving the international performance of manufacturing industry by promoting structure reorganisation. The most significant event in 1968/69 was the merger of G.E.C. and English Electric in the electrical and electronics industry, following up earlier I.R.C. support for G.E.C. in its acquisition of A.E.I. In the field of industrial relations I.R.C. seeks full consultation with trades unions in nationalisation schemes. The I.R.C.'s activities constitute a vital factor in strengthening the balance of payments by increasing the international competitiveness of British industry. In the Board of Trade's view, mergers encouraged by I.R.C. have proved beneficial and this is the reason that so few have been referred to the Monopolies Commission.

The work of the I.R.C. is complemented in the legislative field by the Industrial Expansion Act, 1968.

1. Mr. Edward Heath, now Leader of the Opposition.
2. Such as housing programmes.
3. Hall report on the Economy of Northern Ireland, Cmd 1835, HMSO, 1962.
4. Now Conservative Front Bench spokesman on Social Services.
5. In the first Gwilym Gibbon lecture on 15th April, 1964.
6. Lord Hailsham, Lord President of the Council, subsequently the first Secretary of State for Education and Science (1964). (Now Mr. Quintin Hogg).
7. Mr. Selwyn Lloyd.
8. Now merged in the Confederation of British Industry.
9. The National Coal Board and the Electricity Council.
10. Particularly industrial development.
11. Except the High Peak District.
12. Cmd 2308.
13. The last three being outside S.E. England as now defined.
14. Terence Bendixson, *Guardian* Planning Correspondent, 20th December, 1965.
15. Brunel, City, Essex, Kent, London, Oxford, Reading, Southampton, Surrey, Sussex.
16. Convened by the D.L.G.R.P.
17. He was a member of the English Royal Commission.
18. Published in April, 1966.
19. At Killingholme.
20. At Immingham.
21. An i.d.c. attaches to the *project*, rather than to the *land*; they are now required for certain applications to retain buildings or continuance of land and conditions can be attached. Responsibility has been transferred to Mintech.
22. E.G. china clay, iron ore and quarrying.
23. These will continue at least until 1974.
24. Now Mintech.
25. The present Chairman is Sir Joseph Lockwood; the Deputy Chairman is Lord Stokes.

CHAPTER XXI

PARLIAMENT AND THE MACHINERY
OF GOVERNMENT

Introductory. It is proposed to examine, in this final chapter, the relationship between Parliament and the machinery of the Administration, interpreting the Government or the Administration in the widest sense to embrace the central departments, local authorities, the public corporations and statutory boards. In order to relate this theme to current conditions, the Queen's Speech will be taken as the starting point. Much of the material in the Queen's Speech is implemented by means of legislation but there are other matters, notably the reform of Parliamentary procedure, which can be achieved only by parliamentary administrative action. Turning from Parliament to the organisation of Government Departments, we see the conflicting pressures for a smaller Cabinet on the one hand and more diverse activities on the other. In this connection an examination is made of the Ministry of Technology and its constitutional position in relation to the machinery of government. The Land Commission is taken as a useful example of a statutory board or Commission of fairly recent creation. The need for co-ordination and administrative discretion in all these areas is self-evident but nevertheless poses difficult problems. Finally the linked questions of regionalism and nationalism are discussed, culminating into a glimpse of the future aided by various crystal balls, of which perhaps the Redcliffe-Maud Report is the most potent.

The Queen's Speech. In accordance with tradition and recent practice the Queen's Speech at the Opening of Parliament first dealt with Commonwealth and foreign affairs. If necessary, this subject includes within its scope the allied matters of defence and foreign economic policy. The Monarch addresses both Houses of Parliament but, at a certain point in the Speech, the Queen addresses herself only to the House of Commons, saying "Estimates for the public service will be laid before you", thus acknowledging the complete dominance of the representative

House in this field. Reverting to both Houses, the Speech then mentions proposed legislation. Thus in the Queen's Speech opening the 1968/9 Session of Parliament reference was made to a housing bill to implement the proposals in the White Paper "Old Houses into New Homes"; to a Representation of the People Bill to reform the electoral law; to an immigration appeal bill; and to further legislation required in connection with the proposed change to decimal currency in 1971. We have already seen that the first two bills mentioned have become law as the Housing Act, 1969 and the Representation of the People Act 1969. The Immigration Appeal Act 1969 makes better provision for appeal against the decisions of immigration officials employed by the Home Office relating to admission to the U.K.

The Decimal Currency Board, under the Chairmanship of Lord Fiske, was set up under the Decimal Currency Act, 1967. The 1969 Act provides for practical arrangements necessary to effect the changeover to the new system which will take place on 15 February 1971, from which date decimal currency coinage will be legal tender.

The bill to reform the House of Lords, mentioned in the Queen's Speech was introduced but subsequently dropped. It also proved politically impossible to reform industrial relations by legislation in the 1968/69 session of Parliament, although an Industrial Relations Commission with certain pacifying powers was set up under the Chairmanship of Mr. Woodcock.

An example of legislation incorporating requirements of a treaty or convention is the Nuclear Installations Act, 1969 which amends the 1965 Act to make it comply with international conventions on liability for nuclear damage.

Private members' bills are not, of course, mentioned in the Queen's Speech which is largely concerned with legislation to be brought forward on behalf of the government. However, private members were not idle in promoting legislation during the 1968/69 session of Parliament, notably in the area of divorce law reform.

Reform in Parliamentary Procedure. It has been urged in various quarters in recent years that the work of select committees should be extended over a wide field of public administration. Education, land law, planning and productivity have been mentioned as candidates. Apart from the Select Committee on Procedure, which is of long standing, until recently there was only the Select Committee on Nationalised Industries. In 1968, however, Select Committees on Education, Agriculture, Race Relations and Technology were set up. The Select Committee on Education inquired into the "sit-in" at Guildford College of Art and also at Hornsey College of Art and Essex University but some difficulty was encountered in holding its meetings outside the precincts of the Palace of Westminster. The Select Committee on Agriculture quite properly inquired into the possible effect on British farming of British entry to the E.E.C. It was threatened with extinction for its pains and finally liquidated in February, 1969, at the instance, it is believed, of the Foreign Office.

The modernisation of Parliament is a desirable prospect having regard to the decline in the authority of the House of Commons to which even Ministers of the Crown have drawn attention. A century ago Parliament selected the Premier, was active in policy formulation and partially controlled the work of the departments. Fifty years ago parliamentary government had moved to Cabinet government, under which effective policy-making had been transferred from the public debates in the House to the secret discussions of a Cabinet sustained by a rigid party system. The final stage, according to Mr. R.H.S. Crossman, was Prime Ministerial Government, although 1969 has seen a Prime Minster thwarted three times in succession—on House of Lords reform, industrial relations and redistribution of seats in the course of a single parliamentary session.

Another desirable reform would be more rational hours of attendance and the disappearance of all-night sittings. A start has been made with morning sittings and the introduction of voting machines would save some time. The Opening of Parliament has been televised during the last few years but so far the House of Commons has set its face against its proceedings being televised. This is the age of publicity and it would seem right that facilities extended to the Press should also be accorded to broadcasting and television. The House of Commons now has Select Committees on Public Business and on Broadcasting. A joint Committee of the two Houses of Parliament is currently examining parliamentary privilege.

Private members have to ballot for priority owing to the limited time available to them. Their bills take precedence over government bills on ten Fridays in the Session and also on ten other Fridays but in the latter case only after private members' motions. They also can introduce bills on four days other than Fridays until 7 p.m. There is a case for giving more time to private members, who often promote useful reforms. One suggestion is that private members' bills should be given priority according to the amount of support they gain.

Since 1965 a Minister has been able to table a motion that a Bill be referred to a Second Reading Committee, which is a Standing Committee of between 30 and 80 members nominated by the Committee of Selection. Such a motion can be successfully resisted if not less than 20 members object. A Second Reading Committee reports to the House whether or not they recommend that the Bill ought to be read a second time and, if they report against second reading, they can state reasons. The House decides the question for second reading without amendment or debate. The procedure saves time and facilitates the passage of non-controversial and unopposed bills.

The Royal Assent Act, 1967, simplified the procedure for giving the royal assent to bills. This enables notification to be given to each House by the Speaker of the House of Commons and the Lord Chancellor respectively.

It is appropriate to mention, in connection with the modernisation of Parliament, the proposals for the redevelopment of Whitehall and the whole parliamentary precinct of Westminster. One major aim is to give M.P.s better working conditions and office facilities. The project is being supervised by the Minister of Public Building and Works. Finally, M.P.s are not highly paid and receive no allowances for expenses in respect of their heavy postage bills and secretarial assistance, unlike many other legislators. Adequate expenses to cover such matters are overdue and urgent.

Government Departments and the Machinery of Government. We have seen that the last two or three years have witnessed the emergence of powerful new departments in Whitehall—D.E.P., D.H.S.S., D.L.G.R.P., the amalgamated Foreign and Commonwealth Office and the enlarged Mintech. The short-lived Ministry of Land and Natural Resources has disappeared and the Ministry of Public Building and Works has relinquished administration of the building regulations to M.H.L.G., having been compensated by assuming responsibility from the Ministry of Technology for the Building Research Station. The Defence Department has undergone yet another internal reorganisation so that there are now, under the Secretary of State, two Ministers of Defence, one for Administration and one for Equipment. The Service Ministers are now reduced to the rank of Parliamentary Under-Secretaries of State.

At the time of writing (October, 1969) there are 21 members of the Cabinet although earlier in 1969 the Prime Minster constituted an inner Cabinet of himself and ten others. Secrecy shrouds the exact composition of the inner Cabinet but obviously it includes the Foreign Secretary, the Chancellor of the Exchequer, the House Secretary, the Social Services Secretary, the Employment and Productivity Secretary, the Defence Secretary, the Local Government and Regional Planning Secretary and the Minister of Technology (and probably the Leader of the House of Commons).

Meanwhile the Conservatives thinking is believed to be to enlarge the Broad of Trade into a Ministry of Industry, absorbing most of the present functions of the Ministry of Technology. Under the Conservative scheme, a new Department of Nationalized Industry would probably replace the Ministry of Power and the injection of private capital would be encouraged. In the area of the D.E.P., the N.B.P.I. and the Industrial Relations Commission might be merged and the Industrial Reorganisation Corporation, if it survived, would come under the wing of the Ministry of Industry. It is appropriate at this juncture to take a look at the Ministry of Technology which is bound to be at the centre of technological advance whichever party is in power, even if its name is changed or it is absorbed into another department.

The Ministry of Technology. The booklet Ministry of Technology 1964–69 gives an account of the work of the Ministry as it was until its expansion in October, 1969. The Minister of Technology is assisted by two Ministers of State and three Joint Parliamentary Secretaries. The Minister of State is particularly concerned with the work of the Aviation Group and also has responsibilities for atomic energy and hovercraft activities of the Research Group and for technological collaboration with Western Europe and North America. The Joint Parliamentary Secretaries take questions concerning the work of the remainder of the Research Group, the Engineering Group, aerospace exports and technological collaboration with countries other than Western Europe and North America.

The official head of the Ministry is the Permanent Secretary. The Secretary (Aviation) is in charge of the Aviation Group. Both the Secretaries are Accounting Officers. They are generally responsible for the work of the Ministry and for advising the Ministers on matters of policy.

The Ministry is organized under the general management of the Permanent Secretary into three Groups—Engineering, Research and Aviation; and in addition to these there are common services. There are three Deputy Secretaries and four Controllers, each in charge of a number of Divisions.

The new Ministry's task was defined as being "to guide and stimulate a major national effort to bring advanced technology and new processes into British industry". It took over many of the functions and most of the resources of D.S.I.R., N.R.D.C. and U.K. Atomic Energy Authority. It was also given responsibility for computers, electronics, telecommunications and machine tools and, in 1966, for engineering in general and merchant shipbuilding. The old Ministry of Aviation was merged into Mintech in 1967, the civil aviation functions of the former having been transferred to the Board of Trade in 1966. Thus Mintech acquired responsibility for the aircraft industry and huge research establishments using very advanced technologies.

The responsibilities of Mintech can be summarised:—

(a) Government's relationship with engineering and vehicles industries (the "sponsorship" function).
(b) Merchant shipbuilding (using as agent the Shipbuilding Industry Board).
(c) U.K.A.E.A.
(d) Government research establishments, including N.R.D.C.
(e) Government's relationship with the aircraft, aerospace and nuclear industries (e.g. Concorde).
(f) Government procurement of aircraft, electronics etc. for defence.

(g) Fostering technological advance and research (e.g. through the British Standards Institution and Metrication).

In October, 1969, the Ministry of Technology was enlarged to encompass the functions of the Ministry of Power which ceased to exist as a separate entity; it thus is responsible for the public corporations administering coal, electricity and gas. The enlarged Ministry also assumed the industrial functions of the Board of Trade and the economic planning of D.E.A., other than regional planning. The Minister, now a leading member of the Cabinet, is assisted by the Paymaster-General also in the Cabinet. Mintech. will thus control industrial location and development by means of i.d.cs. as part of national and regional industrial policy. Mintech. will also control all primary fuels and plant industries for electricity generation together with all other power and energy supply and plant industries. Chemical industries and textiles are also transferred from the Board of Trade. The I.R.C., B.S.C. and N.R.D.C. now report to Mintech, to which most mineral development and all metal supply and extraction have been transferred. It is now virtually a Ministry of Industry charged with the vital task of stepping up the pace of modernisation, to be achieved partly by a reduction in inter-departmental committees.

The Board of Trade. The President of the Board of Trade remains in the Cabinet, but with reduced powers. It is now mainly concerned with overseas trade, export promotion and invisible earnings. It is still responsible for the distributive and service trades but loses to the D.E.P. productivity services to industry such as the British Productivity Council and the British Institute of Management. Industrial functions transferred to Mintech. include distribution of industry, planning of new factories, industrial estates in development areas and building grants and loans. The monthly trade figures are still published by the Board and it may well be that in due course the under-recording of exports will eventually be adjusted. The Board of Trade will continue to deal with external commercial policy, including tariff policy and it will, therefore, presumably be one of the departments most closely concerned with the British application to join the E.E.C. Its remaining miscellaneous functions include shipping, tourism, hotels, administration of insurance and companies Acts, patent and copyright. Consumer protection, newspapers, printing and publishing and films. At the time of writing the Board's responsibilities for control of mergers, monopolies and restrictive practices have just been transferred to Mintech.

The Land Commission. The main objects of the Land Commission Act, 1967, were

(i) to ensure that the right land is available at the right time in order to carry into effect national, regional and local plans;

and

(ii) to secure that a substantial part of the development value created by the community returns to the community, and that the cost of land for essential purposes is reduced. The first object is to be achieved by the establishment of a Land Commission; the second by the imposition of a levy on development value realised on the sale of land and in certain other cases.

The Act provides for the establishment of a Land Commission of up to nine members appointed by the Minister; they are Crown servants, in receipt of remuneration and allowances. The Commission can appoint a secretary and other officers. The Commissioners must comply with directions given to them by M.H.L.G. and the Secretary of State for Scotland. Payments of from £45 million to £75 million will be made from time to time from the Consolidated Fund to a Land Acquisition and Management Fund. The Land Commission must submit an annual report and accounts to the two Ministers and must seńd certain of its accounts to the Comptroller and Auditor-General who must lay them before Parliament. The Commission is able to acquire compulsorily or by agreement land which is both suitable for material development and subject to a local planning decision. Standard compulsory purchase procedure applies but in case of objection the Order has to be confirmed by a planning Minister[1] or, where the Commission are buying for the purpose of a public authority, by the Minister who would normally approve the purchase.[2] The Commission has wide powers of management and disposal of land, in some cases subject to covenants restricting future development with a view to retaining future development value. "Concessionary crownhold dispositions" may be made for housing at less than market price subject to covenants, giving rights of pre-emption.

For the purposes of the betterment levy, development value is taken to be realised on the following "chargeable acts or events":—

Case A : Conveyance on sale of a fee simple or the assignment of a tenancy;[3]

Case B : grant of a tenancy;

Case C: project of material development;

Case D : payment of compensation for modification revocation, refusal or conditional grant of planning permission or for certain other planning decisions;

Case E : grant or release of an easement[4] or restrictive right;

Case F : other chargeable acts or events to events to be prescribed by regulations.

The levy is to be charged at a rate to be prescribed by an Order approved by the House of Commons. The White Paper on the Land

Commission[5] said that initially this would be 40 per cent but that it would be increased to 45 per cent and then to 50 per cent at reasonably short intervals. These are modest rates leaving ample incentive to owners to offer their land for development. The rate may be further increased if the Government is satisfied that this would not affect the availability of land for development. There are numerous exemptions for payment of levy, including charities, operational land of statutory undertakings and the National Coal Board, housing associations, and erection of a single dwelling-house for occupation by the owner of the land or by a member of his family if it was in his ownership at the date of publication of the White Paper.

The Act also repeals the provisions of the pre-existing law under which a local or public authority has to pay extra compensation to the original landowner if it obtains a more valuable planning permission within five years of acquiring the land.[6] This protects taxpayers and ratepayers as well as authorities possessing compulsory purchase powers. The Finance Act 1969 provides for certain concessions to small owners.

Co-ordination and administrative discretion. In theory, the Prime Minister is the great co-ordinator at Cabinet level; and at the present time the Prime Minister appears to be performing this function in practice. In the field of local government, for example, the Prime Minister announced in Parliament the decision to appoint the Royal Commissions, as is customary. The Minister of Housing and Local Government answered questions appertaining to the decision which related to the detailed work of his department after the Premier had disposed of more general questions.

The co-ordination of work at the highest level is achieved partly be means of Cabinet Committees, as we have already seen. The overlord system of Ministries, at one time favoured by Sir Winston Churchill, has been revived in a new form. Traditionally, the Prime Minister of the day should take a special interest in foreign affairs. The last Prime Minister to ignore this precept was Baldwin but since the war all the incumbents[7] have observed it, in greater or lesser degree. It is certainly a cardinal principle with the present Prime Minister. It may be that this detracts from the authority of the Foreign Secretary, who is the senior Minister dealing with external affairs. Signs of the times, perhaps, were the incorporation of the old Foreign Service in the new Diplomatic Service at the beginning of 1965 and the subsequent amalgamation of the Foreign and Commonwealth Offices.

Better co-ordination has been achieved in defence matters by the unified, Pentagon-type Ministry of Defence, with the Secretary of State and his Ministers of Defence for Administration and Equipment. Until 1947 the three services were represented by Secretaries of State or their equivalent; the First Lord of the Admiralty in particular was often a leading member of the Cabinet (the post was held by Churchill in 1914 and again in 1939). The creation of a separate Ministry of Defence in 1947 resulted in the exclusion of the Service Ministers from the Cabinet and the reorganisation effected in 1964 was the logical conclusion. There is now an integrated hierarchy for policy-making and decision. The influence of this reorganisation is seen in the creation of D.L.G.R.P.

For decades the Chancellor of the Exchequer has worked closely with the President of the Board of Trade, the latter Minister having been the Chancellor's unofficial deputy. If a vacancy occurs at the Treasury, the Prime Minister of the day may well look to the President as a likely successor (Mr. Maudling was appointed in this way in 1962) but the Paymaster-General and Chief Secretary would now be strong contenders.

Both the Lord Chancellor and the Home Secretary are, or should be, great co-ordinators but this is mainly owing to the multifarious nature of their duties rather than to contact with other departments. The Home Office has numerous links with local government and some with external affairs (immigration and alien control).

Ministers of the Crown have power to take administrative action and this power is often delegated to Civil Servants. As we have seen, a Minister is politically responsible for action taken in his department. Both Ministers and Civil Servants can exercise discretionary power in the interpretation of legislation and in the administration of their departments. Legislative policy may decree an interference with the rights of citizens, for example, the compulsory acquisition of land and slum clearance. The Minister of Housing and Local Government has the power to confirm, modify or reject a compulsory purchase or clearance order; and he must cause a local inquiry to be held if there are objections. This is a classic instance of the exercise of an administrative discretion. Another is the power of the same Minister to designate a particular site as the area of a new town in order to accommodate overspill from an overcrowded city such as Birmingham or inner London.

The courts will interfere with the exercise of an administrative discretion if it has been invoked for an improper purpose or has been used for extraneous considerations or is unreasonable. The main principle here is really one of statutory interpretation, that is, the discretion should be exercised for the statutory purposes, in accordance with the doctrine of the sovereignty of Parliament. Even if the statute allows a Minister to act "if he is satisfied" on a particular point, his decision can be set aside if he acts in bad faith, but this is very difficult to prove. Most of the judicial decisions on unreasonableness or taking extraneous considerations into account concern local authorities but they would also be applicable to Ministerial decisions. In view of the necessity for considerable delegation in modern conditions, Civil Servants exercise numerous administrative discretions on behalf of Ministers, particularly in planning, housing and transport matters.

The co-ordinating role in local government is normally played by the town clerk or clerk, although a strong leader of the council may well prove to be a co-ordinator. Like the Prime Minister in relation to his Cabinet colleagues, the town clerk may be described as "primus inter pares" (first amongst equals) vis-a-vis his fellow chief officers. The town clerk or clerk is usually legally qualified, although the tendency to appoint a chief executive is creeping in. However that may be, the town clerk is responsible for servicing the meeting of committees and of the council. Most town clerks take a particular interest in such matters as housing and planning, although of course other chief officers are also concerned, notably the Medical Officer of Health, the Chief Public Health Inspector, the Architect, the Engineer and Surveyor and the Planning Officer. Most of the larger authorities now have a chief planning officer, who may be an architect or a surveyor, and/or a member of the Town Planning Institute. The town clerk will try and resolve any disputes between chief officers and usually succeeds in doing so. If this is not possible, the remedy is for separate committee reports to be submitted to the council. The new chief executives are said to have been given direct control over the chief officers but a good town clerk already exercised such control albeit unobtrusively.

In theory, the elected councillors are responsible for making policy decisions and the officers are responsible for carrying them out, but in practice it is not so simple. As in the case of the relationship between the Crown and the Prime Minister, it may be said that a town clerk has the right, indeed the duty, to advise, to encourage and to warn his council. The making of policy is thus preceded by a process of consultation, investigation and argument, in all of which senior officers participate. The elected representative must try to carry policy into effect and, in order to do this successfully, there must be substantial delegation of work to the officers. In this connection, it is interesting to note that the reports of the Maud and Mallaby Committees are to some extent being anticipated by local authorities up and down the country in the streamlining of functions and drastic reduction in the numbers of committees. A distinguished town clerk[8] has said that he has always considered that one of his functions was to see that the view and the interest of the individual citizen was in fact represented and not ignored in the consideration of policy. The lawyer's traditional association with the protection of individual liberty is a material factor in this regard. It may perhaps also be said that the elected councillors are responsible for political policy, based on the doctrines of their political parties, whereas the town clerk and other officers are responsible for administrative policy. There is a certain amount of overlapping and the council also has some responsibility for administrative policy, but the officers cannot ever be responsible for the actual *formulation* of political policy, only for carrying it into effect.

Discretionary powers abound in the field of local government. A local housing authority can operate a rent rebate scheme or a differential rents scheme; or it may not do so and the courts have held that it has a complete discretion under the Housing Acts. A local planning authority has a certain amount of discretion in determining applications for planning permission within the area of local policy, although nowadays this is considerably circumscribed by national policy and the wide powers of the Minister. Local authorities have powers to grant or refuse licences to street traders but they must not exercise their power arbitrarily. All applications for licences must be carefully considered and it would be *ultra vires* for a local authority to declare by resolution that in future it would not issue any more licences in any circumstances. The courts will also set aside the decision of a local authority if it is manifestly unreasonable, that is, so unreasonable that Parliament could not possibly have contemplated such action when enacting the statute. Many administrative discretions are nowadays exercised by the town clerk and other officers on behalf of the local authority.

The members of the public corporations in general have much more discretionary power than Civil Servants or local government officers; and the problem of co-ordination, for them, is a purely functional one. Co-ordination at national policy level is the business of the Ministries of Technology, Transport and D.H.S.S. and is exercised mainly in the financial sector. It is only rarely that the relevant Minister takes advantage of his power to issue general mandatory directions. In a sense, there are three different hierarchies of authority in the nationalised industries: the Ministers, the members of the Boards and the officers of the Boards. Apart from what has already been said about Ministers, Board members are responsible for policy to a considerable degree. The functional organisation of most of the public corporations lends itself to smooth administration and it is probably fair to say that the officers are largely concerned with the execution of policy decisions. An Act of Parliament or, exceptionally, a Minister may cause a change of direction. In theory, Ministers are responsible for policy decisions and the Board members for day to day administration; again, this is an over-simplification. The first part is correct, but ministerial policy control may be somewhat tenuous and there is a further delegation of purely administrative matters to the officers of the Boards.

Nationalism and Regionalism. The emergence of Scottish and Welsh Nationalism has been a feature of the last decade resulting in each now having a moderate representative in Parliament. Both Scotland and Wales are separate regions for the purpose of economic planning and regional development. The Secretary of State for Scotland operates jointly from London and Edinburgh. The Scottish Departments of Agriculture and Fisheries; Development; Education; and Home and Health; and the Scottish Law Commission are housed in Edinburgh. The Secretary of State is assisted by Ministers of State and two Parliamentary Under-Secretaries of State. Similarly the Secretary of State for Wales has Welsh Offices in London and Cardiff, the latter including the Community Health, Economic Planning, Hospital Services, Local Government, Housing, Town and Country Planning and Roads Divisions. The Secretary of State is assisted by a Minister of State and a Parliamentary Under-Secretary.

We have seen that considerable aid has been made available to Scotland through the D.E.A., Mintech, the Industrial Expansion Act, 1966 and so forth. Whether this, coupled with the organisation outlined above, will be enough to allay nationalist sentiment remains to be seen. In Wales violence seemed to be gaining the upper hand with extremist elements such as the Free Wales Army coming to the fore. However, the investiture of the Prince of Wales at Caernarvon Castle in 1969 seems to have taken the wind out of the sails of such reckless and untypical elements, at any rate for the time being. John Mackintosh, M.P., postulates separate Assemblies for Scotland and Wales in his book, "Devolution of Power" published by Charles Knight, Ltd. There would also be Scottish and Welsh Prime Ministers; in the case of Scotland Jo Grimond, M.P., the former Liberal leader, is thought to be the natural candidate for this post. In both countries but particularly in Scotland there seems to be a strong affinity between the Nationalists and the Liberals. A Welsh Council has been appointed and Welsh local government is poised for reform. The legislation, when it comes, may be radically influenced by Maud. In Scotland, publication of the Wheatley Royal Commission Report is another factor and Scottish local government is due for genuine recasting. It may well be that a measure of realistic local government reform in both countries, coupled with viable economic and industrial planning and finance would allow the moderate nationalists to be content.

A Blue-print for the Seventies. What, then, is the pattern for the future? In the first place, Parliament should put its house in order—the age old conflict between Lords and Commons should be finally resolved, procedure should be improved to provide a rational working day and back-benchers, too, should receive a greater measure of participation. In this connection, the Whip system should be modified and private members should be given greater opportunities to introduce legislation. It is true that in the 1968/69 session of Parliament numerous Labour M.P.s revolted against the concept of penal sanctions for striking trades unionists and forced the government in general, and the Premier and First Secretary in particular, to drop the industrial relations bill. However, this was a matter in which the unity and even possibly the future existence of the Labour Party was at stake and such a situation is unlikely to recur in the near future.

Next, the streamlining of the machinery of government should continue apace. The Ministries and Departments concerned with local government have settled down and no further reorganisations are called for following the establishment of D.L.G.R.P. and the merger of Health and Social Security. Commerce and industry, however, are a different kettle of fish. The unhappy experiment of D.E.A., which seemed initially to have such great promise, has petered out. The relationship between D.E.P., Technology, Trade and D.L.G.R.P. has been clarified. The proposal to create a Ministry of Industry has much to commend it and this has, in effect, been done by the enlargement of Technology.

The activities of the newer public boards and commissions such as the industrial training boards, Industrial Reorganisation Commission, etc. are having a great impact on industry. The I.T.B.s also appear to be an interesting constitutional innovation in that no single Minister has previously had power to regulate conditions for training in some thirty industries by means of statutory instruments. The key to the future and to reform is to be found in the Redcliffe-Maud Report, with all its imperfections. Provincial Councils may replace the economic planning boards and councils but they should be directly elected. The metropolitan and district authorities are a good idea but there should be a real second tier under the unitary authorities. But above all the central direction of the national resources should be firm and purposeful. The regional and local authorities, like the public corporations, should have sufficient autonomy to act as viable units so that their leaders can make meaningful contributions to their areas. The government should have the courage to make this possible.

1. The Minister of Local Government, the Secretary of State for Scotland, the Secretary of State for Wales.
2. E.g. Secretaries for Social Services, Education, Local Government.
3. In Scotland the grant of a feu or the creation of a ground annual.
4. E.g. right of way, right of light, easement of support.
5. Cmd. 2771 (September, 1965).
6. With a certain limited exception.
7. Attlee, Churchill, Eden, Macmillan, Douglas-Home, Wilson.
8. Mr. G.F. Darlow, C.B.E., Town Clerk of Reading, in a Conference on "Who Are the Policy Makers?" held by the London Regional Group, R.I.P.A., January, 1965.

HER MAJESTY'S GOVERNMENT,
(October, 1969)

The Cabinet

Prime Minister and First Lord of the Treasury (Minister for the Civil Service)
Secretary of State for Foreign and Commonwealth Affairs
Chancellor of the Exchequer
Lord Chancellor
Secretary of State for Social Services
First Secretary of State and Secretary of State for Employment and Productivity
Secretary of State for the Home Department
Secretary of State for Defence
Lord President of the Council and Leader of the House of Commons
Minister without Portfolio
Secretary of State for Local Government and Regional Planning
Secretary of State for Scotland
Minister of Technology
Chancellor of the Duchy of Lancaster (Foreign Office)
Secretary of State for Education and Science
Minister of Agriculture, Fisheries and Food
Lord Privy Seal and Leader of the House of Lords
Secretary of State for Wales
President of the Board of Trade
Chief Secretary to the Treasury
Paymaster General (Ministry of Technology)

Ministers not in the Cabinet

Minister of Housing and Local Government
Minister of Overseas Development

Minister of Transport (Local Government and Regional Planning)
Minister of Public Building and Works
Minister of Posts and Telecommunications
2 Ministers of State, Technology
Financial Secretary, Treasury
Minister of State, Treasury
2 Ministers of State for Foreign and Commonwealth Affairs
Minister for Disarmament
Minister of Defence for Administration
Minister of Defence for Equipment
Minister of State, Home Office
2 Ministers of State, Scottish Office
3 Ministers of State, Education and Science
2 Ministers of State, Board of Trade
Minister of State, Welsh Office
Minister of State, Employment and Productivity
2 Ministers of State, Local Government and Regional Planning
2 Ministers of State, Health and Social Security

Law Officers

Attorney General
Lord Advocate
Solicitor General
Solicitor General for Scotland

Junior Ministers
Agriculture, Fisheries and Food

2 Parliamentary Secretaries

Defence

Under-Secretary for the Royal Navy
Under-Secretary for the Army
Under-Secretary for the R.A.F.

Education and Science

Under-Secretary of State

Employment and Productivity

Under-Secretary

Foreign and Commonwealth Affairs

2 Under-Secretaries

Health and Social Security

2 Under-Secretaries

Home Office

2 Under-Secretaries

Housing and Local Government (Local Government and Regional Planning)

3 Parliamentary Secretaries

Overseas Development

Parliamentary Secretary

Posts and Telecommunications

Parliamentary Secretary

Public Building and Works

Parliamentary Secretary

Scottish Office

2 Under-Secretaries

Technology

3 Parliamentary Secretaries

Trade

Parliamentary Secretary

Transport *(Local Government and Regional Planning)*

2 Parliamentary Secretaries

Treasury (Whips)

Parliamentary Secretary and Government Chief Whip
5 Lords Commissioners (Whips)
5 Assistant Government Whips

Welsh Office

Under-Secretary

Her Majesty's Household

Treasurer (Deputy Chief Whip)
Comptroller
Vice-Chamberlain
Captain, Gentlemen at Arms (Chief Whip, House of Lords)
Captain, Yeomen of the Guard
Lord in Waiting
2 Baronesses in Waiting

Total: *100*

REDISTRIBUTION OF SEATS

In October, 1969, the House of Lords rejected the Commons amendments to the Redistribution of Seats Bill, which had sought to relieve the Home Secretary from statutory liability for failure to comply with the House of Commons (Redistribution of Seats) Act, 1949. Under that Act, following the report of a Boundary Commission, the Home Secretary shall "as soon as may be" lay the report before Parliament together with a draft order in council to give effect to the recommendations. The Commissioners had reported in April and the report was published as a command paper in June. On 14th October, 1969, the Home Secretary informed the House of Commons that all 410 of the Commissioners' proposals and their Report would be laid before Parliament. It is not the government's intention to revive the Bill in 1969/70 session of Parliament and the government's majority in the House of Commons has ensured rejection of the Orders.

Meanwhile an application for an order of *mandamus* had been made by a parliamentary elector to compel the Secretary of State to comply with the requirements of the 1949 Act. The application was dismissed by a Divisional Court of the Q.B.D., following a statement to the Court by the Attorney-General that the Home Secretary would make an *ex gratia* payment towards the applicant's costs. The Attorney-General also gave the court an undertaking that the orders and the report would be laid before Parliament. Each House of Parliament had resolved that the boundary report should not be laid before Parliament during the 1968/69 session. The Attorney-General therefore contended that no order could be sought in relation to an internal matter of Parliament, which has the exclusive right to regulate its composition and procedure, as illustrated in Bradlaugh's case (Bradlaugh v. Gossett [1884] 12 Q.B.D. 271). The Attorney-General also argued that the duty of the Secretary of State under the Act was owed to the Crown or to Parliament and was therefore not enforceable by *mandamus* (which is a prerogative order)–*R. v. Secretary of State for the Home Department ex parte McWhirter* (Times Law Report 20th October, 1969).

THE QUEEN'S SPEECH,
28th OCTOBER 1969

The Speech from the Throne at the Opening of the 1969/70 session of Parliament indicated that Her Majesty's Government would continue their efforts to ensure justice and to promote peace and harmony between all communities in Northern Ireland. Legislation would establish a local defence force for security duties there.

In the ensuing debate the Prime Minister, indicating that there would be legislation to protect human rights, said that the Commons had endorsed government action to ensure that citizens of Northern Ireland had the same rights and freedom from discrimination which had been successfully asserted in the rest of the U.K.

The Speech indicated that at least five bills would be emanating from D.E.P. A bill to reform industrial relations will again be introduced, based largely on the White Paper "In Place of Strife" and on the Donovan Report but this time without any penal clauses. Another bill would amalgamate the Monopolies Commission and the National Board for Prices and Incomes and would rationalise their functions. Legislation would also provide for control of labour-only sub-contracting in the construction industry; equal pay for men and women; and further provision would be made for industrial safety and health.

The Prime Minister subsequently announced that responsibility for monopolies, mergers and restrictive practices would be transferred from the Board of Trade to D.E.P. from the end of October, 1969.

The Queen's Speech referred to a bill to reorganise the ports, which will be nationalised by means of a National Ports Authority. Management of the ports will be delegated to local boards. Such a bill could be introduced by the Secretary of State for Local Government and Regional Planning, the Minister of Technology or the President of the Board of Trade. The President will be concerned with promoting legislation to protect trawlermen and to continue the life of the National Film Finance Corporation until 1980.

The Ministry of Technology will also have much legislation to promote, mostly in the area of the old Ministry of Power. Thus, bills will be introduced to reorganise the electricity supply and gas industries and to enable the Gas Council to refine and market petroleum. The Gas Council would become responsible for the entire industry, including finance and development. A new Electricity Authority will be similarly placed to plan and control the policy of the electricity industry. Powers to help the coal industry under the Coal Industry Act, 1967, will be continued. Legislation will set up the nuclear fuel business of the U.K. Atomic Energy Authority as a separate government-controlled company.

The Minister of Transport will sponsor a bill to create a National Air Holding Board to create closer links between B.E.A. and B.O.A.C., following recommendations of the committee of inquiry into civil air transport.

A bill will be introduced requiring local education authorities to prepare plans for reorganising secondary education on comprehensive lines. Since the departmental circular on this subject in 1965, 128 out of 163 local education authorities have reorganised on comprehensive lines and nineteen others are preparing schemes. Eight have refused to submit a scheme to D.E.S. and eight others have not yet sent one in. The number of comprehensive schools in England and Wales has increased from 262 in 1965 to over a thousand to-day.

The Queen's Speech also provides much material for D.H.S.S. Thus bills are promised to control dangerous drugs more effectively; to introduce new earnings-related schemes of national superannuation and social insurance and to protect occupational pension rights on change of employment (to the satisfaction, it is hoped, of N.A.L.G.O. and other interested parties and associations); and on the Seebohm Report. Another Green Paper on the N.H.S. is promised; the volume of criticism launched against the first has perhaps been heeded. It is believed that the expression "fresh proposals" means a Green Paper rather than legislation. In any event, the government has made it clear that implementation of Seebohm and reorganisation of the N.H.S. will take account of the Maud Report.

Tucked away towards the end of the Gracious Speech is a reference to proposals for the reorganisation of local government in England, Scotland and Wales. Representations from the local authority associations on England are due to be lodged by the end of October, 1969; those on Scotland must be with the Secretary of State by the end of 1969. White Papers will follow and then legislation but probably not until after the general election. M.H.L.G. will introduce a bill to continue in modified form powers to limit increases in rents. This follows the restriction under the Prices and Incomes Act, 1968 and a recommendation of the N.B.P.I.

Finally, the Lord Chancellor's Department will continue its great law reforming activity. An Administration of Justice Bill will abolish imprisonment for debt and reconstitute the divisions of the High Court. A bill would be introduced to abolish the feudal system of land tenure in

Scotland and to improve the organisation of the Sheriffs Courts. Legislation will enlarge the powers of the courts to make financial provision for parties to marriages which have broken down.

It should be borne in mind by students that not all future legislation projected in the Speech from the Throne is necessarily enacted. The Queen's Speech gives an indication of the aspirations and legislative programme of the government of the day. We have seen that three government bills were jettisoned in the 1968/69 session of Parliament (House of Lords reform, industrial relations, redistribution of seats). The 1969 Speech ushered in the fourth session of the present Parliament and it is likely to be its last session. If a general election is held in the spring of 1970 it would be physically impossible for all the proposed legislation outlined above to be enacted by then. It would be incumbent upon the new government to prepare a new Speech and to select all, any or none of the bills which had not yet reached the statute-book. If the general election is held in the autumn of 1970, doubtless more of the projected bills would have been enacted. However, some would not have received royal assent nor would they have even been introduced. A good example would be the bill to reform local government, in view of the consultations and White Papers that are necessary. The last possible date for the next general election is April, 1971, and if it were to be deferred until then, a fifth and final short session of the present Parliament would ensue.

INDEX